Life in Detox

Book Cover photograph ©Dmitry.

Cover design by yours truly, Shawn Van Daele.

First edition 2023

ISBN: 9798377543923

Life in Detox

The beautiful messiness of being human while navigating addiction, recovery, grief and growth.

Shawn Van Daele

For many people, in honour of our unique personal perseverance
through our shared and common struggles, too often fought quietly.

Especially for my parents, whose endless guidance, support, understanding and
endless strength and good examples never fail to inspire me and fuel my fire.

Dad – I hope I finally delivered on
"making a good book."

For my husband Darrell; my rock, my best friend.
My forever.

To Dana, for being you. Always.
I will forever strive to be more like you.
Also, for crafting the subtitle of this book,
not surprisingly, to absolute perfection.

To Lisa, Amanda, my sisters Stacey and Kim, and all of you
who have stood by me when you probably shouldn't have.

To my former husband, 'Hubs' as he's referred to in the following pages,
for your patience during all the years I was spinning out of control.

To Annie Grace, Noah Levine, and Buddha for showing me different paths,
each culminating in a new way of seeing and a new way of being.

And for all of you reading this and helping me get to this point.
Your words of encouragement, endless sense of community and belonging,
and simply helping me feel I wasn't alone when I felt, more than ever, that I was.

And finally, to me.

For making it this far.

Contents

Preface

Bear with me. This journey starts off pretty rocky. Okay. *Really rocky.*

I had to learn to trust myself, to allow and permit myself to be vulnerable, so I could tell these (sadly true) stories in the rawest, most accurate and honest way possible. As you work through these words, I hope you'll see that growth and come along for the ride and grow a little (or a lot), too. Trust me – there's a light at the end of this book, and you don't have to wait for the end to see it. It starts shining the deeper you go.

Every piece to follow is like a little person with their own personality, a story to tell, and a message. Revisiting them is like returning to see an old friend I haven't seen for years and marvelling at how far we've both come. I'm sharing these stories chronologically, which is the most authentic way I can weave a thread through them all; however, I encourage you to make these words *your own.*

Though framed around, at first, my personal struggle with alcohol addiction (and the subsequent shit shows that ensued) – the simple substitution of *one word* can transform each piece into something *uniquely yours.*

Replace *alcohol* with *eating disorder,* overspending, procrastination, gambling, shopping, adultery, lying, negative self-talk, and self-abuse – the list is endless and as vast and varied as each of us. I repeat – *make it your own.*

Whatever the word.

Whatever it takes.

And finally, this can be read in the traditional sense – front to back – and perhaps that's the best way to approach this book, at least the first time around. You'll become part of the *unravelling and coming to terms* with what I had to accept as my reality – and my writing style follows that evolution. But it's also intended to be the type of book you can revisit, like that old friend, whenever you need it, flipping to any page and finding something to take away, something that is possibly *just* what you needed and what you were meant to read that day.

To date, one of my most significant accomplishments has not been overcoming everything that is to follow in this little adventure but *being able to connect and make a difference* to others who are and have felt, *exactly like me*, using what few strengths I have.

I hope these words make a difference to you and those who love you.

xo Shawn

Introduction

I wasn't there when my dad died.

And that's okay because I know it wasn't for lack of trying.

I was close. Like, *15 minutes close.* I guess that's something.

If I hadn't been drunk and three bottles of wine in when my mom called, I may have made it in time to condense 35 years of apologies into one rushed and sad, premature goodbye.

But…I was close, and I'm no stranger to closeness.

Not the intimate, *nuzzle-your-nose-in-my-ear* kind of closeness, but the near misses.

The *almosts.*

The close calls.

I've been close to all corners of the spectrum of success and failure and so very close to the Holy Grail of Sobriety so many times before finally holding it in my hands.

And let me tell you, that is one elusive little grail.

Recovery is not like turning a rock glass upside down over a spider you want to get out of your house. It is not a small, isolated "thing" you can zoom in on, deal with, moving it outside and then assume it's just *gone.* Instead, it's a wide umbrella dripping with your past, your fears, and *all* your anxieties and desires to stay constantly dry in an ever-rainy world.

It's a blanket that reaches to the far corners of every sleepless night in the lonely bed you've been making yourself for decades and years, whether you sleep alone in it or not. Recovery is messy, complicated, terrifying, and endless – it's the beginning of a journey that doesn't have a final destination.

It's a never-ending set of Russian dolls, each smaller and easier to handle than the one before. And it's in the revealing and opening of each hidden layer, each buried regret; each scared little version of yourself that reveals itself the deeper you go that it's *never been alcohol* you need to recover from.

It's from the imaginary world you've built around it in a vain attempt to keep yourself safe.

And this is where the *other kind* of closeness comes in.

The finally moving towards what scares you, instead of away, because that's what we do – we lean *away* – and sometimes run – from the things we don't like in a desperate attempt to find comfort however we can.

Wherever we can.

In the arms of strangers, in the sagging weight of swollen debts and in the murky depths you can only find at the bottom of a bottle.

We are so terrified of feeling discomfort that we end up trying to avoid feeling anything at all. Whatever can numb us, distract us, entertain us and make us forget – we line right up to fill ourselves up. Then we go back for seconds.

And that's how I ended up where I did, a 40-year-old Olympic-level alcoholic who struggled to keep his drinking to *less than four bottles of wine a day* when possible (but in all honesty, by the time I was onto the third bottle and 20th year of heavy drinking, my counting abilities weren't quite the best). I drank as though I believed if I stayed drunk enough, long enough, I could transcend time, undo all my unforgiveables, and finally forget my unforgettables.

Like always, I would get *close* – but never the right kind of close.

I'd get close enough to forget for a little while.

I'd get close enough to forgive myself only through forgetting myself for a little while.

I'd get close enough to *let it all go* into sweet, awful oblivion, one blackout at a time.

And every morning, *there they'd be.*

Every demon I'd been trying to drown was soaked, dripping, and heavier than ever.

There they would be, scattered through my home, mind, and heart and covered in wine stains and disgust. All the spirits I kept pouring into myself to scare my evil spirits away only made for a more crowded hell. They'd return with *more regrets, more* misplaced memories, *more* self-hatred and *more* desire to try and drown them all away again. They would double and triple overnight, and somehow, they would all learn how to swim.

Regret, trauma, sadness, insecurity, anxiety, fear - they are all amphibious.

I spent years – *decades* – first looking the other way as one binge blew into another, then perfecting my arsenal of excuses so I could *justify just one more drink,* later denying wholeheartedly that I even had a problem.

Not only that I *had* a problem – but that I *was* the problem.

I could never figure out how to stop the incredible deception between my hands and intentions.

I can see now it was because I was always leaning the wrong way.

I was always leaning towards whatever would help me forget fastest when all I needed to start doing was lean into all I was trying so desperately to run away from.

To learn how to *pause.*

To learn how to *stay.*

To slow down the ever-accelerating slippery slope, I kept well-lubricated with wine.

The problem though is that alcohol dilutes you.

It thins your courage, and it waters down your strength, stirring you into a sorry, undrinkable cocktail of *So-Many-Reasons-To-Give-Up,* topped up with too many bitters and a garnish of exhaustion. And it's shaken, never stirred.

Always shaken.

Rattled, unsettled, agitated and anxious, with all your parts so mixed up they become lost in the mess.

And there you are, an undrinkable and watered-down disaster. So, as you can imagine, after decades of leaning one way, it isn't the easiest thing to learn how to lean the other way (or even begin to think of how).

Just ask a tree.

Trees give way to the wind.

Trees let themselves be shaped by the conditions around them, leaning towards what serves them – water, light, space. Humans, on the other hand, haven't seemed to have learned a damned thing from the roughly 3 trillion trees on the planet, constantly bending and contorting ourselves in every direction other than towards what serves us.

And we always act *so surprised* when our leaves are brittle, and our roots run dry.

Getting sober was not unlike uprooting myself completely from the depths of a Dark Forest, crooked trunk and all, picking up all my fallen leaves and rotten apples and placing myself properly once and for all in the sun.

Which brings us to a place as good as any to begin this cautionary tale.

PART 1:

Genesis: The Beginning

Well, sort of.
We'll get into that, later.

Think of this part as the unravelling.

The part where I come unstitched so all my
demons can start crawling out of me.

The Dark Forest

I wasn't born in a Dark Forest.

Dark Forests are somewhere you are taken or led, by hand or by hiding, by curiosity or coercion. I wasn't born to abusive addicts, or neglected in a distracted, broken home.

I was born into a loving family, with two parents who offered more and tried harder than any other people I've ever met. We never went without, and if we ever did, we never knew. It was more likely that they themselves went without, so we wouldn't ever have to.

I witness my mother doing this still to this day.

I was far from popular, in the way that most introverts are. Bookish and artsy, I excelled in my classes and failed miserably at pretty much everything else – and at the time, I was beyond okay with it. I wasn't subject to violence or bigotry and escaped being intimately exposed to death until I was nearly in high school. Looking back, until I was 15, I would likely have been nominated as Least Likely to Become an Alcoholic.

It's fair to say that though I wasn't born with a silver spoon in my mouth, the universe was surely feeding me with one as the years passed by.

I've done incredibly self-destructive things but taking for granted the gracious start I was given in life has never been one of them.

Not out loud, anyways.

Never out loud.

The words we *don't* speak can't dissipate into nothingness – they get diverted and packed away inside us like little seeds with the potential to grow into something devastating or breathtaking.

Or, in some cases, maybe something devastatingly breathtaking.

But only if you water them. Or if the world waters them for you. Or your partner, or your boss. Your best friend, your ex-friend, your neighbour or the man who cut you off on the highway, your children or your very own negative self-talk, which *never shuts the fuck up.*

There is never a lack of situations and personalities just lined up and waiting to water each and every one of your insecurities.

And when there isn't, there's always a drug or a drink that'll help do it for you.

It's taken me over 40 years to realize that I was never actually *led* into the Dark Forest, that no one ever actually *put* me there. I grew it myself, around myself, and I watered it with enough drugs and alcohol to fill a moat around the entire damn thing.

So, there I was – alone in the woods with no way out and no way for others to get in.

Perfect.

How did I get here?

JANUARY 31, 2017

**I remember looking at people who were grossly obese, and
wondering how they could let themselves get to that point.
I know. I'm ashamed of myself, truly.**

I would drive past the detox clinic and laugh to myself at the thought that they let
themselves got *that far* gone that they ended up there. I've walked past homeless
people sleeping on the street and couldn't wrap my narrow mind around how their
shit fell so far apart that they found themselves sleeping on concrete. Yet here I
am. Falling apart. Out of control. Needing help. Needing detox.

An alcoholic.

How did I get here.

I've lost sense of time, and I've lost count of bottles. I've lost memories and
friends. I've lost business and money. I've lost respect and trust. I've lost faith,
and I've lost hope.

How did I get here.

Coming to terms with the fact that I need help with my drinking problem has
been the hardest and longest journey. And I'm seeing now that it's just beginning.
I'm frustrated and angry at how difficult – and expensive – it is to get access to
proper assistance in Canada. I feel like I'm contributing too much to the system,
and "they" don't want me to get better. Perhaps a burden on the medical system
(now and later) – but contributing to the economy with every bottle I down and
pack of cigarettes I turn into ashes.

I'm worth much more to them broken than I am fixed.

And that makes me so sad. Because I want help. Badly. And I've tried helping
myself, and it's not working. It's scary to hear you need an actual *medical detox,*
because you could have tremors and seizures – and die. It's scary to be sitting here

at 7 am wanting a drink because turning these feelings into words is terrifying me. It's making it real. I feel like I'm picking at a scab that refuses to heal.

> "Wine hath drowned more men than the sea."
> – *Thomas Fuller*

How did I get here.

I've been looking at detox clinics. I can't afford any of them. I don't want to go to a hospital. I don't want to go to a drop-in centre. Getting the alcohol out of my system alone will not fix my thirst. I won't sweat out the real reasons I drink. You can't detox your soul without proper, professional help, and it's so devastating to find how out of reach proper help is for so many people, just like me.

Wanting help but not being able to get it is one more kick while you're down.

Admitting I need help lit a tiny spark of pride in me, and in the darkness, I saw the outlines of a little bit of hope. Then realizing I can't access the help I want and need draws the shadows back in – and the spark goes out.

I'm going to see my doctor today. Luckily, I have one. And he's lovely. It's a step, at least, so we will see where that goes. And I know I will have only one thought while I am sitting in that waiting room 3 hours from now, and that will be, *'How did I get here?'*

Maybe Tomorrow

JANUARY 31, 2017

I almost made it to 1 pm today.

That was my goal.

12:40 pm was the best I could do. And that'll have to be okay for today because I can't undrink as much as anyone can undo anything. I had my doctor's appointment this morning. It was like going to confession at church.

He gave me a prescription instead of Hail Marys.

Great. Give the guy struggling with addiction a prescription for medication – *fitting.*

This is a massive step for me since I've spent the last year lying to him about the volume of my consumption. I'd usually say I have '2 or 3 drinks' a day, though I have a feeling he knew all along. Today I admitted those drinks are *actually* bottles. The *big ones.*

Also – that I need help.

I think I left my body when the words came out of my mouth because I can picture myself sitting there as though I was suspended from the ceiling, looking down on myself.

How ironic.

I'm beginning to feel like throughout this entire process I keep leaving my body. Escaping the shame somehow. Looking at myself as though I'm a *subject,* a *thing,* a specimen to be examined. Something to be *fixed.* It's making the coming-to-terms easier, but I know I need to step back inside myself if I want to *actually* to *fix* anything. However, the only thing going inside me is more alcohol. Another drink. Another vice.

My doctor agreed that I need to find a program. And he even recommended a couple to me – both out of the budget, despite my miraculous ability to *always* find a way in the budget for bottles of wine and a pack of smokes every day. My dearest friend told me just days ago that my priorities are whacked.

And she's right.

I can find a way to support my habits, but I can't find a way to support *myself*. It's not easy to support yourself when you aren't even inside yourself. The spine of my soul checked out, once upon a time. Like a book trying to hold itself together without a cover, it's hard to hold your head high when you can barely stand being inside your own body.

It's just easier to leave.

And that's where the wine comes in. Every drink is another step away. I can't even imagine how far away from myself I am now, at that rate. I must have walked miles and crossed continents, every drink another step away from *dealing with it*.

If drinks were measured in steps, I should be somewhere on the moon.

Maybe tomorrow I'll do better.

I've said that every day – for years. But I guess that's something. I guess that means I haven't given up on myself just yet. Luckily, I'm not so far away from myself that I can still see myself in the distance. However small. However diminished. However unrecognizable from this distance. But I'm still there. *Somewhere.*

Maybe I'll get a little closer tomorrow.

My hobbies include sleeping and disappointing everyone close to me.

Alcohol: My Most Fucked Up Friend

FEBRUARY 1, 2017

**I really wish I could check in Bridget Jones-style and
log how many drinks I had yesterday.**

But I don't know. I don't remember the last few hours of falling asleep in the chair. Or moving to the couch where I wake up every day. I remember watching a movie (I can't recall which one). And it's always interesting re-reading my texts from last night, because I don't remember sending most of them. I'm coming to admit that drinking is taking so much away from me. I wake up dreading the inbox, with another disappointed person looking for an explanation.

I wake up missing parts of my yesterday.

Drinking is stealing my memories, my money, my relationships and my worth.

I can deal with a hangover. I *can't* continue to deal with the constant losses. Each one is a not-so-gentle reminder of how greedy alcohol is. Like living with an abusive spouse, or a roommate that steals from you, living with alcohol is beating me up every day and taking everything from me. And I'm allowing it to. It calls to me from the store down the street, it trips me up as I walk past it in the kitchen, and it wraps its little arms around me when I need comfort.

If alcohol were a person, it would be my most fucked up friend.

I think that's part of the problem (and there are so many parts). Alcohol is glamourized for many of us. It is literally everywhere and sold to us as an integral part of a lifestyle: luxurious and indulgent while at the same time being the vice we need when times are tough. It offers us answers when we don't have any, a crutch when we are insecure, and sweet oblivion when we feel too much.

It's the perfect solution for every situation.

Until, of course, it isn't.

I confessed to a friend that I have started this journal. A blog for me to talk to myself since I have trouble actually talking about this to *anyone*. She used the word *cathartic* to describe how writing can make you feel.

ca-thar-tic

adjective

1. Providing psychological relief through the open expression of strong emotions; causing catharsis. "Crying is a cathartic release."
2. Medicine: (chiefly of a drug) purgative

Noun

3. Medicine: a purgative drug

Oh, how ironic. I've found psychological release in writing to talk about my problem with how I find psychological relief in drinking. And furthermore – *purgative* is something strongly laxative in effect, designed to release something blocked.

I self-medicate every day to try and release whatever is blocked inside me – *emotions, words, regrets, fears, disappointments, and responsibilities.* And I need to admit that it is not cathartic for me when I drink, but it is quite honestly the opposite. It's so confusing. As Murphy Kennedy said in the *"Alcohol"* version of Visions Journal:

> *"Alcohol worked for me until it didn't work. I then had a serious dilemma: like others who reach their so-called bottom, I faced a situation where the fear of drinking equalled the fear of not drinking."*

I drink for psychological and emotional release from strong emotions – *that are caused by drinking.* There it is again.

Alcohol, my most fucked up friend.

I need it, because of it.

Choosing to stay in an abusive relationship is mental and emotional torture. I *know* I need to (am starting to?) treat alcohol like an abusive partner. Despite how I am the one abusing *it,* drinking is psychologically and emotionally destroying me.

All unhealthy relationships need to end, and watching my friends go through breakups with actual people is sadly liberating. After all, if they can cut it off with another *person,* I should have *no* problem doing it with a bottle. *Right?*

It's not that easy.

It's the coming to terms that you will need to reshape your life without that partner that is the hard part. And the only difference with alcohol is that if I change my mind, I know it will come back in a heartbeat. Without an apology, without explanation – *it will gladly move back in.*

I can't move to another town where I won't bump into them. Everywhere I go, I will see them with someone else. At every restaurant, in every television show, in every magazine. Billboards. Commercials. Conversations. *I will see them loving someone else and reminding me of what I no longer have.*

I guess it's this fear that stalls us. The concept that we will be 'going without' that stops us from walking away from unhealthy relationships. How do you learn to turn that thinking inside out, and realize how much you could actually gain?

Alcohol is definitely the most fucked up friend I have ever had to break up with.

"The thing with broken clocks is you can tell exactly when they stopped ticking. With people, it isn't so easy. Sometimes you can't even tell they're broken."

– N.H.

Kintsugi: Finding Worth in All My Pieces

FEBRUARY 2, 2017

**I was only recently introduced to the concept of *Kintsugi*, which
is the Japanese art of repairing broken pottery with lacquer
dusted or mixed with powdered gold, silver, or platinum.**

*It treats breakage and repair as part of the history of an object rather than something
to disguise.*

This idea took my breath away. *How hauntingly beautiful.* Feeling utterly broken
and crying my eyes out specifically at the time I was told about it, it made my heart
happy to imagine being put back together again. And not only that – but to be put
back together in a way that gives value to all my shattered pieces.

How very Humpty Dumpty.

I've been trying to hold myself together for 20 years with alcohol, which has only
been breaking me down further. Acidic by nature, it's no wonder that wine has
only made my shell weaker as it slowly eats away at all my broken edges, to the
point I feel as though I'll never be put back together quite the same, ever again. I
have such a sense of *shame* for being an alcoholic and for what it has caused me
to do with parts of my life, that being dissolved by drinking is sadly the less scary
option compared to *dealing with it.*

Somehow learning to embrace all of it one day as part of my journey – *as part of
the object's history* – is a lofty and ambitious end goal I am choosing to have for
myself. Visually imagining myself whole one day.

One day, when all my pieces are back together again. When there is gold holding
me together instead of alcohol. When I can see worth in every fracture and fissure
of my being.

*One day, when it won't be all the king's horses, or all the king's men, or three bottles
of wine – but myself who will finally be able to put me back together again.*

Transformation

FEBRUARY 04, 2017

"I only drink a little, but when I do, I turn into another person, and that person drinks a lot."

This quote resonates with me so much. It was supposed to be a funny meme online, but it's hard to laugh at when you're that person. It gave me a little comfort, the concept of taking the disease far away from who I am, and seeing it as something separate. Seeing myself as an *individual with issues,* yet putting the onus on alcohol rather than myself for transforming me into something *so much less* than I am or have the potential to be.

I need to stop blaming myself.

It's the blame that fuels the guilt and lack of self-worth, and it's alone in that dark room where blame lives that I turn to alcohol to help me avoid those feelings. Or sometimes, to glorify them and sit holding hands with my depression some days. What a messed-up thing addiction does to you: *"Let me help you feel better, and while you start feeling better, let me tear you apart."*

What drinking does for you transforms in direct relation to how you, yourself, are being transformed by it.

The more you consume, the more it consumes you.

Today will be a new test. My partner is away all day until sometime after midnight. I have a history of getting absolutely loaded on these days, so today's assignment is to keep myself busy with projects – writing, cleaning and perhaps some actual work-related work. Maybe I'll meditate and devote some time just for me to let some guilt loose.

Today I'll try not to transform.

Coldplay's 'The Scientist' As Heard by an Alcoholic

FEBRUARY 04, 2017

"Tell me your secrets and ask me your questions, oh, let's go back to the start."
– Coldplay, The Scientist

If there were ever a song I could dedicate to myself, it would be this. The journey to sobriety is not unlike ending - or repairing – a relationship. The one you have with yourself. Getting back to yourself and talking to the *you* that you've spent so long estranged from.

The *you* that you left behind. The *you* you've buried under so much hurt, guilt, and self-abuse.

The you you've drowned in bottomless bottles.

The you that has always been waiting for the *courage to be imperfect.*

My favourite version of this song is the cover by Tyler Ward, Kina Grannis, and the love of my life, Lindsey Stirling. It's the most beautiful soundtrack and the inspiration for this written confession. So go ahead and find it wherever you listen to music; it's okay. I'll wait.

I would love for you to read this while the song plays – because it has a way of working its way into your soul.

"I had to find you, tell you I need you"

Finding yourself again is hard. Telling yourself you *need* yourself is even harder – especially when nearly *all* of us are raised not to be 'needy.' Giving yourself worth and forgiveness for not being perfect is sadly a foreign concept that may as well be a secret language with no translation.

I can't put my finger on the day I walked away.

The day I gave up.

The day that alcohol put its hand on my shoulder and changed my course. I suppose it happened in a series of small abandonments, the accumulation of failures and disappointments, eventually turning into a mountain between who I was and who I turned into.

"Nobody said it was easy. It's such a shame for us to part"

And then, I was gone. It's hard to see yourself through a mountain.

Every drink another step away. Every hangover a wrong turn. Every day of drinking bringing another rash of poor decisions, another puzzle with so many missing pieces. And that's the struggle of an alcoholic: you *can* see the big picture. The puzzle. But you don't have all the pieces, having dropped and lost so many on your way. You can't possibly put it all back together when you no longer have all the parts.

"I was just guessing at numbers and figures,
pulling the puzzles apart"

Broken-hearted and broken down, my own two hands pouring every drink, spending every penny and my own two feet taking every stumbling step away from myself, *and not even knowing why – or simply being too afraid to admit it.* Perhaps in the never-lifting drunken fog, I've been aimlessly looking for myself all along. Hoping one day to find my way back, bumping into myself like a stranger in the woods. Maybe one day I will, and I can have that conversation with myself that will answer all my questions as to *how I got here.*

And finally, figure out how a glass of wine became more important than my own peace of mind.

"Tell me you love me. Come back and haunt me.
Oh, and I rush to the start"

It has everything to do with the haunting. The memories. *The regrets.* Everything you haven't forgiven yourself for yet. All your imperfections. Every time you have looked into the mirror of your current situation, and it looked so different from that bigger vision of how you imagined your life would be, with no one to blame but yourself. Every time you've chosen being asleep over being awake, because being awake means thinking – and feeling. Every time you agreed with the ghosts that being numb was easier. And every one of those drinks that have made you numb. And here you are, still running in circles.

"Running in circles, chasing our tails, coming back as we are"

Addiction is the hardest fight I have ever had to fight. Not only are you trying to resist the temptation of the *one thing* that makes you exhale – but you are scratching back at the claws of depression that are trying to pull you back even further. Because *"you don't deserve it."* Because *"who cares."* Because it's just easier closing up and bottoms up.

"Nobody said it was easy, no one ever said it would be this hard"

Every alcoholic, deep down inside, wants to go back to the start, where it all began, and do so many things differently. It's there – *at the start* – that we can confront the demons that help us lift the glass. It's being lost in the meantime which prevents it. I would love nothing more than to sit down with 20-Years-Ago-Me and talk about things that happened generations ago that are outside of my control and remind myself of exactly that. To go back to 10-Year-Old-Me and tell myself it's alright to be confused about being gay. To have a phone call with 5-Years-Ago-Me and explain that I do not have to be everything to everybody. But unfortunately, my only option is to talk to Today-Me and say that everything is, eventually, going to be okay. To tell myself to hold my own hand, instead of a bottle of wine.

"Oh, come up to meet you, tell you I'm sorry,
you don't know how lovely you are"

Your relationship with *yourself* sets the tone for every other relationship you will *ever* have. You don't have to be a scientist to decode that. You *do* have to be strong, though, to forgive yourself. With addiction comes guilt. Guilt that you haven't been strong enough. Guilt that you are weak. Guilt that you've made so many mistakes. Guilt that your addiction gives you courage. It's a horrible cycle, and the only cure is sitting down with yourself and saying you are sorry. Forgiving yourself. Building yourself up instead of tearing yourself down. Every vague promise, every half-assed attempt, every unfulfilled goal – admitting to yourself that it's okay and that none of those things are who you are.

"You don't know how lovely you are" is what every addict needs to hear.

"I'm going back to the start"

I don't have an exact plan. But I do think I have turned around, a little bit. I'm taking steps to drink less and forgive myself more. To commend myself instead of condemning myself. To find my way somehow back to the start, so I can unchain myself from all those little things and reflex habits – *which are the big things* – that cause me to drink.

> "Tell me you love me, come back and haunt me, oh,
> and I rush to the start."

How I wish I could press rewind and walk backwards through time and see the definitive and ignored moments of my life in reverse. *The effect before the cause.* The result before the reason. How I'd have done so many things differently, but still, how many things I would do the same. I'd love to know the moment the path of my happily-ever-after turned into a car crash. That one thing that made me choose the different sliding door that led to addiction.

> "Science and progress, do not speak as loud as my heart."

So – I'm no scientist, but I can't wait for the day to rediscover the chemistry I once had with myself. To meet myself again. To finally forgive myself once and for all and find myself at a new start.

The Dream Box: Reconnecting With My Dead Dad

FEBRUARY 05, 2017

I woke up crying in the middle of the night, covered in a cold sweat.

I dreamt I told my dad (who passed away five years ago from cancer) to fuck off, with a few choice turns of phrase. I can't remember much of what led up to it. *Something about the missing base to a table that had a round glass top. A bicycle with a book in a wicker basket strapped to its side. A cluttered antique shop. My parent's kitchen.* I was irate and angry. Storming out of the room in my dream, I felt instant guilt and went back to apologize. I said I was sorry and hugged him – it was too real. I said, *"I am so sorry. I'm sorry. I have a list 'this long' of things that are bothering me. I'm stressed out. I'm so sorry."* I could feel his skin. He smelled like the factory he worked at when I was a child. Like grease and coal. And he put his lips to the top of my head while I was still crying and said, *'I forgive you. For most of it."*

Then I woke up crying.

For most of it. That's the part that is haunting me.

I had a good day yesterday. It was the first time in God only knows how long that I didn't get totally wasted. The wine just stopped tasting good after a few glasses, so I chose not to drink it (well, I still drank a bottle – but what an improvement from the typical 3, 4 or more.) *I also had a 4-hour 'nap'* from 6-10 pm, my typical tie-one-on time. I've developed a cold, and it's knocking me on my ass – the body gets weak when the heart gets tired.

Perhaps it's the cold that is giving me weird dreams and causing the exhaustion. Perhaps it's all this writing and reflection. Perhaps my dad came by for a visit to help me release some guilt – his and my own. To help me along on this journey. In yesterday's post, I talked about this, and in doing so, I put my dad there.

In my dream box. Where you collect little things subconsciously throughout the day, and they creep out at night because the box has no lock. These scraps of your thoughts and emotions are free to wander and come and go as they please. It's been on my mind of late to write a letter to my father. I've written it 1,000 times in my mind. It's finding the courage actually to write it that I struggle with. Writing it down makes it real. Writing it down would make everything that happened, have happened. I know that much of my anger and addiction is rooted there, so it's somewhere I need to dig. And the truth is – to dig, I have to write.

Words work like a compass for me. I often have no idea where they're pointing, yet I follow them, and it sometimes leaves a beautiful path behind me and before me. On good days, it leads me to somewhere beautiful. Somewhere I didn't know I needed to go.

In the days leading up to his death, I was struggling to find the strength, humility, and courage to have a heart-to-heart conversation for the first time in our lives. And for me to say in words that I forgave *him*. He carried so much guilt his whole life. He'd cry every time I'd leave after a visit over so many things that he did, *that I did, that we never talked about. We had an unspoken, mutual disappointment* with ourselves.

I wanted to clear the air for both of us before he took to the skies.

It never happened.

The thing is, you think you have time.

In fact, there are many letters I should write. This journal is a long one to myself. But there's so many people that deserve an explanation or that I have questions for. Some are still here, some now gone – either by death or distance. Reconnecting is a goal of mine for this year. Reconnecting with myself, my family, estranged friends – *estranged because of me* – people I've pushed away and people that chose to leave. Connecting more with the ones who have stayed. Connecting more with nature and my community. Maybe most importantly – *disconnecting from toxic things in my life.*

I'm borrowing this list from Nicole at Cockatoodledoo, which I read yesterday and was so inspired by:

- Have more open and honest dialogues with my partner.

- Make a better effort to keep in contact with friends (not just on social media).

- Connect with nature, and spend a lot of time outside.

- Connect with my body – use it more, feed it better.

- Connect with my mind – write more, read more, skim less, and spend less time on mindless activities like social media.

- Disconnect from my phone – treat it as a device, not an appendage.

- Pay attention to spending and the things I mindlessly consume.

- Reduce, reuse, recycle.

- Spend more time connecting with my community – volunteer my time somehow.

- Connect with my discovered (and yet to be discovered) skills – take opportunities to learn new things.

- Figure out what work-life balance really means to me.

- Connect with my relationship to alcohol, explore sober connections.

I didn't expect to reconnect with my dead Dad last night. Or to offer him a heartfelt apology through actual tears while sleeping. I am only days into this journey toward sobriety and self-discovery. I am already starting to witness positive changes and tiny miracles, and they're coming to me in the strangest shapes and forms I could never have imagined.

For the first time in a long time, *I am hopeful.*

Thanks, Dad.

On Loss and Losing Grip

FEBRUARY 06, 2017

I've always held worth in paying attention to my dreams.

I'm fascinated by reading (but not defining my life around) their interpretations. I didn't intend to write two posts about my dreams in a row, but they're rarely so vivid and intense, not to mention stickier than marmalade, so I can't really get them off me once I wake up.

Last night, I woke at 4 am (this happens every night) from a particularly disturbing dream: *my left thumb had been severed.*

First, I was with a former colleague/contractor of ours, who was telling me a payment had bounced. I lied and said it wasn't from us but was about to offer to lend her money in the meantime to get her through. Then I looked at my hand and saw I was wearing a silver ring on my thumb that had cut off the circulation, which had swollen to massive proportions. Forward to: my thumb falls off, and I am doing my best to keep my hand upright, so the blood doesn't pool everywhere. I fashion a make-shift reservoir from a small Tupperware-something to catch the blood. I go to my doctor where they are about to try, to my relief, to close it up – just as I awaken.

> *"To dream about a thumb tells you that you must 'get a grip' on life. It represents strength and talent. To dream about not having thumbs symbolizes being poor and friendless." –* Dreamforth.com

Oh, how true. Surprisingly, I still have many friends, though many have given up, so – other than that. This journey towards sobriety is my way of trying to 'get a grip' on so many things. I believe business losses and my relationships falling apart was the final push I needed to admit I needed help and that my alcohol addiction is indeed the cause, despite fighting tooth and nail to remain in denial. Hubs and I have operated our own business for nearly a decade. It involves many people, and over the last year or so, I've done a horrible job of managing things. As a result, our finances have turned chaotic. True honesty? They're in absolute ruins. Our business is losing face. I've made bad business decisions, piled upon countless other bad ones.

It would appear that alcohol can't steer a wheel very well.

Since my husband and I run this business together, the lines between marriage and work often blur daily. And there's a cycle between relationship challenges seeping into our daily work – and our work problems causing arguments and disappointments in our relationship. And repeat.

> *"Dismemberment of a thumb has something to do with negative feelings, like having difficulties and sorrowful instances in life. If the dream is about an injured thumb - like appearing swollen - let it serve as a warning of losing a project or a business that may elicit a negative reaction from partners and people around. Generally, an injured thumb signifies dissatisfaction over things - that the expected result was not achieved since the ability was not maximized." - AuntyFlo.com*

This is the interpretation that bothers me the most. Mainly because I have been trying so hard lately *to have an actual grip instead of letting things fall.* I was at the top of my game five years ago, just before my father died. Then – *my grip just let go.* I didn't have anything left in me to simply *keep holding on.*

This is a post for another day – but in 2012, I found *'my calling.'* I was helping people – everywhere – using my God-given talent and a lot of creativity. I was a philanthropist, and I was changing lives around the world, making dreams come true. I was featured on The Today Show. World News with Diane Sawyer. MTV. Every local news channel. Publications from China to Brazil. Organizations in Russia wanted to fly me out to work with their patients. I was awarded a philanthropy award by a major national hockey team, on the ice and named as one of Facebook's "most-talked-about" in their 2012 year in review. The list goes on.

I simply stopped the project one day. After my dad died, I needed to take a break, and his passing was in the fresh shadow of that entire *half* of my family passing away like dominos over the course of 5 years. My grandfather, my uncle, and my grandmother. My father was burdened with being the last one standing. Talk about guilt. All this loss left an indelible imprint on me that set the tone for my struggles with overcoming and learning how to live through grief for years to come.

It also helped fuel the fire of my addiction.

So far, the break I've taken, stepping down from the highest point of my life, has been five years and counting to the disappointment of so very many people

- notably my mother, family, husband, all those I supported – and who believed and relied on me – *and let's not forget myself.*

I couldn't keep giving.

Fast forward to today. An alcoholic writing a blog about struggling for sobriety, trying to hold my marriage together, and losing the respect of my friends, fans and colleagues to the point of dreaming about losing my grip on everything. I suppose it's easy to lose your grip when you're trying to carry too much. What a steep slope it's been. How did I get here?

One more regret to add to the pile.

"When a thumb is injured in your dream, you may expect business or personal losses; Isolation if you don't have thumbs – This is a very sad sign which will bring you hardship and loneliness in your life, but you can change everything, just put some efforts" – DreamsNet.com

Tell me about it. The good thing about dreams is that they aren't necessarily prophecies. They can serve as warnings. They're the little things you've subconsciously collected and placed in your dream box to deal with later – when you're asleep and your soul is listening, and your goddamn mind shuts up for just a little while. I suppose this is just another awakening, like the Cole's Notes, of what is truly bothering me and worrying me. Maybe it's about the root problems I am looking for answers to at the bottom of a bottle. It's all so intertwined. I have no worries that I won't have plenty to think about today.

I spent some time meditating for the first time in a long time. I discovered a wonderful app which I used for my first session. I'm dedicated to meditating every day for at least ten minutes (because, you know, I've been *so* good at sticking with things lately). I came out of it feeling refreshed, and my mind was clear. It wasn't until immediately after getting up that I had to hold a door to keep myself upright for two minutes while I fought against totally blacking out differently for a change. I was seeing white everywhere. Everything was spinning. The highest pitch ringing in my ears was causing me to want to vomit. It passed eventually.

And that's that. I suppose my intention to gain a grip on things is awakening all the regrets I need to put to rest, so much so that sirens are starting to go off in my head, sounding the alarm on all the business worries I need to deal with head-on.

For a good night's sleep. For a clear conscience. For the chance to take a big step towards self-forgiveness and sobriety.

Off to find my thumb.

Neglect is a Place That Will Tear Your Whole House Down

FEBRUARY 08, 2017

I am sitting to write this morning with mixed emotions.

Hubs and I had a great, two-hour-long conversation last night, revisiting the idea and plausibility of my going to a recovery centre for a month.

A month.

It's not like being gone for the weekend or even a week. But an entire month. The idea is terrifying.

It isn't even the absence or time away worrying me, but the wild unknown of *changing*. It's all the unknowns, like jumping feet first into the blackest ocean, unsure if I will sink or swim or what lies beneath the surface. Maybe that's what I'm most afraid of. Seeing what's beneath my *own* surface that makes me tick, plunged against my will to the uncertain depths below so I can figure out how to swim back out – and all the things that have caused my clock to stop.

Stuck in time.

Like the dreams you have where you are trying to run, but your feet refuse to move.

My broken heart is already there at the recovery centre (I prefer calling it that, over detox, or 'the clinic.' I honestly don't know what the accurate, politically correct term is.). I'm not sure where my pride is yet, or my courage. They are likely lost somewhere between my good intentions and darkest fears.

I've always done a decent job of being able to do whatever I put my mind to (including subconscious neglect of myself and everything that matters to me). That is, until 2012 when I simply *stopped*. We talked a lot about *my potential* last night – and how when my dad died, I put a cap on it, bottled it up, and tucked it away to be forgotten in the corner of the highest shelf. Ever since, I've been filling that void with alcohol, keeping myself as numb as possible.

Absolute, total neglect of as much as possible.

It's not for the lack of *trying* to quit drinking. Over and over and over again. It's not for lack of *wanting* to. This journal, these words, this *opportunity* to go to a recovery centre would not even exist if it wasn't for me wanting to break free from this addiction. Beneath the weight of all the shame, I'm clinging onto that one tiny scrap of pride right now: that I *came to want this on my own.*

Just like the child at the amusement park, who begs all day to go on the scariest ride, then is too terrified to step on when it's his turn, I'm scared to take the next steps and *actually go.*

I keep reminding myself of the scarier alternatives of not going. Losing my marriage. My business. My health. My mind.

I've spent decades neglecting all those things, trying to think clearly between the lightning strikes of torment in my mind. Or my heart. Perhaps both.

Neglect is a plague that will tear your house down.

---

ne-glect

verb

1. Fail to care for properly. "The old churchyard has been sadly neglected."
Synonyms: fail to look after, leave alone, abandon, desert

Noun

1. The state or fact of being uncared for.
"Animals dying through disease or neglect."
Synonyms: disrepair, dilapidation, deterioration, shabbiness, disease, abandonment

---

And that right there is what it all comes down to: *"failure to care for properly."*

It's truly incredible how quickly things can fall apart. How simple it is to care for something, yet how easily we neglect to do so – usually, for the most important things. My mom always says, *"It's amazing how quickly an abandoned house can fall apart. But a house with people living in it seems to hold itself together forever".*

I have a feeling it's time to move back into my "house."

Back into myself.

Last night, I used the words "absolute fucking torment" to describe how it feels inside my head lately. And that isn't fair to anyone involved with dealing with me, helping me, or relying on me.

How long can you go neglecting something – *everything* – until it all just collapses in on itself?

It isn't fair to *me*.

Typing that makes me feel selfish. Leaving for a month to *Kintsugi* my sorry ass makes me feel selfish. Looking back at everything I've neglected makes me feel selfish.

I'm going to close today with something I wrote over 20 years ago in a long-lost journal, but the line has never left me:

> *"Oh, the incredible deception between my hands and intentions."*

I wrote that 20 years ago. Apparently, some things never change.

I Spent the Night in Hell. Again.

FEBRUARY 9, 2017

I feel like hell today.

I feel awful. I haven't been sleeping – maybe four hours max a night. Last night (this morning?) I think I got about three hours. This isn't new. I've been like this for as long as I can remember. Twenty-five years ago, when I was fifteen, I was addicted to caffeine pills. *Shocking.* I took ten, fifteen, or twenty a day, for three years or more. I haven't really slept since then.

I found 3 am romantic.

I find 3 am romantic.

The silence. Like I'm hiding. Or at least safe. Protected from everyone who wants something from me, as they're tucked away in their dreams – I wrap the silence around me where no one is awake to find me.

The faster our world moves, the more priceless these early morning hours have become.

My dreams last night were about fire. Fire, everywhere. Everything was burning Armageddon-style: people, things, livestock.

The earth itself.

But I didn't care. No one cared. Everyone went about their day. In. Out. Work. Eat. Sleep. Repeat. It was the most mundane dream ever – like I was watching a surveillance video of the most absolutely average day.

Except everything was *burning*.

Only when I woke up did I realize how unnatural it was.

I think I may have spent the night in hell.

No wonder I didn't want to go back to sleep after waking up again at 4 am. And I just realized how I started this post – *I feel like hell today*. I tend to name them after they've been written and see where they wanted to go today.

Awake or dreaming, why does my heart need to turn so vividly everything into the most extreme version of whatever is on its mind?

My mind.

Anxiety turns a little wind into a tornado.

I've told Hubs before that I believe I either lucid dream, or that I simply *leave* when I'm asleep – my dreams are *far* too vivid. They are in glorious technicolour, with all my senses present. I've woken up with tastes in my mouth or the lingering smell of something or someone around me. I'll wake up clutching something that isn't there that I was holding in my dream. I am fully present and completely committed in my dreams – the absolute opposite of my waking hours. If I'm not sleepwalking (a post for another day), I am the busiest person in my dreams. Most times, I don't want to go back to sleep after I wake up.

If you weren't before, now I know you must be sure I've lost my mind.

For the most part, I remember my dreams clearly. Usually better than I remember the last few hours spent drunk before falling asleep. Or passing out. I can rewatch them after waking, like thinking back to something I just watched on tv. And in the few hours I actually do "sleep," I'm on a sober adventure somewhere far away. It's so bizarre.

I'm not an alcoholic in my dreams.

When I was very little, thirty-five years ago or more, I started having a repetitive nightmare – eerily similar to my last night. Piles of bodies, burnt beyond recognition. I could see the smoke and steam rising from them. In my limited five-year-old life, there is no way I had ever been exposed to something like that – real, on television, or in stories – that could justify why I would have dreams like that. I could see charred skin. Limbs. Never faces.

And I would have this dream *every night*.

It didn't come with terror or fear – but more confusion and sadness than anything. At five years old, I understood what repetitive dreams were as little as I understood the emotions that came with what I was seeing in my dreams.

I'm not sure when I stopped having that nightmare, but I think I revisited it somewhat last night. I've never forgotten that dream and have told Hubs and others about it many times. If given art supplies, I could paint you the clearest picture of exactly what it looked like – but I *really* don't want to.

The aftermath of everything and everyone on fire.

What the hell is wrong with me?

"I'm not addicted to alcohol
or drugs, I'm addicted to
escaping reality."

– UNKNOWN

I Don't Want to Die Young

FEBRUARY 10, 2017

We sat across the living room from each other, and I could hear the words leaving my mouth, as usual, feeling nothing.

"I don't want to die young. At this rate, I won't make it ten more years."

And there it was.

Admitting that I want to fight. Acknowledging that my fear of change is *not* bigger than my fear of the consequences of not changing.

To look ahead and want *better.* To want more time and more chances to experience life. *That is what hope is,* and in my numbness, it surprised me.

Finally, a glimmer of feeling *something.*

Addiction extinguishes the flame inside you. The one that sometimes burns brightly, and fuels everything of value: passion, creativity, drive, and *hope.* I felt like the fire inside me went out so long ago that everything went with it.

Apparently not.

That's really all you need. To make the decision that you are willing to fight.

To reignite the flame with your own self-worth and give yourself the gift of as many days as possible.

I refuse to die young.

Perhaps it's time to set free all those fires that are raging solely in my dreams so they can set my spirit back aflame.

Mastering the Day, One Step at a Time

FEBRUARY 11, 2017

I don't even know if I'm trying.

I have barely changed my habits. The *desire to change* is there, but not the action.

We had some company two nights ago, and I ended up getting really drunk (not much different from any other night) – but it's that behaviour that worries me. I am lacking self-control. I need limits and boundaries, and I am failing to set them for myself.

I'm still just waiting for something to come along that makes me stop wanting to be so numb.

I need to set a daily goal, which is a much better way of looking at it than thinking of it as 'limiting' myself. I need smaller goals. Instead of looking at the entire staircase, to look at just the first step. Then the next. And the next. In theory, I'll *have* to make it to the top that way.

I don't <u>wake with intention</u>. Quite the opposite, to be honest. It's usually with dread and worries, pouring anxiety into myself from the moment I open my hungover eyes. Painting an image of myself on social media, which I generally hate, that everything is *just perfect* – all the while waiting until noon when I can pour myself that first glorious glass of wine and start the cycle again. My intention every morning is just to make it as long as possible without breaking down.

I wasn't always like this.

It's amazing how you can lose yourself. The *only person* you spend every second of your life with, and you can still manage to lose track of them like a child in the mall. I've taken for granted that I'd always be in control, but the truth is that *I lost control the day the alcohol took over.* Any illusion of being in control checked out the day the alcohol became more important than my health, my goals, and my peace of mind.

33

I just read an interesting article on Unsettle.org about creating morning routines, to set yourself up for success that day – and overall, in your life. I've been doing this. But I've been doing it *so very wrong*. It is one thing to have a morning and daily routine. It's another thing completely when all your routines are destructive and harmful. What it all comes down to is the one thing we all have in common: we want to *succeed*. Not necessarily business or financial success, but success as you define it. That *I made it* moment where you feel you accomplished what you never thought possible.

Today, I'm not going to focus on getting sober.

I'm not going to fixate on all the wrong turns I've made. I *am* going to focus on taking one small step, to master the day. I am going to start my day with *intention*. I am simply going to begin the process of creating a routine that works for me and is in line with those intentions. I already write every morning, regardless of when I wake up – today it was 2 am – despite any number of work-related emails or things that need to be done. I prioritize that habit above all things because it clears my mind and has a positive, healthy reward for me: a little clarity in the fog of my struggles during those rare hours when I'm not stumbling, careless and intoxicated.

Living with intention is the opposite of how I've been feeling. It's the opposite of how addicts and alcoholics live their life, which is totally unbound and out of control.

By acknowledging how you *desire* to feel, you can enter any situation with a whole new sense of being. When you get clear on how you want to feel, you can make clear decisions that create the life you truly desire to live. The moment you tap into the feeling, you get your power back. It's all about embodying your intention.

To get your power back.

That right there is really what it's all about.

My intention for myself, for you, and for all of us, is to get our power back – one small step at a time. Starting, hopefully, with *today*.

Today, I will try my best to love myself, and treat myself better.

"Someone once told me the definition of hell: The last day you have on earth, the person you became will meet the person you could have become."

– UNKNOWN

Missing Pants, Terrifying Stairs, and the Green Fairy

FEBRUARY 12, 2017

It finally happened.

I dreamt I wasn't wearing any pants. But it gets more interesting than that.

I promise there won't be many more crazy ass dream posts; even I'm getting tired of them.

But they fascinate me, like little messengers with a cryptic puzzle I'm supposed to solve, and if I do, I get the prize at the bottom of the box of Cracker Jacks.

These are my favourite blog posts, however, so far. The ones where I get to share the bizarre adventure I just woke up from, pick them apart, and have a little therapy session with myself. I never underestimate the power of dreams and interpreting them. Sometimes it's just a dream – random events from your previous day leaking out of the dream box we place them in so we can ruminate over them without the anxiety of being awake. *Sometimes they're more, however.* Sometimes they're parts of the 'you' you're striving to become, tapping at your subconscious, so you don't forget that they're there.

First, let me tell you about the dream.

I was photographing a wedding, and everything was pretty generic. This is refreshing because my work-related dreams usually entail losing my gear or forgetting that I'm supposed to be shooting at all. Sometimes I'm on the wrong floor of a towering building, and I'm missing the wedding. At least I was present for this one, and I actually *had* my gear with me.

Don't even get me started on the ones where I'm trying to catch a plane.

Along with the whole wedding party, we went to a drama school where the bride apparently went to school. She put on a magical performance of herself as Tinker Bell, I shit you not, where she was literally flying around the room. She was either

Tinker Bell, or, knowing me, more likely the Green Fairy, the Absinthe Goddess. If you aren't sure what this is, Green Fairy, or Green Muse, is another name for the incredibly potent alcohol, absinthe. But she is also a metaphorical concept of artistic enlightenment and exploration, poetic inspiration, a freer state of mind, new ideas, and a changing social order.

Interesting.

I repeat, I'm not an alcoholic in my dreams.

However, it usually finds its way in somehow.

I was sure I would have to photoshop the hell out of these pics because I now seemed to have forgotten how to use a camera.

Finally! It happens in every work-related dream.

There was a special gala for the couple at the drama school, aside from the, you know, otherwise typical wedding reception with the Green Fairy flying around. I was still wearing pants at this point. We leave and go to a coffee shop, and I'm now running up a winding staircase to the attic to get something. I can't recall what; however, attics and staircases are very common in my dreams. I pass a lot of wait staff whom I don't know and who don't recognize me. I try to explain to them that I worked *there* – which I didn't – so I could get to the attic.

Good grief, now I'm lying in my dreams.

I think I was looking for a ruler or a wand. Instead, it was something long and thin, like a walking stick.

I never found it.

Suddenly we're all on our way back to the wedding reception, and a bridesmaid leads us a different way – down a crazy embankment to this set of insanely steep stone steps that are cockeyed and at ridiculous angles, with massive gaping spaces between them where you could fall to your death to rushing water below. My anxiety kicks in full tilt. I'm holding people up behind me and terrified, unable to find my footing, saying, *'I can't. I'm going back."*

I'm so terrified of falling I can't take another step. I'm frozen. Even recalling this to write about it is turning my insides out.

Now we are at someone's house - and this is where I suddenly have no pants on. The bride and all the bridesmaids are doing their thing, and I'm walking around trying to cover myself with my camera bag. I wasn't necessarily embarrassed, and no one was making note of my lack of pants. Sandwiches are delivered, and there are only 2 – they were labelled and had names on them, but I can't remember whose names they were. It seems we were expecting 5. I was starving, but there was no food – this could likely be me just being hungry because I woke up famished.

I go outside for a cigarette, still without pants, trying casually to disguise myself behind bushes in their front yard. Some of the girls are now in the neighbour's house, and I can hear them talking despite them being inside, as though their voices were being broadcast on an outdoor speaker.

"Hey photographer guy, looks like you need to go shopping," one bridesmaid said.

I'm more irritated than embarrassed at this point because I was doing so well at having no one notice I had no pants on.

And then, I wake up.

According to DreamMoods.com:

> *"When you are without your clothes, you are also most vulnerable. There is absolutely nothing that you can hide behind. Thus, the dream may parallel a waking situation where you feel helpless or where you have completely let your guard down."*

Well, I'd have to admit that seems spot on, given how I've been feeling lately. All this writing has been allowing me, for the first time ever, to disclose a lot of things I've kept bottled up and hidden.

A step towards vulnerability.

vul-ner-a-bil-i-ty

The quality or state of being exposed to the possibility of being attacked or harmed, either physically or emotionally

I can't say I fully adopt that definition of vulnerability. Vulnerability can be sexy. It can be positive and productive. *Opening yourself up to possibility* – period. Without being vulnerable, you can't get to the raw emotions that you need to break down and deal with. It's only in our vulnerability that we can truly see what makes us tick. What makes us who we are and allows us to see all the many parts of ourselves we need to work on – and the parts we should be proud of.

I think facing that vulnerability is a huge part of my fear of going to a recovery centre. It's the very same reason I have a hard time talking.

Opening up isn't easy.

Exposing yourself.

Being exposed. And having to *really* look at yourself. All the flaws. The broken parts. And maybe even admit some of the good things, too.

The worst.

Thedreamwell.com has this to say about the scary stairs in my dream:

> *"These dreams may also occur if we feel we are slipping in someone else's esteem of us, if we feel people are "looking down" on us and we are losing some degree of power and confidence. But as with all dreamwork, only you know the entire story of your life, and it is worth remembering that "down" does not equate with "bad." Stairs in dreams going down can also be a symbol for entering our "deeper" self, as when we start dreamwork and start to access our deeper subconscious."*

And according to Dreammoods.com:

> *"To dream that you slip or trip on the stairs signify your lack of self-confidence or conviction in pursuing some endeavour. If you slip going down the stairs, then it suggests that you are moving too quickly in delving into your subconscious. You may not be quite ready to confront your subconscious or repressed thoughts."*

On the surface, it seems obvious that I'm hesitant about quite literally *taking the steps* I need to take at this point in my life. It's fear. Fear of falling, of failure, of being exposed. Addressing repressed thoughts – *and I turn back.*

I was absolutely frozen in my dream. I watched others in front of me navigate the staircase, despite how terrifying it was. But *my* feet wouldn't move.

I was too afraid to take the next step.

I'm beginning to think this is the most profound revelation from my dream. The most honest part. The rest of it seems to be just bookends to the actual chapter, which is about facing my fear of being exposed and vulnerable through taking the steps I need to take.

It's been on my mind so much lately – the desire for change. *The next step.* For weeks now. Months, actually. I'm not surprised it's starting to manifest in my dreams. When that starts to happen, you know you're ignoring something you need to take action on.

PsychicLibrary.com says this about the attic staircase:

> *"Walking or running up the stairs can have several meanings. It can also mean you are reaching toward a higher consciousness."*

Hot damn, there it is.

So, here's my takeaway:

- Shooting the wedding: My reality, my career, my reputation

- Forgetting how to use a camera: Self-doubt

- The Green Fairy: My creativity and passion, fueled by alcohol

- The Attic: Striving for higher self-awareness. Looking for enlightenment

- The Scary Staircase: Fear of taking the next steps to stop drinking, so I can deal with the *real* issues behind my addiction

- Missing pants: Absolute vulnerability. Exposing myself. The real self.

Re-reading everything above, I'm admitting everything that I already know. And I know what that next step is.

It's just getting over the massive fear of taking it.

Broken

FEBRUARY 12, 2017

**"I didn't want to wake up. I was having a much better time asleep.
And that's really sad. It was almost like a reverse nightmare, like when you
wake up from a nightmare you're so relieved. I woke up into a nightmare."
– Ned Vizzini**

I created a very *difficult* surreal photo last April that I named 'Broken', after I made
one of the biggest mistakes of my life. And by *difficult* I don't mean technically
different, even though it was. I mean difficult in the sense that I was confessing
visually to my mistakes, regrets, and turning myself inside out to show what I
truly look and feel like inside

It's a very, very sad photo.

That *biggest mistake of my life* was the turning point for me. It was the point in
time when I realized and acknowledged that I needed help.

Here I am, 10 months later.

So little has changed.

Flashback to April 10, 2016·

> *"I haven't done anything creative in quite a long while. And that's for many
> reasons. I've been broken, and my light went out. Looking back, it was out
> for quite a long while, and it sometimes takes hitting rock bottom to realize
> how far you've fallen. This is for anyone out there dealing with depression
> or anxiety, addiction, or substance abuse - for anyone suffering loss and
> sadness. It's time to reverse the nightmare and get our wings back."*

It would appear that simply admitting that you're broken doesn't do a damn thing
about putting your pieces back together again.

One Rude Little Awakening

FEBRUARY 12, 2017

We're just returning from my nephew's birthday party.
I only had pizza and cake and turned down every drink
– and there was wine.

It was my 40th birthday a few weeks ago, and my sister gave me my belated birthday gift: a gift card for the liquor store, and a flask that reads, *"Alcohol is just awesome water"*.

Oh, right, paired with a gift card for the liquor store, to fill it up. She came by it honestly, so no shame on her – the gift was on point, and I can't deny I gave her two decades worth of reasons why that was indeed the most 'Shawn' gift you could give me.

My sister barely drinks – no one in my family really does. However, my father was a heavy drinker; my uncle was, by my definition, an alcoholic. And, of course, you have yours truly.

Both are dead now.

I'm still here.

It's a rude little awakening for me. Not a surprise, but an awakening to add to my list of recent awakenings. A year ago, I would've thought this was the best gift ever.

And in a way, *it is.*

It's the gift of another reminder that *I don't want to be like this.* Or for people to think of me as though free alcohol and a vessel to carry it in would be *the perfect gift* for me. 20+ years of demonstrating to people that it's what I want – how can I blame them?

It's not her fault. I haven't spoken to my immediate family about where I'm at or that I'm even on this journey. I'm trying to be as anonymous as possible with them so far Because, well, *family.* I know they'd be supportive and would never give me something like this if they knew it was the opposite of what I want and need right now.

The only ones who know about any of this are Hubs, my doctor, three close friends, and *all of you.*

Maybe I'll use it at the gym. Filled with a protein shake or something.

That should make for some interesting reactions.

It's Happening: I'm Going to Rehab

FEBRUARY 13, 2017

Fuck. This is a hard post to write.

The cursor is blinking at me.

What next?

This blank screen is sitting across from me, like a cynical friend, eyebrow raised, waiting for me to tell them the truth. Wanting *the whole story*.

And....?

Fuck it.

I'm going to rehab.

There. I said it. I'm doing it. I'm going.

February 21. A week from tomorrow.

I chatted with the intake specialist last night. I'm calling her at noon to complete the registration, put in my deposit, and make it real.

I fell asleep crying last night. Damn Adele on the Grammy's pushed me over the edge. Hubs and I were having a rare talk, and he wants me to go. He prefaced it with, *"Please, don't misinterpret this, but we need some time apart. To figure out who we are and what we want."*

So I'm going to rehab. For a month.

I can't blame him. It's been 16 years and we've both changed. This addiction and disease have changed me. It has made me do things that aren't *me*, and in turn, have changed *us*.

It broke my heart. Mostly because I knew it was coming, mainly because I've thought the same. That we need time apart. That I need to unload this truckload of baggage.

Thinking about it and hearing it from someone else though, those are two *entirely* different things.

I'm absolutely, fucking terrified.

Sorry for all the 'fucks' this morning, but it's seated in my gut. One huge, ever-growing FUCK, ready to be released after not giving any for so long.

I'm terrified of leaving. Of leaving hubs and the dogs for 4 weeks. Of trying to manage three businesses while away. Of what he'll go through while I'm not here. Of the prospect that he'll realize he's better off without me. That it could be the best 4 weeks of his life. That he can't forgive me, after all, and that the damage I've done is too much to carry.

I'm terrified of confronting whatever is going to break through while I break down. Of going without while I detox, getting it all out of my system first, then my soul. Of changing. Of making the wrong choice of going in the first place or going to the wrong place.

I'm terrified at the prospect of not drinking all day, every single day. Of not smoking. Of having to redefine myself without those two things that have become, sadly, the very essence of who I am and what I do.

I'm terrified of meeting myself again.

I'm terrified of losing more than I can gain.

How the fuck have I fucked up this much.

I made a deal: he'll talk to someone when I'm gone, too. A professional. I've hurt him so much and despite his valiant attempts and dedication to putting it behind him, he has wounds that need to heal and I'm the worst kind of Band-Aid.

Me trying to help him is like using the same knife that stabbed you to sew up the stitches.

So many apologies need to happen.

To each other, to him, to my friends and family.

He said that when I came back from my trip last April (when the Horrible-Awful happened) we did a good job of reconnecting. Of connecting, period. We made changes. We fell in love again.

We realized that all we ever wanted was each other. That we missed lying together. That we missed each other. Talking. *Being friends, instead of colleagues.* That the line between our marriage and our business needed better definition.

And we worked on it.

Then, like all good things around here, it faded back to where things were before I left.

Both of us sad and lonely.

Totally out of control. My drinking, my behaviour, *my indifference to everything.*

Sleeping alone. Drinking alone. Thinking alone.

Thinking too much.

Working side by side, day in and day out, yet totally alone all the time, pouring companionship out of a bottle.

I can't even *try* to fix us until I work on fixing *myself.* A broken vase can't hold any flowers. I'm lucky that he sees that. And oh, does he ever see it. He sees it to the point that he wishes I'd just leave already and go do it.

Do *anything.*

I brought up last night that people always used to ask what "our secret" was. What the trick was to *how happy* we were, how successful we were in love and everything we put our minds to accomplishing.

We would tell people the secret was that *we never expected anything from each other.* That we never asked for something from the other, and that we always supported the other in whatever they wanted to do, think or say.

To just *keep being the person the other fell in love with.*

When the *hell* did that stop?

Oh, right. *When I became an alcoholic.*

Interestingly, I sat to write this morning with very little intention, other than to share that I am finally going to rehab and, in turn, make it real. That I've set a date.

That it's 8 days away.

And here I am, hungover from last night's conversation. Terrified, heartbroken and sad.

I sat there crying and he told me to stop, to be happy about this. To look forward to the transformation, to the journey, to be grateful for the opportunity.

And all I could hear was *"I want you to leave."*

Sort of how I feel about the alcohol.

I have a disease, and he has one, too. *Me.*

I'll write more later today when I've wrapped my head around this hot mess. I'll write more when I'm a little less terrified.

Songs to Cry and Drink To

FEBRUARY 14, 2017

Well, I was a total hot mess last night.

The reality that I'm going to rehab for a month was starting to sink in, and Adele's *"Hello"* on repeat wasn't helping. Neither were the three bottles of wine I drank. Poor Hubs had/has his hands full. I sat bawling my eyes out at the kitchen island for hours, feeling all the feels and having an existential crisis. At one point, I was physically trembling and couldn't stop. It's the closest I think I've been to a total nervous breakdown. He was watching Three's Company.

Ironic.

I always thought it was just the two of us – but it's definitely three.

Hubs, myself – *and the drink.*

I was trembling. All the guilt vibrating inside me, ricocheting off the shame and bouncing against the walls of my being. Wanting out. Knowing it will get out soon. Regret started leaking out of me and fell into my wine glass more than once.

I confessed to a few more friends yesterday.

Confessions and apologies – two things I seem to be doing a lot of lately.

It's amazing how supportive my friends are – I've chosen good people in my life. Or they've chosen me. Perhaps we've chosen each other, like little magnetic puzzle pieces, attracted to one another and fitting together perfectly – two pieces of one bigger, strange picture.

I just don't want anything coming out of left field for them while I'm away, and more importantly, so they'll check in on Hubs while I'm gone. I'm worrying about that the most, feeling selfish that I'm going away for a month to focus on myself while he's stuck here dealing with everything and needing help himself.

He's always been totally selfless like that.

But I'm no good to him as I am right now. I need an overhaul and spiritual oil change.

I started a new playlist last night, because music is one of the few things that still brings me joy. I had the intention that it will be for those times in rehab when I'm journaling or to help me sleep since I'm anticipating continued, wicked insomnia. My BFF said to choose songs that make me happy.

And I tried.

The playlist sounds more like *"Songs to Cry and Drink Alone To."* #PlaylistFail.

But thoughtful music does make me happy because I come alive. It inspires creativity in me. Thoughtfulness. My imagination starts to spread its wings, aloft on the wind of melancholic ballads. It makes me feel *something*, at least, which is a refreshing change from feeling nothing for so long.

No profound revelations. No deep thoughts this morning.

Today, I'm choosing to let it all go.

For today, at least.

Or maybe until noon.

My eyeballs hurt from crying for 4 hours, and my heart hurts from beating itself up so much lately. It feels flat, as though the weight of my anxiety has been sitting on it for too long. Oh right – and I'm also hungover.

Again.

More coffee.

Happy Valentine's Day to us.

Six Days of Drinking

FEBRUARY 14, 2017

19 *litres* of wine. $300 Canadian in wine.
In less than one week. And most are the big bottles.

Hubs says I'm missing some because he took some out already.

The empties just pile up like regrets

FUCK.

The families I could feed with that money. The bills I could pay off. *The life I could live without the regrets.*

The shit I could get done without the hangovers. But honestly, I barely get hungover anymore. My body is just...*nope.* Perhaps I'm in a constant cycle of drunk/hungover, and I can't tell the difference anymore.

6 days. 19 Litres.

Most people don't drink that in a year or more.

I'm placing this here so I can look back one day and realize where I came from.

I'm counting down the hours until I go to rehab *because I can't do this anymore.*

Stuck in the Mud

FEBRUARY 15, 2017

It's been a long week.

And it's only Wednesday. We were having a *really* good day yesterday. Hubs has been focusing on gratitude – for literally everything, and I think that's helping him.

Was helping.

We got into it again last night: a big misunderstanding because my words wouldn't come out properly. It was all to do, again, with me not being able to actually, physically, motivate myself to do things. The simplest tasks – like showering or changing my clothes or climbing the stairs to go to bed - *I just can't.*

It's like my feet are stuck in mud.

And Hubs doesn't get it. *At all.*

I don't believe he thinks the problem is real, or he thinks that I'm just being lazy. He can't see – and I also can't communicate how I'm feeling – that I *do* wish I could do things. Like I *used to be able to*. It's depression, mental illness, or whatever you want to call it.

It feels like the hamsters are dead at the wheel most days.

It makes me sad because I'm going to be gone for a month – and we wasted a perfectly good evening arguing and crying again. Valentine's Day of all days. We didn't even get each other cards.

This year, I gave him disappointment, and he told me I'm disgusting.

Best presents ever.

What a stupid fucking holiday.

All this wasted time, talking in circles. Every drink stretches the circle outwards until we are even further apart and the time it takes to make our way back to each other gets longer and harder.

Wasted. Time. Literally, spent, *wasted and drunk.* How sad. I'm seriously *so tired* of writing these depressing posts. It's not like me at all.

I'm anxious to leave on Tuesday with the prospect of becoming me again. I should be writing about my hopes and learning new ways to cope. I should be focusing on the positive things – but it's so difficult when the condition of the most important thing to me is crumbling on a cracked foundation.

I told my family last night that I'm checking into rehab. That was the hardest, most challenging step so far. But, in true me-fashion, I sent a message, because sitting with them in person and talking about it is the furthest from how anyone in my family works.

Let's just say communication isn't our strong point.

But I did it. I was borderline just going to go away and try and have them not even know I was there. But I know I'm going to need their support, and I know they are all very aware that I'm an alcoholic. I hope it gives them some sort of relief that I'm *finally* getting help.

I apologized for having disappointed them.

They all lied and told me that I never had. Sweet of them, really. But now I'm going to have to tell them that lying to me about it won't help. That it's time for an honest dialogue, so we can put so many things to rest and move forward. In the end, I felt lighter though. A huge weight has lifted for me now that I'm not hiding anymore.

Honesty is helium for your soul.

Sadly, that same honesty can turn into the heaviest of weights for the people you are being honest with.

It's another step.

I'm off to the doctor at some point today to get some baseline blood work done, so it's back before I leave. Hubs is worried about my heart while going through detox. I'm already on two pills for blood pressure, and he's afraid it'll all be too much. He's worried I'll have a heart attack, or my blood pressure will spike or drop like mad.

I'm worried about my heart, too.

Just not in the same way.

I'm worried that as I try to piece all the shattered little bits of it back together, it won't go back the same way ever again.

But *I'm going to try.* Hopefully, with better results than how I tried to explain myself last night and having it all fall back apart at my feet, no matter what I tried to hold it together with. All the pieces of my explanation just kept falling to the floor, breaking into even more pieces, each somehow sharper and more jagged in the end.

Today will be better.

Grief is Just Love with No Place to Go

FEBRUARY 15, 2017

**"Grief, I've learned, is really just love.
It's all the love you want to give, but cannot.
All of that unspent love gathers in the corners of your eyes, the
lump in your throat, and in the hallow part of your chest.
Grief is just love with no place to go."**

Ugh. *My heart.*

When I read this, I came unstitched.

Last night, the sloppy mess that I was, again, kept saying, *"I can't wait to bury my dad,"* – who happened to have died in 2012.

So much grief.

So much left unsaid. Twenty-five of my 40 years just wanting to talk about so much with him – all the conversations that never happened. And in his final days, I had every intention of going to clear the air so we could both carry on with a clear conscience.

So he could take flight with no anchors or regrets.

So we could give each other the apologies we each deserved.

Apologies and acceptance.

It never happened.

> "Looking back, I have this to regret; that too
> often when I loved, I did not say so."
> *– David Grayson*

I did a self-portrait about a month before my dad passed away, a self-portrait of myself, with my face painted white, black paint streaming down my cheeks in tears as dark as ink. I'm surrounded by falling white feathers – feathers from white pigeons, to be exact. He raised birds – exotic & domestic- his entire life. Everything from pigeons to parrots, and some bizarre rodents and marsupials, for good measure.

Feathers and birds will always be symbolic of him to me. I'm going to need to gather all of them over the next month to help me rebuild and spread my wings.

There's so very much that needs to be buried.

Connection

FEBRUARY 16, 2017

"If we have no peace, it is because we have forgotten that we belong to each other."
– Mother Teresa of Calcutta

Finally. We had a nice evening. Uneventful, but in the best way.

Meaning *I didn't lose my shit*

I still managed to polish off 3 Litres of wine yesterday. How is that possible every day? But, Hubs did help with that somewhat. I was sitting in the chair as usual last night, watching Golden Girls – my other addiction – when I realized I wanted to be sitting on the couch with him.

Like we used to.

So, I did.

And, in doing so, *I felt so much better.*

It really is all about connection.

Physical touch – but also the unspoken connection. It's all the things you don't say but can both feel. The invisible threads that bind you together. Born into a world the same way we go out – *alone* – we spend our entire lives seeking connection with others.

"Vulnerability is the only bridge to build connection."

Infants are comforted by the touch of their mother, and seniors' hearts are lifted by the company of visitors. And in that vast amount of time between birth and death – for the lucky ones who are given, or allow themselves, an enormous amount of time – we all just look for that one person or thing we can genuinely connect with.

That person or thing that makes you feel like you're *home.* That person or thing you allow yourself to be *vulnerable* with.

We find comfort in having pets. I have four dogs and my heart is crushed knowing I'll be away from them for an entire month while in recovery. I worry they will miss me, when in all reality, they probably aren't even going to notice. Pets give us an unconditional sense of being needed.

A purpose.

We explore to discover music that aligns with our souls. We look to the soil to garden and connect with the earth. We write blog posts and glue ourselves to social media to find affinity with absolute strangers in exchange for sweet dopamine in the form of likes and comments.

Anything that makes us feel like we aren't alone.

Anything that gives us that sense of connection.

I struggle to connect with so many people and things. Alcohol is the one thing that is always ready, willing and waiting for me. Ready to numb all my connectors so I don't have to think, and I don't have to care. *And music.* Music is always there to try and bring me back to life, or to help me lose myself even more.

We seek asylum in anything that makes us feel connected to something greater than ourselves.

Something bigger than our fears.

Something that wraps itself around you.

Its why hugs make us feel better. Admit it – *everyone wants to be the little spoon.*

There is an unspeakable comfort to be found through connection.

The problem is when we align ourselves with things that break or prevent those connections. Addiction, grief and mental illness does that.

It whispers to you that you don't deserve it.

And I am so very tired of listening to it. I am ready to reconnect with so many things. All my loves fallen (read: *pushed*) to the wayside, that I am finally ready to pick up and wrap myself around again.

If they'll have me.

I am ready to *disconnect* from so many things. All the toxic parts that have blurred my vision and stalled my feet. I am ready to reconnect with *myself.*

I am ready.

PART 2:

Exodus

The Walk of Shame

FEBRUARY 16, 2017

No. Not *that* morning after kind of walk.
The 'It's-12-o-clock-lunch-hour-walk-to-the-liquor-store' walk.

Again.

Just like yesterday.

And the day before. And every day before that. *For the last ten years.*

I am *so not* going to miss that walk or asking Hubs to do it for me. But I know I'm still going to want to make it *every* day. Maybe we'll need to move. Maybe we live too close – literally under a minute door to door. Probably one of the deciding factors on why we moved here.

I sat today trying to remember the last sober day I had. And *I can't.* There isn't one day in recent memory (which is spotty at best, anyhow) where I didn't have a drink.

Actually, *a drink* isn't a fair unit of measure for me.

Allow me to rephrase.

I can't remember a day in the last several years where I haven't polished off bottles, *upon bottles*, of wine. How am I even still here? The human body is a ridiculously, stupidly patient thing.

Until, of course, it isn't.

I've been lucky so far. Getting ready to head to recovery in five sleeps, everything is just starting to sink in. Everything I'm doing seems amplified. Every walk. Every purchase. The clink of every empty bottle as it hits the one next to it.

Lined up like green glass dominoes, ready to make me fall.

There's no anonymity in this town, either. We live in a tiny village outside of a relatively big city. Our liquor store is *also* the variety store. So, it's the same humble people cashing me out every day while I refuse to make eye contact because I know they're aware I've been there, at the same time, every day, since we moved here nearly three years ago. Every day, buying two big bottles of wine, and a pack or two of cigarettes.

The initial *"we're having a party"* and *"company's company"* lies eventually had to stop. Honestly? Did I ever think they believed me? I just said it to make *myself* feel better. They could honestly care less. *Cha-ching.*

I'm back from the walk. Again. *And a bottle is already gone.* I just came in from the kitchen – *yes, to fill up my glass* – and saw that Hubs just wrote on the chalkboard *"Stars need darkness to shine."* Sigh.

I'm working myself up with distractions about going to recovery. What if I don't have access to coffee. Today I discovered I could only bring 200 cigarettes in, and from my math, I'll need 700, if I don't quit or cut back while there. 700. How disgusting. At a pack a day, it adds up quickly. I already know they won't get them for me, and I won't have access to them. I'm worried about withdrawal from technology. I could care less about social media – but I'm concerned about being unable to work while away. Though I know I need to focus on myself and healing, I also need to pay the bills.

I can't imagine how I'd even remotely be navigating this if I had children.

I'm just starting to get worried.

*Pours another drink.

I'm going to keep doing that walk when I get back. But in the *other direction.* When I feel the habit creep back into me, I'll just go and discover a new part of the village. Or wander through the paths I have yet to discover in the woods near our house.

I'll just keep walking until it goes away.

I'm afraid I'll walk so far that I'll never find my way back, because the fear runs deep that it *will never go away.* Is this normal? I don't feel like this is normal. But nothing about my emotions is normal, especially recently. I was so calm this morning, happy with having a nice evening for a change, which sadly only meant: *without uncontrollably bawling my eyes out.*

I can't help but connect the dots that I *only started feeling like this after my daily walk of shame.*

After I had my first drink.

And worse, after my second, and third. Pouring the anxiety down my throat, hoping to drown the anxiety.

Figure that out.

That Time I Pissed Myself in New Orleans

FEBRUARY 17, 2017

This is where the story starts to get good.

It's 2:30 in the morning. I can't sleep, like usual.

Just the regular cycle of passing out/having nightmares/waking up and not being able to turn my brain back off and put it, and everything, to rest. *This post is a long one.*

I've never told this complete story to anyone other than Hubs and my doctor.

I woke up with New Orleans on my mind.

Update from later in the day, while rereading this: *I was just scrolling through my "On This Day" memories on Facebook, and it was three years ago TODAY that I landed in New Orleans for the very first time. How weird.*

It's our home-away-from-home, to the point where we kept an apartment there for several years that we would go and stay at every couple months, or sometimes weeks. Every time, we'd leave recharged and inspired, every one of our senses brought back to life.

The music. The food. The characters we'd meet.

The alcohol.

Well, we left recharged every time, *until the last time.*

It wasn't uncommon for me to have my first round of drinks at 9 am or earlier while in NOLA, because, well – it's encouraged. Before breakfast, I'd have had a few Bloody Mary's, meaning *lots of vodka with a splash of mix*, washed down by a solo cup full of wine in hand on our way downtown at 10 am in search of more drinks. I couldn't leave a restaurant or bar without taking a "traveller" with me, because you can drink freely anywhere and everywhere, 24 hours a day. They have *drive-thru margarita shops,* for Christ's sake.

And boy, did I drink.

Looking back, I am fully aware that part of the allure of that magical city was my subconscious awareness that I could drink all day, every day, everywhere. Don't get me wrong – I fell in love with New Orleans for so many more reasons than that. It's a city that will truly change your soul, and you'll leave parts of it there every time you go. For reasons other than being so drunk you just forgot where you put them or lost them last night on Frenchmen Street.

And just like alcohol, *it calls you back.*

Our last trip was over Halloween a few months ago. *Our wedding anniversary.*

Shit hit the fan so many times between Hubs and I. Our friend tagged along for the trip, and as a result of our beyond-excessive drinking, she got herself into a bit of trouble, too. Nothing serious, but enough to have caused a massive dialogue with her husband when she returned home, which *thank God,* has proven to be for the best in the end.

But it was all because of how drunk we were.

All of it.

Well, *most of it.*

We had a few days left in New Orleans after she left, just the two of us. Most of it was spent apart, not talking. Hubs put it out there that he was coming to terms that maybe we were just meant to have those 15 years together and nothing more. Naturally, I didn't take this well, so I just drank even more. Finally, he promised himself he would stop drinking because we both identified that alcohol was the problem – at the very least, it was the root of our inability to properly communicate anymore.

Happy Fucking Anniversary. We clearly have a problem with special days, and absolutely horrible timing.

You see, a lot was going on with me health-wise at that time, and I didn't say anything to anyone – typical *alcoholic male level of self-care.* I was scared and worried, and it was growling inside me constantly, pacing back and forth, wanting out. Wanting answers. *Wanting to feel better.*

You know – that tiger in your stomach that refuses to sleep.

As usual, I pushed it down by drinking. I distracted my worry with drunkenness until of course, I couldn't anymore. The combination of excessive drinking and what was later diagnosed as a very enlarged prostate (Benign prostatic hyperplasia, or BPH – a common but horribly inconvenient condition in typically older men), led me to actual incontinence and loss of bladder function. I was in incredible pain – bouncing between being unable to go to the bathroom at all, and feeling like I was pissing razors when I actually could piss at all, which wasn't often. The physical pressure was unbearable. This had been going on for years, but the condition was accelerating faster than I cared to acknowledge.

A common symptom of BPH is urgency. Did you know you were signing up for a crash course in the male prostate today? I'll try and make this quick.

There's a complete lack of a warning system. You go from not having to go to the bathroom, to ummm, I'm not going to make it within a matter of seconds. When you're drinking 24 hours a day, the sheer volume of liquid you need to pass is enough on its own, much less when *you physically can't* – and your body just holds it all in. I knew I was having prostate problems, and my father passed away from complications of prostate cancer – so there was an inner terror I was refusing to acknowledge or talk about. Two of my cousins had theirs removed, and my grandfather had BPH as well.

The night, or more accurately, *one of the nights*, when I actually *pissed myself in public* because I couldn't physically hold it any longer, I left Hubs at the store – buying liquor, naturally – so I could try and make it back to our apartment before him. My plan was to nonchalantly throw my pants in the washer, have a shower, and avoid admitting what happened.

He'd never have to know.

Fail.

I was so embarrassed, and in lieu of how awful things were already going on our trip I didn't want to add *one more filthy piece* to the puzzle. Especially because all the pieces were adding up to look like part of a gruesome picture, now pissed on by a goddamn drunk.

The shame was worse than the pain of the symptoms.

He gets back to the apartment, and immediately questions why the washer is on (did I think he wouldn't notice?). Then, with the most disgusted look ever, he says "Oh my god. *Did you actually piss your pants?*" He rolls his eyes and chalks it up to me being a drunk.

I get defensive. Doors slam. There's yelling. We don't talk the rest of the night. The next morning I get up and leave before we even have a chance to see each other.

Beautiful avoidance.

I remember standing in line at Starbucks that morning for what felt like forever. My hangover was the size of the entire French Quarter, and my shame was as big as New Orleans. I was angry at myself, and I was apparently upset that Hubs is not, in fact, a mind reader. In my head, I had convinced myself I'd been so toxic to myself over the years, that I most certainly had prostate cancer, and that I was dying, and by some cruel twist of cause and effect, I also somehow caused it.

Because of guilt. That's what we do.

I may as well have as many drinks as possible in the meantime, so I don't have to deal with it.

We texted each other intermittently throughout the morning. I snuck back to the apartment and sat alone by the pool on the roof, feeling like an absolute useless pile of shit, grateful the rooftop had its own dedicated bathroom for my increasingly disagreeable bladder. The hangover wasn't helping. I had been developing a cold all week and was coughing uncontrollably. This later turned into pneumonia, and I was out for literally ALL of November – I'm still on puffers because of it.

I contemplated everything on that rooftop literally, from killing myself to flying back to Canada.

I eventually needed a drink so bad I summoned the courage to go downstairs to the apartment and get one. I was too tired to go anywhere else. But it was a different kind of tired; my legs could have got me there, and my soul could muster the strength.

This is where the conversation happens, that he tells me he thinks maybe our time is up. That we were just meant to have the time we've had, and that's that. *I refuse to accept it.* I finally spill the tea on how I've been feeling physically, how terrified I am, and explain all my up-until-now unspoken symptoms. That, with the exception of accidentally *pissing myself three times in as many days,* I can't otherwise go to the bathroom. And, when I can, it's essentially a dribble that feels like a combination of burning acid and broken glass. That can make a person a little irritable – and let's add to that impending pneumonia. I explain that my being drunk didn't help my reaction to *his* reaction, and that his lack of understanding only compounded my embarrassment.

Blah, blah, blah.

It's incredible how a little honesty can change the trajectory of a shit show.

> "The worst distance between two people is a misunderstanding."

Things improved slightly and we could actually bear being in each other's company again, however begrudgingly. I commit to seeing a doctor as soon as we return for both the pneumonia developing faster by the minute and the dreaded prostate exam. Initial results were that it was most definitely "remarkably enlarged," and I'm sent for an ultrasound of my prostate.

Yes, the experience was as awful as you might imagine. It was more awful than I even imagined it would be.

Waiting for the results felt like I was holding my breath underwater for two weeks.

It's not cancerous.

Thank God.

I'll be on meds indefinitely to control it and will likely need to have my prostate removed within the next 5 to 10 years. I suppose it's better than the alternative, though, which is dying of cancer. The pills have some awful side effects, to the point where I'm wondering which is the lesser of two evils: taking them and feeling like this, or not taking them and feeling like *that.* Plus, they interact with essentially everything, including my mood, sex drive, and give me wicked vertigo.

How awesome.

So, this is one of those rare situations where I'm going to thank the alcohol for something – saving my life, and possibly my marriage. Things needed to blow up so badly for me to finally address and be honest about my fears, and in turn, it saved my life.

Granted, I'm sure if I weren't an alcoholic, *things would never have gotten to that point in the first place.*

New Orleans has a way of doing this to you. *Changing your life.*

I never imagined it would also save mine.

To Everything, There is a Season

FEBRUARY 17, 2017

"To everything, there is a season, a time for every purpose under the sun."
– Ecclesiastes 3:1-8

I did one of my surreal photos on my father's birthday, 2 years after he passed away.

It's one of my favourites, and I've been thinking about it a lot, lately. Picture a deer standing alone in the middle of a field at dusk, with the to-be-expected evening fog and dew setting itself to sleep for the night; everything orange and brown and looking just like what the word *'October'* feels, plus how it smells like cinnamon and cloves and the way it manages to start soft with cold crisp snaps in the middle and wraps it up with a rolling chill. The deer has no antlers; instead, branches of a tree are in their place, with autumn leaves falling from them and just a few left on the bare twigs bracing themselves for winter.

The phrase above is better known as the lyrics from the #1 song *"Turn! Turn! Turn!"* by The Byrds.

My mom has this hanging, huge, above the fireplace in her living room. The imagery means a lot of different things, to a lot of different people. When I did it, it was way of grieving – of coming to terms that everything happens for a reason.

That everything happens in its own time, in its own season.

That *transformation* is part of the big picture. *The cycle of life, death, and rebirth.* This photo has always spoke to me of grieving and letting go.

Letting go of my dad.

"Autumn shows us how beautiful it is to let things go."

Today, it means something new to me. It's moved into a new season: *rebirth*.

A new season is on the horizon.

Finally.

Time for Transparency and $61,320 Worth of Wine

FEBRUARY 17, 2017

The closer I'm getting to leaving for rehab, the more I'm understanding what is important to me – and the more *transparency* is starting to mean to me.

What's the point if I go into this journey with NO accountability? I'm not doing myself any favours by hiding behind an anonymous gravatars or pseudonyms.

I've changed more in the last 18 days than I care to count, much less the last six years together, or more.

Is it normal to miss those closest to you, before you even leave? Because that's how I'm feeling right now. In all honesty, I've missed them for the last year, two years, and more. Even though I've been right here. *Sort of.*

I want to go barf a little.

Not for leaving, but for leaving that sort of happiness I see in photos of Hubs and I somewhere over the course of the last God knows how many years.

Even then - was I happy? *Because I was still drunk in most of those photos.*

At the rate I've been going – since this photo was taken six years ago, I've drank over 4,380 large bottles of wine.

6,570 LITRES OF FUCKING WINE.

$61,320 worth of wine.

In 6 years.

How's that for transparency?

*I want to go barf **a lot.***

Clock Watching

"Time has a wonderful way of showing us what really matters."
#alcoholicproblems

I spend so much of the day watching the clock. *Spending* my time, like it's a currency. Check to see if it's a decent enough time for a drink. I try to wait until noon every day. Most days I'm successful. It starts when I wake up – usually 3 am, though it's been earlier lately.

Watching the clock.

This morning, watching the clock as I'm nearly out of cigarettes. The store doesn't open until 7am, so I'm dividing them to fit perfectly into that wedge of time, so I don't run out and my mind goes wild and starts catastrophizing.

Checks clock.

Afternoon arrives, and so does the drink. Levels drop – in the bottle, and in my mood. Anxiety arrives, watching the clock in comparison to how much wine is left in the bottle.

Should I go to the store and get more? They close in an hour.

I'm counting the days until I leave for recovery, like a child waiting for Christmas morning, hoping to get exactly what I've asked for, what I've wanted all along.

Time slows.

Days are beginning to feel like months.

I wonder how time will feel, unplugged and dropped into an entirely new life.

I've decided I'm not bringing a watch with me.

Watch.

The word itself *demands* that I give it attention, placing landmarks and permissions at certain numbers and angles, assigning false structure to my day. Clock *watching*, for instruction on what to do next – how much time I have left today, and how much has been spent.

Times of day turn into triggers.

Two little hands, adding up all the time wasted, not waiting for anyone – *they just keep ticking.* Speeding up. Slowing down.

Time is priceless.

Waste it wisely.

Overthinking

FEBRUARY 18, 2017

I've been making the stupid mistake of trying to learn as much about this recovery process I'm about to enter – *and what to expect* – by googling the shit out of it. *Bad. Idea.* Don't *ever* Google health-related anything.

I'm absolutely terrified of the detox and alcohol withdrawal. This morning I came across an interesting chart that plots me as *"high risk for major, life-threatening withdrawal"* based on volume per day and length of consumption.

Um, how about 18 drinks a day for at least the last ten years or more? Where does that fall on the chart? Is there a separate for Olympian-level drinkers? You know. All the fun withdrawal symptoms, like seizures and DT's. Hallucinations, and blood pressure issues, which I already struggle with. Confusion. Agitation. Nightmares. Fever.

Fun times. Though honestly – it's not a far stretch for how I'm feeling right now.

Then again – *I could be fine.* I could pop right out of detox like one of those disturbed and haunted Jack-in-the-Box clowns and into the program with nothing but some insomnia, night sweats and, knowing me, uncontrollable sobbing – not to mention likely scaring everyone else there.

All this overthinking.

I'm trying to figure out which is the chicken, and which is the egg.

Did my mental health cause the addiction? Did the addiction cause and compound the internalized struggles trapped in my head? Is it all part and parcel, each feeding on the other, growing fat and heavy in each other's company like two gluttons just waiting to eat *me,* too?

I'm a *"the more you know"* sort of person. I love to learn. *But damn.* It can work against me sometimes. Too much information, too much misinformation, too many possibilities. I need to learn how to just *let it be.*

Because it's going to be whatever it's going to be, and the only thing I can do about it is accept it and embrace it.

And breathe.

It's part of the process. Right?

"Right now, you might be in a situation that you think you won't survive but six months ago you were in a situation you didn't think you'd survive and two years before that you were in a situation you didn't think you'd survive and the point is you will always surprise yourself and you will always make it through." – Unknown

The World Spins Madly On

FEBRUARY 19, 2017

48 Hours.

That's how long before I'll be on my way to Toronto, getting on a plane alone, and heading for 'recovery,' with my bags packed full of shame and my heart packed full of fear of the unknown.

There I go, watching the clock again.

I have so much to do before I go. The idea of being away for a month is intimidating. I can't say I'm going to resist being forced to unplug when I get there. It's been over a decade since I've spent a day living *instead* of working, scrolling, typing, swiping – and, of course, *drinking.*

"The whole world is moving and I'm standing still."

I don't even know if I'll remember *how* to take care of myself. Not to be confused with being *focused* on myself. Self-interested and self-indulgent, but for a change this time, it's self-*care.*

I'm looking forward to that moment when I realize that life is going on just perfectly well without me in it back home. That the world will keep spinning madly on whether I am lost or whether I am found. That's humbling and very sad all at once, and I can't help but feel lonelier than ever after those words just crawled out of me and on to the page.

"I just got lost and slept right through the dawn" – *The Weepies*

I've been having a tough time turning my brain off this week. More so than usual. When I committed to going to recovery, I cried for two days straight, as though *I just found out my best friend or my dog was dying.* And over the last few days, I've come to realize it's quite the opposite.

It's as though they found a cure for my dying friend. That they're going to be okay, after all.

The only reason I should be crying is with gratitude for this opportunity and the opportunity to *let it all go.*

Finally. *Again.*

Like Being Dead, But Without the Commitment

FEBRUARY 20, 2017

"Drunkenness is temporary suicide."
– Bertrand Russell, *The Consequences of Happiness*

I slept until 8am. For the first time in months (maybe years?) – I think it's mental and emotional exhaustion from all that evil overthinking. I was making great-ish progress on the packing front yesterday, then hit a wall (of bottles) and laid down for what was supposed to be a 20-minute nap, which turned into 4-hours. I woke up, polished off a magnum of wine, then returned to bed. Hubs invited friends over, and the last thing I felt like doing was being social.

With them, *or myself.*

Sleep is just like drinking – the more of it you have, the more of it you want.

It's the perfect avoidance tactic for everything.

Like being dead, but without the commitment.

Which makes it *just* like drinking.

Today is the last day of my life that I am having a drink.

Or drinks. *Or bottles of wine.* Unless I drink on the plane (yes, this scenario has already crossed my mind many times since the day I booked my room at detox – my flight is too early to drink at the airport, otherwise I probably would. Just another example of how I build my life and plans around the bottle). But who am I kidding – of course, I'm going to drink at the airport, and on the plane, and as much and as quickly as I can refuel before my tank gets drained.

Today is the last day of my life that I am having a drink.

I need to stop thinking of it as *going without.* As if *something will be missing* from my life. There will be so many things missing, in all honesty. I will be missing

75

the sense of being absolutely out of control. I will miss trying to get through the day dragging regret behind me like a rug-wrapped corpse that I'm trying to find a secluded woods to bury. I will be missing my lack of confidence that I turn to drinking to replace. I will be missing the guilt I wake up with every morning that bubbles up throughout the day, and also puts me to sleep every night.

Not *missing*. Missing is the wrong word. Missing sounds sad. As in, "*I miss you*".

There will be an absence.

And I'm going to do my best to replace it with things that serve me. Picking up things I left behind: *art, music, writing, friendships*. Cleaning my *house*, so to speak.

Back to my roots. It reminded me of a photo I did six years ago. It's one of the weirder ones I've done.

Imagine the trunk of a tree in the middle of a forest; it's a mystical place you'd picture in a fairy tale. From the tree doesn't stem what should be branches alone, but it's *me*, bursting into life now that I have *roots* and am forever grounded, finally able to lean into the wind, learning to bend instead of break.

I've never understood it, to be honest, and I'm not sure if I'm being born from, or to, the tree. But even then, I felt that hollow in my gut. *The absence.* The gut feeling that something was missing and preventing me from being whole. I was longing for roots and something to nurture me; the earth, the air, and *myself.*

It screams of wanting *to be alive but being caught somewhere in between.*

I'm not even sure where this post is going. On my second cup of coffee, and I'm finally just starting to wake up from that rare, deep sleep I could have gladly lost myself in forever.

And there it is.

Finally, waking up.

That's where I am on this journey. Despite usually only getting three hours of sleep each night, I've been asleep *for years.*

Like being dead, but without the commitment.

I'm eager to see what the morning brings.

Not All Cries Are Created Equal

FEBRUARY 20, 2017

First, there's the type of cry like when you stub your toe and the pain has nowhere to go, so it turns into liquid and forces itself from your eyes.

Then, there's the type of cry that comes from grief. *Sadness for a loss.* It's slow and steady and has been waiting for someone to ask you those impossible words: *how are you doing?* Then it all bursts out of you, like a dam being broken. Finally, the pressure releases, and you pretend to be okay in the end. But it's not the end, and you're not okay.

Then, there is *the* cry that erupts from the depth of your being. Where all the salt has settled from every disappointment in your life. It gets stirred up and spins upward through all your fears and uncertainties and burns you on the way out to the point of not being able to open your eyes. Like fire and regret have turned into tears, and they just want out.

Now.

It's through the burning and stinging, through the pain and the blinking, that all the sorrows and regrets you can't ever speak of just pool out of you.

And you can exhale.

For now.

Short breaths caught quick between sobs.

The poison has left you - *for a little while.*

That's the type of cry I've been having today.

Packing is hard.

Letter for Hubs

FEBRUARY 20, 2017

**It's 10:45 pm and in less than 6 hours, you'll be driving
me to an airport because I'm an alcoholic.**

I am sorry.

And thank you.

Thank you, more than you know.

Thank you for being patient with me. In times when I know you probably want to walk out the door and never look back. In times when you don't understand why something SO SIMPLE can be so HARD for me. For at least *trying* to understand that, even in times when you're tired and you can't. Thank you for allowing me to do this – for myself, and for us. Thank you for this second, third, and *fifteenth* chance. Thank you for your belief in me – for your hope that *maybe this time* I'll get it right.

Thank you for every sleepless night you've spent – apart from me and I from you. Most days, on different floors and in different rooms. Miles and lightyears apart, but still there for me. Always.

I am sorry for all the spilled wine, the slurred words, the thoughts that came out all wrong, and the times I've passed out on the couch or the chair, and every single night you've climbed those stairs alone to bed without me there to crawl into bed with you.

I'm sorry for not being there to have and to hold.

Thank you for whatever it is in you that sees that maybe there's a chance I'm not completely broken, but maybe I've been trying to put myself back together all wrong.

Thank you for every time, while in my darkest moments, your voice has risen up and encouraged me to try *just one more time*. Especially when those days were the hardest for you.

Because of me.

This is the hardest thing I've ever had to do. And you've sat there quietly. Patiently. For years, waiting for the day I would just wake up and realize that this couldn't go on any longer.

I'm sorry.

You deserve a best friend and a husband – *not a drunk.*

And I promise you, I am still in here, somewhere.

I'm still here.

And I'm going to go and find me, for both of us. Because in finding me, I'm only finding *half* of who I am.

Thank you for being that other half…*patiently waiting for me.*

I woke up, I sat down, and I wrote this. It was the first thing on my mind and has been the first thing in my heart for so long now.

Stars need darkness to shine.

I miss you. I love you. I thank you. I am sorry.

Shawn

Let the Games Begin

FEBRUARY 21, 2017

I have an unhealthy Golden Girls obsession.

You've been warned.

Rose: "Well, I'm off!" **Dorothy:** "That would be my diagnosis."

And so am I.

It's 2:35 am, and I'm busy procrastinating on packing those final pieces still.

We leave in 2 hours. And I just *can't*.

Like, *what the fuck is wrong with me.*

I'm sitting here, flipping between coffee and wine – *at nearly 3am* – because it's the last glass I can have. *Until the next one.* But wait – I should have coffee. Then I see the wine. *Maybe one more drink.*

This will be the last one.

Forever.

I knew it would be hard. I didn't think it would be *this* hard.

I'll be surprised if they let me on the plane – I've been crying for 12 hours and look like I've been on a 20-year bender (which I have). I have just under 7 hours to pull myself together before we take off.

The worst of the baggage has been packed for years. *Let's be honest.*

Everything else is just superficial. Things to bring comfort and help me feel like I'm not actually *away*. That I'm not alone.

*Comforts and entitlements...*all the little silver spoons of privileged North American life, rolled up tightly in a suitcase, only to drag it all behind me until it can decompress and cause me anxiety in a new, unfamiliar place.

Thank you.

To whoever reads this. To all of you for encouraging me. To all of you who have walked this walk, and every one of you taking the time to think of me. For every one of you waking up each morning and being strong enough to stay sober one more day and to cheer on total strangers who are fumbling, *just like me.*

THANK YOU.

I feel ridiculously self-indulgent – but all this writing was only ever intended *for me.* I didn't think for a second that anyone would actually *get it.* Or even more terrifying – *read* it. I just thought this was easier than actually, physically writing things down on real-life paper – you know, like the *old days.*

In any case, *I'm off.*

Let the games begin.

PART 3:

Revelations

Not in the biblical sense.
There are no saints to be found here.

30 Hours. Day 1.

FEBRUARY 22, 2017

It seems a silly thing to celebrate.
30 hours of sobriety.

The average person can go 30 days without batting an eye. But here I am – checked into detox and waiting for the gross parts to pass. I can't take credit for most of that sobriety, just yet. They gave me a pill to help me sleep – and sleep I did for 12 hours. I sweat like Niagara Falls and had the worst nightmares of being stuck in a photography dark room sorting through black and white negatives of grotesque murder scenes. I peeled off the t-shirt I slept in like a second skin. *Disgusting.* It should just be burned – and I'm sure all the alcohol that seeped out of me and into it would fuel the fire like gasoline.

Small accomplishment No. 2. *I didn't drink on the plane.*

I wanted to so badly. But I reminded myself that it would just start the cycle over, and I'd be in detox even longer. So, I resisted and pretended my tomato juice was 50% vodka.

Small accomplishment No. 3. *I've eaten. A lot.*

On top of all the alcohol and addiction, I resist eating. Sometimes, I'll go days without food, and fill myself with litres of wine and not a morsel of nutrition. But I've eaten solid since yesterday – including a bag of sour peach candies last night that made me want to be sick, but I needed something to excite my taste buds for the lack of wine. Sugar. *Anything.*

They're feeding me well here (and I can now say I've experienced octopus salad, which was a culinary masterpiece). I will admit I did not want to eat yesterday or today, since I got here.

And I don't think it's because of hunger.

It's because I don't really want to be social just yet. These first few days of detox, I'm allowed to do as I please, for the most part. And talking is among my absolute least favourite things to do on a good day – especially with new people.

And *everyone* here is "new people."

Not many of them, thankfully – there's 7 of us at the moment – but it's like my first day of school and I'd rather wrap my head around the fact that I'm *actually here* rather than start spilling my drunken beans to total strangers.

I have the shakes. I've smoked one extremely long cigarette since I got here – I barely need a lighter because I could light each one after the one before if I cared to. I need to work on that.

For the first time in forever, I'm not listening to music – at home, there is music playing 24 hours a day. *It's my therapy.* Right now, I'm listening to the birds, and the wind. I hear hammering in the distance and someone singing.

I think it's Genevieve. She's a doll. She's the lovely woman who feeds us and keeps us all sane with her smile.

My leg won't stop shaking. I could seriously power a vehicle with it right now, and my head feels like someone is inflating a glass balloon. My stomach has started doing absolutely horrible things, and in the last hour, I've developed a pounding in my ears – not from my heart racing but something beating far deeper inside me.

My nerves.

Tonight, I meet with the doctor again, and we'll discuss my treatment plan. I've already met two of my counsellors; both seem wonderful. I was greeted with the biggest hug when I arrived at the airport. I wasn't expecting that at all.

Funny how your mind can create an entirely different world for you to waste your time and energy dreading. Expecting the worst when only the best is waiting for you. Lining up worst case scenarios like little toy soldiers just waiting to attack you.

I just looked at my hands for the first time. I knew they were shaking. They're *actually trembling* as much as my leg. Sad. It could be the coffee, but even that, I'm trying to moderate. So far, it's not going well on the coffee front.

One day at a time.

And, for the first time in over a decade, I can say *"I didn't have a single drink yesterday."*

Tomorrow, hopefully, I can get out of the detox room and into my actual room. The Detox room is totally depressing. I'm looking forward to 'settling in' – right now, I can't even unpack. The only thing I've unpacked is a toothbrush and four framed photos of my cheering squad back home. *It helps.*

I've been questioning if I belong here since the moment I landed. The guy in the detox room next to me looks like he's been run over by 15 steamrollers. He hasn't slept since he arrived on Monday, and the poor guy is losing his mind. I feel for him – any meds they've given him aren't working. He's been too strung out on opiates for so long that he's literally immune, and his brain just won't shut off. Like one big stationary thunderstorm that won't stop rumbling, and it's just hanging there brewing, not going anywhere.

He has *the thirst* and it's not giving up. But I'm so proud of him for being here – whether it was his choice or not. *I'm rooting for him.*

I'm rooting for myself.

When I question if I belong here, I remember that *I'm out of control.*

So, today is Day 2. *Of forever.*

But all I'm going to worry about today – *is today.*

For a much-welcomed change, I'm not going to spend my day wound up in the last three decades. Or the last year. But I *will* dwell a little on yesterday *because I'm damn proud of it.*

It's still early – 11:17 am (I'll tell you about the significance of 11:17 to me, one day, and how it dominates my life, always showing up like a bill collector – but a welcome one).

Right now, though, I'm fixated on wanting a drink.

I have been craving one badly since my last one at 3 am yesterday, when I made a conscious drunken effort (is that possible? Conscious and drunk in the same sentence?) to remember *every single moment of that last drink,* and the weight of the glass as I placed it in the sink. Bawling my eyes out. I can hear the glass stem hit the metal and could paint you a picture of what it looked like.

My last glass of alcohol, and it was so much heavier than the glass and wine themselves.

Being here - and I mean *really being **here**, in this moment* – is going to be the most challenging part of this journey, I think.

Wish me luck. It's this time every day I start drinking, and I'm literally fixated on that. I just spoke with a fellow patient here and he's suggested I ask for a Valium to chill me the hell out – he noticed my hands shaking and my nervous leg that's pretty much able to vibrate this entire island all the way back to Canada.

Sorry, this has been all over the place. Appropriate for how I'm feeling right now.

One day at a time.

A dragonfly just landed on my laptop.

Day made.

Ready To Start Bleeding

FEBRUARY 22, 2017

I was really hoping that tomorrow, Day 3, I could get out of *detox*.

The word sounds dirty to me. Like I'm contaminated.

No such luck. At least one more day until I can graduate to a regular room, doctor's orders, but they want to try to start me with some counselling (concentration permitting – *not* my forté at the moment). My brain is a freaking pinball machine, and the closest I can come to describe my headache is as though I've hit my head on an anvil then rolled onto a butcher knife, which lodged itself somewhere in between my eyes, while someone is repeatedly punching me at the base of my skull with brass knuckles.

And let's not forget the vertigo and kick drums in my ears.

I have lots of reading but can't imagine focusing on the words. I keep closing my eyes while typing this hoping the butcher knife will fall out for just 2 seconds. I'm getting super sensitive to light and I'm not sure if that's normal withdrawal symptoms or just the headache/migraine/butcher knife-anvil cocktail.

I'm going to crawl back into the stale detox room now because the mosquitos are too brutal. The little bastards are attacking me from every angle, like bad memories.

I keep swatting at them, but they keep coming back to bite me.

I'm actually looking forward to counselling, despite my gut fear of talking and opening up – in person, to an actual *human being* sitting across from me expecting eye contact. Typing is absolutely no problem for me. I can sit here with the biggest pregnant pause, and no one will ever notice. But, in person, it becomes an ever-growing elephant waiting for a peanut...and I'm never certain I have any in my pockets, and the room is starting to get suffocatingly claustrophobic.

But, to actually *talk* about this. *The root of this.* Maybe, one day.

I am still very aware that there are two distinct parts to all of this – the alcohol, *and the glass*. It's that glass I've been carrying around with me for the last 30 years that I'm interested in understanding. *The alcohol has just been there to fill it up, and now that, too is a disease.*

That stupid empty cup, weighing me down and looking for fulfillment. It was only ten days ago that I committed to taking that 40-year bandage off to finally look at the wound.

I'm ready to start picking at the scab.

As terrified as I am, *I'm ready to start bleeding.*

HALT

FEBRUARY 23, 2017

Hungry. Angry. Lonely. Tired.

Today, I had my first two sessions with my counsellors here at the *clinic,* which is how they like to refer to it. I will have three counsellors in total. It was optional since I'm still in *'detox at the clinic'* – they just wanted to give me the option, and I agreed to try because I'm beginning to get bored as hell sitting alone with my brain, which is often the worst company.

I'm still having difficulty focusing, but I participated in a "community" group round table, discussing 'how we were all feeling' today. (Note: this is *not* an AA book, nor does it align with my philosophies – it's not my path, but high-fives to whatever works for you).

This post is more of a "What'd you do in school today, honey?" post. Take from it what you will, but in my current frame of mind I need to write this down, because I want to remember it.

I can't remember what I said at this morning's community session. Or what anyone else said, so there's a good starting point. My contribution was something along the lines of "I'm really fucking tired, dizzy and confused, and still wrapping my head around being here."

Not my most profound moment.

I later had my first meeting with my main counsellor (let's call him Tony for anonymity's sake), who focuses on addiction. They call it Bio-Psycho-Social, essentially dissecting everything about me – from a surface point of view. It was awkward, talking about everything from my sex life to finances. My memory right now is so short-term, but the one little gem I took away was that *addiction is more potent than love.*

It's stronger than our basic need for survival, and that alcoholism and any addiction is a *symptom.*

I was aware of that coming in here – outside of admitting I was/am totally out of control and a raging alcoholic. I committed myself to come here because I need to know *the why* and I have to learn the *how.*

I was given a break to collect myself afterwards because I became a bit emotional leaving the session. I was totally fine during it but experienced another one of those *leaving my body* moments, but this time I left my mind, too. None of it is particularly surprising because my hormones are having the wildest rave ever inside of me right now.

Next, I was able to meet with my other counsellor, a Cognitive Behaviour Therapist who I swear to God is a wizard. He even has the beard, and his magic wand was the ballpoint pen he spun in his hand while maintaining constant eye contact with me, making me feel vulnerable and totally uncomfortable.

And it worked.

The bastard cracked me like an egg in fifteen minutes.

Again, I can't recall everything we talked about. The drugs they're keeping me on are helping big time with the withdrawal; but not so much with my coherency and memory. I had a conversation with another patient here today and asked him the same question three times in less than ten minutes. Thank God he's been here three weeks and gets where I'm at right now. This new counsellor let's call him Frank.

Frank's focus for our session tomorrow is going to be talking about how I avoid *everything*, how I can't say no, and why in the world I have an innate sense to build up bigger-than-life expectations for myself. Why I numb myself with drinking, so I won't have to deal with situations that make me feel as though I'm disappointing someone else. For those expectations I've fabricated entirely in my own mind, remember? Among other things, I'm sure, but again I can't really remember.

It's easier to get and stay drunk than admit to myself or others that I just *can't* <insert the simplest thing here>.

Then in a group session tonight, we read an excerpt from a book (*I Want to Change My Life - How To Overcome Anxiety, Depression & Addiction*) by Steven M. Melemis) that really, really stuck with me, despite the valium/lorazepam-cocktail-fog I'm in. I only know the name and author of the book because I have a printout beside me that I had to reference.

HALT.

Hungry. Angry. Lonely. Tired.

The high-risk situations that trigger my addiction. And for the first time ever, I connected all four of those situations to how I have been feeling for as long as I can recall. Granted, there's been high points where I've felt on top of the world. But they're in between those valleys where I can't imagine ever climbing that mountain again, stuck in a bottle and unable to get out, drowning because I'm too tired to swim.

It's so premature, but I can already connect those dots. Those blurry, messy, ink-blot-like dots that sometimes look like a party, and other days look more like a funeral.

HUNGER: An ongoing eating disorder, for 25 years. I'll go days without eating and not even notice until Hubs reminds me I NEED TO EAT.

ANGER: Anger at myself for failures, for disappointing people, including myself, for the consequences of my actions, and anger at God – or whatever higher power you want to call it (I subscribe to the "universe" as my higher power) – for taking my dad and that *entire side of my family in under 5 short years*. Anger at myself for not being enough and not being able to complete the simplest tasks – in turn disappointing others and myself. Anger for generational guilt over things I have no control over. *Wash and repeat.*

LONELINESS: I've isolated myself from so many people – primarily the ones that mean the most to me (because of feeling undeserving, because of the anger and self-hatred issues). Loneliness in my relationship caused by drinking.

TIRED: In the physical sense, 3-ish hours max a night is not enough, especially for someone who drinks 3 Litres+ of wine a day (20-25 drinks). And I can't call it *sleep*. It's a very short but destructive cycle of passing out and not even waking up but sleepwalking through my day until I pass out again. Then, there's the *really tired kind of being tired*. Like, I just can't do it anymore. *Feeling flat.*

The emotional/mental/spiritual exhaustion has drained me, and I feel like I have nothing more to give to myself or anyone else. The kind of tired when all you can muster saying is, *"I'm done."*

If you can even muster that.

So, despite having the point of this much larger group conversation we had being *"identifying the high-risk situations that may trigger us to drink"* – being new to this program, I was looking *backwards*.

Everyone else there was preparing themselves for the *future*. Many are about to leave and begin their recovery journey and aftercare, whereas *I'm the new guy*.

It felt like my first day in class, learning a brand-new language.

But HALT stuck with me. Not only because of what it stands for and what to watch for – but that every one of those triggers, that have been my literal existence for the last decade or more have literally HALTED my life.

Not only halted but reversed many parts of it.

One drink forward, 10 steps back.

PS: it's been 2 days, 19 hours and 11 minutes since I had my last drink, and I haven't killed anyone yet.

Sing Me to Sleep

FEBRUARY 24, 2017

Someone sing me to sleep.

I've tossed and turned since trying for lights out at 10pm, and I just can't. They halved my dose of lorazepam last night, and I'm wishing they hadn't. I could get the nurse and ask for more but then I'd be asleep all morning, and I don't want that, either. So, I'm stuck in limbo somewhere between being half and completely dead at the moment and dragging myself along zombie-like towards insanity.

I swear that sanity lives in that little part of your brain that allows you to rest. Like a fat little hobbit – you either have one living there that is lazy as fuck and you don't even know they're there, or one that likes to stomp around with hard-soled shoes at all hours of the night on the second-floor apartment above your room, dropping shit and banging pots and pans, replaying all the old home movies from your childhood at the loudest their surround sound system allows.

Pretty sure the latter kind lives in mine.

And he shacked up there so long ago I don't even know when he moved in. He just sort of showed up like a squatter and has never left.

Sleep is something I am so jealous of. I'm not a jealous person. Things and stuff, I can take it or leave it. But those priceless things – like sleep and the clarity of mind it allows upon waking – *that I am jealous of.*

I haven't known it in years. I'd have to go back to grade school to remember when sleep just came unquestioned, like the law of gravity or breathing air. Never having to be thought about, but always, reliably there. Those pubescent years when your body is stronger than your mind, and it silences your thoughts so you can grow.

But no.

Sleep has become a crossword puzzle. Riddles and backwards questions, stacked up in empty boxes needing answers before I can turn the page and shut my eyes. But all the answers are never there, so I'm just stuck here wondering things like 'what's 8,400 letters and starts with B.' And every possibility runs through my head until morning comes with its bags packed full of bricks and regrets, ready to let me drag them around all day.

In the few minutes of sleep I think I managed to get tonight, at least the nightmares didn't creep in. *They usually do* – in that surreal moment of drifting somewhere between "it's happening" and "I'm out" – that weird ether where you're neither here nor there, like a door slowly shutting, the nightmares dart like mice into your mind and start building filthy little nests for you to have to clean up the next morning, piecing them apart and wondering where the hell they came from.

At least I'm just exhausted, which is a step up from *exhausted and disturbed.*

I need to stop expecting things. I was *expecting* to sleep last night, just like the last two nights, medicated but blissful. That stupid asshole of a hobbit that lives upstairs with his wooden clogs danced around again, cataloguing all the new questions and ideas from yesterday, like a drunken librarian tripping over books and theories and falling on his face over and over, only to keep me awake from his endless racket, throwing dictionaries at the wall that were of no help with my crossword puzzles.

I'm tired.

On top of being confused and lonely, I'm disappointed to be *here* again – 3 am, wide awake, with nothing but words to keep me company. Unclear thoughts and jumbled sentences, knocking at my brain and wanting to crawl out my fingers, falling into place on the white space of a computer screen. When I write, I'm usually unsure of where it's going or what I'm saying, until 3 or 4 final words drop themselves in italics, a door slams, and that angry little hobbit goes back to his room.

What a fucking asshole.

Honesty and Self-Love

FEBRUARY 24, 2017

Today was a good day.

I just had to type that, because I can't remember the last time I did – and actually meant it. Despite *still* being sleepless, the highlights of the day outweighed the exhaustion. I'm fully aware we haven't even begun to scratch the surface. The poor counsellors are on a search and rescue mission in my mind, and I'm pretty sure one of them barely made it out alive today.

For the first time since I arrived, I felt some semblance of myself returning today. Not the old, sober me, who I don't remember at all, though I do remember the countless stupid things he still did, but not the man himself. Or the passed out drunk me either, *thank the Universe.* But I feel much more myself than I have the last 4 days. I have blacked out countless times from drinking, and it never dawned on me I'd black out from *not drinking,* too.

Detox is a freaking trip.

It's a bit of a haze, and re-reading some of my posts are like reading something someone else wrote.

Which is exactly why I'm trying to do this every day. Because I never want to forget.

I'm not naive enough to think I can simply (ha!) stop drinking and everything will fall into place. I'm eager to move forward, to be honest, and to embrace this journey and eventually feel the real me – whomever he is or will be – emerging. I'm not expecting miracles or an easy ride – *in the near or distant future.*

The recovery centre (sorry, *clinic,* because I'm sick, remember?) I chose to come to is different, in the most wonderful way. Today I was able to move to my real room, an absolute relief because I could unpack. The transient feeling of living out of my suitcase was making me feel even more lost and lonely – and wanting a drink. I'm literally in the middle of paradise – on a tropical island with sun and sand - a far cry from the dreary dead grey of icy winter in Canada. I am luckier than most.

This is a luxury; despite the torment I'm putting myself through.

I cannot put enough emphasis on how the sun and fresh air is the world's most effective medicine.

This morning, our psychiatrist took us on an outing to the beach to watch the sunrise, and we had an hour to just sit and think. After the last 4 days (read: 15 years) it was the most cathartic experience in recent memory. Some people took long walks. Others sat and just watched the sunrise.

I walked out into the ocean, waves barrelling towards me and just braced myself, letting each one crash past me. I imagined every wave was a challenge or a failure. Some were regrets and some were goals. Some brushed past me like unspoken apologies, and others smacked me in the face like unreceived punishments. I must have stood there for 20 minutes, wave after wave crashing into me, refusing to let them push me back or knock me down. I haven't felt that sort of strength or liberation *in years*.

And, because it's me, *of course I cried.*

Now, don't get me wrong – half the time I wanted to barf because I'm still not feeling 100% and the vertigo has latched onto me like one hundred leeches. But I tolerated it and took in the absolute wonder of the vastness of the ocean and what caused that wave to travel across the globe and end up finding me.

I know. *Pretty deep for a Friday evening.* But I think coming out of the last 4 days of feeling like the world was crashing down, those crashing waves brought me back to life a little.

We returned to the clinic for a couple group meetings – then more interestingly, the completion of my Bio-Psycho-Social evaluation. *I cried again.*

I told one of my counsellors things I have never told another human being. *Ever.* And he thanked me for my honesty, and I thanked him for making me comfortable enough to do so. 3 hours later I had dished more about my life than I even knew I *knew* about my life.

With only 28 days here, I do not plan on wasting even one of them, though it's looking as though I'm going to run out of tears before it's my time to go home.

We drudged up childhood trauma, adolescent trauma, adult trauma. So much heavy stuff, which I'm reserving that for another post on another day when I've had more time to digest and talk about it on this end. Or when I have to at least process it in my cluttered, dusty head. He asked how long I was staying here – I said 28 days, and he replied, *"Good, you're going to need it."*

This man is not only a counsellor, but he's also an absolute mentor to me already. 30 years sober (with bumps along the road) and has a track record so long the internet would have a problem holding it all. *He's been there.* I won't go into his qualifications beyond his life experience, but I have absolute confidence in him. And, in speaking with some new friends I've made that are leaving tomorrow, they've assured me the short time they've spent with him has literally changed their lives, and they're heading home with a sense of confidence and a solid plan.

He took us to downtown Cabarete this evening, to an AA meeting, And I spoke. I shared. *I scared the hell out of myself.* I had no intention of saying a word – I just wanted to take it in and experience the experience. But with 5 minutes left to the meeting, something rose out of me, and it just started flowing.

Those words.

"Hi, I'm Shawn, and I'm an alcoholic."

All the words I wanted to say had been spinning in the pit of my stomach as I listened to everyone else sharing, like they'd been floating in a pool and the drain was pulled – bumping into each other, some disappearing and others rising to the top, all of them in a whirlpool of chaos with only minutes to spare.

I plugged the drain. I opened my mouth.

Honesty and self-love.

I kept it brief, but the topic tonight was "self-love" – and I identified how it took me *so long* to realize (read: *admit*) that my self-destructive behaviour was ruining everything I do love. My marriage, my friendships, my business, my reputation, my finances, and my health, to name just a few.

The total absence of self-love.

And my first step towards achieving it was being **honest** with myself - *for the very first time* – that I needed help, admitting myself into rehab, and accepting that I am worthy of the love and self-care.

Because without it, I am no good to anyone, especially myself.

Whether it is correct or not, or whether I made a fool of myself or not – I explained how I believe/just discovered that *the first step towards self-love is honesty*...and alcohol is the most dishonest thief you'll ever meet. It has lied to me for years and I've believed it. It's tried to convince me that I need it, that it makes me better, more eloquent, more courageous, more immune.

And by being honest with myself that *it is none of those things*, I was able to take was my first step towards real, true self-love, for the first time I can remember in my life.

So, *today was a good day.*

PS: 3 days, 18 hours and 39 minutes sober. Money saved: $161.87 CDN. And I still haven't killed anyone.

The Drawing Hope Project

FEBRUARY 25, 2017

There is a massive weight I've been carrying with me for 5 years.

And it's not my father's passing, though that is obviously a huge component. I've always addressed it as guilt for not fully completing a project, and for letting certain people down because I hit that wall where I simply couldn't do it anymore.

You know the wall.

The one you try to climb, but each time you gain any ground, it just grows taller and taller. Like Jack's Beanstalk, growing to a point where it breaks through the clouds, and you just don't have the strength to keep climbing.

This came up in therapy yesterday, and my counsellor turned it around for me in a way I've never looked at it before, and I had one of those 'huh' moments. *Insert my slowly shaking head and facepalm here.*

It *actually does* start with my father's passing. As some of you know, I do fine art surreal photography, also known as *'those weird photos'*. It's just another way for me to get my thoughts and feelings out into something tangible, that can be translated into every language – *sight and soul.*

Well, my father was very sick, and I wanted to do something to cheer him up, so I took a drawing when I was 5 or 6 which I did for my grandmother, who had recently passed away, and turned it into a photograph. It cheered him up so much – *he was my biggest fan.* In the depths and final days of his cancer, it was a rare thing to see him happy and excited about anything.

Long story short, I started doing this for other families. Children born with life threatening illnesses or fatal diseases would send me their drawings and their personal stories – and I would travel to them, have a super fun photo shoot, then turn their drawings into real-life photos, starring themselves. Essentially, bringing their imaginations to life.

Showing them *their dreams coming true.*

Showing them that *Anything Is Possible.*

It's called The Drawing Hope Project.

I was a wish granter. To the parents and caretakers of these children, it meant the world. They were able to see their child doing things they'd never dream of – and likely wouldn't live long enough to have a chance to do, anyway. To see your children's imagination come to life must be such a wonderful thing for them when they aren't certain about their child's *actual life, aspirations or future* at all.

"When you have a child that goes through a life-threatening illness, every single
picture is so very precious. Each picture you take captures a moment that can
never be repeated. And when your child's future is uncertain, there is nothing
more valuable than those pictures to remind you of all those moments."
– *Joanna Mitchell (Ryley, The Queen of Hearts' mom)*

So, I started turning 'sick kids' into superheroes. Queens and Princesses. Astronauts and magicians. Whatever their mind and heart desired, I waved a camera and a little magic, and turned into a sort-of reality for them. Their reactions were priceless, and for the first time in my life I felt I'd found my calling.

The words *debilitating illness* are ringing me ears. *The irony.*

How did I end up going from that, to here? I was an absolutely functioning alcohol back then, but I still managed to be contributing *something good* to the world.

I did this on my own time, with my own money. Travelling across the county, and even once flying to Las Vegas to work with 7 children in one day at the Nevada Childhood Cancer Centre (ABC World News with Diane Sawyer tagged along to document it that day).

And it continued - it went viral. Every day, I'd receive hundreds of emails from despondent parents asking me to make their child's dream come true. That their son had a terminal brain tumour, and this would be the most priceless gift if I could give it to them.

I wanted to say yes to everyone. *How could I say no?*

Every one of those children became my adopted children in an odd way – they looked up to me, I'd receive cards and random videos with updates, and I'd go for coffee with their parents just to listen. Nevermind my business that pays the bills falling to the wayside because balance isn't my forte – I clearly didn't. I'd bring them bags of art supplies, to encourage them to keep drawing and creating.

I initially wanted to work with 10 children, and take all the characters I've turned them into, and weave them into one magical storybook full of hope. In the end, when I hit that wall, I had worked with well over 60 children and their families in 2 short years. It was covered by The Today Show who flew to Canada for several days to document my work with one child, ABC World News with Diane Sawyer, all the local and national news networks, NBC, and overseas in publications in nearly every country.

And then *I just stopped.*

I carried the stories of every one of those children, including a few we've lost to cancer or other illnesses, with me every single day since I met them. *Including the ones I wasn't able to help.* And it's there, at the bottom of every glass of wine I've drank during and since.

Guilt and regret.

I've always attributed it to not being able to continue or complete the project, and the much-anticipated storybook that everyone has been waiting for as its culmination. *The Book* that some families will only see their child in, now that they're dead and gone and have flown away.

Because I delayed. Because I just *couldn't finish it.*

I isolated and my drinking went through the roof because I couldn't bring myself to saying *no* to any of these families or children anymore. I withdrew because I didn't have answers, at least the ones I wanted to be able to give them, about when I'll be doing this work again, or when the project will be finished.

But I will say, it was the highlight of my life and the most I've ever felt like I was doing something positive with what I've been given to work with this in life.

And I've spent so much of it wasted.

Wasted so much of it wasted.

My counsellor identified it as a trauma – delving into these family's situations and taking them on myself. It was never like I just showed up, took a photo, then left. I became their friends. He explained that it's hard enough for 1 family to go through what they're going through, but I've taken on 60 and feel that for whatever reason it's my responsibility to *make it all better* for them. To be the magician that can take away their pain and give them hope. Oh, and while I'm at it, here's a magical photo of your ailing child riding a rainbow octopus at the bottom of the ocean.

He identifies this as one of the driving forces behind my 'recent' alcoholism, but the root of that empathy and sense of responsibility stems much further and deeper - and we aren't even getting there yet.

So, have a look if you'd like. *Prepare to cry a little.* These little kids have so much strength, and I'm feeling absolutely selfish and awful for wasting so much of my time and my health, taking both for granted in a world where little kids like this are struggling and hoping they'll make it to 10 years old.

I feel like an asshole. So much irreplaceable time wasted, quite literally. And I promise every one of them this morning I am going to channel their strength - the strength of 5 and 6 years olds – to help me through this.

My tiny little inner army.

You can visit the site at www.DrawingHopeProject.ca and see the children's magical drawings and photos, and their stories. Grab the tissues.

I'm can't even proof-read this tonight because it's broken my heart thinking about all of this this morning.

Maybe when I'm strong enough, I'll do a series for recovering addicts and alcoholics? We can definitely all use a little hope as well and could certainly use the reminder that *anything is possible.*

Better Out Than In

FEBRUARY 26, 2017

Forewarning: *Angry Rant Ahead with Lots of Swear Words.*

I'm an irritable fucking mess today. 5 days, 16 hours and 27 minutes since my last drink and I was doing damned good until today.

Today I really want a drink

No. *That's a lie.* I was doing fine for *some* good parts of the day. Then one little thing happened, the trigger was pulled, and the cravings shot off like fireworks in my brain. And it was over the most ridiculous thing ever:

This comment on my blog:

> "It's amazing how articulate you are considering you are newly sober and in rehab. I've been in rehab and I spent years working in a rehab and I seldom met a newcomer able to communicate at this level. This leads me to believe that you are either a well-established author (I hope so) or you're not really newly sober and in rehab. Sorry for my skepticism but I have been in recovery for 32 years and something about this just doesn't seem right. And by the way, *personal journals are meant to be private, not public.*"

First of all, I *should* be flattered that the chaos in my head and my heart is somehow finding order on the page and still has some semblance of sanity. But there's two other parts that really pissed me off, which is great timing, because I've been *in a mood* all day.

"You're not really newly sober and in rehab" and the finally, *"And by the way, personal journals are meant to be private, not public."*

Like...WTF?

Ok. *I'm sure they meant well.*

Thankfully, there are no drinks to be had here, because for some reason it's driving me to want to drink *all the drinks.*

I write for myself, to get my thoughts out.

Words to me are like wool to a loom.

It's a craft I adore, and I spin sentences in my head just walking down the street – forgetting them instantly – but I love to write as much as I do photography and art, in general. They're all connected, and cooking and baking is in there, too. *Creating.* I'm blessed that there are so many of you supporting me on this journey and are taking your time to read whatever nonsense spills out of my fingers each day - *despite all your own challenges, you still take the time to encourage me. It says so very much about your character, and I thank you.*

Like seriously. *You are all amazing.*

I think I was just shocked as shit to essentially read someone suggesting I don't belong *here* and that the absolute reality of what is happening to me and how I'm feeling is a lie, or doesn't fit their concept of what an alcoholic is, how they should write, or how I should be acting. I'm not a stereotype.

Nobody is. We all have our strengths. Writing happens to be one of mine.

How I wish to fuck it was all a fairy tale.

Why am I even caring about this? Why is it bothering me so much?

Maybe because it took me literally a DECADE to come to such a point of honesty that I was able to admit I need help and had no other options. The final straw. The last chance given, knowing there won't be anymore. The 9th life, long gone.

I don't know.

But swallowing what little pride I had left and committing to leaving so as to save myself as well as my marriage, my family, my businesses, and personal potential was among the hardest things I've ever had to do. And, I know the hard part hasn't even started yet. Admitting I've been failing at all of them is a tough to pill to swallow – *especially with nothing to wash it down with anymore.*

Nothing I want, anyway.

I refuse to apologize for what I write here – or that I'm not moving fast enough or I write with an *'emotional fragility"* or *'pretty words'* that are so real to me, still here on the other side, just *days* into a journey many of you have been working an entire lifetime on.

Of course, I'm fucking emotionally fragile right now.

Aside, again: Thank you more than you'll ever know to all of you who have made me feel encouraged and not alone, who've said you know what I'm talking about and that you've been where I'm at. That it gets harder before it gets better, but it's worth it. You know who you are, and though we haven't met, I love you all.

Next - *"a journal should be private, not public."*

I call total bullshit on that one.

This is my experience, my journey, and I'll do whatever I what I want with it. I need this to look back on one day. Perhaps it's generational, and I don't want to scribe my deep dark secrets into a paper journal that will disappear with age, disappear, and be forgotten – as if these emotions never happened. Hidden away like the dirty family secret – *if no one knows, then it never happened.*

Well, *fuck that.*

What if I my struggles can help someone somewhere with theirs?

It's time to talk about shit. *Not* talking about it is how I got here, and I'm not making that mistake ever again. Maybe one day someone will read this, and it'll inspire them to be honest, too, and start a dialogue that will save their own or someone else's life. Maybe it won't. But for right now, it's the best medicine I'm taking every day.

The problem with this world is that *we are told how to feel.* We are told not to talk about it. And we are *told* that we shouldn't be feeling what we are feeling. That, right there, is the biggest problem I have with organized religion. For the record – my parents *never* shamed me. Not once. I'm luckier than I know, and I do my best not to take it for granted.

I *am* a spiritual person. It doesn't mean I need to go to a church.

Going to church doesn't make me a Catholic. I could sit in a garage all day and it doesn't make me a car.

I believe in a Higher Power, most definitely - and I call her the Universe. I see her in trees and in music and the touching of hands. The exchange of energy and the power within us to change our lives based on our thoughts. *But that's another post for another day.* I actually have the words *"Thoughts Become Things"* tattooed on my arm, alongside a Dalai Lama quote about gratitude.

Well holy shit, I'm on a rant, and I apologize. This post is turning more and more into a mirror of my brain at the moment.

Better out than in, I suppose.

I've been doing great trying to adjust and settle in here, having my little moments of pride every time I check my tracker to see how long I've gone without a drink and how much money I've saved. Unfortunately, it doesn't track how many people I *haven't* hurt or things I've screwed up in the meantime, all the while trying to dislodge that stupid butcher knife that is still lodged between my eyes like a never-ending migraine.

One more reason I'm so irritable today.

So, it's water, more water, and eventually a mineral water to give myself some variety. I know, living on the edge over here. I'm very much looking forward to getting into deeper counselling this week, starting tomorrow, *finally.*

After re-reading what I just wrote, *apparently* I need it desperately.

I want to do the work. I can't *wait* to do the work.

I'm quite certain I'm depressed. Nothing new, really. I was depressed when I left home, and I was depressed when I arrived here. Now I'm just depressed, in withdrawal, *and* lonely – despite having made some great friends already.

I'm going to thank that person who left the comment that I didn't *write enough like an alcoholic* - whatever the hell that means. Because without it, I wouldn't have found the courage inside me right now to sweep all this clutter out of my brain.

I have a feeling I'm going to sleep much better tonight.

The Tin Man

FEBRUARY 25, 2017

**"You have a good heart, Nicholas.
That doesn't change."**
– Delilah, Everything Must

Tonight, we watched *'Everything Must Go'* starring Will Farrell. I've seen it before, ~~drunk on the couch, and I believe I passed out before the ending, last time.~~ It felt like I was watching it for the first time, tonight.

Apologies in advance as this post is a little all over the place tonight, but my heart has advised me we won't sleep again tonight unless I set this free. It's not intended as a 'poor me' post, but I need to document a little revelation about how and why I've been feeling like I have been.

That one leading quote in this post just glued itself to my heart and soul about 45 minutes ago. A broken alcoholic, talking to a girl from high school he hasn't seen in over 20 years, diminished by his shortcomings and struggling to find his footing at absolute rock bottom. Feeling unworthy and looking for some reassurance that he does, after all, have value.

I didn't understand until tonight, quite accidentally, that I've been *questioning the integrity of my heart.*

I've been wondering if I'm *actually* a good person or have just been masquerading as one all this time. At some point, the image I have of myself transformed into some avant-garde piece of sculpture made up of tin cans and found objects - hollow and pieced together with good intentions and garbage, held up by two crutches: *one of all my failures and the other my bad decisions.*

I so easily forget all the good things I've done, but keep a very orderly list of every time I've let someone down, myself included.

I regret so badly everything surrounding *"The Horrible Awful"*, a post that may never make it to this blog, but is where my photo *"Broken"* came from, which went down last April – a turning point in my life, but branded forever on my heart, as it very well should be.

"You've ruined everything. You've taken absolutely everything from me. You're a horrible, horrible person." – Hubs

It's hard to forget the events surrounding and leading up to it, and impossible to forget hearing those words. Harder still because they've woven themselves around my heart and ever since, my heart looks different to me.

Thank you, alcohol, for holding my hand on that Choose-Your-Own-Adventure chapter of my life where I chose every wrong page possible.

And ended up here.

Not exactly the ending I had hoped for.

And what *did* I hope for? What did I expect would happen? People who do *very bad things* deserve *very bad endings.*

Prior to that, the collection of disappointments I began hoarding in my business, in The Drawing Hope Project, in even the simplest of tasks and my marriage began disappointing my family, pushing away my friends, ruining work partnerships and there I was, taking everything for granted because I'd rather be drunk and not think about it. I was too busy forgoing life-changing opportunities because the bottle couldn't come along with me.

"You have a good heart, Nicholas. That doesn't change."

I absolutely needed to hear that today.

Because I'm realizing today that it is such a huge part of what has led me here, what threw me into a deep depression, what accelerated my drinking to exponential and unsafe levels, and why I've been crying non-stop for the last 12 months.

I've been grieving the loss of my *heart,* which I always sincerely believed was, indeed, *good.*

And it is.

That doesn't change.

Our choices do. Our circumstances do. Our consequences do. But do you believe people are born with a good heart, or a bad heart? Can people change what type of soul they've been given? Is this a Grinch Who Stole Christmas situation?

Or do we just end up pushing our heart aside, listening to the addiction instead, beating so loudly in our ears we can't hear anything else?

> *"I was standing over there, rusting for the longest time."*
> – The Tin Man, The Wizard of Oz

I have spent so long thinking mine had *actually changed* - and that I was, as I was told, *a bad person*. That has multiplied my grief into feeling absolutely worthless and like an awful person with a black heart. On top of feeling overwhelmingly guilt-ridden, I've been feeling like an impostor, when all along I've *just* been a drunk with a good heart, submerged so deeply in wine and addiction I couldn't see it anymore.

I feel like the Tin Man in the Wizard of Oz, searching for his heart.

Tap away at me and you'll hear the echo – that recurring, hollow absence reminding me that something is missing. Over and over again, bouncing around my insides, searching but finding nothing.

> *"As for you, my galvanized friend, you want a heart. You don't know how lucky you are not to have one. Hearts will never be practical until they can be made unbreakable"*
> – The Wizard of Oz, to the Tin Man

I am hoping that as the fog continues to clear while I am here in recovery, I will discover my good heart is still there and has been all along.

It's still the same heart, just made more beautiful by being broken.

I intend to leave here with gold holding all my broken pieces together again.

> *"If I ever go looking for my heart's desire again, I won't look any further than my own back yard. Because if it isn't there, I never really lost it to begin with."*
> - L. Frank Baum, The Wonderful Wizard of Oz.

Message In a Bottle

FEBRUARY 27, 2017

be-wildered

adjective

1. Confused and indecisive; puzzled.
"He saw the bewildered look on my face."

If I had to choose one word for today, it would be *bewildered*.

Confused and indecisive. Puzzled.

And that's how I felt leaving my first one-on-one session with my psychotherapist, who I love. It started off simply enough, then took the most wicked u-turn and we were suddenly standing on my father's grave with all my regrets and disappointments spilling out of me.

My memory of the session is choppy at best, feeling eerily familiar to every day before rehab when I was too hung-over or freshly drunk to remember what I had said or done the night before. Absolutely bewildered, puzzled by how I got there and completely confused as to what the hell was happening.

Now 6 days sober (but the valium isn't helping) - the fog can only be attributed to my heart and my mind re-learning the new language of sobriety. Emotions are falling out of me like candy from a well-beaten piñata.

My dad. In a nutshell, the simple question she asked was how I felt about my dad and what regrets I have.

The words *"I disappointed him"* fell from my lips and that's when I pretty much lost it.

Scratch the "pretty much" part.

I totally lost it.

This, I know, is going to be a very big part of my healing here. *Grieving. Forgiving. Accepting.* And I am not very good at any of those things.

I'll never forget the night my mom called to say it was time to come home as he'd taken a turn for the worse. Of course, I was in no shape to drive, it was 10 pm and I had at least 3 Litres of wine in me by then.

Two of my best friends had just arrived from my hometown, where he was – after driving several hours and walked through the door the moment the phone rang. Without a second thought they had me in their car and we were flying through the thickest fog, *of course,* at speed limits that were dangerous but necessary, in the dead of night.

The weeks and months leading up to this I had promised myself I was going to clear the air with him, and whether he was coherent enough to understand it, I would forgive him and ask for his forgiveness of me, in return.

About 30-minutes from the hospital, in the backseat of the car, I felt something physically lift from me. The closest I can describe it is as though I became *unstitched*. Everything became looser, like a corset being undone that had been strung up too tight for too long.

I asked my friend to slow down, *because he was gone.*

I knew it.

With every ounce of my being, I knew it. I felt the exact moment my dad passed away, from miles away.

And along with him went all my last chances to give him those words that were waiting in line behind my pride for so many months, or more accurately, years. Like anxious children they nagged me every day – *are we there yet?*

And we never were. In that moment, flying down the highway barely able to navigate between the blackness and fog, I knew we never would be.

So, they crawled back inside me, finding a way to multiply, fertilized with addiction and watered with wine. Both existed before then, but this new crater inside me had made room for more. *And more. And more.*

The thing is, you think you have time.

I had spent several years not speaking with my dad growing up – moving out early because of our disagreements and shaming him for things I wish I had known more about at the time. But we didn't talk.

We'd just trip over the issues every time we walked across the room, as it all piled up beneath the carpet seemingly every problem was swept under. Years of unspoken *everythings* and both our egos were too proud to throw out the carpet and sweep it all out the door.

Years wasted. Things unsaid. The belligerence of time in that it insists on going in only one direction, filling its bags with *what-ifs* along the way.

So, I have a project.

A letter to my father. And I'm to write a little on it every day, as I go through the next 3 weeks here in rehab. Every happy memory, every wish, every disappointment, every question I never asked. A chance to ask why he did what he did, and to be angry at him and myself for having repeated his sins 20-some-odd years later. To tell him I'm proud and upset, that I miss him and every little thing in between.

And there's so many in-betweens.

Right now, all I want is to finally let those nagging little words that sat so patiently in my throat for so long know that yes, *we have, at last, arrived.*

On the final day of rehab, before I climb back on the plane to begin the hardest part of this journey – *learning to live day to day* – we are placing that likely to be 20-page letter in a bottle, and like the fisherman my father was in his heart, *sending it out to sea.*

Quick Purge

FEBRUARY 28, 2017

Today I only have a handful of words to offer, so that I can offload some mental clutter before going into back-to-back sessions, to have my brain and heart dissected.

I feel like I'm going to have a nervous breakdown today. I'm having a very hard time trying to balance some work responsibilities that are necessary while I'm away, and the work I am *really here to do*. I'm usually pretty decent at time management, but right now my mental and emotional state aren't really being conducive to much of anything.

Last night, we had the luxury of being taken downtown to a restaurant for a going away dinner for two fellows who are leaving today.

It was *far too early* for me in this program to be placed in that environment. I had anxiety seeping out every pore on the way there and had to strategically place myself in a position at the table where I was just looking at the wall, so as not to see any other guests in the restaurant that may be having drinks.

Drinks that I am still wanting so badly.

So far, that's my only first strike against this place. *I wasn't ready for that.* It wasn't really fair this early in the game.

Luckily, they had San Pellegrino and I'm pretty sure I drank them out of their entire stock of it.

I could have said no, I'm not ready to go. But that would've meant a counsellor had to stay back with me here at the clinic, and I know they all really wanted to go celebrate the massive success of these two men that have come so far, and may never meet again.

I didn't want to be *that guy* that ruined it for everyone else.

But *I passed the test, somehow* – however I think I'm paying for it today.

114

My stress level is through the roof, like a top being wound up and ready to release any second, spinning out of control and unaware of anything in its path. Today's sessions should be interesting – if I can get through them.

It's lunch now – but I have no appetite. Funny how stress can push aside the most basic of your needs, just like addiction can push away love, push away hope and welcome in all things destructive that it craves and feeds off.

And speaking of *off*, I can't wait to get off this rollercoaster.

I feel like there are three of me here, squeezed into one little box on the ride and eventually one of us, or all three, are going to fall off..

The *me* that just wants to work at becoming stronger. The *me* that still needs to maintain some semblance of responsibility in my businesses back home. And the loudest *me,* that just wants to crawl up in a corner and sleep for the next 3 weeks.

They're all having a wicked battle today and I sure hope the me that came here gets stronger and wins in the end. At this very moment though, it's anyone's game.

Look at me, still sitting back like a spectator, as though I have *no control* over how things are going to turn out.

How a Seashell Saved My Life

MARCH 1, 2017

I'm probably going to say and explain a lot of things incorrectly here about the 12 Steps, but I'm going to do my best – and once again, do *not* worry, this is anything *but* a book about the 12 Steps.

That's not my jam. Everything in the next several paragraphs just sort of *happened to me today. So that's what I have to talk about.*

That, and how a seashell may have happened to save my life, too.

Please remember I'm still new here and still learning. Specifically, I'm going to talk about Steps 2 & 3(ish) and how the last 36 hours that just passed here in rehab played out.

Plus that time I had an epiphany on the beach this morning.

I'm going to try and make this brief, but *I promise the ending is pretty damn cool.*

Post-script: It's not brief. It's pretty long. Apologies.

As I was saying, I'm all new to this. I came here knowing nothing about AA, nothing about the 12 Steps, and only scary horror stories of people's detox nightmares that I read online – plus the ones my actual doctor told me.

What I *did* know, was that I was absolutely powerless when it came to alcohol. I no longer had control, and can admit wholeheartedly that I never did. It's exactly why I'm here right now, and I be an even bigger fool than I am to try and say anything different. That most sincere confession is the very first post I ever made on this blog, *'How Did I get Here', and it's one of the first stories in this book.*

I had been tormented for years and as everything of value in my life spiralled outwards away from me as though repelled and disgusted by my drinking, I came to realize that *this could not go on any longer.*

I have never looked back from my choice to come here. I was beyond willing to go *anywhere* that could assist me. Despite walking into this blindly I could clearly see my destination, which was to find help, *since I was helpless.*

You could call that Step 1.

I gladly raised the hammer and put the nail in the coffin on that part of my life, in admitting I was absolutely powerless and out of control, and in a cycle of insanity.

I was raised Catholic, but we were never devout. *'C&E Catholics'* essentially, meaning we'd go to church on Christmas and Easter, and any unfortunate obligatory funerals or weddings in between. However, even the *'C&E'* fell off our radar and to-do list years ago.

The one thing I have been surprised with is how Step 2 - and essentially every step in general, refers to the Higher Power *of your understanding.*

Pardon my language, but *thank God.*

I know I've explained this before, but I believe in The Universe as my Higher Power. I believe in energy. In the Law of Attraction, essentially, you get what you give, and energy cannot be created or destroyed. I believe in love and compassion, in fairness and equality, though I also believe in an afterlife of sorts. The afterlife to me is not in the conventional sense but far more logical, as I understand it. I find loved ones in storm clouds and heavy leaves dripped with dew in the morning, I see them in birds in flight and certain breezes when they pass me in a certain me. I feel we do carry on, and in the most beautiful way imaginable.

I do not believe there are coincidences, and I believe we all have a path and purpose in life.

I understand that all of that doesn't all fit nicely into one box.

But *I believe.* I definitely believe there is something greater than me, and all of us. I don't have a name for it – so I just call it *The Universe.* I'm sure there's more poetic, specific or appropriate names for it, but that's what resonates with me. Essentially, it is *everything.* I suppose that makes it just like almost every other religion.

The end all, be all.

In a roundabout way, this would be a loose Step 2.

I admit that the Universe has never let me down, and has allowed me to live up to this point, and for some reason, has chosen me to get well.

Perhaps in one of my drunken, sobbing hot-mess disaster evenings, the last of which being a quick and at the same time, never-ending, 9 days ago, I sent yet another pathetic sick plea to the Universe that I just couldn't do this on my own. I had said it so many times, but this time it came from the very hallows of my despair, where it continually caroused with the resentment of myself, and how alcohol had won.

Again. And again. And again.

So, still trying to wrap my slowly-coming-to-consciousness head around all this new information and the evidence behind the 12 Step Program and AA, I find I'm still stumbling on how to approach Step 3.

"To make a decision to turn our will and our lives over to the care of God as we understand Him."

Well, *fuck.*

Inside me, the shutters started rattling and doors start slamming and that wicked west wind started blowing every imaginable option, thought, question and belief around my brain – *a storm was coming and I wasn't prepared.*

For a control-freak, who has been *out of control* for well over 10 years, this a huge step. And there's no way my legs are long enough. The distance between where I'm standing and where I need to be may as well as be at opposite ends of the Grand Canyon.

But *I believe.* I believe in the Universe. I believe, and in the past have proven, that if I ask, it will answer – so long as I'm on a frequency of Gratitude.

Ask. Believe. Receive.

I speak with Frank, one of my counsellors, about this stumbling block I'm having, and for any of his advice on how I can just *release my will to something, and allow it to take charge of my life.* We chat and discuss, and essentially it comes full circle to exactly where I knew it would – that only I can figure that out for myself. It's different for everyone.

And that meant it is no different for me.

I finally made it to bed with no hope of sleeping, again, and put the audiobook of The Secret on to fall asleep to. I have *"Thoughts Become Things"*, which is the essence of the entire book and philosophy, tattooed on my arm as a permanent reminder to check myself. I felt it couldn't hurt for a brief refresher course and quick tune-up. If I was going to put my absolute faith into the care of the Universe to look after me now, it seemed as good a time as ever for a quick re-introduction in case the Universe had forgotten about me in the meantime.

Here's where shit starts to get real.

Sorry for all that crap up above, but I felt it necessary to explain where I was emotionally this morning waking up, sort of hovering between *"I got this"* and *"Holy shit what the hell is happening"*.

Every morning we wake at 5:30 am and head to the ocean for a walk on the beach during sunrise. It's the most therapeutic thing in the entire world, and our psychotherapist comes with us, and we each go our own way. Unlike every other morning, my other counsellor who is guiding me through the alcohol addiction/ AA/12 Step portion of the program happens to be up as well, because there's some mix-up with the car keys.

He's never up at this time, so it was weird to begin with.

I ask if he's coming with us and jokingly, he says, *"No – just bring me back a shell. A nice one – you know, one of those conchs"* as he climbs the stairs back to his room. He's an incredible man with as many stories as there are grains of sand on the beach. A recovered addict, alcoholic, certified relapse counsellor and clean for nearly a decade – he is hands down the exact person I would have chosen to help me, if I had had the choice. He's hit rock bottom so many times he's left an imprint. One day, I'd love to tell his story, and I plan to learn as much from him – and about him – as possible while I'm here.

But that's for another day.

So off we go to the beach. It's one of those beautiful Dominican beaches - clean sand, few pebbles, rolling waves crashing and nothing but palm trees and ocean spreading for miles in every direction It's peaceful, it's quiet. All the tourists are still passed out and hungover in their 5-star resorts, while we addicts and alcoholics are walking the beach searching for our souls.

I become determined to find a shell to bring back for Frank. Thing being, I've never seen a shell on this beach. Little broken-off pieces here and there, but nothing more than worn round pebbles beaten by millennia of travelling across the sea, just to wash up here for a moment and be stolen back by the next wave in a second.

And I think of the Universe. *Asking and receiving, and* where I need to get to with my faith in order to move forward, *eventually,* under the care of that Higher Power I still obviously haven't surrendered to.

I decide to stop looking. I stop walking. I place my request out loud, alone on the beach.

"Please, send me a shell. As a sign, and for Frank. I need this."

I speak it deliberately and with more confidence than I've felt since, well, I don't even know how long. And I leave it there, letting the words wash into the ocean and out of my hands.

I walk further, down the beach. A jogger passes me, and I admire her determination. Her health. I imagine she lives on avocados and overpriced coconut water. Or maybe she's in a loveless marriage and hates her job. I'm sad for a moment when I wonder if maybe she's trying to stay fit because she has fertility problems and would do anything to create an entirely new human inside her, the beginning and birth of a completely new universe.

I've come to learn that nothing is ever as it seems.

That's been my brain lately. Here, there, everywhere. I'm basically a walking Dr. Seuss book without the wholesome moral and adorable drawings. I remember I'm on the beach. I turn to the ocean and let the water rush up around my ankles, washing away the sand beneath my feet as it returns.

One wave. And the water exhales back to the ocean.

Two waves. It is exactly 7 am. Sunrise. The sun crests over the horizon.

And there it is.

The wave washes back, placing at my feet, the most perfect shell.

A conch.

I swear on my father's grave, *I shit you not.* It fucking happened.

It gives me chills typing this. And the only thing that could have blown me away more was if I heard a freaking choir of angels at the same time.

It was like a full-blown epiphany and 10 billion sleeping neurons in my soul sprung to life.

I picked it up and stood there for at least 5 minutes, just taking it in. It wasn't just a shell. It was *exactly* what I asked for – and it was the answer I was looking for, literally within minutes of me asking for it.

I'm not doing a very good job of describing how impactful this was or is for me. If there was ever an ounce of proof, I needed to be able to place, *with absolute surrender and confidence,* my life into the charge of the Universe, I received it this morning *at exactly 7 am, on a beach in Cabarete, Dominican Republic, when the ocean placed a conch shell at my feet.*

The more I looked at it, the more I admired its shape and design – the spiral of the universe itself. It wasn't massive, but it was *absolutely perfect.*

Even more amazing - if you know anything about *"The Golden Ratio"* it gets even more mind-blowing, of which I'll spare you the details, but know it cemented in me the certainty that I am exactly where I need to be right now, at exactly the right time, and the Universe made sure I was standing at that very spot to collect that shell.

Faith and hope that came with it.

Thank you, Universe.

I naturally can't wait to get back to the centre to give it to Frank and see his reaction, especially considering the talk I had with him yesterday about my stumbling over finding the faith to commit my life to something I can't quite define.

We get back to the centre and I give him the shell. He holds it in his hand. He looks at me. He looks at the shell, and he looks at me again.

Silence.

I tell him the story of how I asked, how I stopped looking, and how it found me.

Then he says – *"and it's a conch. It's a baby conch."*

And he starts to cry.

He goes on to explain that despite his years of sobriety, 11 DUI's, 3 suicide attempts, years in jail, and multiple relapses that he is *still in his infancy,* just like this shell. Trust me – the man is a genius, and his life calling is to be here helping addicts and alcoholics. He has a heart of gold, and he's religious beyond belief. His life has been spared so many times so he could help spare mine and so many others. I truly do want to write his story for him one day, because I can't even summarize it here and do it an ounce of justice.

"This is honestly one of the best gifts I've ever been given," he says. "I will keep this forever. *And I mean it."* Clutching it in his hand like it's the first piece of a food a starving man has had in 20 years, he looks me straight in the eyes with tears in his own, and without a word gave a nod, and passed some sort of strength to me that I've never known before.

I just re-read the last few paragraphs, and it makes me sound like I've totally fallen off my already broken rocker.

If I were to explain it any differently, I'd only add more rather than take any away. As time goes on, I'm sure I'll be better able to explain the transformation that happened to me today. It feels as though I'm telling a story that happened to someone else.

But it didn't.

It happened to me.

It may sound like so *much-ado-about nothing*, "Woohoo! You just made me read 2,400 words because you found a stupid shell? *Thanks a lot, Shawn.*"

Yep. That's exactly it. *I found a shell.* And with it came the unquestionable, unwavering answer that I was looking for: that my faith, however I choose to define it, is in the right place.

That I'm in the right place.

That the Universe indeed has my back.

All that, plus everything is going to be okay.

The Good, The Bad, The Ugly
(And a little Buddha, Too)

MARCH 4, 2017

11 Days. 16 hours and 14 minutes.

It feels like a split second, and an eternity, simultaneously.

That's how long it's been since my last drink – and to be completely honest, I don't miss it.

At all.

Words I didn't think I'd ever type, much less this soon.

Don't get me wrong, I *crave it*. And I will for months, and years – who knows how long. Maybe forever. *But I am starting to feel like me again.* Not even the old me, thankfully.

No, a new me, made up of pieces I've found while meditating on the beach, pulled together through my newfound love of yoga, and capitalized with words plucked from books that I can't get enough of. Everything is slowly starting to make sense and I can finally look myself in the mirror again. *It really is faith* – a faith I once had in the Universe, and in my insanity and belligerence, I spent years holding it hard under water and wine, until it drowned and stopped kicking. To clarify once more, faith does *not* mean sitting in a church. It doesn't even mean reading a book.

It only means *you believe in something.*

So long as it good, and pure, and serves others more than it serves yourself.

That, to me, is faith.

Persistent and forgiving little thing, faith can be, because it climbed right back out from its watery grave the moment I asked to come home, it took my hand and said *"That's okay – I forgive you."*

Thank you, again, Universe.

I don't even look the same.

"Well, if you'd stop having *so many damned epiphanies* on the beach," Frank, my addiction counsellor said this evening after dinner about how much I've changed in 11 days.

A tiny (read: *huge*) little moment of terror and pride overtook me, because it's the first time I heard someone else say it, even though I've been thinking it. The hard part hasn't even started yet. I am *more* than well aware of that, I'm not that naive, I promise, but I feel like an almost dead houseplant that was ready to drop its final brittle leaf.

Abandoned on a dusty shelf, then rediscovered and given water for the first time in years, just moments before it was too late to ever grow again.

All that fluffiness above aside, yesterday *totally* sucked. See? It's not all sunshine and rainbows, and I'm not trying to blow either up your ass. So many awful and traumatic things are coming to the surface in my therapy sessions, I often leave feeling and wanting to be physically ill.

Trauma is a patient, vicious, sneaky beast. So far dealing with these issues are proving the hardest for me – going without alcohol is easy in comparison to swallowing the truths that sobriety brings. Family secrets. Family traumas. Toxic communication. Misguided love. The tragedies of broken hearts and broken families. The sick persistence of history repeating itself.

No wonder this entire world drinks.

Side note: Please send tissues, I've gone through every box in the Dominican Republic.

It would seem that with every step forward, there is a bargain and game of poker.

I'll not only match your progress and tiny successes, but I'll raise you 10 resentments and 20 regrets.

Give and take. *Light and dark.* Birth and death. The two sides to a coin, to a soul, *to a life.*

Frank mentioned that recovered alcoholics are among the luckiest people on earth, since they (we? Maybe one day, we?) get to live not just one life, *but two.* We get a second chance, a second life. *A rebirth.* An entirely new gift to not only recover, but to transform and manifest yourself and your life into something completely, entirely new.

A phoenix, if you will.

Not unlike the neglected house plant, leafing out and coming back to life, stronger for its struggle to stay alive.

There's something new about me, *sobriety, perhaps,* but I know it's more than that. I'm not just being romantic, I promise. That shit pisses me off, too. I'm reading literally *everything* that sits still long enough; assigned readings, but also meditations that I'm discovering, or that I believe are discovering *me*. Books are appearing in online searches that are completely unrelated to what I had searched for. So, I download them, and they speak to me as though saying *"I was actually what you were really looking for but didn't know how to ask."*

I've stopped fighting.

I've begun connecting all the dots between my long buried and ignored personal beliefs and faith, the 12 Steps & Traditions, The Big Book, daily meditations and therapy sessions, and it's drawing a picture of whatever my *faith* is that is starting to look very much like a photo I took this morning at the Yoga Temple we go to.

I would spend every waking minute there, if I could.

It's just a photo of Buddha, done in mosaic on the wall behind a waterfall, but somehow when I first set eyes on it, I felt like I had come *home*.

I've been reading *'Mindfulness and the 12 Steps'* and it's been helping me immensely. Not assigned reading as part of the program, but it speaks to me in a language that makes absolute, *to the core*, perfect sense to me. Yesterday morning I spent 40 minutes meditating on the beach at the edge of the ocean, following a meditation suggested in the very first chapter of the book. I imagined I was in an endless, golden field full of my mentors, visionaries and loved ones, some still here, some passed. Great Buddhists, Mother Theresa, Martin Luther King.

You get the idea.

Someone was holding my hand and I couldn't see who it was, but I wasn't alone.

I kept repeating, I am not alone. I am not alone. *I am not alone.*

Now there was no burning bush, nor did the ground rumble beneath my feet. I wasn't enlightened or filled with any awe-inspiring wisdom, connecting with the pulse of the cosmos and every living thing, though that would've been cool, don't get me wrong.

I *can say* I became, for the very first time, *an inner witness*, a neutral observer of the mind. Through my mindfulness practice I am learning to separate from my mind. Can I get a *hallelujah*, because I've been stuck in there far too long.

Amazing what slowly returning to sobriety can do. *My poor brain.* So damaged for so long, with so much recovery ahead.

Plus, a burning bush would probably have freaked me right out.

Interestingly, my grandmother was there in the field, and she took my face in her hands and called me her *Boykin,* as she always did. And she *laughed.* I haven't heard her laugh since before 2007 when grandpa passed away, and especially since *she* passed away, as well. She never drank a drop of alcohol in her life, except a sip at Christmas here and there. But she loved me like no other (well, other than my mom) and I am not surprised in the least she was there to greet me.

Of course, I was crying. It's me after all. You'll get used to it.

Fucking epiphanies.

She, and the millions of other people in that field on the beach passed something to me; a stillness and strength that I wasn't alone in this. Tony, who just left the clinic a few days ago was there, in the field. I miss his calmness already, but I think I've learned it wasn't just *his* calmness. It's a calmness we can all discover, and a calmness he discovered while here. It is definitely contagious. Considering the condition I was in the day I walked in here, I was immediately drawn to his aura of calm – and I knew *I wanted that for myself, too.*

It's amazing to watch people come and go here – everyone at different ends of an all-you-can-eat buffet, and it's truly up to us what we put on our plate and into our souls. The food is there, but no one can make you eat it.

I'm happy to say that I'm totally pigging out, not on actual food, but I *am* gorging myself on this opportunity. I've lost over 4 lbs already; it's amazing what not consuming 3,000 calories of a wine every day can do.

> *"The one in whom no longer exist the craving and thirst that perpetuate becoming; how could you track that Awakened one trackless, and of limitless range?"*
> – The Buddha

I've been writing like a madman, not here on the blog, but in my workbooks. My hands are aching since I'm not used to handwriting anymore. How sad is that? I get frustrated at the lack of space that's allotted in the workbooks because I have so much to say. Two weeks ago, I wouldn't have given two shits and would've had a tough enough time forming a coherent reply to half the self-awareness questions

I'm being asked. Today? I'm Mr. Can-I-Have-4-More-Pages-Because-I-Think-I'm-Just-Starting-To-Get-It-And-These-3-Blank-Lines-Aren't-Going-To-Be-Enough.

I am feeling passion again for the first time in, well, I don't know how long.

Let's just say too long.

Now, to admit with terrible honesty that I'm very afraid of the coming steps, of carrying on when I go home, of the reality of discussions I've had with Frank about the likelihood of relapse and the dangers of my job as a wedding photographer and being surrounded by the worst kind of drunks every Friday, Saturday & Sunday night, each weekend for the next 9 months. The *"Avoid People, Places & Things"* approach does not apply in my world when it comes to my career. It is a certainty and an inevitability that I will need to plan for.

Don't let me down now, Universe.

His forewarning that I will, because of the length and volume of my alcohol abuse, likely experience insane post-acute withdrawal symptoms in several months which could last for months as well, didn't really make my day.

Frank is either very much a realist, or a total asshole sadist. In all honesty, I love him and he's the best thing ever – this place would be nothing within him, Tina and Tony, the therapists. So, I'm going to say he's probably a bit of both. He's been around the block so many times, the man has no time for bullshit.

He's recommending Antabuse for me as a *"level of insurance"* because of the dangers of my job, which are unavoidable. *Awesome.* I'll do and try anything to continue to recover and grow at this point. I was insane to have drank that first drink, every day, and I'd be *beyond* clinically insane to risk doing it ever again.

Relapse is not an option. Drinking *ever* again is not an option.

It's easy to write about the good things, for a change. It's that scary "Oh shit, I have to go back to a new reality in 17 days" that scares me. *It's safe here.* The "Oh now I get to make a 'searching and fearless moral inventory of myself' next step that is making me snap the elastic on my wrist to keep me in the moment and force me to stay with the anxiety until it passes, which is a trick Tony taught me, to help me stop avoiding.

I'm looking forward to the AA Meetings, as bizarre as that sounds, because I also secretly hate them, and have no interest in pursuing them once I leave here. I've already compiled a massive list of every possible one in my home area, organized by day of the week, type of meeting, distance, and time of day, more to appease Frank than anything else.

These next parts are going to hurt, and I know that as well as I know with certainty that the ocean will still be on the beach when we arrive tomorrow morning. It's going to hurt, not like peeling off just one layer of my skin, but every messy layer right down to the bones.

But if I'm doing it, I'm doing it *'all-in'*.

Someone remind me of this over the next couple weeks, in case I try and dance around the dirty parts I don't want to step in.

So, there you go. The good, the bad, and the ugly.

And a little bit of Buddha, too.

I'm alive, and I'm slowly waking up.

*Big Stretch.

Between Two Boats

MARCH 7, 2017

I didn't sleep one single minute last night. I was kept company by Thich Nhat Hanh and his teachings in *'Being Peace'*.

It is saving me.

We went to the beach for our morning walk and found the ocean and sky in absolute turmoil.

As my friend put it, pathetic fallacy at its best.

Today marks my 2nd week of being here in recovery, and 2 weeks of being sober. I didn't expect to grow so much, so quickly. Stripping away all the regret, the grief, the shame, and the guilt, I've uncovered myself again by *giving away my self.*

Surrendering is a beautiful, indescribable thing.

I found a new place to do my morning meditation – it fondly reminded me of Siddhartha Gautama and the Bodhi tree. I'm not one bit surprised that I've walked past it *every* day, and only saw it today for the first time.

A perfect rock, beneath a perfect mango tree, facing this morning's tumultuous ocean, rising up between two boats.

I found my place and made myself as comfortable as possible; my heart this morning and all night being tossed around as though it was riding the waves before me. I used its heaviness at that moment to ground me, solid like a mountain, upright like the tree I was sitting beneath.

I asked for the serenity to accept the things I cannot change, the courage to change the things I can, and the wisdom to know the difference. Since I've stopped fighting and struggling to force change upon the unchangeable, I have become immensely *lighter*. Stripping away the shame, guilt, regret, and grief – *even lighter so.*

I lost (*found?*) myself in meditation for nearly 30 minutes.

My mind wanders less and less each time I sit now, and those 30 minutes are the most precious of my entire day. They're filled with quietude and gratitude, and today, a sort of loving-kindness arose, that I sent to all the broken and hurt parts of me, the people I love, and to those who could use it today. I gave thanks for yesterday's sobriety, for the strength I needed to remain calm and openminded in a heartbreakingly difficult situation last night, and for the limitless opportunity of this day.

I set my willingness to *allow things to be as they are intended to be* at my feet, and the ocean washed it away in a storm of foamy waves. I imagined it being transformed into whatever the ocean desires, and in its own way, know that it will return it to me as it is intended to be – if I'm willing to accept it, as is.

There's a difficult and painful decision that needs to be made in my personal life back home, and it's beyond my control. I release my will to the Universe and ask again for serenity to *accept what I cannot change* – and to allow things to be as they will be, as I cannot control it.

I open my eyes and consider *the two boats* resting before me.

The boat on my left looks perfect and upright, a fine boat that could easily handle the angry waves on a day like today. The other is upside down and beat up, paint peeling and obviously worn from many years of battling angry waves and currents.

I notice the *"perfect"* boat is tethered to the tree, with a worn but well-tied rope and knot, holding it safe from floating off on its own, but imprisoned with no free will at the same time. *It can't sail anywhere.*

The other, *"imperfect boat"* is not.

It's free to sail wherever it wants.

Sometimes, the obvious choice is not the one that will get you where you want to go.

Decisions.

Repeat after me:

I am a fucking awesome person who has dealt with so much shit and I have made it through all of it and am still cute as fuck and smart and funny and nice and intelligent and I kick ass.

Alive and Well

MARCH 10, 2017

Day 17. Already. *How did that happen?*

My friend here described anything bookended with dates, like travelling, studying, or relationships that *it's always about the first 2 days and the final 3.*

Everything in between is white noise.

In most cases, I'd agree. Being in recovery at a rehab centre, though – despite time speeding up and slowing down, the blurry days of detox lending way to early realizations, to *a-ha* moments, hinting at a slow rebirth – all that *white noise* is the most precious thing I've ever experienced.

I'm so effing lucky to be having this, not particularly easy, opportunity. It's not an experience. It's an *opportunity,* a gift. A gift I haven't just given to myself, but to everyone who knows me, loves me, and for everyone I'll ever meet. I'm trying so hard to be present in the moment, not living in the past or the future, but I still struggle with the time wasted, *literally.*

Recovery is a gift to my *body.* My psychotherapist here makes me do an exercise where I sit and go through my body, apologizing for all the hurts I've caused – but *out loud.* It's as ridiculously cathartic as the level of ridiculous I felt the first time doing it.

It's a gift to my *mind.* Being here is that golden paste that is piecing all my broken bits back together. *Kintsugi-ing* myself, so to speak. I am finding myself more beautiful for being broken – no longer ashamed of how *un-whole* I was, and felt, all the time. Every therapy session, every accomplishment however small, I'm slowly discovering how to put myself back to together again.

For myself, meditation along with the practice and study of Buddhism has been my saving grace. I look forward to those quiet moments, getting to know myself, again, for the first time.

The *same* self I couldn't stand being in the same room with, much less share a body with, for what feels like forever.

Everyone has to find their "Higher Power" – whatever that looks like – while going through this process, however you choose to work through it. For me, the accountability of knowing that what I do to myself affects everyone else, *forever,* now and in the future – is a gentle reminder to be compassionate. *Always.* To myself, and all things.

We are all connected.

Interesting story: before I left to come here, our four dogs would always be yapping and fighting, or barking at me. Irritating, really. I arrive at rehab and get an update from home that they're all little angels, now. Peaceful. Quiet. Minding their own. It's no coincidence they were reacting to my energy. Agitated, angry, and all over the place.

Chaos, on 16 legs.

Our energy affects everyone around us.

Another tattoo I have, this one being on my inner right forearm. It's a quote from The Dalai Lama:

> *"Today, I am fortunate. I have a precious human life.*
> *I am not going to waste it. I am going to use all my energies to expand my*
> *heart out to others to achieve enlightenment for the benefit of all beings."*

I've always had good intentions. Unfortunately, though, the alcohol had its own, too.

What an amazing reminder. If only *I had taken the reminder every day I've looked at it for the last 7 years since I got it!* If only.

It looks so different now, through sober eyes. It means something new, again. What a hypocrite I've been, walking around so long with those words permanently staring back at me, while wasting my *'precious human life'* more and more as each day passed. Instead of expanding my heart, alcoholism made me retract and isolate, crawling in, instead of *looking* in, so I could then *reach out.*

I once thought meditation was a means of *escaping the world.* A way to transcend society and find that quiet place where you can meet yourself - your *true* self – again, and possibly for the first time. Don't get me wrong – it absolutely *is* that. But the reason for meditation is *to prepare yourself to reintegrate into society.* To make yourself stronger. To hold together the mind, body, and soul, so you can be a whole person and be better equipped to *contribute back to society.* Not to escape it. It is there for all of us everywhere to learn how to control *how we react to our feelings.*

When you're at peace, it is impossible to be hurtful, or do hurtful things.

Meditation teaches you how to become, and remain, compassionate.

Being belligerently drunk every single day for 15 years does not.

I'm currently working on preparing myself to 'reintegrate' back into the 'real world' in 11 days. I've made lists of all sorts of meeting in my area back home to test the waters, from Refuge Recovery meetings to AA and AlAnon to men's shelter's support groups. I've noted their type, time, and location for every day of the week within 50km of my home, in an impressively organized spreadsheet I can only *hope* I use as a tool and not a scratch pad. I already have a temporary mentor lined up, and have found both a yoga studio and meditation studio I can't wait to join. I'm working at finding a sober companion to support me in the many work commitments I have this year that require me to be around lots, and lots, of really, *really drunk people* – including Hubs. Plus, how to handle all the *free booze* I'm always surrounded by – my life back home is literally an open bar. Awesome. I'm coordinating having Antabuse available for me when I land back home in 11 days, as it isn't available in Ontario, apparently. That goes against everything I want or believe in, but I'm pulling out whatever stops I have to so as not to risk all of this falling apart.

I'm just trying to set myself up for success, so I can just *keep going.*

I made amends with my former personal trainer, who I actively avoided back in November, unfortunately likely affecting his income and well-being, by coming clean that I'm an alcoholic and that I've been in recovery.

His reply was remarkable, thoughtful, and on point: "No stress at all. You'll be a better person for having gone through all of this. *Tough times make for tough people.*"

From a Buddhist perspective, I don't particularly want to be a *"tough person"* - but at the gym I don't mind kicking a little ass again. I haven't been motivated for so long – depression, avoidance, drunkenness, *isolation* all stopping me from anything worth doing. He asked me what time would work best for my sessions – I said it didn't matter, and admitted I only asked for 10 am or 11 am sessions in the past because it was early enough to not significantly cut into my drinking time.

How sad. But, sadly true.

It'll be amazing to experience what working out feels like *not totally hungover, sweating a liquor store onto the floor of the gym.*

So, I am alive, and I am well.

With so much work left to do, I'm looking forward to all of it. This is just the very beginning. I've been having some PAWS (Post-Acute Withdrawal Symptoms) already. Words are escaping me and yesterday I stood on the beach for 5 minutes staring at my phone trying to find the word *"convert"* in my mind so I could google a currency exchange. It was gone. Literally, from my entire vocabulary, despite having typed it about 5 times a day for the last two weeks.

My mood has been steady for the most part, and I've been blessed with understanding and compassion from Hubs back home. *My little Buddha.* He's growing as much through this as I am, and that is the greatest gift. I can learn more from him than from any book or meditation. *He's saved my life as much as this program has.*

My heart is healing, and Hubs gave me the best bandage.

So.

I am alive, and I am well. I haven't been able to say either of those things for many, many, *many* years.

Some Things I've Learned

MARCH 14, 2017

Today I'm celebrating 3 weeks sober, as well as Hubs *and* my sister's birthdays, from 5000km away, in the middle of the ocean.

I've never been able to celebrate *one day* sober much less 21 of them strung together in a row for over 15 years. So, I'm cheers-ing both of them with a Perrier, today. As part of my gift to them and myself, I thought I'd revisit the lessons I'm gathering while here, so as not to forget them. I've had more than a few awakenings while I've been here.

In no particular order, I present to you:

Shawn's List of Shit He's Learned (So Far) In Rehab (Part 1)

1. Beautiful things grow from the darkest of places.

2. Peace is not always quiet.

3. Being alone is the only way to discover how to be with everyone, and everything, else.

4. German Camels are remarkably better than Dominican Marleys. That, and just because something fulfills a need doesn't mean it's good, or good for you.

5. Suntanning can quickly turn into sunburning. The same rule goes for almost everything in life. Too much of anything almost always results in pain.

6. You always have 3 chances to make something right. Before, during, and afterwards. It gets progressively harder with each chance you don't take.

7. Compassion is the only thing that matters. For yourself, and all beings. If you can nail this – everything else will follow.

8.   The Serenity Prayer holds the key to happiness. Stay present and give your precious energy only to things you have control over. If you do not have control over them, you always have control over how you react to them.

9.   Friends who send you new music are the best kind of friends. They're the ones who know what your soul sounds like.

10. The only way to learn anything is by doing it wrong.

11. When you can't live without something, you can probably do without it.

12. You can sail across an ocean with no set destination, and still end up exactly where you're supposed to be.

13. Being apart is the best way to grow closer together.

14. Every regret you let go of can be replaced with a virtue. Virtues weigh significantly less than regret, and the less weight you are carrying, the more you can help others with the load they themselves are carrying.

15. The obvious or easy option is almost always the wrong one.

16. The less you want, the more you will receive. All good things that arrive without expectation are usually the most valuable.

17. If it terrifies you, do it. If it's uncomfortable, do it. The best views are found after the toughest climbs.

18. Breathing is the most valuable, magical tool you own. Use it, listen to it, follow it. It's been trying to tell you something since the day you were born.

19. If you are sad, or angry, or depressed, I can guarantee you are in the past or the future. You do not belong there and can never go there. Be in the present and those feelings will go away (if you struggle with this, see #18).

20. "Early to bed, early to rise, makes a man healthy, wealthy & wise" – is true. True wealth is not found in your wallet.

PART 4:

Resurrection

Of course I relapsed.
But all is not lost.
Some of my best writing
came as the result of it.

Never Stop Starting

FEBRUARY 4, 2018

**"The best day of your life is the one on which you decide your life is your own.
No apologies or excuses. No one to blame.
The gift is yours - it is an amazing journey - and you alone are responsible
for the quality of it. This is the day your life really begins."**
– Moawad

I am back.

At the beginning.

If you haven't noticed, *we skipped nearly an entire year there* – a year where I veritably crucified myself and slipped down a very, very slippery slope, carrying my own cross on my back and a bag full of nails.

I disappeared from here, in true "me" style, because I still somehow struggle with forgiving myself for, or finding a new way to look at, my faults. It's easier to avoid things, than to suffer the pain of *dealing with them*. Thank you to everyone who reached out, and maybe somehow understood my silence meant I was floating somewhere in a bottle.

I wish I could tell you that you were wrong.

But you were very correct.

Albeit the severity of how badly my drinking has affected my life and those in it is nowhere near what it was *my last time around*, I am mindful of the reality that I need to deal with this *again*.

I feel it raging like a never-ending hangover, swollen behind my eyes. A dull headache that just sits there reminding me that I'm unwell.

I won't call it failure because failure would be me never coming back *here*.

Failure would be me refusing to admit I have a problem, *again*.

Never stop starting again, right?

I stopped working on myself and recovery and got cocky. The thirst returned. I quenched it with hesitation after 3 months sober – like a fool –and its grip wrapped around me faster than a bottle of wine gets emptied around here.

So many bottles of wine.

But today is Day One.

Again.

And I'm okay with that because it's better than saying it will be *tomorrow.*

Today's the day I'm taking responsibility for the quality of my life again and going dry. I've learned quite obviously that moderation is not my forté. Acknowledging that fact gives me the power to re-explore my beliefs around drinking and being an alcoholic.

The best day of your life is the one on which you decide your life is your own.

Cheers to beginning again.

Hopefully for the last time.

I also need to add that none of what prefaced this part of the story was wasted; every lesson learned, every painful experience, every raw *dealing with and unearthing truths* – I still carry all of them with me, and somehow, it has changed how I am made up, how my mind works, and how my heart beats.

None of it was wasted, even though I have been, as of late. I've just, like usual, started taking it all for granted.

Alkaline

FEBRUARY 6, 2018

They say we all have cancer inside us.

Something growing, just waiting for something to feed on. Sometimes it's cancer, sometimes it's a thirst. What it comes down to is that it's something eating away at you.

14 months ago, I was in a very dark place. I had been on a 10-year bender and despite having built a remarkably good-looking life, it and I were crumbling from the inside out. I was in a whirlpool that was pulling me down deep to the center, faster and darker every day.

I was physically sick, which is not surprising after pickling myself daily, but that constant cycle of drunk-and-withdrawal was masking other serious health problems that were just below the surface. It's easy to ignore when you are numbed by wine.

I was 39.

2 months later I checked myself into rehab, and luckily managed 3 months sober, and never felt better.

Until I started feeling worse again.

I had done a great deal of work on myself – unloading years of self-sabotage and regret, delving into Buddhism and mindfulness with every ounce of my being, and miraculously managing to detach myself from the incessant sadness I once carried around like my Siamese twin.

However, I had done a lot of damage, too.

So off to the doctor I went. Then a specialist. And another specialist. And another. Then a series of cold bright rooms filled with beds and needles and disgusting procedures where they insert large items into small spaces.

It was terrifying and awful.

Having recently watched my father go through the same process with a premature unhappy ending, it eventually got the best of me and my false belief that wine would make me feel better landed me back in the cycle of drinking daily.

A lot.

And it did make me *'feel better'* for a little while. It worked like an anaesthetic for my fears. But anaesthetics wear off, and fears grow when you feed them, just like what I feared was the cancer growing inside *me.*

It's said that cancer can't grow in an Alkaline environment. Of course, wine is among the most highly acidic of things you can put in your body. And, cancer loves acid, just like me back in high school. So, here I've been feeding what I was already genetically predisposed to having for a good 20 years or more.

Now, my point here is not to tell my story, *but to make you think about yours.*

Cancer is anything growing inside you that you're feeding with bad habits.

Your worries, your fears, your self-destructive false truths that you aren't good enough, you're fat, you aren't worthy or worse.

I'm learning to acknowledge my **false truths** as they trigger me throughout the day, and have started asking myself *"but, is it true?"*

Nearly 100% of the time, they aren't.

Things like *"If I have a drink I can stop worrying about the results of the biopsy,"* or *"If I have a drink I can finally relax,"* or maybe *"If I have a drink, I can escape this nightmare."*

So, that's what I've been doing. Having drink after drink, bottle after bottle, without realizing (read: admitting) that none of those false truths were helping me.

In fact, they've been doing the exact opposite.

I was just feeding the cancer and instead, creating more illness and concern, which I needed never-ending *new* false truths to keep me in denial of.

It had to stop.

The more I was learning about cancer, the more I realized I needed to learn about *health,* instead.

I promised myself and everyone around me that I would, and I quote, *"Give all the fucks"* in trying to combat this and take responsibility for my own well-being. Enter massive diet change on December 28, 2017, roughly 5 or 6 weeks ago. I went vegan. Don't worry, I won't try and convince you, but I will recommend you watch the documentaries *"What The Health"* and *"The C Word"*, and draw your own conclusions.

They are life changing. Or at least they were, to me.

I knew I had to stop feeding the cancer and instead start to starve it. So far, it's going well. And here I am on Day 3 of being sober again. I also won't talk about how I couldn't sleep at all last night, tossing and turning with sweat pouring out and off me like a disgusting beast. Detox is a bitch.

My gut is telling me this is the big Domino that *everything else* is lined up behind.

Becoming Alkaline.

Creating a life where I am *no longer feeding the things that are eating away at me.*

And that's why we drink, right?

To numb those false truths so we don't feel them gnawing away at us from the inside out. And, by 'feeding' I don't mean specifically what we put into our body. It's our thoughts, our actions, and our words as well. Truth is, it feels incredibly empowering to finally be taking responsibility for my own health, wholistically – *physical, mental and spiritual* – instead of relying and waiting on something *outside* of myself.

A doctor. A pill. *A bottle or three.*

So, that hunger and thirst is still there inside me – but this time I don't own it.

I've given it back to whom it belongs.

And I'm going to starve those little bastards.

Red Flags

FEBRUARY 7, 2018

It's Day 4 of being sober, again, and I won't lie by saying say that Day 3 was a breeze.

While it wasn't brutal, I was idle. I was craving. I was *thirsty*.

But I took the time with each craving to *stop* and become aware of what I was feeling at that moment, and the moments and events leading up to it. Was I thinking about the future? Was I stuck in loop in a cyclone of thought over a moment from the past? Was I maybe just hungry or tired?

After years of taking the backseat to my cravings and allowing them to take the wheel, what I had actually and accidentally done was dig a continuously deeper trench, as though we were driving on rails and it was always to the same destination, wheels stuck in gutters we couldn't steer out of.

The bottom of a bottle. And then another. And oftentimes, *another.*

I never stopped to consider why I was climbing in the car – I just knew it would take me to where I wanted to go.

And where I wanted to go, was to feeling numb, *as quickly as possible.* To fixing whatever was causing the discomfort that was in turn causing the *craving.* I never stopped to consider that the craving was just a *red flag.*

red flag

noun

A red flag as a warning of danger or a problem.
"They had overlooked the red flags that should have alerted them to the county's disastrous investment strategy."
A red flag as the symbol of socialist revolution.

You see, I had it all inside-out.

I always assumed that the craving was the actual problem, and that I **needed the wine** to appease the craving.

But the problem was never the wine. The wine was just a patch that numbed the problem. And after years of creating that trench by reacting to my craving with drinking immediately, every time a craving would hit – into the backseat I'd go and like a child on an amusement park train, off we went to Numbville.

I was never in control.

I'm sure this is common with most addicts and alcoholics. After decades of taking the same, shortest route possible to what you think is the "solution" to your pain or discomfort, it's hard to imagine taking the backroads.

But what if the craving is actually a *red flag*? A way that your body is calling for attention, like a tiny siren inside you that makes you anxious and uncomfortable to alert you that *something is wrong.*

My approach yesterday to put my cravings in the backseat for a change was to *start listening.* And guess what?

It worked.

I started being *mindful* of the moments around my cravings, and they were 100% of the time connected to *situations or thoughts* that were making me uncomfortable. And the craving was just my brain's way of offering the fastest solution to making me "comfortable" again, as quickly as possible. Thanks, brain!

My biggest hurdle was always getting past the craving to start pouring wine at lunch. I'd clock-watch until it flipped exactly to 12:00 pm and that first warm burn of shiraz hitting my gut would quench the fire that was smouldering in me all morning. It did more than quench it, though. It also *fueled it.*

I'd barrel through, not having breakfast, or lunch, and usually also skipping supper. I still can go all day, or days, without eating. But drinking 3 Litres of wine a day is beyond easy.

Well, it turns out, *I was just hungry.*

Long story short, I had a quiet eating disorder through most of high school, and well into university. I'm pretty sure there's still an insecure fat boy living inside me, doing his best to not be *"that fat gay kid"* anymore. The thought of eating still triggers an anxiety in me, which my brain quickly responds with *"But wait! Let's go for a quick drive to Numbville and that gross feeling will go away!"*

And we drive as fast we can.

Through listening to my cravings, I'm starting to learn *their language.*

I've turned them inside out. Instead of hearing the craving as *"it's time to drink wine"* I'm translating it into *"what is making me uncomfortable?"*

Then dealing with it.

So far, every discomfort I've recognized connected to my cravings are related to things in the future or the past – or at least my perceived idea of how what's happening in the *present* will affect the *future.*

It's almost always borne from moments of me *trying to control things I simply can't.*

So, when a craving hits and I recognize that I'm tired – *I rest.*

If I recognize that I'm dreading a business call – *I make it and get it over with*

If I tune in to my body and realize I haven't had breakfast or a snack but am craving a drink – *I eat.*

I never actually wanted the wine. It appears I just wanted to *be comfortable.*

And who doesn't?

Here's to another day of learning the language of my cravings and learning a hell of a lot about myself.

The Fear of Being Happy

FEBRUARY 8, 2018

Do you ever have moments where you realize that things are actually going pretty well, that you are feeling pretty good, and you wonder, *"Okay, what's wrong. When is the knife going to drop?"*

I have that stupid Joy-Fear connection.

When things aren't falling apart, I wonder when it's going to start.

It's Day 5 sober today, and I'm feeling a number of things, from pride and confidence to control and health. *I feel lighter.* But tagging along as that loud, rattling fifth wheel is the constant worry of when I'm going to stumble and have a drink again.

Of when I fail at this.

Of already feeling regret for drinking eventually, despite being completely committed to never drinking again, because I've been through this before and know that I can't. To save my damned life, I can't. I just need to get to a point of *not even wanting to.*

It hangs over me like a dull heavy knife on thin, frayed twine.

Worrying about all the inevitable situations where I'll be uncomfortable and tempted.

Why can't I just be here right now, sober on Day 5, and let that be enough? The problem with so many of us is that we are always somewhere else: in the future, in the past; we are always *anywhere but here.*

Worrying is just like any other habit. If you do anything long enough and often enough, it becomes second nature.

"Worry does not empty tomorrow of its sorrow, it empties today of its strength."

I read somewhere that the trick to breaking the Joy-Fear cycle is to replace the "fear" part with moments of simple pleasures. Instead of thinking *"Wow things are going so great, I wonder when something awful is going to happen"* to stop halfway at *"Wow things are going so great"* and follow it by something that brings you calm and happiness. Or to intentionally set out to do activities you know bring you great joy, followed by another experience of something that brings you calm. It's about learning how to *interrupt* the habitual *'but'* we all tend to tack on to everything.

It comes down to turning the Joy-Fear connection into a Joy-Calm connection.

To expect good things. Always.

It doesn't help that that I'm detoxing and going through brutal withdrawal, and my anxiety is already at an all-time high. Yesterday was the worst so far, and midday and I had to lay down for an hour for fear I was going to end up in the Emergency Room or morgue. Impending doom. That's what detoxing mixed with anxiety feels like; a cocktail inside you made up of nausea and too many *I'm-not-strong-enoughs.*

It felt like I was under a blanket made from patches of worry and threads of dread.

It was my 3rd day of not sleeping (like, at all – so let's toss utter exhaustion into the mix, too) and I just stared at the wall wanting to feel better. It passed eventually, but I had to spend the rest of the day trying to keep myself busy, wanting to pick up a bottle but instead picking up pots in the kitchen, cooking food I didn't need or want.

I was trying to turn my anxiety-fed-fear into things that bring me happiness, instead. It sort of worked. Just like any other time I try and change my habits, it's going to take a lot of practice and awareness. *And failures.*

See? I'm already expecting to fail and stumble, regardless of how well things go. Maybe it comes down to those false truths we tell ourselves every day? That voice inside that whispers *"You're doing great, for now."* We've been listening to it for so many damn years that of course we don't question it anymore.

We just silently agree and accept it as truth and wait for the day when we aren't doing great anymore.

And, because we agree with it, expect it, and inherently believe it, *of course we are going to fail.* Because we have a fear of being happy.

I do, anyways.

Did I drink because I was sabotaging myself and my life? Tearing it apart from the foundation because I felt I didn't deserve to be happy or successful? Waiting for all my good things to come toppling down, because I've just been waiting – *forever* – for them to?

I won't get into where I think that deep-rooted belief of mine came from, but I think I know. I will say I know that expecting success is the game changer. Feeling it in my heart and the deepest parts of my gut that my life is so very much better without alcohol and will continue to be. Feeling so completely that the *only possible outcome* is that I can and will totally rock this sobriety thing.

It is not the absence of fear but the courage to take action anyway that determines success.

It's time to start expecting nothing but my wild success, one day at a time.

My only job is to line up all my successful *one-day-at-a-times* into weeks and years and forever and ever-and-evers.

A Letter to Future Me

FEBRUARY 9, 2018

**The other day I stumbled across the coolest corner of the internet.
A little website called FutureMe.org.**

The idea is that you can write yourself a letter that will be emailed to you on a date of your choice, anytime in the future. And because of human nature, chances are I'll forget I've done this, days or months from now.

On February 9, 2019, when the letter I wrote today to my *Future Self* pops into my inbox, I'm hoping I can read it with sober eyes, not hungover, no longer swimming with rogue regrets.

What I wrote was two-fold.

First, I explained how good I'm feeling today. How much happier I am sober. How the quality of my life, in every aspect, is better right now, only Day 6 of being alcohol-free. I painted a picture of my life with and without alcohol, to remind myself clearly of how good clarity feels. As if this entire blog and book shouldn't already be enough.

Then, in the event this plan goes horribly awry, and I stumble, reading that letter through wine-coloured glasses, to serve as a gentle nudge, a *Ghost of Christmas Past* sort of messenger, to take a deeper look and try again. To never stop starting. All of this falls into what I rambled about yesterday: anticipating failure and how it is intrinsically tied to our innately human fear of being happy.

Because really, I should just be envisioning myself 1 year from today sober and thriving. *Not sending letters of encouragement to Future Me saying "try, try again".*

It's not the future I'm afraid of. It's repeating the past that makes me anxious.

I may do a few more letters to *Future Me* this morning. Maybe one to arrive a month from now, when I will have 36 Days sober under my belt, then again in 3 months, and 6, and so on.

Like a parole officer, making me accountable for my sobriety.

And, the only person I'm accountable to is me. My sobriety hinges entirely on my choices, and my choices alone. So why shouldn't I be the one making myself check myself? Probably because I didn't a very good job of it *in the past,* which is why I'm relying on *Future Me,* the only witness I have at this moment to how I feel within and without, to be waiting for me down the road like an old friend. And he'll remind me of that time things were so good, thriving and terrified, and how yet we were so proud of ourself and how we never felt better.

It's an easy feeling to take for granted, because don't feel we deserve it.

I think any of us with an alcohol use disorder can identify with taking things (so many things) for granted. I've reached a point in this journey where I am pulling out any and every stop possible to ensure my success. If that means writing 500 letters to *Future Me,* so be it.

My morning routine this past week takes up at least 3 hours every day. From my readings by the remarkable *Annie Grace,* who is saving my life, to *her inspirational and insightful videos,* to my personal journal, and *then* to writing these posts. It's a fair trade for the 12 hours I used to spend wasted and wasteful every day.

It's time to invest in myself again, no matter what the cost.

I have a feeling Future Me will thank us.

Swallowing My Own Tail

FEBRUARY 10, 2018

Just a little post for this morning, as I'm heading out the door for a photoshoot this morning. I'm a photographer. It's not as glamourous as it sounds.

Though tight on time I refuse to skip my morning routine. Running late? *Write it anyways.* Got the flu? *Write it anyways.* Dog barfed all over the floor? *Write it anyways.* **At least I'm not hungover.**

Journaling is such sweet, priceless therapy.

Today marks Day 7 sober. A small but valiant victory.

I've lost 4 lbs, 5 lbs, as I just weighed myself, saved $170 CAD in booze I didn't buy and gained some self-respect in the process. Not bad for 143 hours.

Today's talk and video in The Alcohol Experiment was about drinking and its link to depression, and vice versa. I admit I've always wondered which came first, the chicken or the egg. Was it my adolescent, and later adult, depression that I reached to drinking to dilute? Or was it my drinking that caused the heavy cloud overhead and within to grow and grow and grow?

I think it's fair to say that each exacerbated the other.

At this point, 28 years after I started "seriously" drinking, it's like the snake who swallowed its tail.

The *Ouroboros.*

Now, if you haven't heard of the Ouroboros, here's a quick synopsis, taken from Tokenrock.com:

> "The ouroboros has several meanings interwoven into it. Foremost is the symbolism of the serpent biting, devouring, or eating its own tail. This symbolizes the cyclic Nature of the Universe: creation out of destruction,

Life out of Death. The ouroboros eats its own tail to sustain its life, in an eternal cycle of renewal."

That's what I have been, albeit subconsciously, trying to do. With every drink, I'd try and get my life back, to temporarily numb the depression, and in turn I would end up even more depressed.

The eternal cycle just got bigger and bigger with each swig. The more I'd take, the more it would take back. The higher the wine brought me, the lower I'd end up.

I've spent my entire life chasing my own tail.

This is a shallow analogy that I hope to explore more, since I think there's a lot of parallels between the Ouroboros and the alcoholic. The only difference being the serpent finds renewal, and alcoholics just get bit. Or maybe, it's a symbol of the *recovering* alcoholic? Maybe that's why it's speaking to me today, on Day 7, finally beginning to remember what being sober feels like?

Finally connecting with myself, like the snake, *at last*, reaching my tail.

Life out of Death.

A snake is often a symbol of resurrection, as it appears to be continually reborn as it sheds its skin.

And today, 1 week sober, I'm beginning to feel like things are beginning to peel.

Car Crash, Train Wreck, Tornado

FEBRUARY 11, 2018

I just finished watching '*Australia's Most Effective Drunk Driving*' advert, according to the video name. Google it. I can't argue with it.

It's worth the 5 minutes – *trust me*. Before I ramble on this morning – *please watch it*. It really hit home for me, and sadly, millions of others too, I'm sure. *I hope.*

And that makes me sad.

Not only does it make me sad that we live in a culture of alcohol, where it's glamourized as the cure-all to making us relaxed, confident, sexy, and most recently, *healthy*, but it stirs up dirty memories of times I was simply *lucky*.

Lucky and *very, very stupid*.

I have not driven drunk often, *to my knowledge or recollection*. It goes without saying that there have likely been innumerable mornings I've woke up mere hours after blacking out and drove *somewhere* with the alcohol still pumping through my veins, my brain, my reactions.

I'll never forget my first attempt at going alcohol free, at a local outpatient Addiction Services program. They were running through the gamut of "intake" questions, and they asked me how I got there that morning. This was after they asked me how much I drank the day before, and when.

I said, *"I drove my truck..."*

And they politely explained that from the volume I drank the day before, I was still very illegally under the influence, and would technically be until later that afternoon.

No matter. I'd have at least another bottle of wine in me by that time.

I had drank so much the day before, and every day before that, that it was going to take at least 24 hours or more of my body fighting to get back under the legal limit.

Hubs drove home.

A few months later, we are having a pool party and the drinks had been flowing since the first early morning "breakfast beer" and it was now about 10:30 at night and a small miracle I could even stand up straight.

Ok, let's face it, I probably wasn't standing very straight or stable.

Long story short, my friend yells my name from inside the house, I rush in and there's one of my dogs with her eyeball *literally hanging down near her jowls,* panting and wanting a treat.

WHAT. IN THE ACTUAL. FUCK.

Her eye literally *fell out.*

I, nor anyone who was over, was in any condition to process what was happening, or what to logically do next. We were all loaded. So naturally, of course, I panicked. Hubs panicked. Everyone panicked. Our dogs are our children.

And what horrible, drunken, useless, irresponsible parents we were in that moment.

So, we did what every negligent, concerned, raging alcoholic *would* do.

We swaddled her up, climbed into the car, hit the gas and flew blindly into the night with reckless abandon, seeing triple and risking everything to get her to the emergency vet. Hubs drove, I tried to comfort her and watched as yellow inner eye fluid began staining my white and still wet swim trunks with a sickly neon-ness I'll never forget.

At 160km/hr (100 miles) we were blaring the horn and flying through red lights across the city core, holding our breath and closing our eyes just hoping we slip through the intersection after intersection.

You know, like in the movies.

We were crossing into oncoming traffic just to pass vehicles in our own lane, flashing our lights and turning corners like we were in *Days of Thunder.* 40 minutes later, we arrive, miraculously unscathed at the emergency vet, stumbling and crying, with absolutely no control over our emotions – because, well, *the alcohol.*

It makes me absolutely sick to my stomach to imagine how things *could have ended up.*

We could have killed someone's mother. Or child. An entire family. A woman on her way to give birth at the hospital. A stranger crossing the street. A teenager on a bike. We could have injured someone and saddled them to a life of pain and therapy, ripping away and transforming their entire life - and the lives of everyone who knows them - in a split second because of our selfish and irresponsible "choice". We could have killed ourselves – but in all honesty, I was at a point in my life where if you had asked me, I would've said that dying wouldn't have been the worst possible outcome.

How sad that an alcoholic's disregard for their own life can overshadow the respect for someone else's.

When you unknowingly cross over to that darker side of drinking (because let's face it, there's no bright side) where you no longer have *any control* over it – you've entered terrifyingly dangerous territory.

You become a car crash waiting to happen, a train wreck – a tornado in the lives of everyone around you.

If you're one of the "lucky" ones, like me, you can claw yourself out with the car crash remaining just a metaphor. But so long as you're not in control of your drinking, you will always be a tornado in the lives of everyone around you.

Uprooting their safety, spinning wildly and unpredictably, with no one in your path being safe from harm.

Pixie ended up having her eye removed. Thankfully, it wasn't her blue one, born with one brown and one blue eye. To this day we still don't really know what happened – not unlike waking up day after day trying to figure out when your drinking problem *became a problem.*

It's a frustrating process, trying to pinpoint that spot in your life where you crossed over into *Tornado Territory,* where you became so numb and your brain so dysfunctional that flying at 100 miles an hour through red lights and intersections in the dark of night when you can't even form a sentence without slurring seems like a good idea, and the only option.

I am so lucky. Not everyone is. And unfortunately, it's the innocent ones that usually end up on the shitty end of the unlucky stick. You know – *the ones in your path.*

I am NOT lucky.

I am stupid.

Correction: I *was* stupid.

I was so stupid on so many occasions, in so many different situations.

Yet here I am, 8 days sober – again – and looking into the remaining blue eye of my baby girl, feeling incredible gratitude for whoever, wherever, cleared those intersections and got us to the emergency vet that night safely – leaving everyone in our path unscathed, *thank the Universe.*

And guess what? *We drove ourselves home, that night, too.*

The only thing worse than an actual tornado, *is a drunk one.*

The Next Right Thing

FEBRUARY 12, 2018

**"Do the right thing, and then do the next right thing, and
that will lead you to the next right thing after that."**
– Michael J. Fox

The whole notion of a *"Day at a Time"* is sometimes bigger than I'm able to digest.

These last 9 days I've been more of a *"Moment at a Time"* sort of guy, trying my best to be mindful of my cravings, aware of the false truths I'm telling myself that just one drink will help me relax, or that I deserve a "reward" for doing so well this week.

That a drink will make me feel even better than I'm feeling at this moment.

Who am I kidding.

That one drink would turn into ten, then three bottles of wine, then four.

I keep having to ask myself – *How well did things go the last time I tried to have "just one drink"?*

It's 6 am, and I'd be lying if I told you drinking hasn't already crossed my mind 20 times since I woke up at 4:30 am. I've never drank at this hour of day – but it doesn't stop the wine from whispering in my ear from the moment I wake up, it's sour breath thick with tannins and lies, keeping my head in a cloud of cravings.

I made it 96 days sober last year, after a month at a recovery clinic, so I know these cravings get quieter, but they never truly go away. It's a voice I'm going to have to learn how to parent, reminding it every time that the candy it's begging for will rot its teeth out.

That the sweet will only bring sour.

So how do I do this? It feels as though I have Hitler in one ear, feeding me propaganda over and over, while Oprah's in the other telling me to breathe, and that I've got this. The dichotomy of this disease has the ability and strength to make a man go mad.

Until that is, you take its strength away.

And where does it get its strength? From promising you *the future.*

A perfect world, with all your problems washed away – for the time being, at least. Sweet, intoxicating, temporary ignorance. The absence of pain and the illusion of pleasure.

Just Drink Me. I'll make you feel so much better.

I think it's fair to say no one has ever found comfort in the uncertain, uncontrollable future. Or the past, for argument's sake. The only *true* comfort you can have is *taking control of your life and actions, and being here in the present moment.*

If we can do that, we take the craving's power away. We can silence the lies, by *mastering this moment.* How long do you think a pusher will keep pushing, to get you to buy their drugs? Eventually they'll give up and go away, *right?*

Just keep doing the next right thing.

Over, and over and *over* again.

As many times as you need to, to get through to the next moment, *"surfing the urge"* until the tide pulls back, and your feet are on the ground again.

It was my last day in rehab, March 21, 2017.

We went for a walk on the beach, the ocean, for a change, louder than the Nazi in my ear.

I wrote a message to myself in the sand, because I learned that the only way I could beat this beast, was to simply *Be Happy Now,* and that's what I wrote, like a message to myself for the ocean to take with it in one retreating wave, to become part of itself, and wash upon shores closer to me, in other places and other times.

It's time, again, to stop buying into the sugary promises of a less painful future.

To stop listening to the voice telling me that a drink will make the next moment better than this one. That what I have right now *isn't quite good enough.*

I listened to my own advice for 66 more days, until the voice came back louder and stronger, and with a brand-new sales pitch.

I bought into it.

And here I am today, starting over again but winning at 9 Days sober.

But what I did, when shit got real again and the shameful pile of empty wine bottles and self-sabotage grew too tall, is *the next right thing*. The fact that I started drinking again last year after rehab doesn't matter – *it's the unchangeable past.* The fact that the voice is back and screaming *"Drink Me!"* with deceitful promises of how much better I'll feel if I do doesn't matter. *It's the uncontrollable future.*

What does matter is the fact that I can, at this very moment, choose to listen to what the little Nazi in my ear is saying, acknowledge it, and confidently say *"I don't believe you anymore."*

It's the only thing I can do in this controllable present moment.

It's time to Be Happy Now.

And now.

And now.

Just keep doing the *Next Right Thing*.

Waking Up

FEBRUARY 13, 2018

**I woke up this morning, 10 days sober, like a kid on Christmas morning.
Excited, full of energy, and full of anticipation for the day ahead.**

Who am I and what the hell happened?

I'm just scratching the surface of this Alcohol Free life, but everything is already
a far cry from rolling off the couch with the hangover-to-end-all-hangovers just
10 mornings ago, unsure if I was already dead or just wanting to die.

It was that fateful morning, preceded by hundreds more just like it, that was the
classic bucket of water thrown on the drunk to wake them up so you can kick
them to the curb.

I don't want to feel like that anymore.

Breaking free from the cycle of drinking & withdrawal, for me, has been a slow
process of *waking up*. It's as though I've been under a mountain of blankets in bed,
keeping me warm every cold dark night for the last 20 plus years.

I never noticed I was sleeping on a bed of snakes.

Each sober day under my belt is lifting a blanket from me, and I'm slowly waking
up and seeing everything for what it *really* is.

It's never *really* been a safe, warm place – *being drunk.*

It's been a trap, and I laid myself down willingly, day after day after day, sleeping
with snakes. I was so used to it, I stopped noticing them writhing around me,
taking grip and keeping me there, *stuck.*

The more I strip away the lies about alcohol that I've grown to believe as absolute
truth, the more I'm revealing soft spots of understanding that I hope to harden
with experience, one day at a time.

It feels a lot like mourning.

If you've ever lost someone, you will understand how you can wake up in the morning, forgetting they are gone. And for a split second, everything is as it was.

Until you remember.

Then it all comes rushing back, the scab is ripped raw, and you truly wake up.

Then, you have to come to terms – *again, and again, and again* – with your loss.

It's basically *Groundhog Day for Grief.*

I'd be lying if I said I haven't been feeling like my good friend just died. I've been looking at this process as "giving up alcohol" – *and therein lies the actual problem.* **It's not a sacrifice.** I haven't *given up* anything. The only thing I've lost are those pain-stricken mornings, the regret, the shame, and the daily abuse I put myself – and everyone else – through.

Perhaps it makes more sense for us to start saying *"I'm getting rid of alcohol",* because that's what you do with things you no longer need and that are no longer serving you.

You get rid of them.

This morning is the first one since going alcohol-free that I can recognize myself in the mirror. Actually, *that's not entirely true.* This morning is the first one since going alcohol-free that I am *willing to actually look at myself* in the mirror.

I'd avoid it as though I was the Elephant Man every day until I was drunk enough to not care what I looked like or how I felt.

Like clockwork, it seems the actual poison has officially left the building, alcohol taking 7 to 10 days to fully leave your bloodstream. I feel like today is the official beginning of my new normal, again. Every challenge and struggle I've pushed through over the last 10 days, every painful, uncomfortable moment I've survived, has been one of those blankets I've spent so long beneath - folded up, and put away.

Good morning.

It feels fantastic to be *awake.*

And I'm never crawling into that bed again.

The Clearance Aisle

FEBRUARY 14, 2018

**It was February 14, 2017.
One year ago, today.**

Valentine's Day.

For the first time in my life, I had *finally* stepped up and admitted I had a drinking problem, and that I needed help.

Talk about romantic.

Okay. It wasn't as simple or romantic as is sounds. The idea of admitting my failures and flaws made me sick to my stomach and broke me down like a wrecking ball.

I knew in my gut that this was something I couldn't do on my own.

Clawing my way out of abysmal chaos wasn't exactly something I had a lot of experience at. But diving straight into it? *Absolutely.* It's eye-opening when your doctor recommends that any alcohol detox be done under medical supervision, because, well, poison leaving your system hurts more than when it goes in.

I was so far gone; I needed a mountain of valium and a team of chaperones to hold my hand in turn while the alcohol left my system.

How terrifying and embarrassing.

I trusted myself so little, I knew I had to be quarantined somewhere without *any* access to alcohol if I was going to make this work.

So off to rehab I went.

Reading my post from exactly 1 year ago today, the sickened self-hatred and loathing I had for myself and the wasteful, painful situation I put myself, and Hubs, and everyone I loved or who trusted in me feels as familiar as if it were yesterday.

Probably because just 12 days ago I was right back where I started.

Here's what I wrote:

February 14, 2017. "6 Days of Drinking"

> *"This. This is what I've drank in the last 6 days.*
>
> *19 litres of wine. $300 (Canadian) in wine. In less than a week.*
>
> *And most are the big bottles.*
>
> *2 of them a day, I'd say. (That's 4 normal bottles at least).*
>
> *Hubs says I'm missing some, because he took some out already.*
>
> The empties just pile up like regrets. *FUCK.*
>
> *The families I could feed with that money. The bills I could pay off.*
>
> The life I could live without the regrets.
>
> *The shit I could get done without the hangovers. But honestly, I barely get hungover anymore. My body is just...nope. Perhaps I'm in a constant cycle of drunk/hungover and I can't tell the difference anymore.*
>
> **6 days. 19 Litres.**
>
> *Most people don't drink that in a year or more.*
>
> I'm just placing this here so I can look back one day, and realize where I came from.
>
> *Because looking at those empties makes me sick.*
>
> *Counting down the hours until I go to rehab.*
>
> Because I can't do this anymore."

It's fair to say I was in a broke-down state, feeling as pathetic as possible.

At rehab, they tried to write us into the pages of *The Big Book*, casting us alongside every other alcoholic: inherently broken, flawed, and absolutely powerless.

We were explained that we were there because of an *"allergy"* we had to alcohol, and if we remained on our own, we'd also remain *as hopeless as we apparently are and will continue to be.* The only possible outcomes for us, *we were told,* were jail, institutions, or death.

I felt generalized, as though all of us there were just 12 Step minions, one no different from the other, connected by the simple fact that we were all intrinsically *broken and incurable.*

So there I was, thinking, *"Well, this sucks."*

I was already about as low as I've ever been. 40 years old, in rehab, and absolutely out of control. I felt I belonged in the clearance aisle with a big sign reading: "BROKEN! But still works!"

Sort of.

The AA approach, thankfully, made me start questioning everything, at least as a jumping off point. Because somewhere deep inside me I knew I wasn't inherently flawed. I *knew* I had a good heart, despite my misgivings, mistakes, or any and all hurts I had caused.

> "You have a good heart, Nicholas. That doesn't change."
> – Delilah, *Everything Must Go (Will Farrell Movie)*

Maybe there wasn't actually *something wrong with* **me.**

Maybe I had just *done something* wrong!

I refused to sit there, pushed to the back of the shelf in the clearance aisle, flawed, chipped, and forgotten.

Forever discounted.

Their approach was to blame the cracks in the pitcher, instead of the gravity that broke it. I was being taught that *I was the problem.* And, for a little while at least, I sadly bought into it.

That is until I reached the point where I started to become angry at the alcohol and the culture that sold me on its necessary allure (not to mention my inability to just simply control myself.)

You need it. Your life is better with it. You're a better version of yourself when you're drunk.

I was NOT okay at the back of the shelf anymore, discounting my worth because *there was something wrong with me.* Maybe there was something wrong with the poison I had been drinking? Or the encouragement from every media outlet and public place to keep drinking it, because it's a reward I deserve for how hard I work. Because *I deserved it.*

Maybe there was actually something wrong with everything else?

It's so easy to get caught in the guilt-trap, beating ourselves up because we react differently to things than others do. Situations, ideas, *drugs.*

What is wrong with me? Why do I have this problem when other people don't?

It also doesn't help getting kicked when you're down, being told that trying to glue yourself together is going to be the hardest thing you've ever done – *and it won't stick* – because you're not like everyone else. You're broken beyond repair.

Well, thanks AA. That's helpful.

Maybe I just became very addicted to a very addictive drug that I was told I needed in my life.

Maybe it's as simple as that.

With the help of Annie Grace's This Naked Mind, not to mention the Dharma, it just recently became obvious that it's time to start questioning *everything*.

And, for the record, there *is* something wrong with me.

My beliefs about alcohol, myself, and how I perceive the world and my place in it.

With each false truth that I strip away about how alcohol benefits me – *and there are no benefits, for the record* – another part of me gets put back together. Each new actual *truth I am willing to accept* is a bead of glue, binding all my broken parts back together, stronger than they were before.

Kintsugi for the soul.

I'm ready to move to the top shelf, where the light can reach me. Where I can be seen, broken parts and all. Without shame.

I no longer believe I deserve to be discounted and pushed to the back of the clearance aisle.

I am *not* my addiction, and I refuse to let anyone tell, *or try to teach me*, that I am.

Especially myself.

I'm ready to move to the Top Shelf, marked up and with a great big sign screaming "New and Improved."

The Three Me's

FEBRUARY 15, 2018

The other day, Hubs looked at me out of the blue and said: *"Do you want to know what I'm loving most about this whole being sober, Alcohol-Free thing?*

And I stabled myself because I don't usually like talking about serious things face to face.

Or, at all.

"I am loving this whole new consistent Shawn. Don't get me wrong, but there was a morning Shawn, an afternoon Shawn, and an evening Shawn."

And I had no choice but to agree.

I was feeling it too, and I'm feeling it more and more each passing, sober day.

Alcoholics put their partners and families through so much shit. We take for granted their patience, and if you're lucky, they are patient; not everyone is. We lie to ourselves that we're only hurting ourselves, if we're aware enough to admit that we're hurting anyone to begin with.

Like playing hide and seek with a toddler, they think no one can see us but they're standing there in plain sight.

It's obvious to everyone else but us.

Being the *Three Me's* was an exhausting, self-deprecating cycle, not unlike the *Evolution of Man*, but in reverse. I'd start my days standing relatively tall, and with each drink as the day went on, I'd take slow but steady steps backwards until I reached the beginning again:

Unable to communicate, slow, confused, and not particularly attractive.

And then, I'd just *pass out.* Every evening I'd reach black-out, like being absorbed into a black-hole and arriving back at the beginning of time. I'd repeat that decline every single day and lie to myself that it's *just who I am.*

I wasn't drunk: *I was tired.* I wasn't drinking too early in the day: *I was stressed out.* It didn't matter how much I was drinking today: *I was going to drink less tomorrow.* It didn't matter the time of day, there was a Shawn standing by to justify drinking and offer an excuse.

Evening, pre-black-out Shawn always had the best arsenal of excuses.

No wonder I was so exhausted all the time. It's hard enough being 1 alcoholic, much less 3 in one day. There was always Morning-Hungover-Shaky-Wanting-A-Drink Shawn, Afternoon-Just-Started-Drinking-And-Procrastinating-Shawn, then the infamous 3-Sheets-To-The-Wind-4-Litres-of-Wine-Later-Shawn.

None of them were very nice to be around.

And poor Hubs, trying to juggle all 3 of Me.

As the day would go on, I'd accomplish less and remember even less than that.

Hubs would bring up the movie we watched the night before and it'd be gone.

No recollection. You could've paid me to tell you the plotline or title and I couldn't.

Dementia must be the most terrifying of diseases. Developing it sits at the top of my list of greatest fears. Yet, I gladly and habitually self-induced it every night.

Evening Shawn had a very bad memory, if he had any at all. He also cried a lot.

Mountains became molehills, the wrong word could turn into a battle cry. Everything became amplified to offset the fact that I was so absolutely numb the world around me had to scream for me to hear it.

How sad that drinking can split a person into thirds, not one of them as good as the whole. It doesn't matter what your intentions are, the size and integrity of your heart, or your goals to simply, somehow, *do better.*

Drinking for me was the classic magician's *"Saw Them in Half"* illusion.

But it wasn't an illusion.

Every day I'd walk (stumble?) on stage, crawl into the box, and let myself be divided.

It's a tiring life, *never feeling whole.* And that's what the alcohol did to me, every day: *it diluted me.* It divided me. It took whatever potential I had as a whole and turned it into fractions. Any effort I made – *at anything* – was always just a thin slice of what I was capable of.

Since going Alcohol Free 12 days ago, I feel myself pulling back together, slowly stitched whole again with threads of sobriety.

It's not an overnight process.

Once you've been in pieces so long, it's not always easy to figure out how things go back together.

But I'm getting there.

The comforting *Consistency of Being Sober* makes literally everything easier.

My job. My marriage. My efforts to untangle my mind. Everything, *somehow*, is starting to seem manageable now that I'm no longer letting the drink divide me.

It's easy to be strong when you are whole, rather than a third of yourself, or less.

I can't say I'm going to miss the 2 Me'u

Not one of them did me any favours, but they'll always be there as parts of me, taking time to heal while I become whole again.

Here's hoping the stitches hold.

The Horrible Book of My Deepest Regrets

FEBRUARY 16, 2018

There is a photo I did 6 years ago of Hubs, in the guest room at our old house. It's called *The Abduction*.

He is floating above himself, somewhere transparently, *above himself,* while his whole self is sleeping, tucked in bed. It's haunting and beautiful all at once.

6 years later, I'm looking at this photo and seeing it for the first time.

It's not obscured through wine-coloured glasses: *it's about becoming an observer in our own lives. Or, maybe it's about escaping reality.*

It's so easy, albeit uncomfortable, to stay harboured within ourselves.

We spend our days quarantined in our bodies, safe from being vulnerable, as though we're tiny Librarians filing away our shame, our guilt, our regret, and our fear like dusty, dog-eared books, and our mind is the dark, dimly lit library itself.

Full of stories we are too afraid to read or tell.

Alcohol put me there.

Lost in the stacks, the library hours would just extend longer day by day and year by year until eventually I simply lived there, re-reading the same old stories. Eventually, Fiction became Truth, and the History section became Current Events.

Stuck in this loop within myself, I felt safe, *but not secure.*

Each time I'd pull *"The Horrible Book of My Deepest Regrets"* from the shelf, it would get heavier, as though the pages would double every time, I closed the cover.

Every page, typed in red wine.

I admit, it was my favourite bedtime story. It was dark and twisted, and every time I'd read a new chapter the story's ending would change itself.

But it was *never* a happy ending.

The longer I stayed there, re-reading the same old stories, the more tragic the tale's ending became. I had become nothing more than an awkward character, poorly written into an otherwise interesting story.

I'd become collateral damage, as though I was just innocently passing by when the Giant landed flat on me, falling from Jack's Bean Stalk. A bean stalk I myself had been fertilizing and watering and encouraging to grow.

I was no longer the main character, *the hero*. I was just another page in a warehouse of similar, sad books. *And the villain always won.*

It took me a really, really long time to realize I wasn't okay with that.

That I was bored and tired of re-reading the same stories that all had the same ending, and tired of becoming a smaller and less significant character in my own twisted biography. I wanted to read a Happy Drama or an Adventure novel; even a Comedy would do.

I was tired of re-reading the same old Tragedy: *Boy drinks wine, then the wine drinks him*. I was ready to become the author again, intent on writing a happier ending where the villain no longer wins.

This time I'd dodge the Giant before he lands on me.

And so, I forced myself to go outside.

Outside of myself, outside of my *comfort zone*, far from the stacks of sad stories that had kept me trapped and enthralled for years. And what I found outside the tall walls of the library was a world of raw, beautiful *vulnerability*.

> "I'm going to leave my body (Moving up to higher ground)
> I'm gonna lose my mind (History keeps pulling me down)"
> – *Leave My Body, Florence + The Machine*

What I believe comes down to is this:

By closing the cover on the story I've been *telling* myself, I have the power to *reimagine and recreate the ending*. Every moment of every day, I have this opportunity.

By being vulnerable and *owning my shame*, I can erase it.

By being mindful of my *self-talk*, I can begin to learn *a new way of speaking to myself.*

In no longer re-reading *"The Horrible Book of My Deepest Regrets"* every day, I can pick up a much more empowering *Choose-Your-Own-Adventure* book, where for a change, *I'm in charge.*

But I can't do any of these things so long as I'm locked in the library, alone with my fairy tales and nightmares, trapped in my history while all I was trying to do was *escape.*

There comes a point where you grow tired of being *abducted* every day.

And that's what drinking did for me. *Or against me.*

It abducted me and threw me straight into the spine of the darkest storybook imaginable.

My self-worth was stolen by bottles and shame, and I transported myself back to the library over and over again, drink by drink, just to re-read my saddest and scariest memoirs. Not once did I learn anything from them, other than realizing how tired I was of that same old story.

I think it's time to tear up my library card.

Today Is Enough

FEBRUARY 17, 2018

I don't intend on getting poetic and fluffy today.

But there's always this incredible deception between my hands and intentions, so there's still a very good chance this post will go rogue, like a drunken mouse in a brand-new maze.

Stay tuned, and we'll see.

I want to celebrate a small success, today.

No, a *huge* success.

Today will mark 2 weeks sober, armed with nothing but logic and understanding, and sweet, beautiful *clarity* for a change.

It's so much easier to see things *as they are*, once you're no longer seeing double.

Some Things I've Learned:

- Waking up knowing my name and where I am is a pretty good start to the day

- 3 Litres of wine a day is not recommended by the Surgeon General

- Pomegranate juice is expensive, but cheaper than regret and self-loathing

- Anticipation is more of a drug than actual drugs

- Time moves more quickly when your senses aren't completely numbed

- Blacking out every evening is probably the least attractive thing ever

- Leaving the house, and being able to drive myself, to places other than the liquor store is a pretty sweet perk of being a grown man. *Who knew?*

- My brain has some pretty cool thoughts when it isn't drowning in wine and dopamine

- Being able to remember those cool thoughts are akin to having them twice

- Annie Grace deserves Sainthood

Now, that's just the short list.

It's the best I can do sober on a Saturday morning at 5am, which is so much better than still being drunk at this hour almost every other Saturday morning for the last two decades.

Okay, I'll be honest.

Every morning for the last two decades.

Today is a checkpoint for me. As humans we love landmarks and flags; markers to tell us how far we've come and how much further we have yet to go. We are plotters who find comfort in seeing *the big picture.*

We love countdowns and diaries.

We are always looking forward and looking back; it's the human condition that once we know where we are, we immediately want to see where we're headed and be able to look back to where we've come from, too.

That's the struggle: allowing where we are right now, *to be enough.*

But it's in these small (read: huge) victories that we arrive at along the way which makes the rest of the journey seem manageable and exciting.

If I can do 14 days, I can do 400. And if I can do 400 days, I can do 40 years.

Right?

Maybe.

I think when we relate where we are *right now,* to where we think we need to be (1 year sober, 10 years, 40) that we not only get intimidated and overwhelmed, but we miss the opportunity to celebrate our win *today.* It also diminishes the success we should be celebrating *right now.*

Because, let's be honest: *there is no finish line in this marathon.*

There is no race. There is only *right now.*

And right now, *this needs to be enough.*

It goes without saying that we need goals. Having something to work towards and look forward to is what gives us momentum. But what fuels our drive to get there?

Feeling good right now.

I can't possibly emphasize that enough.

Because, I know when I feel like a pile of shit within and without, I could care less to take any steps towards *anything* other than my bed. You can't find strength in looking at yesterday's failures, or last years, or even tomorrow's intimidating uncertainty.

You can only draw strength from right now.

It is quite literally the only chance you have to make a decision. You can't re-decide what you chose yesterday, or plan how you'll choose tomorrow.

It's only in this magical, immeasurable, and limitless "*now*" that we have *any* power at all.

We can't change our past choices, *but we can choose better right now.*

We can't predict our future choices, but we can choose better *right now*, so our *future* choices will be easier, not to mention fewer consequences to face down the road.

We can celebrate *today* because it's our first day sober or our fifth year dry.

Both will have the same effect: *feeling good right now.*

And if you're feeling good *right now*, why would you want to dilute it with a drink or twelve? I'm (re)discovering that being *mindful* is the only drug I need.

mind-ful-ness

noun

1. The quality or state of being conscious or aware of something.
"Their mindfulness of the wider cinematic tradition"
2. A mental state achieved by focusing one's awareness on the present moment, while calmy acknowledging and accepting one's feelings, thoughts, and bodily sensations, used as a therapeutic technique.

Well, so much for not getting fluffy and poetic.

But I got excited.

Today, *right now,* is enough.

I'll worry about tomorrow when it gets here.

Stuck In the Lineup

FEBRUARY 18, 2018

**"The golden opportunity you are seeking is in yourself.
It is not in your environment, it is not in luck or chance,
or the help of others; it is in yourself alone."**
– *Orison Swett Marden*

I think it's fair to say we are all prone to waiting for our big opportunity.

Waiting for chances, waiting for the right day, waiting for our a-ha moment, or a time when things are slower, and we can wrap our lazy fear-riddled heads around our ambitions.

So much waiting.

We spend (waste?) a lot of time telling ourselves that now *isn't quite the right time.*

I'll be stronger next week, when _____ is over.

If I try right now, I'll fail because _____.

If it wasn't for _____, I wouldn't _____.

Fill in the blanks however you like, but for me, there was always a long list of justifications waiting to fill up those blank spaces. My life has been so much *heavier* because I've carried around my trusty arsenal of excuses for so long, collecting new ones along the way.

And every time I'd cash one in it was as though I'd get bumped to the back of an ever-growing line.

Forever in queue.

I could always see what I was in line for – *sobriety, eating healthier, going to the gym, going for a walk, writing a novel, cleaning the garage, simply being stronger and more confident, making past due apologies* – but whenever I'd get close,

I'd forfeit my turn with one of a million excuses and pardon myself to the back of the line.

Again.

You know what's weird and interesting about lineups?

*They're made up exclusively of people doing **the exact same thing.***

Checking out. Checking in. Waiting for the same ticket, the same concert, the same clerk to check out our groceries. Waiting in line for an autograph, a drink, a chance at something, or waiting to exchange what we thought we wanted for something we think we'll like better.

The next time you're in a lineup, spare a moment to take it all in: that in a world with 7.6 billion people, all of you managed to arrive at the same place at the same time, spending your time *doing the exact same thing.*

The idea of *spending time* is interesting. The phrase itself tells us that time by its very nature is a *currency.* Yet we spend/waste it freely and without thought, as though it's limitless, and we can somehow make *more of it.*

Until we go bankrupt.

We spend/waste so much time thinking about our ambitions and justifying why this time *right now* isn't the right time, cashing in our currency at horrible exchange rates.

This is how I feel I spent/wasted my time leading up to becoming alcohol free: *Waiting for the perfect opportunity, the right time, and a cure outside of myself.*

In a never-ending queue, mistakenly waiting for someone to just hand me a ticket to Soberville, I settled into the crowd with everyone else, all of us waiting for the exact same thing: *the 'right' opportunity. What we think we want.*

Waiting for some mystical cure to fall from the sky and take away the pain and discomfort of actually, finally, buckling down and doing it.

For freedom, without the rocky road of escape.

The thing with waiting without action, is that it's like quicksand.

The longer you stand there, the further you sink.

I was given pieces to the puzzle though, which came in the form of success stories or brilliant, inspirational prose pulled from my stacks of self-help books.

I collected them like a packrat; hoarding shiny bits of insight and glittering ideas on how to get where I wanted to go, stored far away from where I stole them.

And they piled up, collecting dust, never truly being pieced together.

It took me a long time to realize how far the quicksand had swallowed me while I stood there, sinking in line for so long. It's usually when it's up to your neck and you're running out of time and breath that you realize that freedom and escape is your own responsibility.

I got myself in here, it's time to get myself out.

It was only in that rare, brave moment of taking responsibility and owning the truth that I was in the condition I was in (a raging, sinking alcoholic) and so deep in the quicksand because I *chose* to stay in the lineup, that I was finally able to start pulling myself out.

It was in the moment when I let go of blaming everything outside of myself (*my dad drank a lot so I drink because it's in the house, work stressed me out, so I need this, blah, blah, blah...*) that I was able to begin standing on that nest of prose and inspiration I had squirrelled away.

I was creating my own opportunity to finally be free.

I got myself in here, it's time to get myself out.

Until I became clear on what I was *truly* waiting for in that lineup, I was forever stuck in queue.

And clerks have no time for customers who don't know even know what they're in line for.

"Everyone you meet always asks if you have a career, are married or own a house as if life was some kind of grocery list. But no one ever asks if you are happy."
– *Heath Ledger*

And there it is.

Being happy.

If you take the time to drill down every aspiration, every hope, every dream, craving, desire, wish and ambition you have, they will *all* come down to the end-goal that we just *want to be happy.*

Why is this something we are waiting in line for? Why are we so ashamed of wanting happiness that we'll poison ourselves to numb that desire, or keep ourselves in an eternal loop of going without because we feel we don't deserve it, repeatedly just *wasting* our limited time?

The moment you realize that happiness isn't something that can be handed to you over a counter is the very moment you'll pull yourself from the quicksand and out of the lineup.

That's how it happened for me, anyhow.

The years/decades of standing in line, forever in queue, ended the day I woke up and realized I was tired of sinking. It ended the day I owned the fact, without shame, that *I deserved every bit of happiness possible.*

And in owning something, it becomes yours.

I did another photo 6 years ago, called *Live Your Life*. It's of myself, standing in the middle of a freeway, hundreds of rushing cars flying past me, with my arms and face turns to the sky and my clothes catching the wind with a sort of freedom and fearlessness I can only dream of. It captures *just being in the moment* instead of rushing like everyone else, to whatever is keeping us *busy*.

It's about as close as I can get to showing you what crawling out of the quicksand and getting out of the lineup feels like. When I created that photo, it was just a fantasy; an aspiration to maybe, hopefully, one day feel as free as I look in the picture.

To finally experience what exhilarating and fantastic, absolute *freedom* feels like.

It took time for me to admit that it wasn't waiting for me at the end of a lineup or the bottom of a bottle.

Where it was actually waiting for me was just on the other side of one raw, brave, terrifying moment of honesty and action, followed by another, *and another*.

I discovered that the fantastic, absolute feeling of *freedom* also feels a heck of a lot like *happiness.*

And isn't that what we're all waiting in line for?

As Above, So Much Below

FEBRUARY 19, 2018

"We do not see things as they are, we see things as we are."
– Anais Nin

We use the term "scratch the surface" to describe things of great depth; things that take time to fully understand or uncover.

It's our way of saying *we've only just begun.*

On the surface, it looked as though I *just* needed to stop drinking. Or at least, stop drinking so damn much. It was as though it was too hot outside and if I just took off my jacket, I'd be fine.

I wore my addiction like a heavy winter coat on a stuffy summer's day.

It felt secure and safe, with deep pockets to fill up with my insecurities so I could carry them around regardless of the weather. The more I drank, the heavier the coat became. Every drink was just another layer.

It wasn't until I *stopped* drinking that I was able to start stripping away the layers, one by one until I stood there vulnerable and being seen.

It was only when I stopped drinking and the coat came off that I could see all the scars I had been hiding.

Most I had refused to remember, and some I lied to myself about having forgot.

A lot of them weren't healed, yet.

The longer and harder I drank, the easier it was to cover them up and deal with them *later. Later,* when I wasn't feeling so vulnerable. *Later,* when I could peel back the layers in privacy and look at them myself. *Later,* when I was sober.

Later.

Maybe tomorrow...

It never happened.

This isn't to say I didn't *know* they were there. Most of the scars still hurt, and it was through drinking – *a lot* – that I found I could numb away the attention they were screaming for.

For a little while, anyways.

Getting rid of alcohol I discovered, and in my gut already knew, was just *the tip of the iceberg.* And all humans are like icebergs: *complicated, magnificent, drifting illusions.*

As above, so very much more below.

What I saw on the surface – that I need to stop drinking – was *nothing* compared to what was actually weighing me down. The scars and the hurt were still there, just below the surface, away from the light and submerged in *liquid denial.*

Neatly covered beneath the heavy layers of drunkenness that were cooking me from the inside out.

"We do not see things as they are, we see things as **we** are."

– Anais Nin

I need to share this quote again, because it is exactly how I lived my life for so very long. I only saw a small fraction of my problem and my addiction, because I had drank myself down to a fraction of myself.

That's not entirely true.

I saw it. I just stayed drunk enough so as to not have to admit it.

If I stayed drunk enough, long enough, I could forget about everything going on below the surface.

It was only when I stopped drinking that I was able to shed some light on – and admit to having – my wounds and scars. You know what it feels like when you've burned your hand and you later put it near something hot?

It hurts. In a lingering burning sort of way. Like a memory that is too real of when you burned yourself in the first place. But, somehow, it hurts a lot more, now.

It was in those scary, early days of sobriety that my scars started to scream for attention again, and at just Day 16 this time around, they're still yelling. With the glacial clarity that comes with sobriety, it slowly became obvious that drinking, being only the visible tip of the iceberg, is just a symbol – *a symptom* – of something much, *much* bigger.

Getting rid of alcohol has been the easy part.

The hard part, *the part that is calling on all my courage*, is to dive deep beneath the surface now and start dealing with all the facets that make up the whole. All those hard-to-reach corners where I've stashed my shame and regret, the dark depths where the lies of inadequacy live, and the sad, shadowy parts where I store my fears.

All the heavy things, that ironically keep the iceberg from sinking.

All the *real* reasons I drink. All the years of lies I've woven into layers around me; lies about why I drink, unravelling and undone in a worthless pile at my feet.

It's in the weight of these sober truths that the big picture becomes visible. Every scar, wound, false belief and fear, slowly rising to the surface, thrown into the light and demanding to be *seen*.

This is the hard part.

This is the part where I need to lick my own wounds, without the anesthetic of insobriety.

It's like a reunion of all the things that keep me up at night, finally gathered in the same small room and wanting to catch up with how I've been, since I've been gone so long.

All the painful parts, vying for my attention after years of neglect.

It's in the **diving deep** after we stop drinking that we can start to see everything, for once, *as it really is*. It's in the stripping away the layers of drunkenness that kept me covered and hidden, that I can finally feel and deal with all the hurt parts I've been numbing.

And it's in finally seeing the entire, overwhelming, beautifully complicated iceberg as a whole that I can finally begin to really, truly heal.

First Steps and Failures

FEBRUARY 20, 2018

**"The first step towards getting somewhere is to decide
that you are not going to stay where you are."**
– Unknown

I've never made New Year's Resolutions.

It's sort of surprising, considering I'm the King of Procrastination, always waiting to do something. *Why start today? I'll just wait until and do it later!* I *am* usually rather spontaneous in my decisions, though. If I get it in my mind that I want something *now*, I usually just act on it. Unfortunately, at times, without much forethought or research.

I'm more of a Feet-First-Right-About-Now-Sounds-Good-Resolutionist.

December 28th, 2017, I decided to become vegan. *"Plant based" to be exact.* I had been watching some documentaries and came to finally admitting how much I'd been poisoning myself with not only alcohol, but the food I was consuming. I didn't have to give it much thought. I just took the first step, and here I am 55 days in already. After being scientifically and honestly educated on what my body really needs, and how to starve cancer through diet, I was able to flip the switch and just no longer eat animal products.

It wasn't so easy when I tried to flip the switch and just "no longer drink alcohol".

That "switch" is the motherboard of all motherboards. 10,000 subtle dials and levers all needing to align in unison to unlock the escape hatch.

But that's not what's on my mind today.

Last week I enrolled in an 8 week "Fundamentals of Addiction" online course through the *Canadian Association of Mental Health* that starts at the end of April. It's an introductory course, as the name would suggest, and it's scratching the itch I've had for years to be in school, learning something new.

My problem/challenge, with quite literally everything, is finishing what I've started.

Or even just starting what I've said I was going to do.

How sad that I'm already concerned about my commitment to the course and my ability to stick with something *for once* and see it through to the end, because of my track record. I wouldn't say I get *bored* with things, as its *quite the opposite*. When I really *get into* something, I tend to look like a frantic squirrel darting across a busy highway with blinders on, unable to make up its damned mind.

Commitment is following through with what you said you were going to do, long after the mood you said it in has passed. I think and talk a lot about *being present*. Just being okay with being here, *right now.*

Worrying about my future 10, 20 years from now, and thinking things like *"who would want to hire a 60 year old wedding photographer?"* are pretty counterproductive to the mindfulness approach of just being comfortable right here and now.

Or is it?

Is being decisive in *this* moment, to create moments of *future* happiness, the opposite of being present? Or am I just using my present moment to create pleasant, present moments in the future?

Chances are I'm just overthinking everything as usual.

In any case, I don't have any goals of doing anything specific with that course, or expectations of where it might lead me. But I love learning. And I love writing. And I love the idea of being able to learn things that may help me and others on my own journey through addiction and recovery, and hopefully learn things that I can pull into my writing, too.

Enrolling in that course is just a *first step.* I have no need to understand or even see the whole staircase or any of the steps that may or could follow. One of the magical parts of being sober is that you start hearing the *good* voices inside you again, those little messengers of intuition that rise up when you're listening, pulling you towards something you're supposed to do, or someone you're supposed to meet, or somewhere you're supposed to go.

You can't hear your gut instincts when you're drunk every day. The bar brawl that alcohol creates inside you drowns them all out, and eventually, they stop talking.

It's amazing, with the clarity that comes when you can manage sobriety for a little while, the things you start to hear, and the feelings you start to feel. Once the life comes back to your senses – common sense included – *everything begins to light up* with a newfound sort of electricity that starts to buzz in your veins.

Back to those first steps. *Are you beginning to see how accurate that squirrel on the highway analogy is for how my brain works?*

Those first steps are always the scariest. They're the heaviest ones, carrying the most weight, stamping your intentions like a footprint or a signature: *I am here. I am committing to doing this, leaving a trail of where you've come from in the dust that's collected in all the time you've wasted standing in the same place.*

It feels so much better when you take those inspired, scary, first steps in the moments when you are *still feeling inspired.* No waiting. No procrastinating.

I am doing this. It doesn't matter whether they're steps towards losing 10 lbs, becoming alcohol-free, or that you'll start washing the dishes as you make them dirty. It doesn't matter whether they're first steps towards something overwhelmingly big or incredibly small.

Every first step, regardless of what it is towards, resonates the same to your soul.

Every first step translates into: *I want to do this. I need to do this. I am doing this.*

And all the butterflies in your belly take flight.

Understanding why first steps are so terrifyingly exciting comes down to seeing that they all offer the exact same thing:

The opportunity to no longer be standing where you've been standing for so long, because of your *decision* that you are *no longer going to stay where you've been staying.* Every first step is hinged to the possibility that you can make things different, and better, than how they are right now.

Nothing changes if nothing changes.

First steps are scary because once you've taken one, it opens the floodgates to the unknown and uncharted – *and all the things that could possibly go wrong.* We see ourselves failing. We see ourselves disappointing ourselves and others.

Because let's face it, most of us alcoholics while we are *"deep in it"* are the *best* pessimists and procrastinators out there.

What if we started looking *forward* to things, instead of imagining everything that could go wrong? What if we started *expecting success*? What if we stopped trying to *control* everything for a change, which is where all the suffering that comes with alcoholism is rooted: *being* out of control. What if all our tiny *first* *steps* were seen as monumental victories instead of the first step towards another chance for us to fail?

What if we stopped comparing possibilities to track records?

What's important is *taking the step now*. Taking that first step when you are feeling inspired, when you can still hear the omens of intuition rumbling in your belly, before you've had time to pull out your laundry list of reasons of why you'll fail and why it's a bad idea.

I know that laundry list so well.

About a month ago, I signed up for a 21 Day Men's Yoga-Shred online course. I have a thing for online courses, apparently. It goes without saying that I haven't streamed one video yet or once turned myself into a table or a cobra.

Did I *really think* when I signed up that it was something I was actually going to physically do every day while I was still drinking like it was my job? Because you know, being 2 bottles of wine in at 2pm on a Wednesday afternoon *really* lends itself to the downward dog.

I apparently *did really think* I was going to do it, because I was motivated enough to take the first step and pay for the course.

I'm glad I took the first step of actually signing up – it must have been in one of those rare, quiet moments in the middle of that bar brawl inside me where things fell silent enough for me to hear my gut telling me to do it. Or maybe I was just tense and felt that stretching would do me some good. Or maybe I was feeling out of shape and the idea of a "shred" in 21 days seemed like a fast track to something I know will help me feel better.

It doesn't matter.

What matters is that *I took the first step*. And that's the cool thing about first steps – they'll wait for you, marked with your intention that at some point, before you convinced yourself otherwise, *you truly wanted to do it*. Your footprint will still be there where you left it, pointing you in the direction of where, at some point, you wanted to go.

So long as you can view it as *positive intention*, instead of just another time you didn't finish what you started, it'll always be a step forward. Especially if you return to it time and again, until you're able to take the next step, then the next.

January 31, 2017, I started writing, publicly. I took the first step towards journaling my way through recovery by writing my first post, *How Did I Get Here?*

This post you are reading right now is my 109th since that day.

It's amazing how many steps just naturally followed the terrifying first one of putting my vulnerability and addiction on display for everyone to see; of trying to write my way out of a bottle. Once I pushed through the hard and painful part of writing my first, telling sentence on this blog - the simple loaded question of *"How did I get here?"* - each step that has followed seems to have taken itself.

I took a very big step the other day and decided to print out all my posts from this blog in a terrifying attempt to compile them into something cohesive. It blew my mind to see nearly 400 pages of my thoughts and fears come together in one hard copy of crazy ramblings, drunken confessions, and sober realizations.

It's from those first five words that I wrote - *How did I get here?* - that 400 more pages began to fill themselves. If I hadn't put them to paper and screen that day, I'd have nothing but a stack of blank paper and a tormented, likely forgotten pile of prose inside me.

Imagine a world where everyone is addicted to fearlessly taking first steps, no longer comparing possibilities to track records.

Imagine the pages we'd fill in the *Big Book of Success Stories* if we all stopped being afraid of, well, *everything.* I'd still be eating animal products and I'd still be drinking 3 to 4 litres of wine a day. I wouldn't know how to use my camera, and I wouldn't be writing this post right now, because I'd have never started this blog.

The distance doesn't matter.

The biggest step you'll take is the first one.

Nothing changes if nothing changes.

PS: Eat whatever you want. Bacon is delicious.

Seeing Red

FEBRUARY 21, 2018

**This morning I did an interesting, *literally* eye-opening experiment
that illustrates the power of visualization and the mind.**

Think of this experiment like the tasty tray of sample bites at Costco.

Try it, and if you like it, you can take the whole box home with you.

I've spent many years reading and studying Rhonda Byrne's life-changing book, *The Secret*. It goes heavily into visualization and being on the *"right frequency"* to summon the Law of Attraction. I've loved her approach so much that I have the words *"Thoughts Become Things "*tattooed as part of the sleeve inked forever on my right arm.

So, let's get to it.

If you've done this experiment before, do it again, because it's a great reminder of how involved and in control we actually are, despite feelings of being absolutely *out of control,* sometimes, in the actual creation of our day-to-day reality.

Close your eyes. *Don't. Not just yet.*

Keep reading the instructions, *then* close your eyes.

Once you've closed your eyes, imagine the colour red. Flood your mind with the colour red. Every shade, hue and rich palette of red candy apples, fire engines and roses. Red buttons, red shoes, red walls, red cars, flirty red dresses, and red, flashing lights. Taylor Swift's red lips. Whatever red means to you.

Red wine.

Everything, everywhere, is red.

Stay there for a moment, feeling and admiring red, red, *red.*

Hot tip: *this is the point where you can close your eyes and start picturing the colour red for a minute or two.*

Now, open your eyes. If you're reading this, I'll assume they're open.

Look all around you and notice how you're immediately drawn to each and every red thing in the room. *Aside:* this will likely only work if you actually *have* red things in your room.

I didn't think we had anything red in our kitchen, until I looked around and my eyes zeroed in on a red Betty Crocker spatula, then the red power light on the oil diffuser we keep running in our kitchen. A little bit of red on the birthday card just to my left, which I bought for my nephew. The dogs red water bowl. The round red 'close' button in my browser's window that I'm typing all this in.

I wasn't looking for red things.

My brain just found and brought to my attention what it was I had visualized and made my *dominant thought* with such focused *intent.*

My thoughts *literally* became *things* right before my eyes.

Just because you don't always see something doesn't mean it isn't there. The trick is focusing your attention and energy on what it is you want to see in the world around you.

Now, imagine if we start to apply this witchcraft (I call it witchcraft because a sober mind is truly full of magic) to other parts of our life. Visualize yourself pulling into the best parking spot at the grocery store. And when I say visualize, I mean *really truly envision and feel* yourself pulling into that parking spot. Know what the steering wheel feels like under your hands, see the short distance to the store entrance, see and feel what you're wearing and the way the sunlight reveals all the dust on your dash.

The more senses you can utilize the better.

Now, imagine if we apply it to staying, or becoming, alcohol free, or whatever you're striving for or to overcome. Actually, let's take a step back and look at how the *Seeing Red* theory applies to when we had no control over alcohol.

I clearly remember what it felt like - and I mean *truly felt like* – being in the throes of uncontrollable alcoholism. I was desperate, depressed, and broke down. When I closed my eyes, all I saw was black. An endless, unmanageable loop of more desperate, depressed, broken-down days.

And the past.

Let's face it: as alcoholics, we spend a lot of time trapped inside our heads, all the while feeling as though we're *losing* our minds.

I put so much focus on how awful things were, how out of control my life was, and how I was this destructive tornado in the lives of everyone near me – and guess what?

That's exactly what I got more of.

More depression, more being out of control, more obsession over alcohol, and more rapidly declining feelings of self-worth.

More blackness.

Instead of seeing red, I was seeing in the world exactly what I was giving my attention and energy to.

I was sitting in the hot mess I'd become, and all I could see in the landscape around me was more of what I was focusing on.

The crappy parts.

The dark parts.

The unforgivable, shameful stories of the past that I kept reading to myself night after night and day after day.

Now, let's fast forward to the day I decided to get rid of alcohol, *again*. I shifted my focus and attention to Annie Grace's *The Alcohol Experiment*, to supporting and getting support from like-minded souls stuck in the same struggle, and to climbing my way out of the pit I'd thrown myself in.

I fixed my attention on becoming healthy, helpful, clean, strong, and sober.

I pictured myself succeeding.

I visualized myself in what should be difficult situations, tripping over triggers that would normally land me at the bottom of a bottle. I visualized myself having fun, laughing, comfortable, confident – *and sober.*

I pictured myself getting rid of alcohol as *the easiest thing I've ever done.*

Day by day and trigger by trigger I'm intentionally setting myself up to seek out sobriety and strength in the reality I have within my power to create.

It's been scientifically proven that the act of visualization can literally *rewire* your brain. Plus, it works with everything from seeing red, to finding parking spots, to getting and staying sober and most importantly: *gratitude*.

If you can visualize and feel – and *I mean really, truly feel* – gratitude for what you *do* have, when you open your eyes you will seek out – and the world will present to you – even more people, situations and things *to be grateful for.*

It's cliché, I know.

Mind over matter. But it works.

It's time to start using our *minds* to create what *really matters.*

The New Normal And Becoming Really Real

FEBRUARY 22, 2018

Day 19. It's fair to say not all mornings are created equal.

I usually wake up early. Like, *really* early. 4 am, usually.

I like it.

It's quiet and dark and I can put on my electric violin playlist and lose myself in a few hours of silence, waking slowly, caffeinating quickly, and feeling my way through my morning routine.

Coffee. Cigarette (still have to work on that one). Bathroom. Let the dogs out. Coffee. Cigarette. Let the dogs in. Bathroom. *Annie Grace*. Journaling. Coffee. Let the dogs out. Bathroom. Cigarette. Let the dogs in.

Writing.

You get the idea.

It's pretty uneventful, but there's something almost *mystical and pure* about the alone time before the sun comes up.

Nothing but darkness, silence, and a puzzle of words that I try and fit together, banging around inside me, wanting out.

I wonder when I'll stop *counting days*. Adding up the dollars saved, the drinks I haven't had, the days I've spent sober.

Measuring this newfound clarity against the foggy ruler of twenty drunken years; comparing millimetres to miles.

I'm striving for more balance in my life. I lose myself so completely in things. I am unable to moderate, at quite literally, *everything*. I am *absolutely* all or nothing, and I see myself inside this *recovery bubble* as though I've blown it around myself in all its delicate, soapy iridescence.

It could burst at any second.

New normals are never easy. They feel like you're a stranger in a strange land, a tourist for a time. At first, it's human nature to want to explore the attractions, to discover the alluring highlights that drew you to the destination in the first place. At what point do you stop being a tourist, and start feeling comfortable? Is it even safe to let your guard down and announce, if only to yourself, *"I have arrived."*

But here's the thing: there *is no arriving.* There is *no destination.* It's all just a big, messy journey and we'll forever be learning the language of this new land.

There will always be *where you came from.*

I easily become distracted and obsessed with things. This random segue is a perfect example.

Perhaps it's the passion of the *"creative"* within me, or perhaps it's a chemical flaw. There's always the dichotomy of within and without; the battle between the physical and the fantastic. Some things are more easily explained because you can prove them with science.

The important, undefinable things are more difficult.

Usually because accurate, appropriate words don't exist to describe the sum of your feelings. You can't add adjectives and verbs together or divide prose by pronouns and come to a solution that equals the original equation of your emotions.

In math, it's literally called *"a problem"* that needs, and can, be solved.

Inside me though, where math checked out sometime during the hazy days of high school, there's no solution to the problem of accurately defining how I feel.

Sometimes, things just don't add up.

This morning I'm feeling out of sorts, like an impossible equation without an answer.

I'm tired of being sick, of only getting poor, *awful* sleep, regardless of how well I eat or that I haven't had a drink in 19 days. I'm beginning to grasp at random short straws, now.

Maybe my second chakra is blocked? That'd explain a lot of the physical bullshit going on inside of my body over the last year and a half or more.

Maybe my chemistry is just balancing itself out? Perhaps this becoming vegan thing blended with alcohol withdrawal and my daily handful of medications is messing with my hormone levels? Levels that are already out of check and balance, like a biological budget blown out of the water.

My body has been on a spending spree and now it's time to settle the debt.

Maybe it's the full moon? No, it can't be – there's another week of counting days under my belt ahead of me until that happens.

Maybe I'm just missing an integral piece to fitting all this newness together.

What a curse, sometimes – *being human* and feeling the need to explain the unexplainable. Until we can find a definitive cause to our effect, we feel lost and inadequate, because it's our nature to explain things, *including how and why we feel what we are feeling.*

"Feeling sad" isn't enough. We need to understand and explain *why* we are sad. "Feeling confused" isn't enough. We need to be able to *list all the pieces* that are not making sense to us. Just "feeling happy" isn't enough. We need to *justify* what's causing our joy.

This morning I'm feeling all over the place, exactly like the words I'm sitting here trying to fit together, as though I'm trying to catch a nest of spiders breaking apart in the wind.

Ego is defined as: *"the part of the mind that mediates between the conscious and the unconscious and is responsible for reality testing and a sense of personal identity."*

I wish my ego would just *go.*

Maybe I'm not as *really real* as I think I am, after all.

Maybe I can't accurately define how I'm feeling, because I'm *not actually my feelings?*

Maybe if I step back and just let myself *feel the feelings*, they'll be satisfied by being acknowledged and go merrily on their way? Or do I have to dig deeper and understand where they came from?

Maybe if I give them a name, they'll leave me alone.

So many damn, headache-inducing maybes.

Maybe I just need to chill the hell out.

I'm feeling as tattered and confused as the Velveteen Rabbit today:

"Real isn't how you are made," said the Skin Horse. "It's a thing that happens to you. When a child loves you for a long, long time, not just to play with, but REALLY loves you, then you become Real."

"Does it hurt?" asked the Rabbit.

"Sometimes," said the Skin Horse, for he was always truthful. "When you are Real you don't mind being hurt."

"Does it happen all at once, like being wound up," he asked, "or bit by bit?"

"It doesn't happen all at once," said the Skin Horse. "You become. It takes a long time. That's why it doesn't happen often to people who break easily, or have sharp edges, or who have to be carefully kept. Generally, by the time you are Real, most of your hair has been loved off, and your eyes drop out and you get loose in the joints and very shabby. But these things don't matter at all, because once you are Real you can't be ugly, except to people who don't understand."

Maybe this is just a part of *Becoming,* and in true Shawn style, I'm overthinking everything.

Maybe the rich *new car smell* of sobriety is starting to fade and I'm becoming aware that simply *being sober* doesn't change anything other than my ability to finally see all the things I once ignored and pushed aside more clearly.

Maybe I'm Becoming Really Real.

I feel as though I woke up with growing pains, like something inside me is stretching and in my sleep, I lost the crushed the rose-coloured glasses that I've been wearing for the last 18 days.

I've been looking for my quiet place alone at 4 am, in an empty room full of screaming words and ideas, knowing all the while that it's not where I'm going to find it.

There are quiet places also in the mind, but we build bandstands and factories on them. Deliberately, to put a stop to the quietness. To pretend at any cost that it isn't there.

"Ah, but it is; it is there, in spite of everything. At the back of everything."
– *Aldous Huxley*

The closest I can come to explaining how I feel this morning is to compare it to everything I've written above: all over the place, disjointed, a little off-centre, and pursuing something I can't define that is just out of reach.

Scattered.

And that's okay.

I'm still learning the language of this new land and *Becoming Really Real* is going to take time. Plus, I never was very good at math.

Muddy Waters

FEBRUARY 23, 2018

**"Muddy Water, Let Stand,
Becomes Clear."**
– Lao Tzu

Throughout the great philosophers and leaders from Buddha to Lao Tzu and The Beatles lies a timeless, beautiful truth: *Let it be.*

Yesterday, I was feeling out of sorts.

I felt outside of my skin and as though my mind was amplifying everything.

A clown car of thoughts where more and more just kept spilling out in an endless line of absurdity.

Half of my thoughts didn't even make sense. All my irrational fears and dormant regrets were stirred up into a gloriously muddy, messy pool of anxiety.

I don't even know why.

I can't put my finger on what triggered it, other than our highs need lows and that hormones are just awesome. Maybe it's because I'm starting to feel all the feels via this newfound sobriety, no longer numbing myself into one long, drawn out emotion of *"everything is blah"*.

Whether what triggered it was a chemical, mental or spiritual imbalance, I somehow found myself smack dab in the middle of the Addicts Trifecta: *Bad Chemistry, Bad Thoughts, and Bad Self-Image.*

Just overall...bad.

Old *drunk* Shawn would have readily waded knee-deep into the waters, losing himself more and more below the murky surface the further out he'd go.

And the more he'd muck around in the waters, the more dirt he'd stir up.

Addiction encouraged me to lose myself in the mud.

And when the waters get muddy, it all starts to look the same: dark and cloudy, with all the heavy things unsettled and adrift. The more I'd poke around, the farther out I'd go, the more I tried to push down the dirt, the muddier and messier things became.

It's fair to say that when you're "in it" you can't control it.

And now, it's story time:

> "Buddha was once travelling with a few of his followers.
>
> While they were passing a lake, Buddha told one of his disciples, "I am thirsty. Do get me some water from the lake."
>
> The disciple walked up to the lake.
>
> At that moment, a bullock cart started crossing through the lake. As a result, the water became very muddy and turbid. The disciple thought, "How can I give this muddy water to Buddha to drink?"
>
> So, he came back and told Buddha, "The water in there is very muddy. I don't think it is fit to drink."
>
> After about half an hour, again Buddha asked the same disciple to go back to the lake.
>
> The disciple went back and found that the water was still muddy. He returned and informed Buddha about the same.
>
> After some time, again Buddha asked the same disciple to go back.
>
> This time, the disciple found the mud had settled down, and the water was clean and clear. So, he collected some water in a pot and brought it to Buddha.
>
> Buddha looked at the water, and then he looked up at the disciple and said, "See what you did to make the water clean. *You let it be*, and the mud settled down on its own, and you have clear water.
>
> *Your mind is like that too.*
>
> When it is disturbed, just *let it be*. Give it a little time. It will settle down on its own. You don't have to put in any effort to calm it down. It will happen. It is effortless."

Yesterday, I had to get myself out of the water. *What is it with alcoholics being drawn to liquids?*

I had to keep myself busy, turn off my thinker, and let the mud settle.

Just a few weeks ago with muddy water up to my neck, I would have just drowned myself in it and a few bottles of wine, grateful for the blindness that comes with trying to see through the dirt.

New and improved *Sober Shawn* had a rare and increasingly more common moment of clarity.

Just walk away.

Stop trying to control it.

Stop trying to understand it.

Stop trying to push the dirt down.

Just let it settle and *let it be.*

I threw myself into my work, spent some time on self-care and reading, spent some time in the kitchen, which is my happy place. What I *didn't* spend time on was trying to decipher, explain or otherwise *justify* my feelings.

Acknowledging them was enough.

Knowing they were there and just *letting them be* was enough. You know, all that fun *"feel the feels"* stuff.

Emotions are essentially toddlers. Unstable and wobbly, full of repetition and difficult questions, growth spurts and tumbles, constantly vying for attention.

But, with a little love and nurturing, they can grow into themselves, strong and whole-hearted and full of potential. Often, they learn best when left to their own devices, comforted in knowing you are nearby, but able to explore and discover on their own.

Emotions, like toddlers, need room to grow.

When you're hovering over them and trying to control them you just end up *standing in the figurative muddy waters, stirring up more muck.*

The Serenity Prayer

"God, grant me the serenity to accept the things I cannot change,

The courage to change the things I can, And the wisdom to know the difference."

I often turn to the cliché *Serenity Prayer* when I feel uncomfortable, because it's basically a magical decoder ring for your feelings that holds the power to instantly snap yourself back to reality.

Are you anxious? *Get out of the future, and just let it be.* Are you sad? *Get out of the past, and just let it be.*

Both are having the grace and serenity to *accept things you cannot change, and to simply let them be.* As alcoholics, we're blessed/cursed with the frustrating condition of being *absolutely out of control,* while trying and forever failing to control quite literally *everything* around us.

The *wisdom* happens when you know to get out of the water and just allow everything to settle into undisturbed, crystal-clear clarity.

That right there is having the courage to change the things you can.

"There will be an answer, Let it be.
Speaking words of wisdom, Let it be."
– The Beatles

The Ghost Hangover

FEBRUARY 24, 2018

The only time I ever sleep in is when I have to be somewhere.

Even when I woke every single day into the most swollen of hangovers, I'd wake up at 3 am, regardless of the time I blacked out in the living room chair. Hangovers can be wicked, that way.

"Oh no, honey. No sleep for you. I wouldn't want you to miss this joyride of nausea, vertigo, and regret. It's what you signed up for, isn't it?"

I'm off to an early morning photo shoot today, so of course I slept in later than I wanted to. In all honesty, I don't trust or understand people who want their photo taken before the forgiving light of 5pm. It's probably fair to say they aren't raging alcoholics prone to puffy mornings filled with bloodshot eyes, wine-stained lips and mysteriously missing memories from last night.

They aren't afraid of what they look like because they probably didn't spend most of yesterday beating themselves up.

Old me would have loved/hated today's early morning appointment. The key to an alcoholic's calendar is to schedule your To-Do's early enough in the day so that they don't interfere with wine-time – which was any time after 12 pm. I'm still adjusting to the idea that I can be sober, present, and presentable at dinnertime and beyond.

I'm getting there.

Today marks my 3-week checkpoint: 21 Days Sober.

That happened quickly.

However, every morning since I've got rid of alcohol I've been waking into the weirdest of phenomena: *the ghost hangover.*

I don't know if this is actually a thing.

Or, if it's ever happened to anyone else. Maybe it's common, or maybe I'm one of the lucky ones who get a hangover from Pomegranate Juice.

Regardless, I still spend the first few minutes of my day groggy and grumpy, habitually rubbing my forehead as though I'm soothing a headache.

A headache I don't even have.

I try and piece together the night before, *with surprising ability, clarity, and success.*

What the hell. *Why do I feel like shit when I didn't even drink last night?*

I'm dragging my feet, would do anything for a gallon of water, and in my mind's eye imagine what I must look like: inflated and red, my eyes glossed over in their bloodshot jaundiced glory, and deep pillow creases down my cheek from where I passed out, and remained.

Then, like clockwork, the negative self-talk begins.

Ughhhhh I feel like crap. What is wrong with me. I feel puffy. I can only imagine how washed up and broke down I look. Why do I do this. There's no amount of coffee that can make this go away. I hate everything.

Checks clock – 5 hours until drinking time...

But wait.

I'm not even hungover. I *don't* actually look like a bag of shit. And I don't even drink alcohol anymore.

I haven't had a drink in 21 days.

How strong is this drug and how long have I spent every single morning sluggishly running the nausea-and-regret-riddled gamut, that even sober I go through the same motions, just this time tending to a *ghost* hangover?

I've conditioned myself to expect my mornings to be awful, despite them being my favourite time of day. Maybe I wake up early so I can wallow in self-loathing for a while in peace and quiet. Maybe it's the decades of negative self-talk I've endured every morning that can't wait for me to wake up:

"Hey Shawn, it's time to get up. You deserve to feel like a bag of crap, and I don't want you to miss anything by sleeping it away."

21 Days in and still haunted by ghosts.

After my grandfather passed away in 2007, my grandma spent at least a month or two still putting his morning medications out with breakfast. Meals she would still cook two for two, despite there being only one of them left.

And every day she'd cry when she realized what she had done. She'd cry when the new normal came rushing back, reminding her that every morning forward would never be like any of the mornings before.

I guess that's what happens when you've been married to someone for 63 years. Your routines become as much a part of you as your limbs. Death, loss, transformation, and tragedy can leave you feeling as though part of you has been amputated. A part of you that has always been there, a habit you have always done *– instantly absent, but still tied directly to your emotions, habits, and daily motions.*

Like a ghost.

And ghosts are just emotions that are bent out of shape.

There's a syndrome known as *Phantom Limb Syndrome:*

> A *phantom limb* is the sensation that an amputated or missing limb is still attached. Approximately 60 to 80% of individuals with an amputation experience phantom sensations in their amputated limb, and the majority of the sensations are painful.

Maybe that helps to explain my ghost hangovers.

I severed such a huge part of *how I defined myself* when I stopped drinking and I'm not sure if all of my parts received the memo. That part of my brain that helps me get going in the morning – *the auto-pilot* – just moves me through the motions without much conscious thought on my part, until adequate levels of caffeine have been established.

Exactly like I always have. Until I slowly begin to wake up.

It seems a lot of people who get rid of alcohol start bouncing out of bed like Tigger on crack every morning: refreshed and made of shiny, freshly oiled new springs.

Not me. Not lately, anyhow.

I'm still putting out grandpa's medication.

I'm still cooking breakfast for two.

I can still feel pain in my phantom limbs.

I think it's time to have *another* good honest talk with myself, admitting once and for all that the parts I severed were not a loss, but actually cutting out an illness. And, now that it's gone, there's no need to dress and lick my wounds every morning.

I just need to let it be, and let things heal.

Shoshin: The Beginner's Mind
And Other Sad Tales

FEBRUARY 25, 2018

I'm still counting days.

Every evening as my relatively clear-thinking sober head lays down to rest, I check off one more day, as though I'm collecting gold stars for good behaviour. My sleep is still broken. Every night I'm up 3, 4 or more times; a combination of habit, anxiety, weird-ass dreams and having to deal with an already broke-down prostate and bladder, now in full revolt of all the juice and tea I had in lieu of wine the night before.

That's okay. *It's a transition.*

It'll get easier.

Waking up each morning feels like Day 1 all over again. Every morning, I'm back at the beginning, armed with good intentions and backed by a terrifying track record I hope to never repeat. I wake up into the same funnel I woke every drunken day before, with the simple but overwhelming desire to *not drink today*.

Today marks 22 days sober.

I feel stronger, but still unprepared. 16 or more sober hours stretch out before me, undoubtedly littered with triggers and hurdles to avoid and to jump.

Every day feels like Orientation Day, like it's Day 1 all over again.

And I'm grateful for that.

The moment we begin to believe that we know what we're doing is the very moment we get ourselves in trouble.

Now, 22 days sober is just a drop in the ocean compared to the 7,300 days I consecutively spent drunk (yes, I just did the quick, very disgusting math). But it doesn't stop me from patting myself on the back a little. The trick is in being able to quietly celebrate each success, tuck it in my pocket, and keep building on my strength each day as though it's my first day walking without crutches.

Each day my confidence becomes a little bigger, a little stronger. I wobble a little less on my new legs. My mind becomes a little wiser and the hurdles become a little easier. But in the deep, honest bellows of my gut I know that I will never really truly *"get there"*.

Because there is no destination. Being present in every moment on this journey of recovery *is* the destination if there has to be one.

I wonder if it's true, that we will forever be *recovering* alcoholics. No matter how far we've come, there will always be that scar inside where we remain a little broken, that swells up in times of trouble, and reminds us of where we came from despite how much we've grown.

We are born into every new day as a *beginner*.

Shoshin is a word from Zen Buddhism meaning **"beginner's mind."** It refers to having an attitude of openness, eagerness, and lack of preconceptions when studying a subject, even when studying at an advanced level, just as a *beginner* would.

> "In the beginner's mind there are many possibilities.
> In the expert's mind there are few."
> – Shunryu Suzuki

It was late May of last year – I don't know the exact date, but it was close to what should have been my 100 Days Sober celebration. I had been diligent, dry, worked hard, and didn't slip once on my cunning, clumsy escape from the bottom of the Pitcher Plant. If you haven't read Andrew Carr's Pitcher Plant analogy for alcoholism yet, I recommend searching it out and having a read.

I was cocky and confident, and Hubs and I agreed that a bottle of wine couldn't do much harm.

Wrong.

I'd "obviously proven" that I could take it or leave it. 100 days, almost, was nothing to balk at, so off I went to collect my prize winnings at the liquor store.

Because I deserved it, of course.

I stood gazing at the endless shelves of wine as though I had finally made my once-in-a-lifetime pilgrimage to Mecca. The bottles sparkled and their sexy labels began to speak to me. I was so close to bowing down before the shrine of what used to be my god, after nearly 100 days without a sip or a sermon.

I searched the store and sought out the most expensive, deliciously poisonous reward I could find.

And we drank it, underwhelmed by how *not awesome* I felt.

There weren't any fireworks going off at my first sip. The choir of angels I was hoping for were apparently out for lunch. My stomach flared up with the familiar burn of acid hitting my insides, and I refused to admit it *wasn't actually doing anything for me.*

In fact, I just got *tired.* So of course, I just kept drinking.

And drinking, and drinking, and drinking.

So much more drinking, that the one "innocent" bottle I tried to moderate with turned into 4, 5 or 6 bottles a day.

For 8 more months.

I had lost my Beginner's Mind.

I had outgrown, in my mind, the humility that comes with *beginning.* I'm not sure if "outgrown" is the right word. Maybe "abandoned" is more fitting.

I had abandoned my delicate *beginner's mind* in trade for the delusion that I was, however delusionally, *in control.*

In hindsight, that was a pretty shitty trade.

It's human nature to want to move forward, to grow, to learn and to explore. But it's also important – *critically important* – to stay rooted in what originally helped us to grow. If you uproot a tree, its roots become exposed, weak, and endangered.

Uproot our progress and the same happens to us.

What's important here is that we keep our roots reaching deep, where it all started.

To stay where the seed was planted and where the sprout began to grow. It's the roots that help a tree stay strong and stable, not the branches. And the strongest trees grow in the midst of the strongest winds.

I think we all know that person who knows everything. You know that guy who is an expert on every topic, has been there, and is certain to make sure you're well aware that he does, in fact, know everything.

He's unlikable, and in all honestly and likelihood, pretty insecure, too.

That's essentially who we turn into when we lose our beginner's mind. It's in that moment of unconsciously and/or insecurely believing we have it all figured out that we start undoing anything we actually *have* figured out.

We unknowingly become that unlikeable, obnoxious know-it-all, who ends up making himself look like an idiot.

Olympic athletes don't stop training every day just because they've won a gold medal.

It's with a beginner's mind that they know there is always more to learn. They know there is always more room to grow, and always someone to learn from. They keep training and never forget the first day they laced up their skates.

It may be Day 22 for me today, but it's also Day 1 again.

I'm approaching each morning with the openness and eagerness of simply learning new ways *and reasons* to not drink *today*.

And in doing so, *I'm watering my roots* because it's entirely up to me how strong this tree is going to grow.

Of Mice and Men And Providence

FEBRUARY 26, 2018

**"If the only thing that people learned was not to be afraid of
their experience, that alone would change the world."**
– Sydney Banks

I'm 41 years old and still need to look up the meaning of some words now and then.

Providence is just one of them.

I've heard it used my entire life, and other than being a city in Rhode Island I knew it had *something* to do with nature and/or god or some sort of otherworldly something-or-other.

I wasn't too far off, with my favourite definition of *"Providence"* falling to its synonyms: *foresight, fate, destiny, and common sense.*

prov-i-dence

noun

1. The protective care of god or of nature as a spiritual power.
"They found their trust in divine providence to be a
source of comfort"
Synonyms: fate, destiny, nemesis, kismet, god's will, divine
intervention, predestination, predetermination, the stars.
2. God or nature as providing protective or spiritual care.
"I live out my life as Providence decrees"
3. Timely preparation for future eventualities.
"It was considered a duty to encourage providence"
Synonyms: prudence, foresight, forethought, farsightedness,
judiciousness, shrewdness, circumspection, wisdom, sagacity,
common sense

I also rather enjoy the last one: *"timely preparation for future eventualities."*

It just sounds so...*grown up and responsible.*

Sometimes I get a word stuck in my head, repeating itself like a scratched, skipping record (am I dating myself here by making vinyl LP references?) The word *"Providence"* has been rattling around my brain over the last few days, and I have no idea why or where it came from. Numbers do the same for me. If I measure something and it's 16" for example, 16 repeats sometimes for hours in my mind.

Maybe it means I'm on the right path.

It's as though there's been someone hanging over my shoulder, whispering it in my ear nonstop and it keeps replaying in my head, beyond my control, just like when T Swift dropped *"Shake It Off"*.

Providence. On repeat.

Just because you don't choose or want to hear it, doesn't mean your mind isn't going to keep playing it.

Like when I'm craving a drink or ten, or unconsciously hearing my nagging, negative self-talk, it just stays there, *stuck*, until I acknowledge it, give in to it, or deconstruct it and send it on its way.

When something is stuck in my head, it won't go away until I deal with it, as though it's been placed on my path for me to learn from or create from. I'm slowly getting better at recognizing repetition in my life as a sign that I'm supposed to do *something*.

That's sort of how it happened when my life seemed stuck on repeat, every morning jumping back to the same low, hungover spot, willing to trade anything for another chance at some sort of sobriety.

Desperately grasping for even a shred of control over my life again.

I had to make the record stop skipping somehow. I was getting so very tired of the same old song.

A similar thing happened before I created another photo, inspired and titled after one of my favourite novels, *Of Mice and Men*, by John Steinbeck. I couldn't get the story out of my head until I eventually channeled it into an image of myself in a black top hat, on a black background, with window light dramatically landing on my profile and my hand, in which sat a tiny little mouse, and we are both just *staring* at each other.

> "Maybe everybody in the whole damn world is scared of each other"
> – *Slim, Of Mice and Men*

That quote from the novel *is everything*.

If you haven't read or watched *Of Mice and Men* yet, I'll try and summarize the story's moral for you, as I understand it.

It's about the universal struggle for survival that is shared by most living things, from mice to men. It's about how no one trusts one another, how we are all lonely, scared and alone, and regardless of our best-laid plans (Providence, *if you will*), *things will still go wrong no matter how carefully we plan or prepare.*

How joyously optimistic.

Let's just say the book is *brilliant*, but not the most cheerful of tales with its grim and sadly accurate commentary on the nature of our existence. Plus, a puppy dies, and that's about the worst possible scenario imaginable.

Honesty is usually pretty ugly.

I think it's this innate, human condition of *feeling alone and scared*, which drives so many of us to the point of addiction and beyond. It's what drives us to do things that help us feel as though *we belong*.

As humans, we not only crave connection, but *we require it.*

Feeling "alone" drives us to all sorts of things, from isolation, depression, self-abuse, negative self-talk and self-sabotage or suicide, just to name a few that I'm intimately, *and sadly*, very familiar with.

The worst kind of feeling alone is when you aren't alone at all. It's when you're in the company of others but feel light-years apart.

We drink to escape, seeking comfort and company in bottles and bars. Our attempts to feel as though we *belong* just leave us feeling more alone. Our plans and intentions fall apart, we break down a little more, and we get stuck on repeat.

Just like Taylor's "Shake It Off" being trapped in your head, we get stuck in the loop, unable to shake it off no matter how hard we try. And the longer we stay in the loop, the more we begin to wonder what makes us so different from everyone else. Why are we stuck and why can't we get our shit together like it seems everyone else can?

What if we started asking ourselves *"Why am I so damn hard on myself"* instead?

> "If the only thing that people learned was not to be afraid of
> their experience, that alone would change the world."
> – *Sydney Banks*

If only we were fearless, everything would be so much easier.

Breaking away from our fears of failure, and oddly enough, *success,* gives way for Providence to hold our hand as we boldly, *and scared shitlessly,* move forward with terrifying, positive attempts at bringing change to our life.

And that change usually only begins when we courageously stop and try to listen to whatever is playing on repeat in our heads.

We *have to listen* to understand.

And we *have to understand* before we can *act.*

And let's face it, as alcoholics, we aren't really known for our well-thought-out actions. It's usually only when things get really, really (*like, really*) bad and we are pushed to such an extreme level of self-disgust that we feel almost forced to change our behaviour.

Essentially, we finally get tired of our own bullshit.

Breaking away from what has always been a really scary thing. Change itself is made up of uncertainty and risk, *and uncertainty and risk are really, really, uncomfortable.* Especially when it feels like we are diving into it alone.

What if I fail? What if my cravings are stronger than my best intentions?

Oh, but darling, what if you don't, and what if they aren't?

What if you're so much stronger than you've been telling yourself you are?

Fear stops us, stalls us, and it digs our isolated hole of loneliness deeper and deeper the longer we just sit there, as though gravity just keeps getting heavier.

We need to be fearless. We need to become lighter. We need to rise up.

We need to trust that Providence has our back, and whatever we need on the journey ahead will somehow be there for us.

The word Providence itself has *"Provide"* within it.

Think of Providence as *having faith,* however you define it, and in whatever you define it by. Whether you believe it's in the stars aligning, my personal belief that the universe is conspiring with you, or that its god's hand leading you, it all comes down to the same comfort: *that we are being looked after.*

And if we are being looked after, what do we have to be afraid of?

The day I committed, again, to getting rid of alcohol, *once and for all,* I immediately became intimidated by the long, lonely, struggle ahead of me.

Because that's what I was told to expect.

Thankfully, Providence was there to remind me that I'm not alone, but I was in it together with so many others just like myself.

Mice, men, and everything in between. We are all connected. We are all in it, and we are *all struggling.*

Once I committed to changing my life, groups of like-minded, terrified, incredibly strong people seemed to start popping up out of nowhere. From the Alcohol Experiment community to my new friends at the Recovery Elevator, I didn't find my tribe – my tribe found me.

Providence was there to show me that even though my best-laid plans and intentions may not play out as I hope (or, perhaps they actually will), there will always be comfort in the collective.

> "Dear Prudence open up your eyes
> Dear Prudence see the sunny skies
> The wind is low the birds will sing
> That you are part of everything
> Dear Prudence won't you open up your eyes?"
> – Dear Prudence, The Beatles

Maybe we aren't alone on this journey, after all. Maybe we aren't all drifting in our own one-man lifeboats, scared and afraid.

Perhaps we're all sailing the same choppy waters on the same big ship. Perhaps we've *belonged* all along, and we are all more alike than we are different.

Maybe the only thing we have worth being afraid of is staying in the same sad place? Maybe all we have left to do is take our fear and *Shake It Off,* once and for all. Just imagine if we all stopped being afraid of *failing,* and started to celebrate *trying,* instead?

Sometimes a little blind faith is the only thing that can send fear on its way.

> "The moment one definitely commits oneself, then Providence moves too."
> – William Hutchison Murray

The Meditation Room

FEBRUARY 27, 2018

I need to retract my comment the other day where I said,
I wake up early every day – like, 4 am, early".

I slept in until 8:30am today.

I feel as though I time travelled and woke up in some alternate universe where people get a good night's rest, the sun is shining, and they wake up feeling brand new.

I am not used to this.

The last 24 days have been the fastest and slowest 24 days in recent memory.

Actually they're just the *clearest* days in recent memory, because my memories before going alcohol-free are pretty sketchy and foggy to say the least. I've been spending a tonne of time on self-care: *reading, writing, relaxing, detoxing and not putting a lot of pressure on myself to be doing anything in particular other than adjusting to this new normal.*

Today's goal is to rediscover my meditation and mindfulness practice.

I was doing so good for so long.

After returning from rehab last spring, I flipped one of our spare bedrooms into a meditation room, and it's still one of my favourite rooms in the house – despite not visiting it very often. Sadly, it's become the room where we "shove the things" when company is coming, or we're too lazy to put them where they actually belong, usually meaning the garbage or the garage.

I think we all have a space like that, *within our homes, and within ourselves.*

You know, *that place you take for granted.* That secret hiding place where you pile up your procrastinations and hide away things you don't really want to deal with just yet.

That piece of furniture that doesn't have a home. The stack of magazines you subscribe to but never read. The feelings of inadequacy and anxiety you promise yourself you're going to deal with.

Just not today.

A junk drawer for all your ugly emotions.

It's not like I didn't *want* to spend daily quality time alone with my thoughts, or lack of thoughts, in my Meditation Room. I just couldn't, well, *be present* when I was 4 bottles of wine in and unsure of what time it was much less focus on my wine breath going in and going out for 20 minutes without barfing.

Meditation and mindfulness require you *to be fully present* so you can clear your mind and observe what's passing by. Sort of like sitting on a park bench and people watching, but instead you're sitting with yourself and watching all your distractions drift past and just letting them.

It's also fair to say that being drunk is basically *the opposite of meditation.*

Being drunk allowed me to take a lot for granted: the meditation room, as well as the equally safe, quiet space inside me that I was able to carve out during my 5 months of daily mindfulness practice.

It's amazing how quickly I filled it back up with trash when I started drinking again. I'd just take all my uncomfortable feelings and hide them there behind closed doors.

If meditation is *engaging in contemplation or reflection* (read: chilling the hell out), the *opposite* of meditation is *confusion and disorder* (read: freaking the hell out).

What I did externally to my precious meditation room by filling it with garbage is exactly what I did *internally* to my clarity of mind and calm when I returned to drinking every day: *I filled it with clutter and turmoil, every day shoving more things in that I didn't want or know how to deal with.*

And I'd just close the door and walk away.

All the way back to the liquor store.

Once you've tried or done something long enough that really, truly makes you feel good, it's impossible to forget. Once you've had the best pizza of your life, every other pizza you try will just remind you of that time you had *an even better pizza.*

The Best. Pizza. Ever.

That magical slice will haunt you for the rest of your life.

The same goes for when we do things that make ourselves feel good. *Meditation, going to the gym, eating healthy, becoming, and staying, sober.* Once you've tried it and know intrinsically how much better it makes you feel, you'll always think of it when you recognize how good you *aren't* feeling.

Or when you *are* feeling good and want to *continue feeling better.*

Today I'm feeling ready and able to clear out the meditation room - *inside, and out.*

I'm going to reclaim my safe space. My quiet place.

My refuge in recovery.

In clearing out the meditation room in my house, I allow myself to begin clearing out the clutter in my mind at the same time. I'm tired of feeling claustrophobic and overwhelmed, sitting alone with my thoughts in a room full of the mental and emotional rubbish I've been hoarding.

It's time to dump the junk drawer on the floor and finally start sorting out what's worth keeping.

Weapons Of Self-Destruction

FEBRUARY 28, 2018

Today is my last day as a smoker.

That took long enough.

25 years, to be exact.

And it's been 25 days since I had my last drink.

I'm lining up my poisons like dominoes to topple; *a delicate chain reaction that's taken years of habit and ritual to build, finally falling from nothing but the strength of my fingertip.*

The morning I woke up knowing that I wanted/*needed* to get rid of alcohol once and for all, again, I promised myself I would treat it as *the easiest thing I have ever done.*

It surely hasn't been.

Not even close.

But here I am, 3 and a half weeks later. The sky hasn't fallen, my world hasn't tumbled around me, and my worst fears of *never being relaxed or having fun again* have shrunk away in the shadow of *how much more relaxed and sober fun I'm having.*

All the hypothetical, horribly uncomfortable future scenarios I imagined never transpired. The days keep rolling forward as they always have, regardless of my anxiety or insecurities over dry lunches and un-tanked evenings.

99% of what we worry about never happens. The process to this point hasn't been easy and it's been riddled with roadblocks and triggers ready to burst. But so far, I've made it this far. I've had to watch my every step, and that isn't going to change for a really, really long time.

The landscape we live in is littered with landmines just waiting to blow us back to the beginning. From blatant advertising (not of a bottle of wine, but of how *fabulous* that wine will make us) to the more subtle *social language* of liquor (if you drink with us and like us, *you can belong*, like we do) the path to recovery is made up of a million carefully calculated steps.

It usually takes something extreme to snap our immature *"but I want it"* mentality back to reality.

Like a health scare. The death of a relative or friend.

A tragic loss that drops all your priorities into perspective like pianos falling from the sky.

Sometimes it takes something terrifying and obvious to fall at our feet before we finally open our eyes.

When Hubs and I decided to finally overhaul our diets last December, I made a quiet but wholehearted promise to myself that if I could first take control of that, then next I would tackle drinking responsibly and my obsessive and destructive alcohol addiction. *Then* I would take on the intimidating beast that's been riding my back for 25 years: *the 25 smokes I smoke each day.*

The more negative things you remove from your life, the bigger and more obvious the negative parts that remain become.

If I'm doing the work to eat healthier and smarter, why am I washing it all down with poison?

That was a key motivator for me in getting a grip on my drinking: *common sense.* If I kept drinking, *while eating to stay alive*, it was like I had willingly shackled myself to a treadmill.

I was never going to get anywhere.

And now that I'm feeling somewhat in control of my diet and drinking, it's time to shake off one last demon that's equally cunning and sly.

At least smoking, unlike alcohol, is socially shamed now. I've grown really tired of being the social pariah, the only one still sneaking out for cigarettes.

It's like I'm still listening to *New Kids On The Block* while everyone is blasting Drake.

It's like when words fall out of vogue, or never rising to become *in vogue* in the first place. You don't want to be the only one *still* describing something as *"so fetch"*. Mean Girls reference.

It's just easier to stop using it.

Right?

Here's hoping. I'm not naive enough to pretend or entertain the delusion that getting rid of cigarettes is going to be easy. Cutting out 25 times a day routine of filling myself up with smoke and mirrors, pretending each cigarette *"helps me relax"*, opens up 25 times a day where I'm going to have to be *really freaking present, really freaking aware and really freaking strong.*

I'm not usually an idiot.

I know how awful smoking is for me. I am beyond aware of how wasteful it is to my health, my finances, and my time. Plus, it smells really, really bad, and even worse after you butt the cigarette out, the stink sticking to you like one more thing you desperately need to shake off.

It's stealing my time right now, and decades from my future.

We trade our future health and wellbeing for false, fleeting comforts in the now, that only leave us feeling even *more* uncomfortable and *more* unwell.

What a shitty deal.

And we repeat it over and over, hour after hour, day after decade, until it kills us.

Smoking is just another big sledgehammer in my arsenal of self-destruction.

We're so counterproductive and love to live in loops. "I'm going to eat healthy"– *and we wash it down with wine.* "I'm going to stop drinking" – *and fill those dry gaps with even more cigarettes.* "I'm going to quit smoking" – *and fill that new void with...what?*

We are always seeking a substitution. Another vice. Another poison.

I'm trying to get my life back to where simply being alive is enough.

The sort of life where I can understand and reclaim what truly *being alive* actually feels like, without crutches.

Without weapons of self-destruction.

And I can only start by removing the things that are killing me.

Shattered

MARCH 1, 2018

I have a piece of glass stuck in my foot, and it's been there for days.

I can't *see* it, but I can *feel* it.

Whenever I take a step, I swear it just buries itself deeper, carving out new ways to make itself known. It's amazing how the tiniest sliver of glass can feel bigger than the object it came from.

Just a tiny little painful piece of something larger, left behind.

The fallen plate. The shattered glass of wine. The glass ceiling that came crashing down when you broke free.

Leftover shards of something once whole, always there to remind you to watch your step.

I'm pretty sure that no matter how long I survive/thrive without alcohol there will always be those little pieces left behind, dug deep under my skin as a reminder of where I came from. I guess that's what addiction is: *something buried deep inside you that needs a lot of work and pain to deal with and try to remove.*

As best as you can, anyhow.

Addiction, trauma, disappointment, anxiety, false-hopes and betrayal, they all shatter and break you into so many slivers it's impossible to completely pick up *all* the pieces. It's not a situation a simple set of tweezers can relieve.

The bits left behind from when you were broken aren't always as obvious as the glass in your foot. They get stirred up when a feeling, or memory, or craving pushes against them. The pain swells up to sharply reminding you that it's *still there,* and probably always will be, especially when you take one wrong step.

Forever lodged in your history as proof of your wounds.

A sliver of the old you, the old hurt, and all the old reasons excuses for why you did what you did, and why you were the way you were.

Evidence of all those wasted years, trapped inside the unbroken bottle that just kept on breaking you.

Time has a way of leaving small secret scars for us to look back on.

Not to dwell upon, but to keep us humble.

Our histories are as varied as the reasons we drink/drank to excess. Sometimes it was because it looked like we had no other choice than to walk across a floor full of broken glass, towards the only door we could see.

I did the best I knew how, with what I knew then. Now that I know better, I will do better.

Maybe the leftover hurts we all carry with us are there to remind us how quickly things can break down again. All the good things, *the important, irreplaceable things*, are as delicate as glass and can slip through our fingers, crashing to the floor with one misstep or stumble.

One wrong choice.

Shattered.

> "Scars have the strange power to remind us that our past is real."
> – Cormac McCarthy, All the Pretty Horses

If there's someone who doesn't need a reminder that the past is real, it's an alcoholic. Oh boy, *do we ever know*. At least the parts we can remember. And, when we manage to finally break through the glass ceiling we trapped ourselves beneath, moving forward with the freedom of wild horses and upwards with the velocity of a rocket, we want to ride as fast and far away from that past as we can.

I've been on an intoxicating *sober high* the last 26 days, just now able to see the first of what will hopefully be many finish lines. 30 days, soon. 1 month alcohol free.

And my scars have barely screamed.

But I know that they're still there, as proof that I'm healing. Proof that *so far*, I've survived.

> "Scars are not injuries. A scar is a healing.
> After injury, a scar is what makes you whole."
> – China Miéville, The Scar

Uphill, Both Ways

MARCH 2, 2018

**"Growth is painful. Change is painful. But nothing is as
painful as staying stuck where you do not belong."**
N.R. Narayana Murthy

My parents were always very good at reminding me how rough they had it as kids. Their treacherous, daily hike to and from their one-room country schoolhouse seemed to always be in the midst of a snowstorm, walking a million miles to school each day. Sometimes barefoot, because, of course, why not. For dramatic effect.

Uphill, both ways.

It's a miracle they survived (insert eye roll here). But in the moment back in the day, it helped to put into perspective whatever minor inconvenience I was likely whining about at the time.

And my trusting naive child's mind believed them.

When I set out on this journey to reclaiming my sobriety, and in turn *my life*, I knew it would be an uphill battle. If sobriety were a switch we could flip and suddenly turn the A-Ha! lights on, we wouldn't learn anything or truly be able to see how far we've come.

We'd just be standing in a bright room without purpose, without understanding, and without any real appreciation of what we've accomplished or why.

It takes that gradual, slow illumination like sunrise for our eyes to adjust. It works just the same for the soul.

True appreciation requires patience, time, *and work.*

It's universally agreed that addiction is a downward spiral. A steep, slippery slope that we slide down until we hit the first of many rock bottoms. And it's true, just like Alan Carr's *"Pitcher Plant"* analogy: you don't even realize how far you've fallen until it's too late, and you're trapped.

But now, looking back from this 27th day sober, I admit that getting to the point of addiction which I did *required effort*.

The momentum happened naturally.

But to *really* get to the *"Overachiever Level"* of addiction that I did took a lot of time and a lot of energy.

And a lot of work.

If the path to addiction is a slow slippery slope, why did every day feel like an uphill battle? My daily trek to the liquor store wasn't so unlike my parents daily uphill, both ways, trek to school.

Keeping up with the demands my addiction required basically turned my life into a hostage situation.

If I'd satisfy its requirements, it would let me survive just one more day.

That was the easy part. Feeding it.

The exhausting, daily uphill battle became made up the simple things. The things that shouldn't take any effort, unless of course, you're an addict who struggles with the most basic shit non-alcoholics take for granted.

Finishing what you've started. Starting what you need to begin. Keeping in touch with family and friends. Being social. Paying bills. Keeping promises. Eating. Doing the work. Getting out of bed. Showering.

Looking forward to anything instead of dreading everything.

As much as addiction pulled me down, it was a daily uphill battle to willingly keep myself there. I can see now that it wasn't just alcohol creating that hill, it was me.

I kept myself there, bound to the bottle like a prisoner.

And feeling like a prisoner is emotionally exhausting.

Everything became difficult, as though I was trying to climb an escalator that was forever going down.

So much effort just to stay stuck in the same place.

One day, for lucky ones like me, you finally break free from the hostage situation that alcohol has been keeping you in. You devise your escape plan. You arm yourself with tools and ideas that will help you in the steep uphill climb out of the pit where it kept you, and that you kept yourself. You're lifted out by your own perseverance, blind faith, and the hands of others just like yourself, all of us caught in different stages of entrapment and escape.

All of us on our way up the hill.

The world isn't flat.

And neither is our experience on it.

It's uphill, both ways.

And the most important thing we can learn is to *just keep climbing.*

Shit Cakes And The Happiness Trifecta

MARCH 3, 2018

Throughout this process of reclaiming my life, sobriety *and happiness*, I've grown to be very good at easily and freely forgiving myself.

Handling myself more gently. Giving myself time to rest and adjust – and room to make mistakes.

Old 3-or-4-Litres-of-Wine-a-Day-Shawn was, rather ironically, *a perfectionist.*

That is exactly why nothing was even *remotely* close to perfect, and why things never got completed, and why some things didn't even get started.

> "The pursuit of excellence is gratifying and healthy.
> The pursuit of perfection is frustrating, neurotic, and a terrible waste of time."
> – *Edwin Bliss*

It's become crystal clear to me that I was pursuing all the wrong things. I believe I was pursuing them with the *right intentions*, but it was only in the early, waking days of sobriety that I was finally able to see I was only chasing my own tail.

I thought I wanted perfection.

I thought I wanted everything to be *"just so"*. I thought I wanted to be liked and admired when all I wanted was just *to be happy.*

> "Happiness is pretty simple: Someone to love, something
> to do, and something to look forward to."
> – Rita Mae Brown

The best thing about what I call the *Recipe for Happiness* quote above is that is works for everyone.

It works for the people at "the top" as well as all of us at the bottom. It's the holy trinity of happiness: *The Trifecta.*

The trick is having a conscious, sober inventory of what those three things are made up of in *your* life.

You know, making sure your ingredients are made up of the good stuff.

If you're using cheap, crappy ingredients, you're just going to bake a cheap, crappy cake.

I believe we all unconsciously build our lives around the Happiness Trifecta, since it hits on all the things that make us tick. They're the gears of the clock that are meant to keep us on track - and happy - over time.

To help us create, grow, and nurture happiness in our lives.

We don't actually *consciously* think about it, because it's our human nature to satisfy our needs, *and to survive*, no matter what. How well we are satisfied, and how well we survive, hinges on our level of happiness. You can see why and how The Happiness Trifecta has the power to create the balance each and every one of us is seeking:

Someone to love: This satisfies our innate human *need* for connection and belonging.

Something to do: This hits on our need to feel like we are *worthy*, important, useful and unique.

Something to look forward to: This gives us the motivation and persistence to *keep moving forward*, even during difficult times.

> "To plant a garden is to believe in tomorrow."
> – *Audrey Hepburn*

When I was drinking, my trifecta sort of looked like this:

Someone to love: *Obviously* not myself. I loved the wine that I treated like a best friend. After all, it's who I hung out with all day, literally every day.

Something to do: Drink, get drunk, get drunker, and black out. Avoid doing *anything*. Repeat.

Something to look forward to: Drinking. Getting drunk and looking forward to forgetting about all my problems and imperfections. Blacking out. And *repeat*.

It's no surprise that my cake ended up tasting like absolute shit, considering the ingredients I was putting into it.

And here I am, saying that Old 3-or-4-Litres-of-Wine-a-Day-Shawn was a perfectionist.

That list certainly doesn't make me look like one.

I believe it was partly because of the unattainable, impossible drive for perfection that drove me, and drives so many other, to the point of absolute unravelling where I ended up. No matter how hard I tried, I couldn't hold myself, or anything, together perfectly. So naturally I and everything started to become unstitched.

The more things I failed at starting, finishing, or fixing, the less perfect I and everything felt, because the ingredients I was using to *seek happiness* were designed *to take it away and keep me chasing after it, and they were slowly poisoning me.*

My trifecta was flawed.

I no longer want, *or need*, a perfect life, or a perfect *anything*. I don't want or need the perfect cake, but I *do* want something palatable that tastes pretty damn sweet.

I'm tired of using really shitty ingredients and expecting really stellar results. I'm tired of eating the shit-cake I've always made and choking it down pretending that I like it.

It took the clarity of being sober for more than a few minutes to be able to step back and look at the pantry of ingredients I had been using all along: *they were all cheap, expired, and long passed needing to be tossed in the bin.*

All my old habits and beliefs were rotting in waiting, and the longer I kept using them the sicker they were making me.

It was time to try a new recipe, full of fresh, healthy ingredients:

Someone to love: *Myself,* for a change. *Self-care* has become the Magic Baking Powder˙ that is helping everything in my life to rise.

Something to do: Reading, writing, cooking and *creating*. Sometimes my *"something to do"* is doing *absolutely nothing* and being 100% wholeheartedly okay with that. What's important is that *whatever* I'm doing nurtures my spirit.

Something to look forward to: This one surprised me, because it's not an ingredient I could intentionally add to the mix. The moment I overhauled my personal recipe for happiness, this ingredient opened wide like floodgates.

Suddenly...*I'm looking forward to everything.*

In Cajun cooking, there's something called the *Holy Trinity,* and every good recipe begins with it because it's tried, true, it's delicious and *it works.* It's the solid base all delicious southern recipes start with, and every *other* ingredient you add to the pot comes alive.

Onions, bell peppers, and celery.

I'm sure it took centuries of experimentation, trial and error, and a lot of really disgusting dishes to finally nail down the tastiest, most reliable combination.

But once they nailed it, it stuck.

If you don't start your gumbo with it, it isn't *really* gumbo. (Well, that and okra).

I feel like an early Cajun, testing out a bit of this, and a bit of that, creating my own Holy Trinity of ingredients so my entire life tastes better.

I'm getting rid of expired ingredients and throwing away old recipes that never tasted good and were only making me sick.

There will be no more shit cakes.

I'm ready to start baking a little Happiness Pie. It may not be perfect, but it's made up of ingredients that feed my soul, and that's as close to perfect as you can get.

That, and it tastes absolutely, freaking delicious.

This Is Where I (Usually) Where I Stop

MARCH 4, 2018

**February 4, 2018, I committed to 30 consecutive days of sobriety.
Again.**

No wine. No beer. No 8 am Hair-of-the-Dog.

Nothing but my own sober self to spend some much-needed quality time with.

You know, so I could start sorting out some of the clutter in my head. Just 30 days of clarity to try and make sense of the mental clutter that weighed me down and helped me sink back into drinking all day, every day.

Drinking every day, regardless of a solid month in rehab, and regardless of my deep, impossible-to-ignore *desire* to no longer drink.

Today is Day 29 of my 30 Day Alcohol Experiment.

This is usually where I stop almost everything that I start.

Right at the finish line. Just before reaching the top of the mountain.

It usually doesn't matter how long I've been running or how far I've climbed. This is the point where the anxiety *always* swells up like a tsunami and washes me back to the beginning.

And I let it.

I have always allowed myself to get dragged away in the undertow the closer I get to shore. For as much as I write and as much as I talk, I admit I don't really know very much. I know *how I feel,* and that's about as scientific as things get over here.

And feelings are crafty little things.

They're like an army of *Transformers* that live inside you, morphing, changing, turning from one thing into another.

They are never static and one thought or situation or memory can turn them into something entirely different.

How do you give a name to something like that?

Naming something takes the fear away. Labels and definitions begin filling the void where uncertainty and the unknown used to be. Labels and definitions help to contain something, creating edges and boundaries – applying limitations to something otherwise limitless: *This feeling is sadness. And this one is joy. This is empathy, and this is regret.*

So here I am, not knowing what to name my chronic inability to finish what I start.

Procrastination? Fear of success? Fear of failure?

They all sound too cliché, even though *fear* is probably at the deep and dirty root of it. Neither ‹fear of success› or ‹fear of failure› seems to make sense, since I start projects and journeys in *order* to succeed.

It doesn't make sense to start things you have no intention of finishing, or that you intend to fail at. Right?

That would be insanity. Then again – there's nearly 200 pages leading up to this that prove that maybe I've made some pretty insane choices in my life, repeatedly.

So why is it that when I get *so close* to my goal, so close that I can see it on the horizon and almost feel it in my hands, that I throw my hands up and abandon ship?

I'm not even exaggerating here, kids.

I do it all the time.

Maybe it's the classic *Rabbit & The Hare* story. I fly too quickly out of the gate and spend all my momentum in the start-up and not the finish.

But even that doesn't feel quite right.

It's just weird, because where I am right now is in a place where I honestly *do not want to drink.* Not at this moment, not tonight, not tomorrow, and not on our vacation in New Orleans just 10 days from today.

So why am I feeling this crazy anxiety over *actually accomplishing* what I set out to do? Why does wrapping up tomorrow's 30 Sober Days make me want to be physically sick to my stomach?

I feel as though a bomb is about to drop.

I should be celebrating.

The more I ramble the more it's starting to make a *little* more sense to me. Thanks for sticking with me here.

Maybe it's the *infinite unknown* of what happens *after* accomplishing what I set out to do, that sends me into the backward, downward spiral? Maybe all along I've been forgetting to look at and aim for the *next step* that comes after finally reaching this one?

Maybe I've always just seen the forest, and overlooked the trees?

I admit I'm a "big picture" sort of person, and I also admit that I think it's time I become a little more of a "task oriented" sort of person. Knowing my next step, my next goal, might take away the *terror* that kicks in when I see the finish line and immediately get the *"Holy-shit-what-now?"* feeling that gnaws away at me.

What now.

That's the scary part.

It's the moment when the training wheels come off and you're suddenly on your own. You've accomplished what you set out to, and now there's expectations of what you need to accomplish next.

Expectations, but from who?

Maybe I've made up the idea that *everyone else* is expecting something from me, and I can't let them down. That's a pretty narcissistic idea, now that I come to think of it. Now would be a really good time to remind myself that everyone else is knee-deep in their own shit and what I'm doing with my own life is likely pretty low on their scale of things they lay awake at night thinking about.

But it's a theory, albeit a really self-interested one.

Am I afraid of letting everyone else down, if I fail? Am I afraid of what they'll expect of me next if I succeed? Am I afraid of allowing myself to live the life I've dreamt of? Am I afraid of feeling like I deserve my dream life?

Am I afraid of owning the fact that I'm worth it?

Whoever told me that I wasn't? *Probably me.* Maybe it was mass marketing. Maybe it was those grade school bullies from 30 years ago or maybe it's the newsstands that tell us what *"true success"* is *"supposed"* to look like, not to mention the perfect body, home, and bank account.

So many theories, and I think each one has at least a little bit of truth to it.

What I *need* to do is *stop stopping.*

Coincidentally, the first entry I made when I started writing again on Day 1 2.0 of this 30 Day "experiment" was titled *"Never Stop Starting"*.

And here I am, encouraging myself to finally *stop stopping.* To keep going. To keep climbing. Keep swimming. Keep achieving. Striving. Working. Growing. To stop being fearful of the unknown and infinite that sprawls out after the finish line, but instead to line it with smaller, achievable goals that lay out a path for me to follow.

My challenge has never been in the starting – *I excel at beginnings.*

Maybe I just need to start looking at endings and accomplishments from the other side. The side that looks like the beginning of something else.

The first step of the next step.

Forfeit is the only thing worse than failure.

Sober Vows And Flattened Squirrels

MARCH 5, 2018

"Life is a matter of choices. And every choice you make, makes you."
– John C. Maxwell

We are always just one decision away from a completely different life.

30 days ago, I made the hard and fast choice to try Annie Grace's Alcohol Experiment, as you're well aware, because well, I felt like a torn-apart bag of hungover trash that smelled like a winery and looked even worse.

I'm pretty sure that morning, not unlike most others in the months, years and decades before it, I woke up with wine stains on my shirt, my lips, my teeth and at least 3 or more spots on the floor and random pieces of furniture. I'm sure a few drops even landed on the dogs.

I had pickled myself again.

And I was well beyond tired of it.

Tired of my old bullshit. Tired of running. Of hiding. Of numbing and avoiding.

Of ruining everything: my happiness and health included.

I wasn't just tired of it – I was sick of it, *quite literally*. Sick of keeping myself in a constant state of illness. Who in their right mind willingly volunteers to fill themselves with *a disease* every day? The cycle of self-sabotage was dizzying, and I wanted off.

So, I made the decision to end it, without the safe word of *"maybe"*. I knew there wasn't room for *"maybe I'll try it"* or *"maybe it's time"*. I had to put aside my wishy-washy tendency of sitting on the fence, perched somewhere between optimistically committed and fearfully uncertain.

I had to climb down and choose a side.

Was I going to side with the part of me that thought I could *maybe* try and stop drinking for 30 days, and see how it goes? Or was I going to side with the part of me that was screaming for *certainty and decisiveness*, and a solid commitment without grey areas, and without maybes.

Because maybe almost always mean no.

I had to be all in. I had to throw my *maybes* to the curb and put my big boy pants on and make the *decision* that no matter what, I was no longer going to drink. That I was done taking my happiness and health for granted and that I could admit with every ounce of my worn out being that after 2 decades of hardcore daily research – *I was never going to find anything worth keeping at the bottom of any bottle.*

I had never found anything in the past other than sickness, shame, debt, loss and regret. Why in the world I thought the results would be different each time I drank is beyond me.

You don't keep doing something you know and have proven time and again to yourself only causes pain, like stubbing your toe on the corner of the bed. We don't keep walking over and kicking it every morning after we've done it once and realize it hurts like a bitch.

We know it hurts and we know it causes us pain.

So why do we keep popping corks every day and guzzling down what we know only makes us sick and sad?

It's fascinating to step back from your life just enough to deconstruct it into all the choices and decisions that we've made, that in turn, *have made us*. To look at all the sliding doors we have walked through, and to see that *we are where we are because of the choices we have made*, whether conscious or not.

I *decided* to drink every day. I felt out of control, and indeed I was, but I still *chose* to keep myself there. I *chose* to buy the wine, I *chose* to open it, and as ritualistic and routine as it all became, I still *chose* to pour it down my throat.

I put, *and kept* myself there every day through my choices. It only makes sense that making new and better choices are what's going to get, and *keep*, me out.

Imagine if we all invested as much time and energy as we do satisfying our urges to drink into *not drinking*?

Holy crap. Just imagine.

I've proven I can summon an army and align all the stars of the universe to ensure I could get drunk every day. Now, I'm deciding to prove to myself that I can draw on that same reserve of determination to ensure I never have to drink again.

It comes down to whether I want to use my powers for good or evil.

That's the decision I made 30 days ago.

I decided to put as much effort into my health, happiness, and wellbeing as I had been giving to drinking. And today, I'm renewing that commitment and decision to keep going, free of the *"maybe's"* and *"we'll see's"*.

Be decisive. The road of life is paved with flat squirrels who couldn't make a decision. I don't know about you, but I'm pretty tired of spending my life like a flattened squirrel. Run down day after day by indecision because I was too damned scared to make changes and *do for myself* what I've spent my whole life wishing for others: *an easy, unsaddled life full of freedom, wellbeing, and joy.*

The only thing separating where we are and where we hope to be, are our solid, committed decisions to get there. *Without any grey areas. Without the emergency escape route that "maybes" allow.*

I know I'm repetitive today, but I'm trying to drill it home as deep into my brain as I was able to drill in my desire to drink and self-destruct. I know I'm also a little more passionate than usual, but reaching 30 days sober today has helped me to hopefully put all my *maybes* to bed once and for all.

I'm leaving all of these words here so I can come back from time to time and remind myself of my sober vow that *I no longer welcome in my life what has only taken my life from me.*

> "First we make our habits, and then our habits make us."
> – *John Dryden*

I don't feel as though I need to recommit to my decision every day, anymore. Now that I've wholeheartedly decided, *it just is*. Like cement. There's no more *maybes*. No more *we'll sees*. No more *counting days*.

There's incredible, sweet relief in no longer having to make choice after choice every single day, of whether I'm going to drink, or maybe have one later, or next week. The triggers will still be there. The roadblocks will still appear. But knowing I've already made my *choice* to no longer drink makes every day that much easier.

Whenever the option to drink falls in my lap or slaps me in the face, deciding what to do is a no-brainer. It's a no-brainer because the *only choice that aligns with my best interests is the one I've already made.*

That drinking is no longer an option.

Nothing else has changed other than my mindset, and the firm decision that I've made to never drink again. And, in turn, *everything* has changed.

There is absolute freedom in committing to a decision that feels as permanent as a tattoo.

And there's sweet relief in knowing that I never, ever have to kick that damned bed frame ever again.

Consumption

MARCH 6, 2018

**It became obvious to me last night that I don't just have a drinking problem.
*I have a consumption problem.***

My hobbies apparently include *having as much of anything and everything as possible*. From my once 3-4 litres of wine and pack of smokes a day to last night's half loaf of banana bread and 2 litres of juice, to this morning's 48 ounces of coffee that I'll pour down my throat by the time I'm done writing this post.

I am constantly reaching for things to collect and consume.

In excess.

I feel as though I need more of *everything*, grasping at anything of substance that I can pour into myself as though I'm filling some bottomless void. It's a one-way high-speed highway where I'm trying to get things into me as quickly as possible, at all times.

I'm not picky. Whatever quells the hunger in the moment is usually pretty good by me.

The problem is that the hunger feels insatiable – *and yet I'm not even hungry*. I need to be drinking something constantly – *even though I'm not thirsty*.

It would be easy to chalk it up to an *addictive personality*, if I didn't think that term was absolute rubbish. I wasn't *born* addicted to anything. My parents didn't *raise* me to obsess over things, and I wasn't raised in an environment of scarcity, predisposed to coveting things in fear of drought or lack.

My "personality" is the combination of quirks and qualities that form my distinctive *character*.

My *behaviour*, on the other hand, is made up of my *actions and reactions*.

That would make addiction a *behaviour*. It's *not* my personality, and it's *not* who I am; although it's important to note my behaviour as an addict absolutely changed my personality.

But here I am anyhow, alcohol free, *and still obsessed with consuming*.

When I was drinking, it was easy to ignore, because I barely ate. So long as there was wine, *in volume*, it would be consumed *en masse*. In the rare times I wasn't guzzling wine (basically in that tiny window between waking up and noon) you could find me guzzling black coffee *like it was my job*. The only thing that's changed is that my wine has turned into water, kombucha, juice or whatever else I can keep pouring out and keep pouring in.

Fill in the gaps with cigarettes and sweets, and *I'm still as addicted to consumption as I ever was.*

There's still something deeper within me that's *starving*; something with a thirst so strong it never feels quenched. Maybe it's just the North American code of *more, more, more*. Afterall, I'm the guy who when he finds the perfect pair of boots goes ahead and buys them in every colour, with a backup pair *just in case*. I do the same with shirts. And jeans. And pretty much anything I enjoy, from savoury dips to puppy dogs *(because how can you possibly have enough hummus or Boston Terriers?)*

It's a fair trade in hindsight, swapping alcohol for almost *anything* else. But now I'm struggling with being mindful of moderating my *new* addictions. I've been giving them free reign because "I'm in recovery".

Because I need "to be gentle with myself right now."

Well, if I keep staying this gentle with myself, I'm going to need bigger pants and a catheter because I can barely keep up with the volume of food and fluids I'm devouring.

And really, to feed what?

What in the world am I try to feed and what is this appetite I'm pouring anything and everything on top of to try and satisfy?

It's something deeper that alcohol obviously couldn't gratify regardless of how hard I tried every day, paying my ransom with bottles and blackouts. I'm still here, eating and drinking my feelings, only now I'm sober enough to sense the bottomless well I'm pouring it all into.

At least it isn't poison that I'm pouring, this time around.

Okay. Now I'm just being over dramatic.

It's not that bad. It's not as though I'm sitting here rocking in a corner wondering when I can have my next V8, Kit Kat bar, bag of chips, or feeling despondent and empty, or that my life is meaningless and unfulfilling without a glass of cabernet or 2 litre tub of mint chocolate chip ice cream.

It's not like that.

I love my life. *Especially this sparkly new sober one.* I just wish I could figure out this endless *thirst* that I thought would go away. I'm still fresh out of the alcohol-free gate so it's nice to imagine that over time the thirst will lessen or leave, but most addictions and obsessions *just grow.*

Just like weeds, out of control and never where you want them.

Just like my *waistline* if I don't get a damn grip on my consumption of anything and everything that sits still long enough.

I don't believe it's gluttony and I don't believe it's greed.

I practice being grateful as a way of life, and I'm truly thankful for every little bit of each and every corner of my life, and that gratitude is growing exponentially with each sober day.

But still, there is this persistent, gnawing feeling that I'm not fully *complete* without something in my hand to eat, drink or otherwise consume. Like I'm not enough *as-is* and that I need something from outside of myself to make me whole.

What in the world am I trying to satisfy?

The beautiful dark side of sobriety appears when you begin to reclaim your clarity, and rediscover your ability to *listen to your body,* allowing the *roots* of your addiction to rise to the surface where you can't ignore them anymore.

And when they rise up they become so much easier to trip over.

It's as though I'm finally turning the volume down enough to hear my inner hollows bellow and growl. Whatever thirst was briefly silenced by booze is still there bubbling below the surface begging for more. The same hunger that craved another and another is still there growling, empty, and wanting satisfaction.

And nothing I consume seems to satisfy it.

Peeling alcohol from my life is no different than removing a bandage and revealing the wound.

The last time I felt *truly full* was when I was giving myself away and being of service without expecting anything in return. It was when I was using the talents I've been given combined with a healthy dose of passion and philanthropy, and I was overflowing with so much gratitude that it began spilling over everywhere I went.

It's ironic and incredible how by pouring whatever you have to give into another's cup, you can in turn fill up your own.

Perhaps that's the void I'm trying to fill.

Feeling useful.

Feeling beneficial, like I'm *contributing* somehow instead of always taking, always fixated on myself and my desires. These are all textbook "alcoholic" tendencies.

The more I consume, the less fulfilled I feel.

The more I give, the less I need to take.

Maybe I don't have a consumption problem after all. Maybe the hunger and thirst I'm trying to quiet inside me is just unused potential that's been buried too long, wanting to be released. Maybe there's nothing I can put *in* me to feel complete again, but instead, *something I need to put out.*

Maybe the only thing I'm *really* thirsty for is the taste of wholeheartedly doing something worthwhile again. Of that feeling I once had of being *so full from contributing* that there's no room left for *obsessive over-consuming.*

> "We make a living by what we get. But we make a life by what we give."
> – *Winston Churchill*

I think I'm ready to start **making a life** again.

Rear-view Mirrors

MARCH 7, 2018

**"There's a reason the windshield is much bigger than the rear-view mirror.
Where you are going is so much better than where you have been."**
– Unknown

Have you ever tried to drive down the highway looking at nothing but the rear-view mirror? *It's as though you're asking for a car crash.*

It doesn't work.

You need to know where you are, and where you are heading. Where you've been doesn't matter anymore, unless you've *just* passed a service station and you need a bathroom, then there's some value in turning back. Anyone who has travelled with me will, unfortunately, vouch for this.

My decision to become alcohol-free was borne of a dark place made up of walls plastered with the past, and a lofty, soaring ceiling made up of my desire for a better future. And me, sitting on the damp dirt floor of what felt like, and was, a prison.

There I was, never present, torn between where I had trapped myself and where I wanted to be. Until I could finally focus and turn my eyes away from the walls of past regrets and failures that formed my cage, I wasn't able to turn my eyes upward and aim at climbing out.

The longer I stared at the walls, the taller they became.

A million years ago, when I was first learning to drive, I clearly remember Betty (my Drivers Ed. Instructor) explaining how in order to stay between the lines, it was best to look towards and follow the car in front of you. Now, this approach only works if the car you are following knows what the hell *they're* doing.

In my experience though, no one has led me into a ditch yet.

Thankfully.

You know those evenings when it's snowing so hard and you're driving somewhere? Those nightmare drives where you're absolutely swallowed by tunnel vision, where everything is blinding and you're clinging to the taillights of the stranger in front of you?

That's how it feels getting to this point of sobriety.

Keeping my eyes locked on the road and the people before me.

Because I want to be where they are.

Despite the snowstorm around me, getting there requires following with a little courage and a lot of blind faith in the path left from those in front of me; driving forward, riddled with butterflies, white knuckles and a pinch of thrill all at the same time, *but knowing that we're getting there.*

If that driver in front me started staring at my headlights in *their* rear-view, there'd be a good chance we'd all end up steering ourselves into a ditch, or worse.

It only works – *moving forward and getting there* – by looking at what's right in front of your face and where you are headed – *not behind you.*

We don't have eyes in the back of our heads *because we aren't headed that way.*

Rear-view mirrors can be shifty little things though, *like circus mirrors.* They warp and distort where you came from, somehow making everything seem shinier than it was. They make emotions and memories appear larger than they were and sugar coat them to lure you back.

It's like how my grandparents would always refer to their life back in the *"Old Country"* as something that always sounded like Disneyland, despite barely having 2 pennies to rub together and blisters from decades of simply trying to get by.

But their memories sparkled. *The grass was always greener back home.*

They were convinced that everything was *Bigger and Better in Belgium.*

That's how the rear-view mirror tries to get your attention, by dangling bedazzled and blinding memories to distract you and drive you off the road.

The more you stare, the more fixated you become. And the more fixated you become, the more you start to believe that things were better than they actually ever were.

Looking backwards, everything becomes *censored.* Drunken nights full of laughs rise to the top, and the feelings of death the next day somehow sink to the bottom. Celebrations and glasses clinking start to resonate and remind you of how much fun you once had; the rear-view mirror has no room for reminders of the times alcohol made you say things you shouldn't have, do things you wished you hadn't, or for the thousands upon thousands of dollars of poison you drank.

"It has been a mistake living my life in the past.
One cannot ride a horse backwards and still hold its reins."
– Richard Paul Evans

It's tempting, looking back. And at times, it's actually healthy. Knowing where you came from is humbling and grounding, but clinging to it is a recipe for disaster, driving you into the figurative ditch.

So long as you believe your past was better than your present or future, you may as well just pull over, get out, and walk back to wherever you came from. You're going to be driving all over the damn highway since you're looking anywhere and everywhere *but at the road ahead.*

And if you're anything like me, you've wasted more than enough time being that guy on the road – hopefully just figuratively, but probably and sadly, *literally* too. The drunk driver, swerving everywhere and putting everything and everyone in your path in danger.

At first, when I was just learning to drive this sober highway, I admit I was everywhere. On the shoulder, staring in the rear-view, hoping there was a licensed bar ahead where I could even just smell some booze in the air. I was driving through the snowstorm totally blind. It wasn't until I started following the taillights before me that I was able to start feeling confident that I wasn't going to crash after all, and that I wasn't alone on this highway.

From books like Annie Grace's *"This Naked Mind"* and Catherine Gray's *"The Unexpected Joy of Being Sober"* to the vibrant and vulnerable online communities of everyone else on this road, such as *"Recovery Elevator"*, *"The Alcohol Experiment"*, and *"Club Soda UK"* – they've all given me taillights to follow.

And the more I look forward, the more taillights I see.

There's so much more to look forward to, knowing I'm not alone on the highway in the midst of a snowstorm, but part of a caravan slowly and surely moving forward and guiding each other as we go.

The only use I have for my rear-view mirror anymore is to see how far I've come.

15 Awesome & Unexpected Things That Happened When I Quit Drinking For 30 Days

MARCH 8, 2018

The transition from daily drinker to alcohol-free-zealot is full of daily discoveries, and they're all part of *finally* waking up from a 2-decade-long drunken haze.

From tripping up over triggers to trying to master mind-over-matter from moment-to-moment, I give so much of my energy to exploring and trying to understand – and overcome – the *challenge*s of becoming, and staying, sober.

Today, I want to focus on the successes, instead.

So, I present to you my list of **15 Awesome & Unexpected Things That Happened When I Quit Drinking for 30 Days** (in no particular order):

1. I'm Way Less Bitchy. Yep, I'm starting right out of the gate with the most unexpected one of them all. And yep, I'll admit I was a pretty unlovable demon the first couple of days. But, as I tuck day after sober day under my belt, I'm finding I'm becoming exponentially more patient, and hopefully, likeable. It's amazing how it's so much easier to be pleasant when you aren't fighting cravings, plotting your route so can swing by the liquor store, or stuck in a constant cycle of drunkenness/ hangover/withdrawal.

2. I'm Dressing Better. This baby is two-fold. First, I'm actually leaving the house again, to go places other than the liquor store and then straight back home to perfect my performance of "Anti-Social Alcoholic Introvert". I'm actually putting myself together in something other than the clothes I blacked out in last night, and often, the night before too. Secondly, I can afford to buy myself new clothes with the money I'm saving every day. I was spending $40 Canadian or more a day on alcohol, which is $1200 a month. Oh, the shoes I could buy with that!

3. I'm Wearing My Glasses Less. It's fair to say my vision is far less than 20/20. When I was demolishing 4 litres of wine a day, on top of being blind, I usually looked like I'd been punched in both eyes and hadn't slept in weeks. I'd try and disguise this behind whatever thick-rimmed eyewear I could, paired up with a hat to cast as much shadow on my face as possible. Now that I'm starting to look significantly less abused, I can now enjoy stumbling around bumping into things simply because I'm blind, instead of blind and drunk.

4. I Realized I'm Not Depressed. I spent a really, really, really long time believing I was depressed. I assumed it was my predisposition and that melancholy was just my destiny. Turns out, I'm not depressed after all, but consuming 1,460 litres of liquid depressant a year can definitely make you think you are. Before the alcohol and all its supporting hormonal demons even left my bloodstream after my last drink, my mood improved because I was excited for the possibilities. Now that all my chemistry is starting to level out, I'm as far from depressed as I used to be deeply rooted in it.

5. I Have Much More Time. This perk of not drinking wasn't as unexpected as some of the others. I knew how much time I wasted supporting drinking like I did. From thinking about it, going to get it, hiding it, planning my day around it and creating make-work projects because of it, I spent/wasted a good portion of every day (because really, how productive is starting to drink at noon, until you pass out later that evening?) I've traded in drunk and passed out at 8pm for coffee dates with myself and a book or meditating in the hot tub with a glass of juice. I'm consciously reinvesting this new-found time on myself, and things that nurture my recovery.

6. I've Realized Everything Isn't Awful This one is close to #4, realizing I'm not actually depressed, but it's different. Feeling depressed was basically never wanting to do anything at all. Like, ever. Realizing that everything isn't in fact awful has reopened up the gates of gratitude in my life. When I was drunk all the time, I was never present, and never truly appreciated anything. I took everything for granted. It's hard to feel grateful when you're numb. Hell, it's hard to feel anything but flat and half dead. Each sober day as the sensation of being alive returns, the more I'm finding that everything is in fact incredible and amazing.

7. I've Become Way More Forgiving. Mostly to myself. Drunk/hungover me was pretty hard on himself. For as much as I was the King of Procrastination I was also the Fool of Perfection. I strived for it, demanded it from myself, and to be honest, I expected it from others, too. It's ironic in hindsight since I was stuck in the throes of imperfection all the time. Sober me is a much more forgiving guy; of myself, everyone,

and everything. "Good enough" and sober is so much better than drunk and "never perfect".

8. I Can Form Proper Sentences. This one seems pretty obvious. Drunks aren't really synonymous with eloquence. I'm pretty sure, when drunk out of my mind, that I believed whatever nonsense was spewing out of my mouth (usually on repeat) was profound. But the truth is, I could barely string together cohesive thoughts without distraction or forgetting what the hell I was talking about to begin with. Sober me is relishing in reclaiming the English language again, and better yet, remembering what I opened my mouth to talk about in the first place.

9. Recycling Day Is Nothing To Be Afraid Of. Okay. You've been there. That ear-shattering crash when you hear your recycling bin being dumped into the garbage truck. The type of crash that sounds like a mix of embarrassment, tragedy, and shame, and is loud enough to wake up people in a coma three towns over. Listening to that once a week was surprisingly easier than dealing with the awkward judgement of returning them in such overwhelming volume to the liquor store for a refund. It was like I was leaving bins full of my confessions at the curb, and the garbage men were priests who could haul away my sins and nobody would ever need to know. Now sober, recycling day sounds a lot more like the soft plink of plastic juice bottles and the snoring of all my neighbours who get to sleep through it.

10. I'm Hella Confident. I've always been a relatively confident guy, despite my downward spiral into alcoholism, believe it or not.

11. I clumsily faked it as well as I could, for as long as possible, but relied heavily on that confidence arriving in liquid form. The idea of not drinking however, could transport me to full-fledged anxiety in a split second, and I'd stay there until I knew a drink was on its way. Being sober allows me to pull my confidence from healthier places, like knowing I'm not only good enough, but I am better now than I ever have been. And I'll never trade that feeling in for a drink, ever.

12. I've Discovered That Feeling Good is Contagious. No, I haven't converted or will try to convert, anyone to anything. But as part of my own transition from "struggling, sick drunkard" to "happy, patient, sober dude" I'm now wanting that feeling of recovery and strength to spread to every part of my life. Being sober is making me want to improve literally everything in my life, from my overall health and diet to my marriage, career, and to resurrect long dormant passions. Sobriety has given me the desire to enhance and nurture all the things that really mean something to me.

13. I'm Way More Sensitive. You'd think it'd be the other way around. Alcohol always made me cry. But that wasn't being sensitive, that was being a hormonal mess and being overwhelmed by emotions I had no idea how to deal with or react to. Sobriety brings with it this wide-open space of clarity where you can pause and actually be present with your feelings, and see them for what they really are, not for what alcohol has distorted them to feel like. I can feel and recognize my emotions now, instead of living in a constant state of feeling like an overwhelmed, drunken hot mess.

14. I Look Forward To Things. There was nothing worse than the dread that came with drunkenness. I would dread literally everything. Going to the store. Going to a photo shoot for work. Going out for dinner with friends. Friends coming over. Going to family events. Planning my life around drinking, and putting my life on hold for it, was a full-time job. Anything outside of that was terms for avoiding or cancelling. Being sober is helping me become more social, and truly valuing the variety of life I'm able to experience and remember.

15. Mirrors Aren't The Enemy Anymore. I wouldn't even dare look at myself in the mirror in the morning, and tried to avoid it all day if I could. If I looked half as bad as I felt, it was nothing I wanted staring back at me. Since all the booze has left the building and my body, I'm already noticeably less Pillsbury-Dough-Boy-Level-Puffed-Up, the whites of my eyes actually are white for a change, and my skin has evened out, and is no longer a weird combination of pretty much every skin type imaginable.

16. Movie Endings Are Pretty Cool. I love me some Netflix. I love murder mysteries, scary movies, true crime, and psychological thrillers. You know what I also love, now that I'm sober? Finally, being able to make it to the ending. I'm pretty sure I've watched every movie ever made, and probably made it to the end of about 3 of them – and that was only because we watched it early enough in the day. Drunk me always fell asleep passing out about halfway through every movie. Luckily, the next day hungover-me couldn't remember what movie we watched the night before, anyways. Sober-me, now able to stay awake, is discovering that the endings are usually the best part. Here's hoping mine (and yours) is, too.

This list is just a very small drop in the figurative wine barrel of all the amazing things that are starting to happen in my first short month of sobriety. So, let's just call this Part 1, since every day I'm discovering new and unexpected benefits of being alcohol-free.

Sobriety really does deliver everything that alcohol promises.

Dodging Triggers: How Not To Drink in New Orleans

MARCH 10, 2018

"I survived because the fire inside me burned brighter than the fire around me."
– Joshua Graham

In 4 short sleeps we will be heading to the airport on our way to New Orleans for my first alcohol-free vacation.

We used to keep an apartment there, since after our first visit we fell so much in love with the city and how it made us feel, that it was cheaper to rent an apartment than to keep renting hotels each time we'd go down, which was *a lot*. New Orleans, as it does, crept inside me like all other addictions: *I had to have it, and as much of it as possible.*

Now, if you know anything about *The Big Easy*, it probably has something to do with Mardi Gras parades, beignets, beads, Jazz, parties and drinking topless in the street. They have drive-thru daiquiri shops, for Christ's sake.

If there was ever a city built around binge drinking, NOLA is it.

Every time we'd head down to the Crescent City, my drinking would start, obviously, on the flight down. I would plan my arrival *(drinking)* at the apartment ahead of time, and order wine delivery by the case, so it would be waiting for me when I got there: everything from day-drinking wine to enough vodka and mix to sustain very strongly mixed Bloody Mary's from breakfast thru to dinner. Of course, also sleeves of red Solo cups, so wherever we were going, I could bring a drink with me, too.

It's worth noting that a red Solo cup is 16oz, and I've learned that about 3/4 of a bottle of wine can fit in one, which make it the perfect "traveller" to take with you on your way to breakfast.

I'd be lying if I said I wasn't a little nervous about what feels like crawling straight into the lion's mouth. After all, Bob Dylan put it best:

"Everything is a good idea in New Orleans."

No, everything is *not* a good idea in New Orleans.

Getting to this early point of sobriety has required me to rethink everything, including having to sort out the cognitive dissonance. You know, *those inconsistent thoughts I have about drinking,* in my brain. Thoughts like *"but you have to drink when you're in New Orleans,"* when I know in fact I *don't* have to and I *don't* want to because I know how shit has gone down in the past and I never want to repeat it.

I don't want to repeat the time I actually tipped over, while squat down watching a parade after about 3 bottles of wine, then sort of rolled away down the sidewalk. Yeah, it happened and there's photo evidence.

I don't want to repeat spending the first few hours of each day of vacation nursing the day before's bad decisions, trying to drown out the hangover under buckets of even stronger Bloody Mary's.

I don't want to repeat the arguments that Hubs and I have had while there, or the time we barely spoke for two days of vacation, because we were so belligerently drunk we couldn't get on the same page. Probably because we were both so hammered, our pages weren't even in the same book anymore. Or library.

I don't want to repeat going through my phone each morning, so I can rebuild my memories of *what the hell happened* last night, based solely on whatever photos are in my camera roll, that I had absolutely forgotten taking. That, and the absolute dread of checking what I posted to social media. Face palm goes here.

And I *absolutely do not want to repeat* that time *I pissed myself in New Orleans.*

The problem/challenge with returning *sober for the first time ever,* will be handling the inevitable barrage of triggers encouraging me to drink in excess with the same level of control, patience, clarity, and confidence that have helped me get this far.

Because really, what else has changed, other than the landscape? There's no reason why staying sober in *The Big Easy* has to be *The Big Impossible,* if my heart and my mind have already decided it'll be a breeze.

If I can do it here, I can do it anywhere. Right?

I sure hope so.

The best time to stretch my sober muscle is *right now,* before I'm even packed.

Right now, before I'm even on a plane and *right now,* before I'm knee-deep in drunks and dripping of FOMO all over Bourbon Street.

In Cajun cooking, you almost always start your recipe with a roux. It's the *foundation* that all delicious southern dishes are created from. Today I'm making myself a little *roux for my soul,* made up of equal parts preparation, foresight, courage, and decisiveness so I can cook up the best, alcohol-free vacation possible.

> "By failing to prepare, you are preparing to fail."
> *– Benjamin Franklin*

Addiction triggers come neatly packaged in three different sizes: *environmental, social, and emotional.* They also usually come straight out of left field when you're unprepared, and they're aimed right at your head so they can knock you out of balance and get you when you're down. I can't make these triggers go away. They're what make up the booze-stained fabric of New Orleans, the *Paris of the South.*

What I *can* do however, is *take control of how I react to these triggers.* That's where my power is. I can prepare for them, anticipate them, and totally crush them.

Making sure my Happiness Trifecta is made up of healthy ingredients, and looking forward to coming home after vacation with the overwhelming pride that *I did it* also helps a lot, too.

Dealing with *environmental triggers* when trying not to drink is likely the easiest. Just don't walk into or up to the bar. Don't wander down Bourbon Street where every 10 inches is another sign boasting 3-for-1 drinks and buckets of NOLA's signature poison, the *Hurricane* (they're disgusting, don't ever try one).

When you're trying to avoid drinking and the drinking culture, it seems the most sensible thing to do is to *avoid the places where drinking happens.*

Except drinking happens, *and is encouraged,* literally *everywhere* in New Orleans.

It's like trying to go outside and avoid the air.

The best way of dealing with the *environmental triggers* is pretty obvious: *I have to change the environment.* It's time to explore corners of the city we've never been to and discover landmarks and places that inspire creativity and culture. There is *so much culture* in New Orleans, from her rich history to live jazz and the best cuisine in the world. It's time to create a new list of my "*favourite places in NOLA*" based on how good they make me feel, instead of how quickly and affordably they can make me numb.

The excitement of discovering new reasons to love a city I already adore is pretty awesome and I'm not even there yet.

Now, *social triggers* are a little harder. These are the *situations* I'll find myself in, and the people I'll be around, not just the physical environments. This is where the FOMO kicks in *hard*, seeing everyone else *"having such a good time"*. This is where I need to picture them hungover and vomiting later. This is the St. Patrick's Day parade during March Break, and the table next to me at Muriel's Jackson Square enjoying their second bottle of wine to wash down their crawfish crepes. This is watching everyone having *so much drunken "fun"* and reminding myself of the consequences they'll suffer through later, the money they're wasting, and the fact that they probably wish they could stop drinking, too.

And how it used to be *me*.

This is where the last 5 weeks of sitting with my cognitive dissonance comes in. Bringing what I believe, *and what is actually true*, back into balance and reminding myself as often as needed that the only things I'm *actually* missing out on are:

- hangovers
- embarrassment
- memory loss
- regret
- bad decisions
- vomiting
- arguments
- blackouts
- wasting money
- empty calories
- shame

I'm creating a *new sober social trigger* for myself, where every time I see someone *"enjoying"* a drink and the FOMO kicks in, I'm going to picture a time I walked past someone passed out on their face on a street in New Orleans. Or that time I just *rolled away.*

So now that brings me to the more complicated, *emotional triggers*. You know the ones you carry with you everywhere, regardless of where you are or who you're with. The memories, the mental health stuff. Those deep sprawling roots of the big drunk tree. They can appear out of nowhere, riding on the scents wafting from the open patio doors of a restaurant, to the sights of an old watering hole, or the tastes of a meal you always paired with Shiraz.

It's *nostalgia* and those memories come with feelings that pull on your little alcoholic heart strings.

Those "feelings" that we alcoholics have so much fun dealing with – or more often than not, numbing and ignoring them with an endless stream of liquid ignorance.

Reacting positively to my nostalgic, emotional triggers is something I can only prepare for with a backup escape plan. Premediated *choices*. Dealing with the environmental and social triggers above can, and probably will, trigger *anxiety* and *frustration* — two very tough emotional triggers to deal with, that can leave you feeling vulnerable and exposed.

The easiest way to cope with feeling vulnerable, for me, is by having *accountability*.

Luckily, Hubs will be there, and I will have *all of you*. I have an entire world full of cheerleaders wanting to see me succeed, and better yet, who *understand*. I have an apartment to go back to where I can write and relax if I get overwhelmed, and I have a rooftop where I can meditate if I need to *bring myself back* if I begin to drift or wander.

Keeping this arsenal of self-defence tools front of mind is critical, since New Orleans is a city that ignites all your senses. And it's through those sensory triggers that all my memories of *"the good old days"* spent stumbling through the streets will come rushing back and try to seduce me, stripping away all the crap happened in the past, so I only see the sparkle.

It's up to me to remember that those *"good old days"* almost always ended up *not so good* in the end.

I'm all for being present and in the moment, trying *not* to control the past and the future by just letting things be as they are, and being okay with it. But this, and all situations where you're outnumbered by triggers, is a time where *focusing on the future* is not only important, but imperative.

I need to know how I want to feel in the morning. I need to be accountable for my actions today, so my tomorrow can be incredible.

Incredible, and free of guilt, shame, regret and nausea.

I want to be so present, taking it all in like it's the first time I've ever truly seen New Orleans. I want to be so *in the moment* that I forget that drinking is an option.

I want to enjoy every minute of vacation so much that I would never want to obscure my memories of it.

The fire inside me has to burn brighter than the fire all around me.

I don't want to forfeit the priceless feeling of coming home and knowing that *I did it, and it was the best vacation ever.* I want to stick this sober vacation like a feather into my cap, so future situations can be less intimidating.

The only difference between visiting New Orleans and staying in my own neighbourhood at home is that in New Orleans, I get to watch tens of thousands of people demonstrate all day, every day, *exactly why I stopped drinking.*

> "What happens in Vegas, stays in Vegas.
> But what happens in New Orleans goes home with you."
> – *Laurel K. Hamilton*

Flipping The Switch

MARCH 11, 2018

I mentioned something to Hubs the other day about cravings and my nerves around placing myself around other heavy drinkers right now.

He looked at me surprised and said *"Oh, I didn't know you were still having problems with it, I thought you were fine."* I got a little defensive, *as I do,* and said *"It's not a switch. It's not like I can just turn it off after 20 years of drinking every day."*

I thought you were fine.

I *am* fine. *Ish.*

But how I wish it was as easy to *turn it all off* as flipping a switch, taking all my dirty habits, destructive routines and triggers, and just placing them all back in the dark.

Lord knows they've been in the spotlight long enough.

Getting rid of alcohol and learning to become comfortable with this *brave new normal* happens over time in proportion to how long it took to get to the point of addiction in the first place. Like losing weight or building muscle, growing your hair or building a home, it's an obvious observation, but *these things take time.*

Yep, the cliché *"Rome wasn't built in a day"* is a cliché because it's true.

There is no fast lane, no express aisle, and *definitely no switch* that can be flipped to transform your life overnight.

It takes longer to repair than unravel.

It takes time to learn a new language, and even more time yet to speak it fluently and with confidence. It takes a lot of work, commitment, and practice – and an unwavering desire to learn and get there no matter what.

You're going to say things wrong at first. You're going to have to think about translations and verbs and tenses and slang. And, you're going to have to immerse yourself in that new language and culture, or it won't ever actually *stick*.

Reading a book on how to ride a bike is useless if you never put yourself on one and figure it out for yourself. There will be falling over, there will be learning how to brake and at first there will most definitely be a lot of wobbling your way down the street.

And then one day, you just get on your bike and you're no longer thinking about it anymore.

You just go.

One day, you open your mouth and you're speaking that new language you've been learning, without premeditating each and every word. The sentences begin to form themselves, and a whole new world opens up.

Because the language has become a part of you.

Sobriety and breaking free from age-old addictions and habits works exactly the same.

There's no switch you can flip to learn anything worth knowing, or to get anywhere worth going.

It's more of a slow, gradual sunrise.

> "We burn so hard, but we shed so little light."
> – Clive Barker

It's in the long-drawn-out darkness of addiction where the decision to walk towards the sunrise finally happens. After who knows how long you've been facing West, chasing sunsets and keeping yourself in the dark, you make an about-face and choose to turn East, towards the sun and the promises that come with it.

You become tired of living, if you can call it that, blindly in the dark.

Slowly, everything slowly becomes illuminated. At first, the outlines of new ideas and shapes start to define themselves, and you start to see new paths and opportunities you could never see at night.

There's no more fumbling to find your way. Time slowly allows everything to become clear as everything begins to fall into the light. Shadows draw back and day breaks and your eyes begin to adjust.

If sunrises were on switches, they would lose their magic.

The magnificent colours that leak out over the horizon as it rises would be gone.

No one ever says *"Oh the sun looks beautiful today"* at 3:00 in the afternoon. Its beauty is revered because of those early morning sunrises, at the time of day where everything is still new and uncertain, still tossed between darkness and light, *and yet, it rises anyways.*

"I love that this morning's sunrise does not define itself by last night's sunset."
– *Steve Maraboli*

Recovery is so very much like a sunrise.

A slow awakening. A gradual rising. A steadily growing glow of light after a long period of darkness.

Thankfully there is no switch that turns night to day, or addiction to sobriety, because the beauty is in *the rising*. It's in the appreciation and gratitude that grows with the gradual clarity that gets brighter after the dawn. It's found in the learning, the stumbling, the falling off your bike and the poorly phrased bad translations as you stutter your way through conversations in the new language you're just learning how to speak.

The cure is found in the journey, not the destination.

The sun is most beautiful when it is just waking up.

The Inevitability Of Things Sucking (AKA: No, There is Nothing Wrong With You)

MARCH 12, 2018

There's a tonne of research to back up the theory that addiction is not a substance use disorder, but a *social* one.

This ties into the definition of addiction itself, and what the opposite of addiction actually is. The opposite of addiction is not sobriety. The opposite of addiction is *connection.*

Having real, one-on-one, flesh and blood connections with other human beings, in meaningful and honest ways is the *actual* cure for addiction. Developing reasons to get out of bed in the morning that connect you with purpose and pride, whether it's a job you love or a person you can't live without, that's the soul-fulfilling connection a lot of addicts *need* in order to leave substance abuse behind.

And it's hard.

It's hard because we live in a society that is *saturated with ideals of perfection.* From Instafamous strangers to Faccbook *friendquaintances* (I just made that word up, and I like it) every waking moment of our lives, our senses are overwhelmed by images and stories of *everyone else's* successes, perfectly curated so only the pretty parts show.

And here *we* are, broke-down and falling apart with so much *"wrong with us"* that we want to make right, wondering what the hell our problem is and wondering why we can't get our shit together like everyone else.

It feels like you arrived at the party underdressed and uninvited.

Well, here's a newsflash: *There is nothing wrong with you.*

Let me repeat.

There is Nothing. Wrong. With. You.

We've come to a point where *"things sucking"* no longer has anything to do with circumstance, but instead we believe it has *everything to do with us.*

*If things suck, it has to be because **we** suck.*

We believe that things in our life suck because we aren't *good enough.*

We haven't *tried* hard enough. We don't *want it* enough.

We aren't *worthy* enough, *skinny* enough, *smart* enough or *pretty* enough.

The word *"enough"* used to mean sufficient, adequate, ample, and plentiful.

We're now in a world where *enough is no longer ever enough.*

We measure our worth in comparison to the curated perfection of complete strangers and wonder why we end up feeling inadequate. Its these feelings of inadequacy that stall our relationships. They make us underperform at work, in our marriages, our friendships, and in *actively participating in our very own lives.*

When our lives don't look just like the *unsucky lives* of everyone we see on social media (and tv, movies, magazines, billboards, etc.) it's easy to feel disconnected, and most definitely *not good enough.* We isolate and withdraw, turning to self-sabotage and *connecting* with what we know best – drinking or whatever poison feeds our addiction, or our *need* to form a connection, with *anything.* We turn to whatever feeds our primal need to feel connected and whatever makes our feelings of inadequacy fall to the wayside, at least for a little while.

Life sucks, and then it gets better, and then it sucks again. And repeat.

If the opposite of addiction is in fact *connection,* then that would make addiction itself the same as *disconnection.* We disconnect from people and situations, we disconnect from our true selves, and we disconnect from accepting the reality that sometimes yes, *life sucks,* and there isn't anything we can do about it.

We don't do it consciously, but we also don't absorb the destructive ideas that we're *not good enough* consciously, either. It all happens without us noticing, until things to start suck even more, and the cycle repeats. *We repel the idea that it's okay for things to suck sometimes, that it's okay to be struggling or stumbling, because we're told we aren't good enough if our lives aren't tied up nicely into a perfect bow.*

When our lives don't match the glossy ones we are being force-fed non-stop every day it's easy to ask yourself: *what is wrong with me?* Then, when you start having thoughts like that, it's just easier to drink and make those uncomfortable feelings you don't have answers to go away. It's easier to get drunk than to accept the possibility that maybe, just maybe, there's *actually nothing wrong with you.*

Maybe there's something wrong with the image we've been sold of *what our lives should look like:* shiny, flawless, and definitely without any sucky parts.

Being famous on Instagram is like being rich in Monopoly.

It was my habit of refusing to accept the sucky parts of my life that drove me to drink in excess. The more I refused to accept that sometimes *things just suck,* the suckier things became. I made a career out of trying to drown out the shitty parts with bottles of wine instead of embracing them as part of the unpredictable, wonderful experience of being alive. Since my life seemed to be as far as humanly possible from the scale of success I adopted (read: *was brainwashed into believing*) I defaulted to assuming I was forever flawed, and that was that.

I forfeited so many years of my life to drinking because I felt I didn't know how to "do life" quite right, in comparison to everyone else, regardless of how hard I tried.

What we forget to remember, and what we are rarely told, is that sometimes life just sucks, *and that's okay.* What is *not* okay is believing that because *some things* may suck, that means that *we suck,* too.

Sometimes the hands we're dealt are actually pretty shitty. Sometimes we make bad choices that in turn can make our lives suck even more for a little while. It's the inevitability of being alive: *things will suck. Things will never be perfect.*

Our job is to *make it work anyways.*

It's not only our job – it is our life's work. It's in the lining up of all those days of *"making it work anyways"* that add up to a life well lived, instead of a life well avoided.

Clinging to the social media induced ideal that we aren't allowed to be *beautifully imperfect* is the cornerstone of 21st century addiction. *Suffering* is a human condition – unchangeable and inevitable, and even the Instafamous and curated Facebook *friendquaintances* experience suffering in their lives, every single day. Don't fool yourself into believing anything else.

Here's the truth. Sometimes life does suck. Sometimes other people will do *really sucky things* that will make your life suck in return. Sometimes we're actually the person doing the thing that sucks, and *we* make other people's lives suck as a result.

And what sucks most, is owning the shame that comes with believing that because things in life sometime suck, we do, too.

Trying to *remove the suck* from your life (or trying to drown it in booze, instead) will forever and always only cause more feelings that everything sucks and cause more things to actually suck more for a bit, too. *Putting your life on hold until things stop sucking is the same as saying you're never going to do it.* Embrace the suckiness, because it's as much a part of being human as the air we breathe.

You can take all of this as the most depressing thing you've ever read, or you can take it as an inspiring and freeing way of looking at everything, *starting with everyone and everything you see on social media.*

You can allow yourself to embrace the sucky parts of life instead of hiding from them. You can admit to yourself that there is *nothing wrong with you.* What *is wrong* is our generally shared inability to allow the sucky parts of our life to shine, because I believe that's where we'll find the honest and true connections we're seeking, in others.

> "Human connections are deeply nurtured in the field of a shared story."
> – *Jean Houston*

Let go of comparing your life, however unconsciously, to the lives of strangers and *friendquaintances.* Stop clinging to ideals that in no way serve you. And most of all, find peace and balance with the sucky parts of your life. Don't immerse yourself in them, but also stop pretending they don't exist.

Accept the sucky parts, stop trying to control them, and stop defining yourself by them.

Suck happens.

If we all wore our *challenges* on our sleeves, instead of our accomplishments, what a beautifully supportive and humble world we'd live in.

Find your tribe.

Surround yourself with people who see that *stumbling and trying* is more beautiful and inspiring than perfection ever could be. That's the only place - *in the company of our tribe* - that we can find the true and real connections we are all looking for, and that is we all need.

That's where the real cure is.

Integrity: Waiting For My Cake

MARCH 13, 2018

Today is the eve of my first alcohol free vacation. Ever.

I've likely been on 30 or more vacations, and each one was spent for the most part absolutely oblivious and in a constant cycle of drunk/hungover.

The bartering has already started in my head.

"Maybe I'll just have *one* drink with dinner tomorrow – you know, to celebrate Hubs› birthday and to kick off our vacation. What if I set a boundary to *only drink after 8pm,* and to not let any alcohol into the apartment. Maybe I won't drink for the whole week, then we can *really* let loose on our last night there...»

Maybes, what ifs, and how abouts. I only need to look at my track record to know exactly how those always end up when they involve drinking.

Badly.

Things *always* end badly.

Instead of setting false boundaries that I know I won't keep, I need more of a *"this/ or"* approach. Like negotiating with a child. *Well, you can have one slice now, or if you can wait and if you behave yourself, tomorrow you can eat the entire cake".*

Waking up without a hangover, without the guilt of having given in to the alcohol trap, without undoing all the progress I've made, without an empty wallet and pockets full of regret – *that right there is my cake.*

That's what *really* satisfies my sweet tooth.

I respond much better to praise than punishment. Who doesn't? It's a pretty simple choice: to wake up feeling *accomplished,* or to wake up feeling *abolished.* The options are crystal clear: *drink now, suffer later. Stand strong tonight, celebrate tomorrow.*

So why is it so hard? Why is my brain already trying to convince me that I'll have a much better time on vacation if I waste *it* drinking constantly? Obviously, returning to vacation in the one place *synonymous* with drinking was probably not my brightest move. Every memory I have of vacations in New Orleans revolve around drinking: what we were drinking, where we were drinking, who we were drinking with, and how much I'd had to drink at that point – and how drunk I was by the end of the night. Or least how drunk I was *told* I was by the end of the night.

Well, at least I'm consistent.

Where I'm *not* consistent is in considering my *options*. And there are *always* options. I tend to jump at the first impulse, latching on to what I've always done and somehow expecting different results.

Not only am I consistent, but I'm also very predictable.

It takes awareness to catch myself when I start heading down the same habitual streets that all lead to the same place: *drinking my face off*. Making a fool of myself. Wasting my money and my health. Spending the entire next day chasing another high to somehow mask how awful I feel, only leading to another new low. Missing out on so much because I can't bring myself to feel anything other than absolutely gross.

It comes down to integrity

in-teg-rity

noun

An undivided or unbroken completeness or totality
with nothing wanting.

Nothing wanting. Unbroken completeness.

The absence of need. Completeness. Being okay with things *as they are,* without giving in to the idea that adding alcohol will "somehow improve" what should already be enough, when I know in fact it will do exactly the opposite.

Other synonyms and definitions for *integrity* include: *honesty, being final, goodness, morality, freedom from guilt; principles, wholeness, dignity, and strength.* Each one is an ingredient I need to measure and add to the mix, so I can *enjoy my cake tomorrow:*

Honesty: Stripping away the *false truths* that are going to inevitably be whispering in my ear that maybe just one drink will help me relax or have more fun. I need absolute transparency and honesty with myself about what alcohol *truly* does to me, and how much it takes away.

Being Final: *Decisiveness.* No wishy-washy-sitting-on-the-fence-deliberating bullshit. Like dropping the gavel, I need to affirm my decision that under no circumstances am I going to drink. Final answer? *Final answer.*

Goodness: Appreciating the grace and worthiness within me that deserves to be healthy and happy, free of regret and remorse. Being grateful for the goodness around me, without the illusory lies that adding alcohol could somehow make things better. *Celebrating the goodness within and without,* and looking forward to how good I'll feel eating that cake in the morning.

Morality: Unwaveringly standing by my new standards of behaviour and beliefs about what is and is not acceptable for me any longer. Being upright and decent and no matter what not giving in to my impulses to drink and degrade myself.

Freedom from Guilt: This one is the kicker! Guilt is freaking heavy. Not having to haul that around every day makes everything easier and lighter. This is the icing on the cake, the sugar that I'm craving.

Principles: This is my code. My beliefs. My creed. These are my new standards about what I allow, and no longer allow, in my life. This is knowing the *why* behind why I don't want a drink after all. *This is honouring what my best self deserves.*

Wholeness: Knowing with my *whole heart* that I have everything I need, and that alcohol will not add to, but instead take away from, that wholeness. *And I want to eat that whole damned cake tomorrow, so...*

Dignity: Self-respect. Plain and simple. Keeping it and gaining it. Nurturing it and coming to understand that no glass or bottle of wine can possibly add to my feelings of dignity or self-respect, plus looking forward to my well-deserved sense of success in the morning after retaining my dignity the night before.

Strength: This is that binding ingredient that holds the whole cake together. It's the courage to push through when I'm uncomfortable; to leave a room if I have to, and to remind myself of this list. It's the strength to say "No" right now, because saying "Yes" to feeling great later is worth *so very much more.*

It's time to start packing.

The first thing in my suitcase is going to be the *integrity* to be true to what I know in my heart I desire more than a drink, and I'm going to wear it like my favourite shirt all week.

I'm going to pack a fork, because I want more than just a slice of dessert.

I want to eat the whole damn cake.

Sober In New Orleans: Day 1

MARCH 15, 2018

This is it. This is what I've been waiting for.

Waking up and eating my King Cake. *(If you know anything about New Orleans, King Cake is one of the things you should know.)*

Each day that goes by without alcohol is getting easier, even though my brain likes to try and convince me that *things I'm about to do will be harder than when I've done them in the past because now, I'm doing them sober.*

And it's such a little liar.

Since I booked this trip to New Orleans, I've spent most of my time dreading a lot of the situations I was willingly placing myself in, instead of looking forward to all the *awesome* I'll experience doing them sober. Like not drinking at the airport. Not drinking on the plane. Not stopping for wine on our way to the apartment. Not drinking with dinner. Not drinking even more *(and more, and more)* after dinner. Avoiding certain neighbourhoods. Avoiding that trench that always leads me to getting embarrassingly hammered, because I've always followed the same path *each and every time* we've come here.

It's fair to say that trench has been worn down pretty deep.

We had an easy flight, and my first worries of drinking at the airport were quelled instantly without having to calm myself down like a traumatized child who couldn't have what they wanted.

It was early, maybe 8:30am. We're walking through the concourse at the airport looking for breakfast. Most places are serving a few people, with the exception of course of the massive lineup at Starbucks, the lineup being as iconic as the brand and the coffee itself. Then, we spot a place that is literally packed - *standing room only* - filled to the brim with travellers killing time, but no one was eating.

Hockey Town. A Detroit Red Wing's themed "restaurant" that seemed to have nothing to do with hockey, or food.

I should have taken a picture. There must have been 100 people in there, everyone with this obscene, oversized stein of draught beer with empties piled up on their tables, drinking their faces off at 8:30 in the morning. *That used to be me.*

Because that's what you do when you're allowed to.

That's the magic of airports. Everything tries to run like clockwork in an environment where time doesn't care what you do, and you're free to check your moral compass at the same time you check your bags. When you can't legally serve alcohol until 11am at most places (in Canada, anyway) the airport doesn't care, *it's 5:00 somewhere.* And those airport drinks at 8:30 am just seem to *hit differently.*

I was afraid of this, leading up to the trip. Seeing everyone so "relaxed" and "having fun" while they killed more than time waiting for their flights, and wishing I were one of them.

Because that's what I've always done.

I'm coming to learn that just because it's what I've always done, that doesn't mean it's what I always have to do.

It's like I've always chosen Door #1 each and every time, and kept winning a damned toaster oven, when meanwhile a shiny brand-new car has always been waiting for me behind Door #2.

I had never boarded a plane in the past with anything less than 4 or 5 drinks in me, regardless of the time of day; usually most of them doubles. Part of the "fun" of flying was the no-holds-barred access to booze at the airport and in the air itself. I was that guy that would order 2 drinks at a time on the plane, and sometimes get Hubs to order 2 as well – *for me, of course* – so I wouldn't have to call the attendant back to top me up.

Seeing it in action from just *barely* on the other side at 39 days sober (40 days, today) turned my stomach instantly. Picturing myself there in *Hockey Town*, bloating myself with beer at 8:30 am made me anxious, claustrophobic and a little bit sick. I must be doing something right with this cognitive dissonance thing, trying to keep my unconscious and conscious minds in balance, because the battle I had been bracing for leading up to the trip simply *didn't happen.*

I just kept walking. I didn't want it, and I didn't envy a single person in that bar, enjoying their liquid breakfast. I was looking forward **more** *to the feeling of not being groggy and irritable on the plane* than what a beer or three would give me for a few fleeting, overpriced minutes.

Sober Me: 1 Alcohol & Lies: 0

As a result of *not drinking* at the airport or on the plane, here's a few things that *didn't happen*:

- **We didn't spend at least $100.** That›s probably what we would have spent between the airport and in the air on alcohol for just 1 flight (at the inflated prices airlines charge, not to mention my level of consumption.)

- **I didn't have to excuse myself and climb over the poor soul in the aisle seat so I could relieve myself 8-10 times during the flight.** You know how 1 drink goes in and 3 come out? I certainly didn›t miss *that* magic trick your bladder plays on you while you're drinking.

- **I wasn't irritable** at how long it would have taken for service, or refills, at the bar in the airport. I didn't have the thoughts that *"this place is so understaffed"* or *"as if there's only 1 bartender working"* or *"I may as well just order 2 because it's going to take them so long to bring me a refill."*

- **I wasn't irritable** at how long it was taking the *airline attendants* to start the beverage service when we were in flight. It›s usually 20 minutes or so before they start. When you›re needing a drink, that can feel like hours.

- **I wasn't irritable** at how long it was taking them to return with more drinks after I slammed back the two I would have started with and finished, before they even made it to the back of the plane.

- **I didn't have to buffer the shame** that comes with drinking 4 beers or (airplane-sized) bottles of wine at 9 am, thinking *"Ughhh this airline attendant must think I really have a problem..."*

- **I didn't have to buffer the next wave of shame** that arrives after the earlier worry of what the airline attendant must think of me, because it would always lead to me thinking *"Ughhhh what is wrong with me, I have such a problem..."*

- **I didn't have to ask the taxi driver to pull over somewhere** so I could relieve myself, *again,* on our way to the apartment after the flight, after likely having gone 3-4 times at baggage claim, too. *Seriously, this has happened before.* I›ve had to beg a taxi driver to just pull over *anywhere* because I couldn›t hold it any longer because I was carrying an entire winery inside my bladder.

- **I didn't feel like I needed to have a nap to be remotely tolerable** once we reached our apartment, from that increasing sleepiness that arrives with gusto once we've landed and the flow of drinks comes to an end, until...

- **I didn't have to run to the closest CVS to buy** 4 x 1.5 L bottles of whatever wine was closest to the checkout.

I think you get the idea.

The list of awful, uncomfortable, expensive, and awkward, soul-sucking moments that *didn't happen* are enough to prove, again, to myself that getting rid of alcohol, even while travelling, is the best choice I've made.

Without feeding you a *"this is what I did today at school"* diary of the rest of our day, in short we had an absolutely amazing dinner at our favourite restaurant (*Lüke*, on St. Charles) and I opted for a virgin Bloody Mary to sip on while we slurped back 4 dozen oysters. We had an early night, because waking at 3am to catch your flight lends to a really freaking long day, and I had an *amazing sleep.*

I woke up to the biggest, figurate cake this morning. I didn't once give in to the non-stop brainwashing propaganda *begging me to drink yesterday.*

And I didn't even want to.

I didn't trade my great big King Cake this morning for a crappy little slice yesterday.

Plus, I woke up *happy.*

Time for Day 2 and discovering the *NEW* New Orleans.

Sober In New Orleans: Day 2

MARCH 16, 2018

One of my favourite songs is by Louis Armstrong:
Do You Know What It Means, To Miss New Orleans?

"Do you know what it means to miss New Orleans
When that's where you left your heart
And there's one thing more, I miss the one I care for
More than I miss New Orleans"

Every other time I've been here, which is at least a dozen times, now, I would start to miss this city before I even left. The feelings of stripping away my inhibitions in exchange for absolute freedom to be whoever I wanted to be and of the inspiration that would fill me to overflowing, just like the drinks all the way down Bourbon Street.

I always felt like *I had found myself again.* Like I had been missing myself, as if a part of me always stayed behind here, when I climbed nauseously, hungover and with black gaping holes where memories should be, onto the plane to head home. But I was always what *I thought* was satisfied, my inner gremlin well fed and wet.

It was an all day, every day, post-midnight debacle where he'd burst out of his soft and fuzzy facade he tried to hold together all the time back home.

He always had room to stretch his claws in New Orleans.

You see, travelling in general was always an opportunity to allow myself to "let loose" and lose my inhibitions. To give in to the daily, non-stop desire to *drink, drink, drink* as much as I could possibly drink. Travelling was an easy way to excuse my behaviour, because well, *I was on vacation.* It's no wonder I was so terrified of coming here this time. I wasn't able to pack my excuses.

I left all the lies I would enable myself with while here back on a closet shelf in Canada.

But no worry, there's no lack of encouragement to drink, drink, drink, as much as I could possibly drink, quite literally every 3 feet – and sometimes even less than that. From chalkboard street signs to 3-for-1 *"Big Ass Beers"* and Happy Hour Specials that are available 23 hours a day, you're in luck if you're looking for a destination that is eager to serve up ridiculously affordable entitlement alongside your Sazerac or French 75. Oh, it doesn't stop there. I can't forget to mention the walking billboards. I lost count of teenagers and adults alike wearing shirts that read *"Hooray For Rosé"* and *"Irish I Were Drinking"* (it's St. Patrick's Day tomorrow).

In New Orleans, there are more references to alcohol and overconsumption than there are not.

From being offered mimosa's, beer, and Bloody Mary's with breakfast to beginning to notice how the wine list is always placed on top of the food menu by the waiter, it's becoming more and more obvious how priorities stack up around here (and to be honest, everywhere.)

Luckily, I'm aware. For a change.

My favourite street sign yesterday, of the likely 200 I noticed, and probably 20,000 I passed, read:

Education is Important *but* **Daiquiris is Importanter.**
Well, that about sums it all up right there.
Thanks, Gazebo Café Nola.

And how very thankful I am for the education I did pack on this trip. The readings and magical voodoo of Annie Grace's *This Naked Mind* and the *Alcohol Experiment,* Brené Brown's *Daring Greatly*, and Catherine Gray's *The Unexpected Joy of Being Sober*, which I am currently reading daily while here, among others.

Packing those in my arsenal before arriving here is proving more *"importanter"* than the corkscrew (and backup corkscrew, just in case) that I would once upon a time never leave home without. Corkscrews *and* my bottomless bag of excuses I'd pull from to enable my rapid descent into the seedy, intoxicating underbelly of New Orleans.

Yesterday was incredible and exhausting. I'm not sure why I was so tired. I was brimming with coffee, fresh air, sunshine, and sobriety. We strolled, we tanned, we ate (and ate, and ate) and I made awful footwear choices.

Nice change from the awful choices I used to make while here.

At least these blisters will heal.

I think the exhaustion was from being overwhelmed, in a really good way, of taking it all in. By which I mean, really, for once, *taking it all in*. Awareness is priceless, but boy can it be draining. I'm still in the infancy of being alcohol free. My legs are still wobbly, and my mind hasn't quite made it across the tight rope yet.

Falling would be easy.

And it's such a far way down, with no guarantee of a safety net.

Everything I see, everything I feel, everything I think is being run through my internal Google Translator: *"Okay, what does this really mean? What's the actual internal dialogue I'm having below the surface?"*

I'm stopping to be *aware* of every urge, every habit, every patten, trying to understand and reroute my thinking and understand *the why* behind a wave of *"a drink would be great right now"* or when fleeting moments of unexplainable irritability wash over me, telling myself that I'm simply *not going to have a drink* isn't quite enough just yet. I have to explain to myself, again and again *why* I'm not having a drink right now. It's a constant, ongoing battle of deflecting triggers. I picture myself like Neo in *The Matrix*, twisting and turning, writhing my brain and my body to avoid a nonstop attack of bullets, loaded with liquor and all aimed right at me.

And that takes energy. I'm not going to lie: *it's exhausting*, especially in a place that is so very saturated with triggers. Thinking takes energy. Making decisions takes energy. Understanding doesn't always come free with purchase. It's an add-on.

And it takes as much energy as running a country mile.

Which brings me back to my awful footwear choices yesterday.

I won't go into depth on how packing (and wearing) new shoes when you're headed to a city where you walk everywhere all day every day is a dumb idea. But as I was hobbling through the French Quarter, during which I'm certain I looked drunk from how I was walking (the irony wasn't lost on me) I thought about how my years of out-of-control drinking was just like wearing really bad, uncomfortable shoes.

I know. *Me and my damn analogies, right?*

Anyways. Drinking for me was exactly like waking up every day and putting on the same pair of painful shoes. They didn't fit, and I'd try to squeeze myself in them like Cinderella's evil stepsisters, dying to win the Prince when all I'd ever win, *over and over again*, was embarrassment, anger and disappointment. But even though I knew the shoe would never fit, I'd try it on every day, and it would only bring me pain.

Alcohol was that stupid glass slipper.

Promises of paradise, of riches, and of happily ever after – everything I always wanted, but would never get so long as I kept trying to walk in shoes that were never intended for me. It wasn't until I stopped trying on that glass slipper could I finally walk barefoot to my own freedom, where I could make and create my own paradise.

Then go shoe shopping.

So today is another day – our third one in New Orleans, and my 41st day spent sober. I have some wicked tan lines from my sunglasses, but for once I wasn't hiding behind them to disguise my hangover and bloodshot eyes. I have some blisters and my feet are barking, but it's not from trying to fit into shoes that could never give me what they promised and which I clearly paid too much for. I may be a little tired, but it's not from depleting my body and spirit of the last bits of life left in me on a bender, or from fighting with my gremlins since I landed in New Orleans.

My awareness shield is strong today. Time to caffeinate and find some new shoes.

Just no glass slippers.

Sober In New Orleans: Day 3

MARCH 17, 2018

**Yesterday was weird, awesome, exhausting,
inspiring, exhilarating and eye-opening.**

It's nice to be able to remember the events of last night and yesterday, instead of trying to piece it all together between forgotten "WTF have I done?" text messages, questionable social media posts and random photos in my phone's camera roll of strangers and places I don't remember hanging out with or going to, or strange objects laying around the apartment of which I have no recollection of where they came from, plus the never even fascination of *"how did I not actually lose my keys, my wallets, or my phone last night?"*

It's also nice to be able to say I had a sweeping range of emotions throughout the day, instead of just *numbed indifference* as endless and flat as the Canadian prairies.

I had highs and lows as dramatic and epic as the Norwegian Fjords.

It was a bit of a *Treat Yo Self Day*, from our 80-minute morning massages to an indulgent shopping spree at the outlets – and of course a *lot* of eating in between. Truly, the cuisine in New Orleans is reason alone to visit this city. I was in great spirits all day *until* we were about to meet up with some friends across the street at the posh new NOPSI Hotel *"for drinks"* and to watch the ultra-talented and soulful YaDonna West (friend of a friend) sing. And boy, *can she sing.*

A headache arrived, everything was hurting, and waves of vertigo had me spinning like Dorothy on her way to Oz. Somehow, I think my body knew what I was getting myself into, it's little but loud alarm system sounding off as best it knew how.

Yesterday I just thought I was overtired. Today I'm pretty sure it was anxiety.

This was the first time I was putting myself in a social situation – with friends, other than Hubs – where there would be more than a lot of drinking. It's somehow different from watching strangers across a dining room enjoying some wine.

This was an intimate, in-my-face, smell-it-on-their-breath, extended evening of god-only-knows-what-the-hell-is-going-to-happen.

Plus, it was Friday night of St. Patrick's Day weekend in New Orleans.

The perfect storm to fall from grace.

Here's the abridged version of how things went down:

5:30 pm – Hubs and I head over to meet our friends, after I kill a couple superman-strength Advil washed down with kombucha. I was a little cranky because I was feeling fat and gross after trying on clothes at the outlet – great perk of being drunk all the time in the past is that I didn't really care how I felt, so long as I was – for the most part –*clothed*. Sober me really wishes he had stuck with the gym over the last year.

5:45 pm – The lounge is breathtaking. Swanky and sexy. The type of place that begs for the clink of ice cubes and expensive scotch, spotless wineglasses and the swirl of shiraz and overpriced handbags. Funny how just a hotel lobby can make you feel like a drink would complete you. And *fancy*. Lobbies can make you feel fancy. C arrives and her rosé starts flowing. I encourage Hubs to order a drink. He doesn't really want one but gets a French 75. I opt for a Virgin Bloody Mary and the biggest bottle of Perrier they have.

6:00 pm – I'm grateful no one is drinking red wine. Red wine was my thing. I start thinking that I could handle having just one glass. *It's Friday night after all.* I catch myself and have a tiny internal dialogue, miniature Annie Grace stepping up in my mind to ask if I'm willing to trade 30 minutes of "comfort" for hours of riding a dynorphin waterslide into a pool of regret. I decide to head out for a smoke instead of making a splash.

6:30 pm – I come back to see 3 more people have joined us, whom I haven't met, and someone has taken my seat. I shuffle over my virgin Bloody Mary and Perrier, and she immediately strikes up a conversation, *sort of*. She's already slurring her words at 6:10 pm. She has two whiskies on the rocks in front of her, and for some reason is taking turns drinking from each.

7:05 pm – I go out for another smoke to escape the awkward conversation, and to text my BFF in Calgary: *"Best cure for cravings? Talk to really drunk people."*

8:00 pm – I've officially fallen in love with YaDonna, who is singing Sinatra's *"Summer Wind"*. Everyone else is sort of listening, but no one is truly paying attention, other than an elderly, humble looking grandma who is slow dancing with a newborn while the baby's parents are sitting at the bar.

8:30 pm – I'm starving. I've eaten a pack of cigarettes and have made about 10 trips to the restroom, having to pass that sexy bar twice on each trip. I recognize bottles and labels. Of course, everyone sitting around the bar is drinking red wine. *Goddamnit.* I can literally *smell* it. I order a Red Bull. I don't even like Red Bull.

9:00 pm – C is getting really drunk at this point. The waitress has just been topping up her wine glass free-pour, before it's even empty. Chair-thief is still talking, primarily about herself, on repeat, and keeps explaining how she only drinks socially. I'm reminded of how I was her for 20 years. I'm still irritable but no longer annoyed by her. I feel sorry for her, and grateful for my Perrier.

9:30 pm – We've managed to coordinate our plans enough to make a communal decision to head to this apparently random Ramen Pop-Up at a nearby bar I've never heard of. At this point I'd eat a chair, so I'm just happy a decision has been made. Coordinating this, however, is like herding feral cats.

10:00 pm – We arrive at the Ramen Pop-Up, and it's hosted in the seediest, skankiest hole-in-the-wall you can imagine. It's exactly the opposite of where we just came from. The irony of how quickly we descended from high-end-downtown posh hotel lobby with soulful live Jazz to sticky table-top, dark and dingy bar blasting some sort of angry garage band isn't lost on me. As within, so without.

10:05 pm – I'm transported back to my 3-Pitchers-of-Beer lunches I'd have at Sneaky Dee's in Toronto when I was in University, before heading back to class. The ramen ended up being delicious and the crowd around the bar once again gives me as many reasons as there were people for why I most certainly do *not* want a drink. There's yelling, screaming, and some dude is repeatedly punching his fist on a table almost in tears. I think another drunk kicked him in the balls and left. It also smelled *really* weird in there. At least the ramen was good.

11:00 pm – Apparently, now we're heading *back* to the swanky hotel: there's a live DJ, dancing and a rooftop pool party. Chair thief bails and stumbles home. Hopefully. We arrive and I must admit – the view was breathtaking. The music was incredible. I discovered that dancing sober is akin to playing pin-the-tail-on-the-donkey. I was blindly aiming at some sort of rhythm and looking drunk, even though it was just club soda in my glass. At least I blended in. Hubs is fine, C brought him a rosé that he says tastes disgusting. She keeps encouraging me to drink, over and over again, and pouts when I keep declining. Why can't I just explain to her the truth? Clearly, I still packed my shame along for the trip.

11:30 pm – I'm entertained by more than half of the crowd on the roof and start really thinking about what's actually happening. Everyone is standing in small circles, with the exception of the exceptionally drunk, who are dancing like no one is watching, even though everyone can't take their eyes off the spectacle, and no one is really talking to each other, as you honestly really can't over the loud music. But this is what we call *being social:* spending money on an evening that will barely be remembered, while barely talking to each other. We call it a night (thank god) because C is sort of everywhere and I'm terrified the hot mess of a stranger next to me is going to topple off the rooftop in her 8» heels while she's busting a move to apparently a different song than the one that's playing. Her rhythm is as sharp as a ball of dough.

12:00 pm – We're back at our building. C decides we should all go up to the rooftop for a nightcap. I still have Red Bull regretfully racing through me, so I agree. Hubs and I zip to our apartment for a second then head up to the roof. C never arrives. *Shocking.*

I put myself to bed, grateful for the money in my pocket, the ramen in my belly, and only regretting the Red Bull that should be banned from human consumption.

I'm grateful for last night. It was as though 20 different former-me's were summoned so I could watch myself, like Ebenezer Scrooge in *A Christmas Carol.* All the awful "Old Me's" parading before my very eyes making me question every choice of from past.

> *"What's to-day, my fine fellow?" said Scrooge.*
> *"Today!" replied the boy. "Why, Christmas Day."*
> *"It's Christmas Day!" said Scrooge to himself. "I haven't missed it."*

It's 42 days without a drink today – and especially after last night, it's fair to say, "I haven't missed it."

Sober In New Orleans: Day 4

MARCH 18, 2018

**"Everything in this world seems to improve when
you make a robust change to the music."**
– Some dude in my dream, 3.18.18

Well, this has never happened before.

I was laying fast asleep in bed, dreaming of driving recklessly all over the place, when my dream flipped over to some dude pointing to some written words on a blackboard.

He was using a pointing stick to tap out the words on the board: *Everything in this world seems to improve when you make a robust change to the music.*

Click click click.

He tapped out each syllable as he went over the phrase over and over again, as though I was some dense student who couldn't grasp the concept or being reprimanded *for just not getting it*

He repeated it a few times, placing emphasis on *different* words each time, as though it were a lesson I was in class to learn and never forget. *Then I woke up.* I laid there for a second in typical waking *where-the-hell-am-I* transition. I was rocking my head from side to side, my neck stiff from cheap pillows, still repeating the words in my head. Then I stopped at centre, my eyes snapped wide open, inspired and absolutely awake, still mouthing the words from my dream:

Everything in this world seems to improve when you make a robust change to the music.

I grabbed my phone to stick the line in Evernote, so I wouldn't forget it, as if I actually could if I tried. I even wrote down the date, 3.18.18, along with New Orleans, Louisiana beneath it. I attributed it to *"some dude in my dream."* I didn't know exactly what it meant yet or who this mystery teacher was (because I hadn't had *any* coffee yet) but what I *did* know is that it was something I wasn't supposed to – and didn't want – to forget.

I'm writing all of this about 15 minutes after everything above just happened. The slippery way that times handles sleeping and dreams is that it already feels like it happened to someone else 10 years ago, not me, just 15 feet from where I'm sitting right now typing this. I guess that makes it easier to write about, since it feels like I'm telling someone else's story.

The word *robust* is jumping out at me. It's the one word that's sticking out, so I have to call on Miriam-Webster. Here are my favourites of what I found for the meaning of *robust*:

- Sturdy and strong in form, constitution, or construction

- Marked by richness and fullness of flavour

- Strong enough to withstand or overcome challenges or adversity

Everything we do, every moment of the day, creates our personal soundtrack. Some days we create soothing, classical scores, and some days we sound a lot more like the Muppets theme song. In movies and television, the soundtrack creates the tone, mood and the overall *feeling* of what we are experiencing.

Our thoughts create our personal *soundtrack*. Our actions, beliefs, environment, inner dialogue and fears create our *thoughts*.

Do you want to listen to the soundtrack of a horror movie or an inspiring adventure?

If we don't like what we're listening to, we have to change what is creating the music.

You can be having the perfect day, cool Jazz be-bopping you along until BAM! you're in the middle of a situation and your soundtrack starts to sound more like those *impending doom* moments in *Jaws*. It rises up from your belly, *dun dunnn... dun dunnn...dun dun dun dun dun dunnnn*, swirling around and out into the world, changing how you perceive everything.

Something bad is about to happen.

I spent so very long listening to a soundtrack that kept me in a constant state of suspense, tossed between the saddest drama and epic tragedy. The way I was living my life created it, because I kept playing the exact same notes over and over again. *Dun dunnn...dun dunnn...dun dun dun dun dun dunnn.*

Drinking to excess and tearing my life apart from the inside out kept me on repeat, always feeling like Jaws was about to attack.

What I'm learning is that if you don't like the music – *change it*. If you don't like the movie – *leave the theatre*. If you're tired of watching the same old re-runs – *change the channel*. If you're sick of the song – *change the notes you keep playing*.

You have to make a robust change to the music.

Every single experience can be transformed if you choose to transform it.

Change it by adjusting your attitude, switching to a new environment, shifting your perspective or deconstructing your patterns and habits. What is important is that *when you become aware that you don't like what you're experiencing*, or you hate what your soundtrack sounds like, you change it, no matter what it takes.

Seek out and create a soundtrack that soothes your soul.

Last night, Day 4 of our vacation here in New Orleans, Hubs and I had a nice dinner before we intended to take in the Saint Patrick's Day Parade, then meet up with some friends for live jazz at a favourite spot of ours, Fritzel's European Jazz Bar, unfortunately located towards the end of Bourbon Street.

Everything went from calm, cool and collected to slowly unravelling chaos in a matter of seconds. The difference in environment between the restaurant and the debauchery of NOLA's historically famous drinking district was alarming. It was no surprise. We've bumbled along like cattle down the Bourbon Street corral countless times before, corralled and channeled into bars and pubs against our better judgment, but never against our will. Never really seeing we were all being led to slaughter…just not the kind we thought.

Hell, some nights I felt like I was leading the damned Drunk Parade.

Claustrophobia was kicking in and I was getting increasingly irritated by the minute. The sheer volume of screaming, bead-tossing drunks was scraping on my freshly sober nerves.

GET ME THE FUCK OUT.

I didn't like this soundtrack *at all*.

A quick detour and I was exhaling my tension on much more tolerable side streets, my music changing from soul splitting horror flick to a much more tolerable (but still annoying) Von Trapp Family Singers from *The Sound of Music*.

It was better, but the hills were still very much alive with the sound of obnoxious drunk people, of which I was one, not so long ago.

I'm bitterly reminded of how many years I spent wasted, and how many years I spent listening to *(and creating)* a soundtrack that only made me wish I'd go deaf. It took a long time to figure out I had to change the notes I was playing if I was ever going to enjoy what I was hearing.

We arrive at Fritzel's, and I find some harmony between the amazing 3-piece band that's playing Countess Ada de Lachau's *Little Liza Jane* and the tonic water I'm sipping. The music is as much of a tonic as my drink. It washes over me taking with it the remnants of the discord outside that we just escaped.

Our friends never make it. One is still hungover and immobile from last night's escapades.

An overly affectionate, obviously very intoxicated couple comes and sits in front of us (it's worth noting that the seating in Fritzel's is a small step up from sitting on one another's laps. To call it tight quarters is an understatement.) She's eating her beads. She's all over the place and almost knocks my tonic water over about 8 times. I'm losing focus on the incredible live music and become fixated on plotting ways to injure her without actually hurting her or landing myself in prison.

I promise I'm not a bad or remotely violent person, but my patience lately, *especially around crowds of the obnoxiously intoxicated*, has grown to be shorter than Peter Dinklage. Again, the reminder that I was that obnoxiously intoxicated drunk only weeks ago, is not forgotten by me and if anything, the reminder is more clear than ever, reverberating in my ears like a kick drum.

They finally leave, thank god. A pair of drunk frat boys on a St. Paddy's Day tear takes their place. *Bloody hell.* These two are worse than the bead-eater. One of them is hollering and fist-pumping over the band's sweet rendition of Louis Armstrong's *St. James Infirmary* as if he was watching Mayweather vs. McGregor fight it out instead of a soulful musical performance. He yells something that sounds like *"Fuck yaaaaa bass player bug dum loooooo me go yeahhhhhhh."*

He's sweating buckets of pure, cheap, 3-for-1 draught beer.

We have to leave. Hubs agrees.

At this point, I've lost all interest in catching – *or being anywhere near* – the parade. We head over to see YaDonna sing at the Omni Hotel, since she told us the night before she'd be there from 8:30 until late. And this lady can sing the phone book. She covers Adele better than Adele can do Adele.

The moment we step through the doors of the hotel my soundtrack skips from Nine Inch Nails to Norah Jones. The lobby alone is soothing (and clean, for a refreshing change). We find YaDonna and are introduced to her friends, as well as her cousin and Aunt who would be singing with her.

I quickly find out that they're the holy trinity of my soul's soundtrack.

I feel like I've found my family.

No, *seriously.*

I LOVE THESE PEOPLE. They're sober. They're sweet. They're sincere, authentic, soulful, welcoming, pure Southern class and brimming with Grammy-deserved talent. I'm left speechless when she starts her set, and forget entirely about my virgin Mojito when she dedicates a funky, jazzy rendition of *"My Guy"* to Hubs and I.

I have a video of it that I one day I'll share. It was *a moment.*

Finally, my soundtrack found its groove.

Hubs is about to burst, inspired and in love with literally everything.

So am I.

We stay chatting with everyone at the end of the evening, wrapping things up around 11:30pm, making future plans for dinners and for everyone to come visit us one day in Canada. All of our notes play together like one perfect, harmonious chord.

Music to my ears and to my soul.

So much of the evening before arriving at the Omni was spent stuck on a soundtrack that sounded like nails on a chalkboard. So much of my *life* has been spent composing it.

And I don't want to listen to that anymore.

I had to make terrifying, sweeping changes in my life to finally start hearing something that sounds like the beginning of an album I could listen to forever. I've had to start swimming in different waters, where Jaws is no longer welcome. I've had to put the Von Trapp Family Singers to bed, and wish them *so long, farewell, auch wiedersehen, goodbye.*

Everything in this world seems to improve when you make a robust change to the music.

Robust: *Strong enough to withstand or overcome challenges or adversity.*

This is the NEW New Orleans I've been looking for. This is the soundtrack of my soul I've been searching out, only in all the wrong bars and all the wrongs places, surrounded by all the wrong people. Of all the times we've been here, this is the first time we've made real, authentic connections – unobscured by alcohol, with all of us playing in the same, sweet band.

I can't wait to hear what today sounds like.

How I Survived Being Sober In New Orleans

MARCH 20, 2018

I'm all packed up and from the outside it looks as though I'm ready to go home, my *first sober vacation ever* neatly tucked like a feather in my cap.

On the inside, I'm kicking and screaming and wanting to chain myself to the nearest dead weight so I can stay in New Orleans another day. Or week. *Or forever.*

It's day 7 of our trip, and my 45th day sober. Our flight leaves in a few hours. I'm not ready to go home just yet. I feel like a regular still sitting at the bar after last call and lights on, squinting at the reality of everything now that the music has stopped, and the pub is empty.

Everyone has gone home, but I was just getting started.

I have a little confession for you. Leading up to this trip, I was pulling up my big boy pants and trying to be as brave as possible, holding my breath while deep inside absolute terror was stirring inside me at the idea of an alcohol-free week in New Orleans – though I'm pretty sure I led on to that, and it was pretty darn evident if you read between the lines. I was committed to not drinking, and I'm proud to be able to say I did not have a single drop. But the house alcoholic that lives inside me still had his fingers crossed behind his back when I climbed on that plane last week.

Suuuuuuuuure you aren't going to drink. Whatever you say, Shawn.

As much as I said – *and truly meant* – that I was not going to drink on this vacation, old-me was inside heckling, like it was opening night and my first time on stage. I was filled with visions of flying tomatoes being flung at my head while I bombed my performance.

Here's a few things that helped me along:

- **Accountability.** I may as well start with this one, since it›s one of the biggest. No matter what you attempt to do without some kind of *accountability* leaves the emergency exit flown wide open. One eye on

283

the prize and one on the easy way out. Hubs knew my intentions and supported me wholeheartedly leading up to and during the entire trip. My BFF sent me encouraging texts every day and GIFs of cake (see the entry, *Waiting For My Cake*). I made my intentions clear here on the blog and in a few online alcohol-free communities. If I gave in and drank, I wasn't just disappointing and failing myself: I was failing a whole a crowd of people who were rooting for me to kick it out of the ballpark. Pride can be a nasty thing, but it can also be a *really* motivational tool.

- **I Spoiled Myself.** I ate everything. I shopped like it was Black Friday. I indulged in massages and small treats that helped me stay occupied and entertained. In the infancy of sobriety, it's easy to experience feelings of *going without,* no matter how strong your positive, rational, sober self-talk game is *(see my next point).* I can't say I saved any money on this trip by *not* drinking, since I easily spent what I *would* have drank in the past on significantly more enjoyable, hangover-free things that brought me joy. I didn't care if it was a new hat or a hamburger. *they were mine.*

- **I Rehearsed My Lines** Cravings are crafty little things. They're sneaky. They're incredibly good at hide and seek. They're nowhere to be seen, until they pop out of nowhere and scare you shitless. You're bumbling along having the best day ever, on top of your game and crushing the whole sober-on-vacation thing when BAM! a brick wall pops up and you walk smack right into it. *A glass of wine would be awesome right now.* Fuck. Knowing this will happen – *and it will happen* – is half the battle. Knowing *how* you're going to deal with it when it happens, and following through, is the *other* half. I kept a few simple, easy to call on *self-talks* in my back pocket. Not literally, but if writing them down and keeping the list in your wallet, purse or pocket works, then do it. Whatever resonates with you and reminds you of your WHY. *Why you aren't drinking.* Why a drink right now – you know, that *just one drink* that seems like a good idea – is actually a *really* bad idea. My go-to is always *"Do I really want to trade the 30-minute sort-of-high I'll get – and $8.00 I'll spend) – on a drink for the 2 or 3 hours of coming down from it – or worse, dealing with the regret of the six I'll have afterwards? Is the regret and shame of starting back at Day 1 worth a few empty unfulfilling sips? Do I want to feel tired and groggy in 30 minutes, and want a nap?"* I almost always follow that up with *"How well has having that just one drink gone for you in the past, Shawn? Have you ever had just one? Hasn't it always turned into 20, served up with a side of hot mess and hangover?"*

- **Remove The Guess Work.** Back to that vision of being on stage. The days leading up to this trip began to feel like I had signed up for Improv Night with *zero* idea of what the hell I had actually signed up for, and *zero* experience of being on stage. I've actually had nightmares where I'm in this situation. Improv requires you to be quick witted and sure of yourself: two things I have none of this early on in sobriety. *I needed to have a plan.* I needed to rehearse some lines that would work in most situations. I knew in advance what go-to alcohol-free drinks I would order or ask for. Instead of standing at a bar or frantically searching for options on a wine menu, I narrowed it down - *in advance* - to a few things I'd order wherever I went: Perrier or sparkling water, a virgin Bloody Mary, virgin Mojito, or alcohol-free beer. That's it. Those were my options. This saved me the temptation of mulling over drink menus or staring at shelves of sparkling liquor bottles. Simply put – *it was one less decision I had to make on the spot in order to stay sober.* I avoided temptation by knowing and choosing in advance the *only* options I had to choose from.

- **I Kept Moving.** The longer I'm sober, the more I'm realizing I drank as much out of boredom as I did out of habit and addiction. And boredom is this weird little thing. You can be super busy and *still* be bored. The trick is being *stimulated.* Luckily, New Orleans is one of the most stimulating cities on earth. If reading is your thing, pack a whack of books to read each morning that will give your brain something creative to mull over during the day *instead* of wandering to thoughts of drinking. Search out live music you love and look forward to. Talk to sober strangers (*or really drunk ones* – they're pretty good reminders of why you got rid of alcohol in the first place). I didn't allow myself to be bored because in the past, being bored always led to being drunk.

- **Make Plans – And Keep Them.** Drunk Shawn was the best at cancelling plans. I'd make them knowing 200% that I was going to cancel them. I don't even know why. Dinner reservations, visiting with friends, FaceTime chats, meetings with clients, going to shows or weekends away – they all sounded like great ideas until they were made – then the procrastination game would start, and I'd wait until the absolute last minute to bail on every one of them. Or, just not show up and be the asshole who disappeared into thin air. This trip, we made plans and stuck to them. We met some truly amazing people over the last week, and I'm beyond grateful that I kept my word with each of them on dinner plans and beyond. Last night was the best night of the week, and it's because we stuck to our plan of meeting up with some new friends for dinner and drinks. They drank, I didn't, and I loved it. We discovered new areas of town we'd never been to, an incredible restaurant we would never have found, and quite literally, the best-kept-secret rooftop view of the New Orleans skyline that only locals would know about. Plus, they're "our people" who I know we will keep in touch with. None of that would have happened if I had fallen back onto my *"errrrrr...I'm not feeling so well so we can't make it, but maybe next time!"* routine. Meaning I'd just go get drunk somewhere else, without them.

- **Not Working Works.** Maybe you're like me, but really relaxing isn't my strong point. I work on vacation. Well, I used to, anyways. I'd wake up early to go through emails, send out contracts, do some marketing and get a day's worth of work under my belt before the sun even came up. You know what that does? *Keeps me in work mode.* You know what work mode does? *Makes me want to drink.* Leave work where you left it before you left for vacation, because your work drove you to *needing* a vacation in the first place. I promise you it'll be there when you go back. I took the time I used to spend working and channeled that energy into writing, and eating, instead.

- **Run If You Have To.** This is my final point, and is similar to the first one - being accountable. In order to *be accountable to yourself, you need* to give yourself permission to run if you have to. If you're in a bar, or a restaurant, or on a streetcar or the sidewalk and shit just begins to get too real and the cravings or temptations are steering you in the wrong direction - RUN. Go. Change your scenery. Leave the bar. Abandon your friends. Walk out. Walk ANYWHERE. The *only* thing that matters is that you *don't drink.* No matter the implications, no matter who you leave behind, no matter what show you miss the ending of – *leave.* Leave so that you can stay sober. So that you can stay accountable to what you know in your soul you want more than anything. Nothing is more important right now. **Do whatever you have to.**

And that's it. Easy, right? Clear as mud, I know. That's the tiny (read: massive) toolbox I borrowed from over the last 7 days to stay sober in New Orleans. And it worked. It works on vacation, and it'll work at home.

It'll work anywhere, *if you work it.*

> *"To be prepared is half the victory."*
> – Miguel De Cervantes

Learning To Laugh At It All

MARCH 21, 2018

Finally – I'm home from a vacation *that I don't need a vacation from.*

I managed to wrap up so much work – *that I mindfully neglected all week while away* – this morning. I'm left feeling accomplished and sort of unsure of what to do with myself. Since getting rid of alcohol, I'm finding I have so much more time on my hands.

Ugh. It's so sad how much time I used to give to drinking. It's sad because it's true.

I didn't just spend/waste my time drinking, I spent/wasted it *thinking* about drinking, *going to get* the actual wine (and more wine, when I'd inevitably run out), then hours spent wasted wallowing in self-loathing the more drunk I would get. Plus, let's not forget the hours of nursing the hangover the next day until the cycle would start again. It's fair to say I was working 2 full-time jobs: Professional Photographer on one hand, Accredited Alcoholic on the other.

The only problem is I was just the middleman between both, stuck in limbo, passing along what I earned from one of them to pay for the other. It's sad and unfortunate, and it's also laughable.

Hubs and I were chatting at the airport yesterday while we waited for our flight.

I brought up how being able to *laugh at the whole situation* is so important. Nothing good ever comes from self-loathing or regret, no matter how dire things are. You *have* to be able to laugh at that stuff, or it'll weigh you down faster than a tonne of bricks. Admittedly, being faced with the *big stuff* – losing your home, your job, your relationships and more – is anything but laughable.

When you're in the thick of it - knee deep in the quicksand of *What-Is-Wrong-With-Me's,* laughing at your situation seems *impossible.* When all you're armed with are good intentions of escaping the cycle, but you're still shackled to the bottle - laughing is the *last* thing on your mind.

How can you possibly laugh at your situation when you're sinking faster than you can clamber out? Don't you realize how serious this is? I have a disease! I'm trapped! I'm stuck!

I didn't laugh *once* while I was in it. Looking back, I wish I had. *I certainly cried enough to overflow the Grand Canyon.* Learning to laugh at yourself and your situation takes the terrifying seriousness away from it. It creates a lightness that makes everything seem possible.

Laughter pulls the drawstring of your parachute after you've jumped and you're free-falling fast.

Suddenly you aren't falling anymore.

You're flying.

I had built alcohol up to be this gilded demigod – a grandiose and glorious superior being to be worshipped, that provided me my daily bread, sent down from the heavens in a bottle. *I was stuck in the Secret Cult of Addiction.* I wanted out, but everything just felt so very much bigger than me. I had gone from toe-dipping curiosity *(my early days of drinking, 20 years ago)* to fully committed member, locked into the ritual whether I wanted to be or not. At some point, and I'm not 100% sure when this happened, but I had signed on the dotted line and was officially admitted, signing up for a lifetime membership. I clearly didn't read the fine print.

Cults can be sneaky like that.

All that was missing were some black cloaks and naked virgins dancing around a fire.

I gave more power to what I *thought* drinking gave me, than to my own ability to *choose*.

Looking back, I can see how ridiculous my situation was. I felt as though I was locked in a cage – I could see the rolling hills, I could see the blue skies, I could see *freedom* – but I couldn't ever reach them. I felt trapped. I couldn't *not* drink. I had walked into the cage, and it slammed shut once I was inside.

I can see now though that the door never locked behind me.

I could have walked out at any time I wanted, exactly the same way I walked in in the first place.

Sort of.

The thing is – it had been so long since I entered the cage, the path I took was now overgrown with all sorts of thorns and vines, a veritable forest of thatch and brush to machete my way out of *a la Indiana Jones.*

Just like joining some whack-job cult or signing up for online subscriptions: *cancelling is never, ever as easy as signing up. Sometimes trying to cancel your subscription feels like jumping through moving, flaming hoops while wearing a blindfold and shoes made of cement.*

But when you finally get through to the accounting department – it's worth it. When they stop withdrawing your payment every month for something you never got anything out of, you can look back at the heavy-footed-hoop-jumping and laugh.

Remember that time I was on hold for 18 years with <insert your bad commitment here> trying to cancel my subscription? Oh my, what a time that was!

Remember when I joined that crazy cult that one time? What was I thinking!

Remember how I used to spend 120% of my monthly income on wine? How silly!

Remember when I went to rehab, had 3 months without a drink, then had that 8-month bender? That wasn't my smartest move, but oh well! Won't make that slip-up again! (this one is from my very own relapse adventure last year).

And then, *you carry on.* You carry on without the guilt and without the regret. Being able to laugh at your situation unlocks the iron shackles of shame and swings opens the door for you to walk out into wild, limitless freedom, arms wide open with the wind in your hair and at your back.

It's a hell of a lot nicer than sitting in the dark with your sorrows, reliving them in circles.

> "Do not take life too seriously. You will never get out of it alive anyhow."
> – *Elbert Hubbard*

I know I've spent more than my fair share of time hating on myself for things I've done, and things I didn't do. I've eaten regret for breakfast, tallied up my losses for lunch, and dined with all the people I've ever hurt for dinner.

All I've ever gained from eating my mistakes like that is more hunger. There is no satisfaction to be found by breaking bread with your heartache.

Where I've been able to find real satisfaction is being able to laugh at the ridiculousness of some of the situations I've put myself in. I committed myself more fully to an inanimate bottle of wine, over and over again, every day for two decades – than I ever did to pretty much any other relationship, project, or goal.

I basically married an inanimate object. And not just any inanimate object.

A bottle of *rotten juice.*

What was I thinking?

Shakes head and chuckles

Time to laugh, *learn from it,* leave it behind, and walk out of that cage.

Grabs machete and Indiana Jones hat.

> "Leave your front door and your back door open.
> Allow your thoughts to come and go. Just don't serve them tea."
> Shunryu Suzuki

A Recipe For Relapse

MARCH 22, 2018

**Today marks the 1-year anniversary of when I returned from rehab.
I'm supposed to be celebrating 396 days sober today.**

However, I'm celebrating Day 47.

I returned home from rehab optimistic, calm, clean, and *super tanned* – a definite perk of choosing a recovery centre in the Dominican Republic, when you're a helpless drunk white boy in snowy, cold Canada.

I cannot over emphasize how the sun, the sea and the sand can heal your soul.

I was 30 days sober for the first time in 20 years. I could hold a cup of coffee without my hands shaking violently, and I could hold a conversation without my mind wandering to when the other person would shut up so I could go find another drink.

It was, quite literally, *a whole new world*. I was flying through the air like Jasmine and Aladdin on a weak, freshly woven magic carpet made up of thin frayed threads and heading into a landscape of terrifying *firsts*.

The first time coming home from a photo shoot and not stopping at the liquor store.

The first time out for dinner without doubling my bill with booze.

The first time at a family function without the bloody hangover or pre-numbing with a drink or three – usually doubles.

All these firsts rose up on the horizon like terrifying towers armed with snipers wanting to take me out, and I had to learn to navigate my way through as if everything I needed to survive was just on the other side. I had to learn to walk again on my shaky new legs, so that I could someday learn to run.

It's called recovery for a reason, as though I'd somehow survived a head-on collision that shattered me into a thousand pieces. I was both the car crash and the tree it ran into. I was the train wreck, and the tracks it jumped.

The victim *and* the violence.

I had come home carrying a bag of truths I now needed to unpack and deal with *for the first time*. You know, all the *ugly stuff*: the monsters that used to chase me to the liquor store every day, nipping at my heels just to keep me running. So long as I kept feeding them, they would leave me alone. Now that I was sober, I had to find a new way of dealing with them.

It was like I was at a fancy dinner party, and they were the loud-mouthed friend that kept telling all my secrets, spilling my confessions into the gravy boat. Kicking at them under the table to make them shut up wouldn't work anymore. Dinner was over and the table was gone, and there we were sitting together, totally exposed.

I was looking forward to facing all my demons eye to eye as much as I was going for a root canal without anaesthetic.

It was going to hurt like hell, but it had to be done.

While I was away at rehab, writing worked. It was my morning confessional and my evening prayer; I poured myself onto the page as a sort of bloodletting. Writing released the pressure and the poison.

I was far from home and anonymous, able to extract all my rotten parts without anyone really seeing the bloody mess. I was able to stare my demons in the eye and sort them out on the page. Now that I was home, I felt transplanted. It was going to take time for my roots to reach out into new soil.

My strategy was to carry on as though the only thing that had changed was my ability to finally walk a straight line on demand.

That was my first mistake.

I stopped writing. I closed up that chapter of rehab like an old textbook I didn't need anymore, and stowed my pen away forgetting I hadn't yet written the test. It's no big surprise that I failed. Somehow, I had convinced myself that all I had to do was *not drink*. Looking back, I'm pretty sure that was just me being me and avoiding the uncomfortable parts.

I wanted dessert but refused to eat my vegetables.

You know when you're sick and start taking antibiotics, and they tell you to keep taking them even after you start to feel better? That's what recovery is like. It's an ongoing prescription you need to take daily, even when the symptoms have gone away. Just because you don't feel sick anymore doesn't mean it's not still inside you, waiting for just the right conditions to flare up and take you down.

Had I kept writing after I came home from rehab, I'm pretty sure I wouldn't have had *that fatal first drink* just a couple months later.

I started to take my sobriety for granted.

By no longer writing every day, I in turn *stopped taking my medicine.* Writing was how I dealt with the ugly parts, the jumbled bits inside me that would somehow fall out and arrange themselves into sensible sentences, revealing what I was feeling and couldn't otherwise express. It didn't matter how gross and distorted the feeling or how uncomfortable the confession: *there were words for it.*

Some people find their medicine at the gym or through exercise, others through yoga, some through cooking, music, or coffee dates with long lost abandoned friends. It doesn't matter where you find your medicine or what it is – so long as it helps to heal your demons and sets them free.

What matters the most is that you never stop taking it.

You'll never win the lottery if you never buy a ticket. The same logic works with healing. You'll never get, *and stay,* healthy if you don't take your medicine.

A couple months of white knuckling my way through sobriety pass, clinging to my weakening willpower as my demons grew fatter and heavier. I paraded around as though I had this thing in the bag. *Like I was winning.* But the less I wrote, the more those demons grew, needing an outlet. The antibiotics wore off and they started to colonize. The sickness was growing inside me again.

I was hanging on to the belly of airplane at 30,000 feet and was about to fall – but I couldn't and wouldn't admit it. I was airborne, but I wasn't flying the plane.

Hubs and I decided we'd celebrate *what seemed like success* with a bottle of wine. I was 96 days sober, and you know how it goes. I was sure I could handle just one drink. Or maybe two. We'd just see how it goes. The thirsty parts inside cheered me on: *"You've gone this long, sober Shawn, you've proven you can take it or leave it. Go on. You deserve it. Have a drink."*

So, I did.

It seemed like a good idea at the time (aka: *The Alcoholic's Anthem* and the title track of the score to my sobriety's demise).

*Let the record state that it was **not** a good idea.*

That first drink was underwhelming. It didn't deliver the choir of angels I was hoping for. But somehow, at a point I can't even put my finger on today looking back, that first drink opened the floodgates, and I was washed away.

Washed back to the beginning. Back to before rehab, as though everything I had written while there was erased or scribed by someone else. That one drink turned into *8 more months of nonstop drinking*, the scary part being the transition from *just 1 drink to 4 bottles of wine a day* was so subtle I have no clue when I lost control again.

Actually, I do.

I lost control long before that fatal first drink.

I lost control when I started taking my sobriety for granted.

I lost control when I stopped taking my medicine.

> "I only drink a little, but when I do, I turn into another
> person, and that person likes to drink a lot."
> – Unknown

Almost a year to the day that I *first* admitted I needed help and prepared myself for rehab (January 31, 2017 – also, my first day I started writing about my struggles) – I woke up quite certain that I was in hell, and I had died what felt like a miserable, painful death. It was the only explanation for why I felt so awful.

Oh wait.

No, it was just another epic hangover that happened to feel like the sum of every single hangover on earth that morning, squeezed tightly inside my head and overflowing into my heart. For the first time in 328 days, I sat down to write in lieu of what seemed like the impossible feat of simply focusing my bloodshot eyes.

It was the first dose of *medicine* I'd had in nearly a year, like a drop of water had fallen into a dish of oil. It was a small bit of clarity in a sticky situation.

I haven't stopped writing since, now just 47 days into the *absolutely awesome* new normal of *thriving sober*, but well aware of my ballsy (read: stupid) mistakes the first time around. I treated my recovery as though it had bookends, like it was a tidy little collection of things I could check off, held together neatly with a beginning, a middle, and an end.

A sort of To-Do List to undo addiction.

We all know how wrong that is. It's an ongoing, never-ending novel that requires constant editing, proofing, re-writing, and re-reading – and there are many, many sequels to be written. It's a bottomless bottle of medicine that I need my dose of daily, and these writings are my pillbox.

Welcome to my pharmacy.

"You know when you're sick and start taking antibiotics, and they tell you to keep taking them even after you start to feel better?

That's what recovery is like.

It's an ongoing prescription you need to take daily, even when the symptoms have gone away. Just because you don't feel sick anymore doesn't mean it's not still inside you waiting for just the right conditions to flare up and take you down."

– SHAWN VAN DAELE, LIFE IN DETOX

Recovering Out Loud

MARCH 23, 2018

**This afternoon I'm heading out to have some more ink done on my sleeve.
My left arm is a work in-progress, my right arm is finally complete,
including my favourite quotes by the Dalai Lama and Rhonda Byrne.**

I love my tattoos and wear them proudly like the skin they're now a permanent part of. They're no different than a scar that commemorates a time in my life or a place in my past, the quotes reminding me of where I am and who I strive to be.

Some tattoos you can't see, tucked away on lower backs and shoulder blades, beautiful secrets known only to those you're intimately close with.

Recovery is sometimes like that. A painful process with a lovely outcome, quietly hidden from view like a dirty secret only we know about, permanently inked as part of who we are, and where we've come from.

And no one is supposed to know about it.

It's supposed to be a secret, hidden from parents, bosses, friends.

I want to live my recovery out loud, like a tattoo you can't cover up. But like so many in recovery, my shame-game is *strong*. I parade around the keyboard as transparent as glass, but it's like I'm still stuck in the tattoo parlour. I haven't quite left the building just yet to show anyone else. And when I do, I keep covering it up with long sleeves and coats – my own little secret, just for now. The only people who know are the ones who came along for the ride.

I want to shout it from the rooftops, but only loud enough for the birds to hear.

I want to tell my truths, but only quietly like whispered confessions on a Sunday morning or inaudible prayers before bed.

I want to be proud of where I've come from, but I don't want anyone to know where that is.

It's easy to celebrate in the company of everyone at the tattoo shop. We all have something in common, and the *why's* don't need to be explained. The *how-did-*

you-let-yourself-get-like-that's are all too familiar. Our quiet, closed communities – online or in the rooms – offer a space where we can take our jackets off and wear our tattoos without judgement or shame.

A place where there is nothing but appreciation for the beautifully painful process that has now become a part of us; and appreciation for the healing that now needs to happen.

We hide our recovery like it's something to be ashamed of instead of celebrated.

People are more what they hide than what they show.

It's hard to walk into a crowd of death metal fans and start strumming John Lennon on your guitar. No one likes being the odd man out, especially when you aren't sure how to reply to the barrage of *Wow-I-Never-Knews* when you're standing there exposed with your dirty little secret finally on display.

Everyone close to me *(who are a very small but irreplaceable circle)* know about '*my situation*'. They've been along for the ride since the beginning. They're the ones who bit their tongues for decades. The ones who wanted to grab my arm and drag me into the tattoo parlour, so I'd finally just *get on with it already*. They're the ones who could always see what I needed, but were loving enough to allow me to reach that transformative place where I finally saw it for myself.

They're the ones who knew I had to walk in there on my own.

If I had quit smoking (which I still haven't, for the record) – *I'd be raised up onto the shoulders of strangers and crowds.*

If I escaped being held hostage in a prison for 20 years – *there'd be a massive coming-home celebration.*

If I announce that I'm in recovery from an overwhelming addiction to alcohol *crickets.*

Suddenly, I'm *"Shawn-The-Recovering-Alcoholic"*. Shawn, who they never knew *had a problem*. Shawn, who you need to tip-toe around and stop inviting out because, well, *he doesn't drink and that's awkward. Plus, what if he slips? What if he's not fun anymore?*

The way our world sees alcohol makes is incredibly difficult – or maybe not *difficult* but *intimidating* – to recover out loud. Afterall, the number one support network for *imbibing overachievers* is called Alcoholics *Anonymous.*

No one is supposed to know.

I think what this world needs now more than ever are people who aren't afraid to bare their truths like tattoos in the most obvious of places. People whose pride of their resilience in overcoming the *world's deadliest drug* outweigh their fear of the shame labels that come slapped along with it. People who aren't okay with being *anonymous*.

I really want to be one of those people.

I just started an Instagram profile for Life in Detox (@lifeindetox) and it is absolutely *mind-boggling* how many millions upon millions of people are out there in recovery, or wishing they were. **Millions.** How many people are walking around with the ink of their battles below their skin but covered and hidden so no one can see? What if we (me?) approached *recovering out loud* with the understanding that there are probably more people than not who would admire the honesty and braveness of our truth, because maybe it's something they want for themselves, too.

Wow, you got a tattoo? Didn't that hurt? I've always wanted one, but I'm afraid...

How is that any different from

Wow, you got sober? That must've been a hard and painful process! I wish I could drink less or not at all, too...

What if instead of assuming people will see being in recovery from alcohol as something that makes us somehow *less than,* we started to expect people to see it as something to be *admired?*

Luckily, we're led by the brave. The Annie Grace's, Brené Brown's and Catherine Gray's of the world. People unashamed and unapologetic for wearing their ink where everyone can see, cutting down the stigma that has grown so tall and too often only throws shade. People just like us, but who have traded their shame for the absolute freedom that comes with fearlessly *living and owning their truth.*

As long as we keep our tattoos concealed, we'll always be stuck living a half-life. It's like winning the lottery but being unable to spend it, wanting to scream but only being able to squeak. Or wanting to dress yourself in the entire rainbow, but always dressing in blacks and greys.

I'm hoping the kind of raw courage where we allow ourselves to bare our scars without fear of judgement is waiting somewhere along this path for all of us.

I want the *overcoming* to be more important than *what it is we overcame.*

We've gone through a lot of pain for that beautiful ink, and I believe it's something everyone should see.

"Recovery is like a tattoo.

A painful process with a lovely outcome, quietly hidden from view like a dirty secret on we know about, permanently inked as part of who we are, and where we've come from.

Its time wear our recovery like a tattoo that everyone can see."

– SHAWN VAN DAELE, LIFE IN DETOX

PART 5:

Ascension

Eventually, we all rise.

Unbecoming

MARCH 24, 2018

**From an early age, we are trained to always be
working towards "becoming someone".**

To know how to answer the question of *what we want to be when we grow up*. To *become* someone somehow better than we are, with a tidy label to define our choice. I am a teacher. I am a writer. I am a mechanic. I am a mother.

It's probably fair to say that none of us grew up saying *I can't wait to become an alcoholic*. We don't set out to abuse alcohol in the same way we set out to become a farmer or a chemist. There are no textbooks to read that prepare you for *How to Drink Effectively at 11 am* or exams to write that prove your knowledge of *North America's Most Harrowing Hangovers*.

It just happens, and one day you wake up and realize you've become top of your class.

The problem is *it was never a class you wanted to take.*

I remember the slow waking process of coming to realize that *I had never signed up for all of this*. That I had become someone (*something?*) I had never set out to be. That not once did I add *"ability to drink 4 litres of wine before 8pm every day"* to my wish list, but somehow, it happened. It's not like you can just accidentally become a firefighter or unknowingly turn into a nuclear scientist. But you can easily become someone who loses their control over alcohol. If you're here and you're reading this, *you know*. And I'm pretty sure it was never on your short-list of *Who You Want To Be When You Grow Up*, either.

Do you remember who you were before the world told you who you should be?

Maybe the journey isn't so much about *becoming* anything. Maybe it's about *unbecoming* everything that you actually *aren't*, so you can be who you were meant to be in the first place?

The you that your intentions aimed for, but somehow missed.

In our goal-setting society, shaping our life into something we love usually starts with making clear goals: learning new skills, trying new things, stepping outside of our comfort zones. Adding more and more to who we are, like unnecessary accessories to an already beautiful outfit.

What if we turned our idea of what *"becoming"* is inside out, and started peeling away what no longer serves us – *and what we likely didn't consciously sign up for in the first place* – instead of piling more things on top of it? It's like wanting to redecorate your living room, but instead of clearing things out, you just fill it with more and more furniture. Tchotchkes that collect dust, and rolled up rugs that trip you up. It becomes overwhelming, cluttered, and claustrophobic.

Without knowing, *we hoard beliefs of who we are supposed to be* as readily as we collect garbage that overflows our homes.

And that's the stuff that drives you to drink.

You have to remove everything first and get to the bare bones of the room. It has to *unbecome* what it is before it can *become* a space you want to sit in. You need to lay it all out and keep only the pieces you chose for yourself, tossing all the hand-me-downs and things you never asked for, *but took in anyhow,* to the curb.

It's fair to say I am made up of more pieces I never intended to become, than pieces I did.

The first step of *unbecoming* is to start dragging that shit out as you trip over it. And by *shit*, I mean all those thoughts and feelings that stop you and weigh you down. The *I'm-Not-Good-Enoughs* and *What's-My-Problems*. If you aren't feeling good, chances are there's something playing on repeat in your head. It all starts with awareness and stopping to notice what you're *actually thinking about* as that gross feeling trips you up in the first place.

You need to drag those thoughts and false beliefs out like an ugly sofa that the cat scratched to shreds and take a good, close look at it – *is this really what I want?*

Is this where I want to sit?

We need to stop owning that shit. We need to drag it into the light and call it out as the garbage that it is, tossing it in the bin or out the window and onto the lawn like your cheating ex's clothes. *Get rid of it.* Over time, the algorithm that feeds us our thoughts takes note that we're no longer entertaining the self-destruction anymore, and those negative thoughts *eventually with time* go away.

And you'll have taken a small step in *unbecoming.*

It doesn't happen overnight. *Unbecoming takes time.* It's an ongoing unravelling of all the beliefs we've been wound up in, undone with gentle, and sometimes painful, honesty. And as you remove more and more things that you were never meant to carry, you'll have a life that's increasingly more and more abundant.

It's curious math, subtracting from the whole and ending up with more than you started with. Where do you even start to sort out an equation like that?

Back where it all started.

What do you want to be when you grow up?

I'm certain if you asked 1,000 people that question, most people without overthinking it would come up with a loud and resounding *"To be happy".*

That's where everything we actually *want* to become is rooted. When we ask ourselves or others what career path to choose, it almost always starts with *"Well, what would make you happy?"* We all share the unfailing desire to simply *be* happy. No one sets out to intentionally create or invite unhappiness into their life.

And yet, we do, and here we are: sitting in cluttered overstuffed rooms, uncomfortable and wanting to be sitting somewhere, anywhere, else.

What I'm learning is that *happiness happens naturally* when three simple (okay, maybe not simple, but *important)* things fall into harmony:

- What you are thinking

- What you are saying

- What you are doing

When those three notes play together, they make the most beautiful music, and it will almost always sound like what you wanted to *become* when you grew up: *happy.* It's when one or all of those notes aren't in harmony with the others that the music starts to sound more like a piano that just fell from the sky.

First, I had to recognize and *admit* that I was unhappy, which is *the opposite of what I'd hope to become and* acknowledge that I was tired of covering my ears against the ugly music I was creating by drinking to excess. I had to look at the biggest pieces of furniture I kept tripping over and remove them *first* from that overcrowded room I was stuck in.

And I was able to do that by taking an inventory.

What was I thinking? *I want to feel better. I want to feel like I'm in control of my life, instead of being sucked into this pit every day. I want to save some money. I just want to be happy.*

What was I saying? Things like *"I'm fine!"* or *"Today is the last day"* or *"I'm not drinking tomorrow"* and my favourite *"I can stop anytime I want to."* All those things, and a lot of other lies.

What was I doing? Going to the liquor store every day. Procrastinating. Numbing. Avoiding. Over-spending. *Drinking more than ever.*

It was glaringly obvious that I wasn't setting my life up to sound like the most beautiful symphony you've ever heard. All my notes were off, and my orchestra was not only in shambles, but the entire brass section was drunk and the strings players were blacked out in the basement. It's as though there were 3 different people in charge of my life: *one for my thoughts, one for my words and another for my actions.*

I had unknowingly become three people.

- The person I wanted to be

- The person everyone else wanted me to be (or who I thought I was *supposed* to be)

- The person I had become

Shit had to change. I had to *unbecome* the divided mess I was doing a sloppy job of juggling.

Through the slow and ongoing alignment of making sure that what I'm thinking, saying, and doing are in harmony, I am finally beginning to become what I always wanted to be when I grew up.

Happy.

So long as there was that drunken division between my thoughts, words, and actions, I was always going to be unhappy. *There would always be conflict.*

Getting rid of alcohol was the first step in clearing out that over-crowded room I had barricaded myself in. It was also the biggest, ugliest piece of furniture that took up the most space and was also blocking the exit. By removing it, it gave way to finally being able to see all the other areas where things had piled up, giving me room to lay them out and sort through them one by one, keeping what serves me and saying goodbye to what no longer does.

Ideas like what my bank balance should look like, what *I myself* should actually look like (damn you, *Men's Health* magazine), what a productive day should be made of, what my self-worth is actually worth, what defines a career, and most importantly, what *personal happiness* actually looks like. It's only now with the clarity of mind that comes with getting rid of alcohol that I can begin *unbecoming* all those ideals that I never wanted and were never mine to own.

So I can become who I was before I became who I thought I should be.

The longer I'm sober, the less fucks I'm giving – it's the paradox of drinking. We chase a bottle to put a cork in our cares, and all it gives back are even more upsetting and uncomfortable situations like the ones we were trying to avoid.

My "room" is getting a little less cluttered every day. It's not perfect, but I've managed to drag a lot of the big ugly things to the curb, where they belong. I still have a lot of piles of crap to go through, but this room – *my life* – is slowly turning into a space I can breathe in again.

The first trick is being certain that what I'm thinking, saying, and doing are in harmony, and that they are contributing to, or leading towards, happiness.

The second trick is to stop taking in everyone else's furniture.

"Unbecoming takes time.

It's an ongoing unravelling of all the beliefs we've been wound up in, undone with gentle and sometimes painful honesty.

And as you remove more and more things that you were never meant to carry, you'll have a life that's increasingly more and more abundant."

– SHAWN VAN DAELE, LIFE IN DETOX

Mind Full, or Mindful?

MARCH 25, 2018

When I first decided to get rid of alcohol, all I knew was that it had to happen.

No matter what.

My spirit was so soggy and bruised all I wanted was to wrap it in a big, sober bandage and give it time to heal and dry up. I searched for that bandage for a long time – "in the rooms" and in the books, always somewhere outside of myself. *Waiting for someone or something to come along and fix you is absolute torture, and you'll be waiting a very long time. I tried everything from counselling to pills and kept coming back to the same place: stuck, and sinking, and feeling like shit.*

It wasn't until I realized I had to *be my own nurse* that was I finally able to move forward and *into* recovery. Until then, it was as though I was just standing outside the hospital needing and wanting in, but all the doors were locked.

My brain was one big, messy *connect-the-dots* puzzle. My thoughts were all over the place and the dots were so scattered, all I was drawing was a scribbled, confusing mess. I'd grown so tired of chasing dots from one corner of the page to the other, ignoring some and overlooking others, I was terrified of all the new dots that would appear when I did, finally, indeed, one day, eventually, *you know...* stop drinking.

You see, we have this *monkey mind* that swings from limb to limb and tree to tree, all across the forest, back and forth, up and down, day in, day out.

Unsettled and restless, inconstant, confused, indecisive and uncontrollable.

Alcohol does nothing to help calm that already crazy monkey, hopping from thought to thought and never actually getting anywhere.

If anything, drinking only adds more branches to jump to and vines to fall from.

In the early days of sobriety my poor drunken monkey wasn't only crazed and confused but completely overwhelmed.

I drank because I wanted to put the damn monkey to bed.

Drinking was like a sedative I could feed it to slow it's swinging from limb to limb. Drinking became the earplugs I'd wear to drown out the screeching of the jungle inside my head. It was the blindfold I'd put on to stop the dizzying, relentless jumping from tree to tree.

Addiction brought me to a point where all I dreamt of and wanted was *less*.

Less worry, less regret, less shame, less debt, less hangovers, less sadness, less grief, less obsession, less feeling out of control, less confusion, less indifference, and less anger. My mind was *full*. The forest was overgrown, and my poor little monkey was not only exhausted – he was absolutely and utterly *lost*.

The day I left for rehab was the first day I had gone from a multi-decade, 4-bottles-of-wine-a-day habit to complete abstinence. You may as well have stitched my mouth shut and plugged my nose: it felt like my oxygen supply had been cut off. My *monkey mind* went into overdrive and I'm pretty sure he found a stash of speed somewhere up in those trees, because I couldn't keep up or make sense of the chaos that was starting to unfold in the forest.

Do you know what they did when I first arrived at rehab?

They left me absolutely alone. I was given 3 days of detox to *"adjust"* –without therapy, counselling, or advice, while my body did what it does and started to evict the poison from my bloodstream like a squatter that had overstayed their welcome. But what I really needed was immediate help with the poison *in my head*.

There was a full-on revolt happening up there and the monkeys were getting angry

The everyday, wasteful chaos of my addict's mind had turned into the island from *Lord of the Flies* and there was a beast on the prowl and war about to erupt.

> "Maybe there is a beast…maybe it's only us."
> – *William Golding, Lord of the Flies*

Drinking allowed me to numb and drown out my feelings, and now, with nothing left to drink, I had no other choice but to start dealing with them. Before, when I could just slip that monkey mind of mine some sedative, he'd get drowsy and pass out. But now, he was in withdrawal and had grown to King Kong proportions and was screaming in my face, beating his chest, and terrifying me.

Rehab was okay, but I can't say they really gave us any tools to help deal with the mental anguish or overgrown jungle of tangled thoughts; in hindsight, it wasn't the facility I had chosen, but the sun, sea, and sand that helped me find the path I *needed*. It was from this frustration and desperation to tame that now *very angry gorilla* in my head that I sought out alternatives to the AA conveyor belt they stuck us on. And it was by doing so that I stumbled across Thich Nhat Hanh and *mindfulness*. After reading just the first few pages of Thay's *Being Peace* it was as though the King Kong in my mind finally came down from the Empire State Building, raised an eyebrow and pulled up a seat right next to me.

I won't go at length to explain what mindfulness is, or how to introduce it into your life as the internet is saturated with this already and it's sprinkled throughout this entire book, between the lines. But in a nutshell, mindfulness is a mental state achieved by *focusing your awareness on the present moment*, while calmly acknowledging and accepting your feelings, thoughts, and bodily sensations.

In other words, telling your monkey mind to slow the hell down and pick a damn tree already.

This was foreign to me. Whenever I felt or thought anything remotely uncomfortable, my unconscious and automatic reaction was to *always just drink those feelings away* and lock them up in the liquor cabinet. Now, I had no other option than to deal with and acknowledge them as I didn't have any other choice.

By removing all the liquor from the cabinet, all those ugly feelings I had stashed away there came spilling out all over the floor.

All the ugly feelings were now louder than ever. You know – all the ones I used to drink to shut up. Well, now they were the equivalent of a room full of screaming newborns and I had no experience with comforting babies, and they had no language available to be able to explain to me what was wrong. I had to sit with each one and soothe it as best I could, instead of slamming the door shut and walking away like old Shawn always would, covering his ears and muttering "*blah blah blah I can't hear you*" under his breath.

Instead of pushing the discomfort away as I always had, denying that the ugly parts were as much a part of me as anything, I now had to learn how to introduce myself to them. And there they all were, waiting in line, still wet and dripping from all the years I kept them drenched and drowned in wine.

Hello fear, anxiety, and insecurity. How are you today?

My slowly waking awareness and acceptance that I was made up of all kinds of different parts and emotions – *some equally as gorgeous as others were offensive* – allowed me to start to calm them just by *sitting* with them.

Just like a screaming newborn can be comforted by their mother holding them, all the feels I was feeling began to settle the more I just held their hand.

310

Mindfulness is the mother that cares for your feelings. She may not at first understand why her baby is crying but when she takes him in her arms and accepts him, screaming, crying, and absolutely *as-is*, eventually, *they calm down.* And, once they're calm, you can begin to look deeper and begin to discover the cause of their crying.

I had to learn how to be a mother to myself and my emotions with superhero hearing, so I could listen for when my feelings started to stir. I had to learn how to *stop telling them to be quiet*, and how to stop closing the door and just walking away. I had to learn how to embrace them and allow them to just *let it all out* without expecting them to change.

I had to accept my feelings as *a part of me*, no different from how a child is a part of his mother, no different than them being an extension of myself, that by wishing them away would leave me incomplete.

Wishing that certain feelings would just go away is no different than wishing someone would come along and take away one of your legs.

I've spent a good majority of my life reacting and avoiding – two super-skills that come free with purchase when you flash your frequent drinker card. Problem is, when I wasn't avoiding things altogether, I was reacting really poorly to them.

I began to learn that my feelings reacted in relation to my reactions to them. Through the slow and gentle transformation that came through 1) sobriety and 2) mindfulness, I was able to start *mindfully* reacting to my feelings, shifting my condition from being mind *full* to simply *mindful.*

I stopped blaming, and started owning.

I stopped projecting, and starting reflecting.

I stopped avoiding, and started engaging.

I stopped pushing and started embracing.

I stopped controlling, and started observing.

Then, I began to watch that monkey mind of mine start to slow down. King Kong had finally climbed down from the building and my sweet little monkey was happily hanging out, content in just *being,* and no longer swinging from vine to vine chasing something impossible to catch. This was the banana he was always searching for.

What I learned in this newfound space between being mind *full* and *mindful* is that the magic – *and my power* – lies in releasing the ingrained impulse to *control everything.* I had to stop *trying to control* my feelings, by trying to make them go away, or to wish they would change. Afterall, it was that lack of control in the first place that drove me to drink, and all it returned was – *you guessed it* – even more feelings of being out of control.

I had to learn to stop *reacting* to my feelings (feelings that were freshly bubbling to the surface now that I was sober enough to allow them to) and to accept them simply as parts of myself, no different than how clouds are just part of the sky.

And, just like clouds, *all feelings pass.*

> "Fancy thinking the Beast was something you could hunt and kill!
> You knew, didn't you? I'm part of you? Close, close, close!
> I'm the reason why it's no go? Why things are what they are?"
> – *William Golding, Lord of the Flies*

When I was mind *full*, my monkey was constantly swinging from the past to the future, always looking for the next tree to jump to and leaving a hot mess in his path. All the vines were in knots, and everything was tangled. He was always looking ahead to the next tree, or at the trees he left behind.

He was never just okay being in the tree he was in.

When I began practicing being *mindful* on the other hand, that little monkey started to learn how to simply be okay where he is, sober and satisfied, content in his canopy. Happy to simply be *present*, without a drink in his hand and a vine in the other, flying from limb to limb avoiding the feelings that drove me to the bottom of endless bottles.

I'm still connecting dots, *but the lines are getting straighter.* The picture is growing clearer, and the pages full of scribbled messy chaos have been turned.

The jungle in my head is growing quieter every day now that I'm shifting from mind *full* to *mindful.*

It's amazing what a little space can do.

Dear You, Me, And All of Us

"Everything you need to accomplish your goals is in you already"

I can't do justice to explain how next to simply *not drinking,* the encouragement of everyone in my sobriety circuits have helped me get to this point of sober success.

I'd like to pay it forward a little.

Because a little encouragement can go a really, really, *really* long way.

Sometimes, the words of others behave like fallen seeds. You don't realize they've rooted until they start to grow. And today, *I'd like to plant a little garden.*

Dear You, Me, and All of Us:

Never forget that you are made up of stars. The same stars that manage to grow brighter while everything around them dims – you are made of the same stuff that fuels their flame. You have inside you the same brightness and ability to shine as boldly as any other in the endless, relentless, ever-changing sky.

You don't have to blaze through the night collecting the wishes of witnesses lucky enough to behold you. *All you need to do is keep granting your own.*

And there will be times when you flicker and question yourself, swallowed up in the seeming anonymity of night. Never forget that *you are not nameless;* someone has followed you through their own darkness and it was your light that led them home.

There will be days you feel common and forget where you came from, as if you're just another pale pinpoint next to countless others shining brighter than you. Never forget you were born of the same breathtaking burst that placed us all together, all equal, into the same dark sky with the beautiful intent that we all *glow together.*

And as you continue to glow, you will *grow*. Like trees that bend and curve to their own unique shape, allow the wind to form you. Troubles will blow through your branches and try to break you, but do not buckle. Never forget your roots reach deeper than you know. When storms erupt and howl through your limbs, remember it's their rain you'll be drinking tomorrow.

At times you will lose yourself in the shadow of bigger and bolder trees, but *keep growing*. Every taller tree is a seedling that kept reaching for the sun; a sun that nourishes without judgement regardless of what shape of tree you've become.

Your leaves deserve her light as much as any other in the woods.

Some days you will rage with the strength of the sea, and some days you'll flow surely downstream. Never forget you are both the endless ocean and the impermanent wave. Your mysterious and marvellous unexplored depths are magical and matchless – *discover them*. Dive deep with curious courage but allow yourself to simply drift on the surface at times, too.

And though you have within yourself the power to burn as bright as you'd like, be gentle so you don't burn out too soon. Find what it is that fuels your flame and with temperance learn how to nurture that as well. When what inspires you runs out, so will your fire. Care for what sparks your passion with perennial gratitude.

Never forget that your truth needs to breathe. Set it free from its cage and let it soar over your turbulent seas, let it follow and fly by the light of the stars and build a home in your unyielding branches. Allow your truth to warm itself by your fevered flames when the sun slips low, and nighttime nears.

In those timid moments of indecision and uncertainty, always remember that everything you require is already within you. You are made of the same matter as everlasting stars, witness to the immutable cycle of trial and triumph, and shining more brightly for it.

With much love & gratitude, Shawn xo

Shipwrecks & Glow Sticks

MARCH 27, 2018

I think the hardest part of recovery (other than simply not drinking, surfing the urges, learning to be a functioning, productive human being again, eating everything in sight and undoing 2 decades of damage among other things) is coming to terms with all my wasted years.

Wasted, quite literally.

The past is not usually a place I like to hang out, mostly because it's so damn dark. In the timeline of my life, everything starts out like this somewhat intentional, organized chaos with erratic bursts of colour, like a Jackson Pollock painting.

You know it's beautiful and everyone agrees, but you aren't entirely sure why.

Then, things start to get a little (lot) fuzzier and dark, more à la Francisco de Goya just without all the blood and gore. Eventually, things just go black – *there are no lights at the bottom of a bottle.*

It may as well have been the ocean floor, filled with curious creatures that can light up on demand, but in the end they're all still blind. *That's what addiction feels like* – being stuck at the bottom of the ocean in absolute darkness with this Pacific-sized pressure holding you down with no hope of ever breaking the surface. You can't breathe, you can't see, and you can't swim away.

Basically, you're a shipwreck with more complicated emotions.

That's the period of my life I have *had* a hard time looking at. I would try and focus to make out the shape of something – *anything* – in the murky abyss I call my memories, and almost always come up disappointed. It was like dredging the ocean floor for treasure and only pulling up garbage.

I knew it had to be cleaned up, but it wasn't what I was hoping for.

I spent a really, *really* long time just clinging to that trash. I refused to throw it back, but I also didn't know how to deal with it, either. And by clinging to it so relentlessly, I brought that darkness along with me wherever I went, *including straight into rehab*. I had basically stalled my healing before it even began by overthinking, expecting, worrying, and doubting. My mind stiffened with rigor mortis and refused to let go. I was clutching onto every failure and all the damage I'd done for 2 decades like it was the last thing I was clinging to when I died.

I was too heavy to escape the depths of my watery hell and knew that in order to float my way to the top I needed to unload all the things that were weighing me down.

Well, that's all fine and good except I didn't know where to start and could barely see to find my way. I was lacking the strength to pull out the heaviest stuff first, so I started dismantling things one little lightweight bit at a time as best I could. And the more I did, the more I dismantled my sunken ship, breaking it into smaller, manageable, less heavy pieces to bring to the surface.

Journaling *really* helped me tackle the bottom-feeders.

First, I tackled my tiny regrets, like *that time I said that thing,* or the *little white lies* that caused no real harm. For some reason they were all still in there, my emotional packrat having stashed them away for me to joyously mull over while lying awake every night at 3 am. These were all the *life goes on* sort of regrets. *The kind that no one remembers but you.* Small but mighty, they still all add up to an incredibly wasteful weight, easily released by admitting they no longer matter and that you have no reason to be carrying them around anymore. It felt like I was a grow man, but still walking around wearing my grade school nap sack. *Even though I had outgrown it, I still carried it everywhere.*

I didn't truly feel the weight of everything I had been carrying until I finally let it all go.

"Oh, what we could be if we stopped carrying the remains of who we were."
– *Tyler Knott Gregson*

I slowly began to feel lighter. I was about a week or so into rehab and had started cognitive behavioural therapy. It felt like once or twice a day I'd climb into a claustrophobia-inducing submarine and sink down to the depths again to shine a little light on everything, illuminating all the dark and dirty parts. Some days, I'd even resurface with something I hadn't seen before or long forgotten.

And almost all days I cried more than Mae Whitman in *Hope Floats*.

It was/*is* an ongoing journey of breaking off small pieces that are manageable, so you can sit with them and turn them over in the hands of your heart.

I began to realize I needed to come apart before I could go back together.

Like a glow stick, the more I cracked, the more I lit up.

It took a really long time before I came to learn that *sometimes you have to break before you shine.*

I started hauling to the surface a lot of the heavier stuff – *failures, betrayal, disappointment, self-loathing, insecurity, fear, financial chaos, my father's passing, broken promises* – and they all had something very ugly and very much in common. They all came down to the heartbreaking epiphany that *I didn't love myself.*

This realization turned my entire recovery on its head (and I'm still in a wobbly sort of headstand most days.) I figured out that the goal wasn't to be sober, or just to simply stop drinking.

The goal became *to love myself so much that I didn't need to drink.*

So basically, I was now sitting with a whole bunch of crap I didn't know how to deal with (feelings and memories) and discovering that in order to pry my fingers loose from clinging to all the ugly stuff, I had to start doing something I had no idea how to do: *start loving myself, as is.*

No longer drinking 4 litres of wine a day, by comparison, *was easy.*

I hated adding up – *and taking responsibility for* – all my wasted years and forfeited opportunities. I hated the rollercoaster of feeling all the new and different kinds of sadness and different, foreign kinds of joy. As awful as it was, feeling *flat* was so much *easier.*

Easier, but not better.

I wish I could give you a shortlist of how I've dealt with all the uglies, but it's honestly been a potpourri mix of *mindfulness, writing, apologies, and most importantly – action.* Merely *thinking* about things only stirs them up and makes the water muddy. I have had to sit with my feelings and accept them for what they are, no matter how painful or gross they feel. I have to look deeply and see what cure they want – *and give it to them* – so that they can finally swim away.

These are the big fish. *The ones that have shacked up in my ship.*

I had to truly come to understand that pain is not a punishment, and pleasure is not a reward.

They are two sides to the only coin we have.

And it's only through *engaged action* have I been able to float slowly but surely back towards the surface. If I uncover a hurt I have caused – *I apologize.* If I have loose ends (and there are still so many) that keep me anchored to the deep, I either cut my losses or tie that shit up. It's only through *actual action* that I've finally been able to start scaring away all those big fish.

I am learning that coming to love myself is a long and beautifully complicated process of acceptance, surrender, holding and releasing – and above all, *forgiving.* Forgiving myself for all the irretrievable time now long gone under the bridge, forgiving myself for all the bridges I have burnt, and forgiving myself for not doing my best at times, and *my worst* at others. It's an ongoing process of untying myself from all the anchors that have kept me on the muddy ocean floor.

Forgive yourself for not knowing what you didn't know before you learned it.

It's been through the painful process of breaking myself down like the little glow stick that I am, have I finally – however slowly – started to shine.

Boiling The Big Bad Wolf

MARCH 28, 2018

I was in the bookstore the other day, hunting down more Brené Brown books to add to my *"Must Read Soon So As To Save My Life"* mini library I've started to build.

And Brené? She's the solid and brave foundation I'm building that library on, held fast together with the mindful mortar of Thich Nhat Hahn and the likes of Jack Canfield and Tara Brach. I eventually found what I was looking for, in the Self-Development section. I love how the genre has outgrown the label of *"Self Help"*, as if each book came with a hidden life preserver inside. *Self-Development*, on the other hand – that's the stuff that you can build on. It may just be semantics, but it sits so much better with me. It leaves me feeling like I'm gathering tools to aide myself in building something better, instead of reaching for anyone or anything to just *pull me out of this mess already.* Sometimes *needing help* sounds dirty.

The insight I'm garnering from all those *Self-Development* wizards is helping me to (slowly) pull it all together into a solid, wonky sort of fortress of awareness that even the *Big Bad Wolf* can't blow down. It's a far cry from the flimsy straw and stick huts I've holed myself up in for so long, like the ones the first two lazy pigs built in the story of *The 3 Little Pigs*.

No wonder they ended up getting eaten.

Alcohol (barrels of wine, in particular) has always been that Big Bad Wolf for me, always waiting for me just outside my door, ready and waiting to blow my house down. And he's come pretty damn close more than once, and I'm sure he would have if I hadn't just been standing there the whole time holding the door wide open, inviting him in.

Instead of devouring me in one fell swoop, he'd just nibble a little of me away every day.

I could have prepared and built a house of brick with enough padlocks to put Fort Knox to shame. But no. It was *easier* to just grab at whatever was close enough and good enough, throw it all together and call it a day. I was more concerned with making sure the Big Bad Wolf had a comfortable seat in my house each night than I was of my own well-being. And every day, he'd creep back in, taking a little more of me with him when he left.

When I'd hear him holler *"Little pig, little pig, let me come in"* I never once replied *"Not by the hair on my chinny chin chin"* but something more along the lines of *"Finally, Mr. Wolf, it's about time! Come in, come in, and bring your bottles of wine!"*

I may as well have just sprinkled salt on myself, sitting there like a pound of bacon waiting to be devoured, still sizzling in the pan.

Meanwhile, just down the street was the sweet wee pig I really *wanted* to be.

Whole, complete, and not picked apart into shreds of himself by the Big Bad Wolf. Secure and safe in his little brick house because *he hadn't been afraid of doing the work.* He knew his survival depended on the walls he built around himself, and he prioritized that above the *immediate gratification* I myself always gave in to.

It took way too long before I started to realize/admit that the wolf was taking more than just pieces of *me* with him every night. He had started stealing *all the things* I held dear. And one by one, my house grew emptier, until he stopped coming by every day – and officially *moved in*, instead.

I had become a hostage to the very guest I had willingly invited into my home.

I lived like that for years – shrinking, insecure, and living with a roommate I never wanted, but thought I couldn't live without. Always jealous of everyone safe and sound in their homes of stone, while mine shuddered and swayed in the barest of breezes.

The Big Bad Wolf had won, and his crap was spread all over my stupid straw house.

In a terrifying moment of courage, I promised myself I was going to kick him out. For years, I sabotaged my dreams of freedom from captivity by the wolf by fixating on all the horrible, scary possibilities, and stalling myself because I was afraid of the pain, and the work, and the discomfort. I finally managed to come to terms that *the pain of what I was about to go through to* escape him was much less than *the pain of nothing ever changing and remaining trapped here forever.*

Eventually, there would be nothing left of me.

After all, it was my apathy in the first place that got me into this hostage situation.

And so, I sucked it up and started doing the hard work. I began laying bricks, one by one. My back hurt. My heart hurt. I wanted to be sick, but I wanted to be safe even more. I wanted to be rid of the wolf once and for all.

It took a long time, and a lot of bricks – *and it's still not complete.* The wolf, of course, lost his shit and started banging on my door all day, every day, once he realized he was no longer welcome. He started staring through my windows and hiding behind trees – he was stalking me wherever I went, leaving me notes to remind me of *all those good times we shared.*

He never bothered to remind me of how much he had stolen and the mess he left behind. Plus, wolves aren't known for smelling the best – he left a scent behind that lingers. And lingers.

You already know how the story ends. The Big Bad Wolf tries to sneak in through the chimney and lands straight in the cauldron of hot water left waiting for him, *a fitting end considering all the hot water he used to get me in.*

All those *self-development* books, all the gross, uncomfortable days of transition and withdrawal, all the people I've met on this journey of sobriety – you know, the ones who have successfully managed to kick that wolf out once and for all – *they're my bricks.* My burning desire to never be held hostage like that again, or to be consumed bit by bit, day by day – that's what stokes the fire and keeps the cauldron boiling.

For a welcome change, I'm prepared and ready to catch him when he tries to sneak back in.

And he will.

At some point every day, I see him.

There are always more Big Bad Wolves.

But for now, I'm happy to be holed up in my little brick house, built by doing the *hard work* and lifting the heavy stuff for a change. When the wolf comes around and *he huffs and he puffs,* the only thing coming down are the blinds on my windows, because I'm *really* tired of looking at his face.

Learn To Exhale

MARCH 30, 2018

Few television shows have rocked me to my very core like *This Is Us.*

It was time for Season 2 to come to a close because I was well beyond ready for a reprieve from my weekly weeping fits. While I was still drinking 4 litres of wine a day, my *what-should-be-passing-tears* turned into torrential *Niagara Falls-esque* sobbing for hours, forgetting entirely that I was even *watching* a TV show.

My drunken tears would start flowing and I'd get washed away with my tsunami-strength sobs each week, ending up beached on a desert island of my deepest regrets every time. *I was a very, very sad drunk.*

The storyline of the episode never mattered. There would always be tears.

Lots of them.

There should really be a disclaimer at the beginning of that show, like when they say *"contains violence, coarse language and adult themes"* – a little *"don't ever watch this when you're drunk unless you want to jump down the rabbit hole of your already unbalanced emotions"* could be useful. Not like I would've listened.

I loved the raw pain of it all.

"This Is Us" is like a gateway drug. It looks like an innocent drama on the surface, but in truth it's a door to the *Narnia of Emotions,* a dangerous land where everyone is ugly crying and tissues are required and as abundant as oxygen. It's bad (good?) enough sober. Watching it drunk, though? That's like unwrapping the *Golden Ticket* and getting a private jet to every painful memory you've ever hoarded in your boarded up, dusty little heart.

The last thing a drunk person needs is more drama, but I chugged this show like cheap wine each week because it *allowed* me to wallow and feel all the feels. I was buying it *in bulk.*

It gave me permission to be broken and scared and sad and still clinging to once-upon-a-time's and never-to-be-fulfilled-happily-ever-afters. It gave me the much-needed reminder that despite everything that's left behind, I am still alive, and time relentlessly keeps moving on.

This Is Us was never just about the Pearsons. It was always about you and me, too. The cumulative, *we-are-all-in-this-together* form of "us". **And don't worry, my blog and this book are *not* turning into the TV Guide or Entertainment Weekly.** All of this is just so I can get to that *one scene* that heart-wrenchingly kicked me in my core and knocked all the wind out of me once and for all.

I wasn't prepared for my soul-strings to be pulled so strongly during Kate & Toby's wedding reception scene. (*Spoiler alert). You know – the one where Kevin calls on his family, after years of holding their breath after Jack's death, to finally just *exhale*.

To let it all out.

"If you don't allow yourself to grieve dad's death, it will be like taking a giant breath in and just holding it there for the rest of your life." He then asks each Pearson to take that deep breath and let go. In a beautiful, quiet sequence, we watch them inhale and exhale, one by one.

I died. Like, seriously. Dead. Gone. I couldn't even deal.

> "Grief, I've learned, is really just love. It's all the love you want to give, but cannot. All that unspent love gathers up in the corners of your eyes, the lump in your throat, and in that hollow part of your chest. Grief is just love with no place to go."
> *– Jamie Anderson*

I've talked a lot about how I like to think of this recovery journey as *"getting rid of alcohol"* instead of *"giving it up"*. It's the difference between kicking out an abusive partner and losing the love of your life in an accident. The first brings freedom, the latter brings loss. Despite what I told myself, I downed my *last and final drink ever* and held it down beneath the biggest breath I could muster. I said I was *getting rid of alcohol,* but I wasn't quite ready to let it all go just yet.

And that was me, the Professional Breath Holder.

I held my breath when my dad fell sick. When I quit my well-paying job to become a photographer. When I came out of the closet. When my marriage nearly fell apart. When I chose to go to rehab. When I left for rehab. When I relapsed. When I got sick. When friendships dissolved. When half of my family passed away like dominoes. When I had to walk my sister down the aisle on her wedding day because my dad was rushed to the hospital the evening before. When my dad died 2 weeks later. When I ceremoniously brought that last glass of wine to my lips.

In, in, in – holding it all in like I could keep it there, safe in my lungs, safe from exhaling and being gone forever. Safe from it all escaping like ten thousand butterflies in a windstorm.

That's how the first few weeks of being alcohol-free felt, as though I was holding my breath and just hoping to get through it. That one day, I'd reach a point where I could finally exhale and say that *I've made it* – but I learned that there is no *making it*. There's no destination. It's about the journey *through* the highs and lows, the cravings and withdrawal, the struggles, and the successes. It's in the overcoming big moments of heartbreak and celebrating tiny times of triumph.

It's the thousands of *little in-and-out breaths* that keep you alive, not the terrified and tense deep breath you try and hold in forever.

The longer I continued drinking, the closer to suffocating I became. Wine, somehow, helped me keep all those deep breaths held down. It allowed me to get to a *deep-sea-diver-scuba-guru-level* of holding my breath for so long I was on the verge of drowning.

And just like diving, it took a long, slow exhale to safely, and finally, rise back to the surface where I could breathe normally again.

I started writing this post at 3 am, because my sleep patterns are still as messed up as Lindsay Lohan's career. At around 5 am, an email popped into my inbox announcing James Bay's new single, *"Us"*.

It couldn't be more beautiful or more perfectly timed *(I don't believe in coincidences)*:

> *"Sometimes I'm beaten Sometimes I'm broke 'Cause sometimes this is nothing but smoke. Is there a secret? Is there a code? Can we make it better?*
> *'Cause I'm losing hope*
> *Tell me how to be in this world Tell me how to breathe in and feel no hurt*
> *Tell me how 'cause I believe in something I believe in us"*
> *– James Bay, "Us"*

Tell me how to breathe in and feel no hurt.

Well, James, it hurts the most when the air has nowhere to go. When you're *full*. When you've been holding it all in for so long you're now stretched to the gills and ready to burst.

Breathing in finally stops hurting once you've made room for fresh air.

The Best Parts of Being Sober

MARCH 31, 2018

Yesterday I posted this question on Instagram:

"Finish this sentence...the best part of being sober is..."

It wasn't my intention to write about this today when I posted it on Instagram yesterday. So, it became a bit of an *accidental Instagram experiment.*

I woke up this morning overwhelmed by the number of comments. Comments by incredibly brave people who are in active recovery and are connected by the common threads of discovering and living, finally, the benefits of sobriety.

Their comments have helped me make a connection between *staying sober and having the motivation to do so.*

Here's some of the comments, and feel free to check it on Instagram (@ lifeindetox) and leave your own, too! It's a lengthy list that is worth the read because the *obvious things* we all have in common become impossible to ignore:

- Feeling free – free from the pull of alcohol. Free from its hold on my mind and body. Free from the guilt. Free from the shame. Free!

- I feel free, being my own sober woman

- Actually knowing why people are mad at me the next day LOL

- Feeling – whether it's joy, sadness, pride, anger – feeling the emotions, living through them without using to numb them

- Being present for every minute of my waking day! My kids being super proud of me

- Friends and family being proud of me, waking up every morning without a hangover, and no drunk texting my exes

- Regaining my energy and health. Saving so much money. I remember almost everything!

- The clear-headed confidence

- Not repeating the same mistakes and then being angry with the myself over things I felt I should be in control of, but wasn't

- Freedom

- My renewed level of awareness

- Not seeing if I could top a .7 BAC

- Mental, emotional & physical health!

- Being in control of my emotions. Not feeling like every day was the end of the world and masking it with alcohol

- The clarity

- A good night's sleep! Not waking up in the middle of the night with a nasty taste in my mouth, remorse sweeping over about "how much" then hours of anxiety about it all

- Waking up and actually enjoying life. Even the ups and downs, it's nice to be off the hamster wheel

- Life

- Being my authentic self

- Not waking up at 3 am full of regret and disgust with myself

- Never having to wake up worrying about what I said or did. I hated the mornings!

- Clarity

- Living a great life of peace, love, and contentment

- Being honest, clear, and present

- Seeing my babies with the clearest of eyes. I'm a better Mom.

- I am truly living. I am reborn. I am present. I can feel.

- Freedom

- Oh, where to begin. I can look at myself in the mirror and feel good about what I see, not feel ashamed. I've been able to get my life together, start my own business and a project. Be ok without a man and the best part is having my family back in my life. There's definitely more...

- Waking up knowing exactly what happened yesterday, no panic, and feeling clear headed to face the day

- Being in complete control of my choices, actions, and words

- Being proud of myself!

- Having control and feeling healthy

And there's more. But what is there not to love about sobriety.

I mean, *come on*. That's a pretty impressive list of benefits.

They almost all come down to freedom, feeling, clarity, control, and pride.

No one said they were so happy their chances of a stroke had been slashed to a fraction of what it was, or that their outrageously high blood pressure had finally regulated (I could have listed that one, myself). No one said they were thrilled that being sober meant their liver was less fatty or that they're now absorbing vitamins better than they did while drinking. These are obviously massive health benefits – but it's *not* what helps to keep someone sober.

Everyone said that above all their *freedom and reclaimed clarity* were the best parts of sobriety, meaning that their drinking days left them feeling *out of control, imprisoned, and blind.*

I can definitely relate.

By nature, we are very impatient creatures. We drink because we wanted to feel better and numb ourselves *now*. We drink because we wanted to relax/escape reality *now*.

And in sobriety – the benefits we celebrate, and that *motivate* us are equally as immediate, as they should be. They give us the opportunity to start living our lives more fully *right now*. This minute. With each breath.

The primary, priceless benefit of sobriety as proven above is that we get a second chance at *being alive*.

Nelson Mandela when freed from prison after 27 years probably didn't think about how 5 years down the road his freedom would feel that much better. He relished his freedom with each and every step, *grateful for every day he was no longer a prisoner.*

It's easy to get caught up and lose sight of our *why's*, and to start taking for granted the benefits of sobriety when they become less lustrous and new, and start being more every day and ordinary. Like a child with a shiny new toy, the excitement eventually dulls and eventually it becomes *just another toy.*

Without noticing, it stops being that *thrilling thing they always wanted,* and risks being forgotten altogether.

I'll be the first to admit that in sobriety, I'm guilty of listing all my wrongs and all the *horrible awfuls* that drinking brought me to do. When I think of being sober, it's far too easy to associate it with all the things I *don't do anymore*, instead of thinking of sobriety and *all the things I now can.* It's a sort of *this within and that without* sort of situation, where I can focus on what drinking took away from me – or I can think of what *sobriety has given me.*

Our sobriety needs to be treated better than that toy we always wanted and would have done anything to get. It can't ever be lost in the pile of all our other desires or grow dusty and neglected. We need to enjoy it every day and keep it well-oiled, so it continues to work forever.

We need to remember, always, how badly we wanted it before we had it.

And I'll close with one of my favourites from that Instagram list of *The Best Part of Being Sober:*

"I am truly living. I am reborn. I am present. I can feel."

There isn't a drink in the universe that can make me feel any better than that.

Rocks, Pebbles, Sand

APRIL 2, 2018

**I remember my early days in rehab like I imagine someone waking
from a coma remembers their first few days of coming to.**

The details are there but they're fuzzy and filled with a lot of *what-happeneds* and *where-am-I's*. One thing that stands out the most (aside from the sleepless nights, alcohol withdrawal, sweats, loneliness, shaking hands, and wondering what the hell I had gotten myself into) are the emotional, tear-filled early therapy sessions.

Specifically, the day I learned about rocks, pebbles and sand.

I eat analogies for breakfast, so it only makes sense I fell in love with this idea, despite it meaning I had to spill my stones all over the place so I could begin sorting through what I'd been carrying around so long.

I didn't change. My priorities did.

A philosophy professor once stood before his class with a large empty jar. He filled the jar to the top with large rocks and asked his students if the jar was full.

The students said that yes, the jar was indeed full.

He then added small pebbles to the jar and gave the jar a bit of a shake so the pebbles could settle among the larger rocks. Then he asked again, "Is the jar full now?"

The students agreed that the jar was still full.

The professor then poured sand into the jar to fill up any remaining empty space.

The students then agreed that the jar was completely full.

The professor went on to explain that the jar represents *everything that is in one's life*. **The rocks** are equivalent to *the most important things* in your life, such as spending time with your family and maintaining your health. This means that if the pebbles and the sand were lost, *the jar would still be full,* and your life would still have meaning.

The pebbles represent things in your life that matter, *but that you could live without*. The pebbles are certainly things that give your life meaning (such as your job, house, hobbies, and certain friendships), but they are *not critical for you to have a meaningful life*. These things often come and go and are not permanent or essential to your overall well-being.

Finally, **the sand** represents material possessions and the *remaining filler "stuff"* in your life. These could be small things like watching television or running errands. These things don't mean much to your life as a whole and are likely done to *waste time or get small tasks accomplished*.

The lesson here is that if you start by putting sand into the jar, there will be no room for rocks and pebbles. This holds true with the things you *let into* your life. If you spend all your time on the small and insignificant things, you will run out of room for the things that are most important.

It was my job, and critical to my sobriety, to take a long deep look at what I had filled my jar with.

At first glance, all I could see was sand.

When you're deep into drinking and have lost your grip on the bottle and it's now gripping *you*, the priorities in your life start toppling down like *Jenga: Mid-Life Crisis Edition* where the blocks are all wonky and it's impossible to stay balanced. The more big, important pieces you remove, the closer you get to total collapse.

If there were any rocks left in my jar, they were obscured by sand and buried in a stony grave of pebbles.

Alcohol and my obsession with it had become the sand, overflowing my jar, and leaving no room for rocks. You see, sand slips into every crevice and congests the little pockets of air where you can breathe. It overtakes and obscures the big stuff to the point where you start tossing your rocks away just to make room for more sand. If I could paint a picture of my journey up to that point of my addiction, it would look like *Hansel & Gretel* and the trail of white rocks they left behind on their journey through the woods.

I had left a trail of everything important to me behind in favour of filling my jar with more sand.

Of trading the big stuff for the bottled stuff.

> "Action expresses priority."
> – *Gandhi*

Judging from my actions and behaviour in the years/decades leading up to this point of finding myself on a remote island in rehab for alcohol addiction *(like, what? Seriously? This happens to other people, not me)* it was becoming crystal clear how my priorities had changed. I had become Shawn, *Certified Sand Specialist.*

Before I could start making room for any rocks in my jar, I first had to come to admit – and own – the very hard and real truth that *I had chosen alcohol over what I valued most, over and over again.* And that's an uncomfortable thing to own, like trying to squeeze into leather pants two sizes too small (I haven't ever tried this, for the record. Honestly.)

It doesn't look good, it doesn't feel good, and you certainly don't want them hanging in your closet anymore.

I began by making lists and not overthinking it. One for rocks. One for pebbles. And one for sand. Like, *really real lists* – with a paper and a pen and a very open, broken heart. Then I started digging deep to discover where everything in my life landed on those lists. What were my absolute non-negotiables, the things I valued the most and would defend to my last breath?

Essentially, all the rocks I had left behind me on my path to this point in favour of that one big Everest-sized alcoholic mountain of sand.

And I did the same for pebbles – *the stuff that enriches my life but doesn't define it.*

And sand – *the small stuff that is wasteful of my time, health, or relationships.*

The stuff I can happily live without (but had drunkenly fixated on for decades).

The booze, the bad habits, the isolating and procrastinating.

It turned out I had my entire jar filled backwards and inside-out. It was no surprise. It's the nature of alcohol to displace all the good from your life until you find yourself sinking in quicksand.

Sending myself to rehab – or even that fatefully honest day where I *finally* admitted I needed help – was the first step in spilling my jar all over the place so that I could start filling it back up, properly, for a change.

So, I could place my priorities back in order and stop carrying around all the sand that was only weighing me down. *Sobriety had to become one of my big rocks,* and so long as I treated it like a pebble or sand, I would never have a jar that made me happy.

It's easy for me to sit here and say *"this is what I did, and this is how I thrived"* but I'd be feeding you a great big pile of bullshit. It wasn't cut and dry, and let's not forget my *epic eight-month relapse* just a couple of months after returning home from my month-long, turbulent recovery adventure in the Dominican Republic.

It's a process. It's a series of spilling your jar repeatedly until your rocks are always there – *the first ones in and the last ones out*. It's learning to see the sand as it starts to collect again – and trust me, *it collects* and creeps in without you knowing, just like how it ends up all over your car after a day at the beach.

Sand has a way of coming along for the ride, whether it's been invited or not.

The trick is in keeping your jar so full of rocks and polished pebbles that there's less room for all that small stuff.

What I Learned from Not Watching
The Film 'Walk with Me'

APRIL 3, 2018

It's been nearly a year that I've been waiting to see the film *"Walk with Me"*, a mindfulness documentary that takes you into Plum Village, Thich Nhat Hahn's Buddhist monastery in the south of France, narrated by Benedict Cumberbatch (which is reason enough to go see it).

So, you can imagine my excitement when I learned it was *finally* being screened in Waterloo – about an hour and a half from here.

Sobriety Perk #1: *I knew I'd be sober and able to actually drive there for the 5:30 showing. Old Drunk Me would have dismissed it immediately because I'd "normally" be at least 2 bottles of wine in by that time, unable to drive and definitely unwilling to leave the house.*

I ordered my tickets online and looked forward to it with the excitement of a kid at Christmas. Hubs opted out when the time came to leave, since there was some actual "work-work" to be wrapped up, so I decided to go by myself.

Sobriety Perk #2: *Drunk Me would never have gone to see a film on my own, because it was easier to just wait for it on Netflix, where I could cozy up to watch it with a gallon of wine and fall asleep in the chair during the first 3 minutes.*

I set my GPS and off I went, listening to my *"Peaceful Instrumental Movie Scores"* playlist like I was a truck-driving Sober Zen Master. Most of the commute was on backcountry roads, so of course I imagined I was in some ambient music video on my way to absolute enlightenment. I was already in full-on *Mindfulness Mode,* and I hadn't even reached the theatre.

Sobriety Perk #3: *The ability to actually recount everything that happened yesterday. Drunk Me would have been a passenger and obviously not driving – if we ended up going at all – and would have forgotten most of the trip there, except for the multiple washroom breaks I'd have required. Plus, I would have spent most* *of the drive just googling licenced bars within walking distance of the theatre for before, and of course after, the show. How very 'mindful'. Insert eye roll here.*

I arrive. I park. I am at the wrong theatre.

I obviously need more practice at this whole leaving the house and doing stuff thing. Last Friday we made it downtown for my first sober concert, and I left the tickets at home. Sober me is definitely more outgoing, but his memory still sucks.

I walk *(a delightful change from stumbling)* my way back to the truck. I'm seriously impressed with myself, because just 2 months ago this situation would have made me irate. I'd have been cranky, blaming, frustrated, and wanting a drink or six. Despite the calming nature of the film, I would have been heading into it like a raging bull. But instead, I took my time, didn't panic, admired the old architecture of downtown Waterloo, and took some nice deep breaths of Spring.

Sobriety Perk #4: *I am 2 billion percent less reactionary. When things didn't go according to plan, or situations of spontaneity popped up, Drunk Me would either a) pull up my defences à la Jackie Chan or b) turtle and withdraw à la Cowardly Lion. There was no in between. Sober Me is happy to go with the flow, more à la Autumn Leaf on a Babbling Brook.*

It's at this point, a couple city blocks later and closing in on showtime, that I figure out the correct theatre was literally *around the corner* from the one I just came from. In my defence, I'm not from Waterloo. I'm also not particularly adept at directions. I finally arrive, back where I started – the irony not being lost on me – and head in to pick up my tickets. It's a charming theatre that smells like a bottled-up retirement home. There's only one screen, and the box office is also the concession stand – cash only, of which I have none.

Sobriety Perk #5: *Old Drunk Me would have panicked at this point (and likely went on a rant about how ridiculous it is to not accept cards in 2018 of all things, and on and on and on...) because the idea of sitting through a 90-minute film without something to drink – even water – was unheard of. I needed to be always drinking something like a liquid pacifier locked to my lips. Sober Me? Totally happy to find myself a seat, people watch, and appreciate how I just saved myself from buying a $9.00 bottle of water.*

Time passes, and we're 10, 15, 20 minutes past showtime (luckily, I had my phone and Zen Koi game to play...it's oddly therapeutic). People were becoming *mindfully impatient,* until a theatre rep explains there had been a power outage in the projector room, and it would be another 10 or 15 minutes. No big deal, I was oddly content, alone in the theatre staring at a big, blank screen. *I was learning so much already and the film hadn't even started.*

Sobriety Perk #6: *The longer I'm sober, the more patient I'm becoming.*

The classic "One Day at a Time" *mantra applies to literally everything in my life now, not only sobriety. And sometimes it's just one moment at a time, or just one second, but I am shockingly more tolerant of pretty much everything (other than talking politics – ain't nobody got time for that). Drunk Me, in classic addict fashion, demanded immediate gratification.* I didn't want to wait for life, despite me giving life no option but to wait for me for so long. *In recovery, I've learned to happily let life take its time, as it's in those moments of waiting that life is actually happening. Drunk Me was always searching for that* "life" *like it was the prize at the bottom of the Cracker Jack box. It took sobriety for me to notice that the real prize was the enjoyment of all that sugary caramel-coated popcorn on the way down.*

Eventually, another theatre rep appears to explain with sincere remorse that the projector had overheated, and the showing was, indeed, officially cancelled. *"Walk With Me"* would not be watched by me, or any of us. I expected rotten tomatoes to be thrown, or for belligerent boos to erupt. But instead, people applauded him for his efforts (plus, we all felt bad for him because he was obviously terrified of getting up in front of the crowd to announce this). I suppose that's the sort of crowd a documentary about mindfulness and a bunch of Buddhist monks in the South of France attracts.

Peaceful, calm, understanding, and accepting people.

I hate to say it, but if we had been there for a screening of *Jackass: The Movie*, I'm certain the crowd would have gone wild, and not in a celebratory football touchdown sort of way, but more of a, well, *jackass* sort of way.

Mindfulness attracts mindfulness, as jackassery attracts jackassery.

Sobriety Perk #7: *This is where Drunk Me would have escalated. First it would have started with feeling like all the muscles inside me were angry and contracting, my internal body temperature would have flushed my face and I'd immediately source out the nearest open bar and bottle. It's quite possible that Drunk Me would have been secretly pleased, since it would have meant I was that much closer to drinking myself to sleep that night. I would have been angry – just in general. Drunk Me did not like surprises, of any sort, ever. But I was good. I was content. I gathered my things and made my way outside, collecting my complimentary pass for the next show (which I likely won't go to see because of the distance). I wasn't fixated on how the show was cancelled, but instead enjoyed how it was still sunny outside, observing that I was a little bit hungry, and that all in all this Comedy of Errors was pretty entertaining.*

I was so in control of my emotions and my *non*-reaction to everything that had just happened, I felt my inner Buddha stirring with pride (and a little hunger – I'm actually beginning to *notice* when I'm hungry, now.) It was okay. *I was okay.*

The waves of anger and disappointment, frustration and blaming that would have normally turned this molehill into a mountain didn't arrive. And it wasn't waiting for me around the corner, or across the street. *I'd know, because I walked around for quite a while before I finally found my truck (I told you I have navigation issues.)*

It was glaringly obvious that *alcohol was truly the fuel that turned all of my smallest fires into infernos.* It *is* ethanol, after all, so it's no surprise that pouring buckets of it on top of my generally already volatile and fiery emotions would only give the smallest spark more gas to burn.

Alcohol turned all my first world problems into explosive, first world Armageddons.

I climbed back into my truck (found it right where I left it), discovered my new favourite playlist (*Buddha Beach*, on TuneIn Radio), and made the one-and-a-half-hour drive back home as a witness to one of the prettiest sunsets ever. I was as content or more than if I had seen the film I had waited an entire year to apparently, *not see.*

Sometimes, the anticipation of something is better than finally getting it. I would always feel relaxed *immediately* when I was buying the wine – *not necessarily drinking it.* I would feel relief in a restaurant after ordering a bottle – *not when it arrived.* Knowing the prize at the bottom of the Cracker Jack box was waiting for me made all the caramel corn along the way taste that much better.

vor-freude

noun

1. The joyful, intense anticipation that comes from imagining future pleasures

Ya, that's a new word for me, too, and apparently, it's in German. But the feeling is more than familiar, regardless of what language it is. The rush of anticipation is universal. From drinking, to watching (or not watching) the film last night, to looking forward to a vacation 8 months from now – that's the real prize.

That's the popcorn on the way down.

Perhaps I've always just been addicted to having something to look forward to, because that's where *living and being alive* actually takes place: right between the wanting and the getting, in those aching, anxious moments of imagination where simply looking forward to it is enough.

Resurrected & Infected

APRIL 4, 2018

"The past is never where you think you left it."
- Katherine Anne Porter

Oh, how sweet life would be if the past sat still, well-behaved like a service dog for the blind, waiting to be called on until you need their eyes. How easy life could be if the future had patience, instead of always rushing at you with *what-ifs*. How easy recovery could be if all your wrongs untied themselves with each passing sober day.

Wrongs that hang there like double knots in your lifeline, shortening your rope and holding you back like an anchor dropped at sea.

You're still floating, but you're held in one place.

I think I'm pretty good (and getting better) at *simply being present*, bearing witness to the past as it taps on my shoulder and the future as it pours sugar down my imagination's throat. I try to let them arrive and depart like unexpected guests, with no feeling of obligation to either entertain them or serve them tea. Like Shunryu Suzuki said, *"Leave your front door and your back door open. Allow your thoughts to come and go."*

When you're in recovery, you could charge a cover at the door. All your past wrongs line up and camp out overnight just waiting to get in so they can drag their dirt all through your house. All the *drunken deeds* you thought you had buried come parading back to you like *The Walking Dead*, resurrected and infected.

But what happens when you aren't the one with the shovel in hand, digging them up and setting them free. What do you do when the ones you hurt while *soberly challenged* are still hurting? How do you raise the anchor so you can both sail forward, no longer tethered in place, moored by the actions that *Drunk You* did?

I wish I knew.

The best apology is changed behaviour.

I wish that healing was contagious, and that we could spread it like the common cold. That just by being near someone, you could undo their hurt and untie their knots.

That apologies could disinfect the past.

I wish I could pour my sobriety on all the open wounds I've left in my path and help them close without scars. I wish I could properly explain the dark and passive indifference that consumes you when you're sitting there at rock bottom. I wish I could explain how in the unawareness of addiction I couldn't see who I was hurting, while I was spinning wildly and blindly with a knife in my hand.

Maybe it's in the slow untying of those knots in sobriety that your rope grows longer so you can throw it out to others. So, the ones you dragged down with you to that lower, darker, painful new depth can begin to climb back out.

When you make amends, you hand someone a bandage – but you don't get to decide if they choose to use it on the wounds you carved. When you explain that you stumbled when you barely knew how to walk – it's not up to you if they remember your fall, or instead, your struggle.

Sometimes you need to make peace with making peace.

We are all characters in each other's stories, and we hold no control over how we are written into anyone else's. Despite starring in a new role in your own, you may always be a flashback in someone else's, forever repeating the same horror scene until they choose to change the channel.

These are the truths that come with recovery.

When you slowly and finally wake into sobriety from the nightmare of addiction, a time arrives when you need to admit that it wasn't just your own bad dream, but you were the monster under other people's beds, too.

Sobriety cannot be selfish.

You can't stand there and release your regrets like balloons to the sky without noticing who you've left burst and deflated. Just because you've buried *your* demons doesn't mean *others* have put theirs to bed, too.

To bed, where they will eventually wake up.

To bed, where they're just resting.

To bed, where you can still hear them snoring, always reminding you that they're still there.

So far, one of the hardest parts of recovery is realizing that my past is not only *my* past. It's a poorly coloured picture that spills over the lines, my mess marked in ink and impossible to erase. It's the rear-view mirror I try and check only to see how far I've come, but at times I'm called out and forced to stare in the eye all the horrible things I've left behind and can't undo.

> "The past is never where you think you left it."
> – *Katherine Anne Porter*

It's never where you think you left it because it's been scattered across the many pasts and paths of everyone you drove off the road on the highway of your addiction. But how do you try and help others see that a flat tire is no reason to get rid of the whole car?

And even though you're now sailing on the sober open road, sometimes you need to turn around and tend to those you left in ditches. Sometimes you need to try and help people see that just because you lost control once doesn't mean you're a bad driver. And sometimes, that means you need to return to the scene of the crime, as ugly and painful and uncomfortable as it may be.

> "Only the one that hurts you can make you feel better
> Only the one that inflicts the pain can take it away"
> – *Madonna, Erotica*

Part of recovery is coming to accept that there are many things I cannot control – notably the future, the past, and how others have written me into their stories.

I can't control if I'm thought of as an explosive trainwreck or *The Little Engine That Could.*

And I can, and I did, and I am.

I also can't control whether others want to forgive me enough to come along for the ride.

This Time Around

APRIL 6, 2018

The morning after my last drink brought with it both a mammoth-sized hangover, and an impossible-to-ignore, starving sensation of *wanting*.

I had relapsed from my first, short-lived attempt at sobriety, and I was waking (dead for the most part) after an 8-month bender that could put Betty Ford to shame.

The Wanting: *I wanted to never feel that awful again.* I wanted to stop having to beat myself up every morning over my weakness the night before. I wanted to stop once and for all the lying about how I *"wasn't ever going to drink again."* I wanted to be in control of my actions and my decisions, for a change. I wanted *off* the ride that was only making me sick, over, and over – *and over* – again. I wanted all the losses and hurts to stop. I wanted everything to cease being *so hard* because I was always so drunk. I wanted to stop wanting *all of this*.

Every. Damn. Morning.

The Willingness: I had finally reached the decisive tipping point of *wanting freedom* more than I was willing to *deal with the suffering* that came with addiction. I was finally willing to do the hard work (whatever that was because at this point,

I wasn't too sure) – and *change*.

No matter what it involved. No matter how uncomfortable. If I didn't change, I was going to either have a stroke, have an accident, or take my own life – physically or figuratively. I was 8 months into my relapse, and life was again starting to feel like

I was racing full speed ahead towards a busy intersection and not sure if I wanted to slam on the brakes, or just fly headlong into and under the transport trucks in my path.

And yet, every time, I'd hit the brakes just in time.

I'd hit the brakes because somewhere, something inside me, however small, was still conscious and beating hard enough to know that I didn't *really* want to die.

All I *really* wanted, was to *change.*

And the most important ingredient for change is willingness. Change is born from the *very core* of dissatisfaction. Change comes from that place where you *want something more than what you already have or what you are getting.* This also helps to explain why I relapsed so *very* magnificently.

What I always wanted *most* was the *temporary pleasure* that drinking gave me, and I kept ordering it like it was my favourite appetizer before the same meal every night, knowing full-well it was going to poison me and leave me ill just like it always did. The alcohol *always* won when it came to what I wanted more, because there was nothing I wanted *more* than the fastest route to blackout possible.

The Inspiration: *The next most important ingredient for change is inspiration.*

Throughout my drinking career, I was seldom in the company of *the sober.*

Barely anyone in my family drinks (other than my dad and uncle, both of whom are dead now – *ironic*), and only a handful of my close friends drink at the gold-medal-Olympic-level that I did. However, my social circuit still flowed religiously on bubbles of Prosecco and bottles of Becks.

What I *needed* was to be in the company of *the recovered,* not simply *the sober,* or those bizarre anomalies of nature who are somehow able to moderate (I swear they are aliens). I didn't have access to that intimate, life changing *inspiration* from others ahead of me in recovery, the kind who can see your spark and pour their own success story on it like fuel to ignite you. I sought them out in books and podcasts, AA and Refuge Recovery rooms, and by lifting rocks wherever I could to see if maybe the right person or idea was hiding there waiting for me, but I kept coming up empty.

I needed someone or something *outside of myself* to help put my recovery into practical action, as though I had been reading how-to books on swimming but had never stepped foot in a pool.

"I did it, and so can you" are possibly the 7 most inspiring, motivational words you can string together, especially for a despairing addict. I needed someone to come along and hand me that seed, but I *also* needed to open myself up to the very attainable possibility that I could grow into sobriety just as they had, too. Plus,

I needed the willingness to both *plant* and *care for the seed once planted.*

I needed *the wanting, the willingness, and the inspiration* to come together in one powerfully decisive moment of desire and courage, like a trio of superheroes ready to swoop down and carry me to safety. I was stranded, and I needed all three of them to arrive and coordinate my rescue.

Post-Rehab/Pre-Relapse: When I came home from rehab in the winter of 2017,

I truly felt as though I was doing it alone. It was impossible for me to feel any other way about it. I was being handled with white gloves and people started tiptoeing around me because I *went to rehab,* and because I *have a problem.* It was hard to feel anything *other* than different from everybody else.

Looking back now, I'm sure it was all in my head.

My close friends and family were encouraging and supportive, but I always felt outside of the tribe. *I was unofficially the sober pariah, sitting on the sidelines.* There was always that *one thing* separating me from all of them: the fact that I *wasn't allowed* to have a drink.

In the same way I had no control over my drinking, I now felt as though I had no control over my *not* drinking. As we never really got to the *why* of my drinking in rehab, they sent me on my way with one very specific rule, and that was simply *that I was not* **allowed** *to drink.*

Leaving rehab left me feeling as though my new normal meant I had to *go without,* and from that day on I'd forever be window shopping, but never buying. Socializing with friends felt like showing up to the party with a contagious disease;

I may have arrived, but I probably shouldn't have been there, and no one really wanted me near them anyhow (Edit: this was written pre-Covid, but the feeling was akin to being *that guy* who was positive for Covid and still came to the party without wearing a mask.) This probably isn't how everyone else saw things, but it's how I *felt* them. Everything felt like a *sacrifice.* A sacrifice that I was making by *not drinking,* or a sacrifice that *everyone else* was making in my honour, *by not drinking around me.*

That was a recipe for disaster, and disaster it surely became.

As long as I felt that I was doing this alone without any real accountability, and that I was making a sacrifice and *going without,* it was only a matter of time before I started drinking again with the thirst of a man long lost in the desert. You can only chase a carrot that's been dangling in front of you for so long until you eventually stop running, grab the damned thing and slam 'er back like the drunk uncle at Thanksgiving Dinner who hasn't eaten for a year. My entire sobriety was being propelled by willpower, and the propellers were tired and starting to get jammed.

I had been sailing fatefully through sobriety like the Titanic, and I was heading straight for an iceberg.

I sank 8 weeks later.

One of these days, I'll fill in the *gaping 240-day hole* in this blog about my relapse *(short story: insert at least 960 bottles of wine, true story)* because I think it's as important to understand where things went wrong, as it is to celebrate everything that went right.

This Time Around: I've never been more grateful for such a crippling hangover in my life than I am of my last and final one on February 4, 2018. I certainly know how to go out with a bang, even though I had no idea it was my final performance of *Leaving Las Vegas, Shawn Edition.* I quite literally drank myself to the point of my body and soul *demanding sobriety or else.*

I'm grateful because it brought with it the *sincere wanting and willingness* to change. It also stamped itself in my memory the same way as if I been hit by a speeding car and left for dead or trampled by ten thousand running bulls in Pamplona.

You know, the sort of life-changing thing you don't simply just forget about.

The kind of thing that leaves a scar.

I had officially grown tired of my own bullshit, and I believe my relapse was absolutely necessary since my first attempt at sobriety was thrown together with unsustainable pieces that never really matched up. Without my relapse, I would never have arrived at the point of desperate sincerity that I did that. The point where I finally learned that my success could *never* be built on willpower and feelings of going without but needed to grow from a place of *wanting better.*

Wanting better *more* than I wanted a drink.

The Right Kind of Wanting: My first attempt at sailing the sober seas, I *did indeed* want to change – but it was more out of a *hope for redemption* than it was an aching desire to *live fully.* And there's an important difference. The former was hoping for and grasping at the forgiveness of others, and the latter was wanting/ *needing* to forgive *myself.* It's cliché, but in my first attempt at getting sober (where I failed gloriously), I was doing it for everyone else. I was doing it for all the people I had hurt, as a demonstration of my commitment to no longer being everyone's *round-the-clock handful.*

This time around, I wanted more than anything to finally be introduced to *my authentic self.* To be *whole-hearted* and fully alive, so that whatever I put my head and my heart into (like my writing), I was putting *all* of it in. If I could get to that point, I could finally become someone who doesn't need forgiveness or approval, because there's no room for self-destruction in authenticity, unless it's in the tearing down of all the parts of you *that aren't you.* It comes with its share of messes, when all those complicated *real* parts of you start spilling out – but as they say – *better out than in.*

My best advice: *be sure you are doing this for yourself first. In taking care of yourself, you can better take care of literally everything. It's not selfish, it's shameless. And there is no room for shame in recovery.*

Writing My Way Right: I penned my days through rehab like a child writing home from summer camp, then stowed it all away like my dirty little secret the day that I left. One of the most ill-fated mistakes I made was overlooking how journaling was in fact the most effective medicine for me and the closest I had found to a cure outside of meditation and mindfulness. This time, I've kept writing. I write like I need it to keep my heart pumping and to keep my blood flowing. It's become as much a part of my day and recovery regime as breathing air and drinking water.

I've found true accountability to myself and all of you, which is both inspiring and motivating. When I stopped writing last year, I always had one eye on the emergency exit, knowing I could relapse quietly without anyone knowing, slipping out the side door where no one could see.

My writing keeps me honest.

My best advice: *find something that keeps you accountable and keeps you moving through recovery. Never become complacent in your sobriety, as that's the first step down a very slippery slope.*

I Did It, And So Can You: Accountability is critical because it makes me *want* to show up – for myself, for everyone who wants me to succeed wildly, and for everyone who just like me was looking for someone to hand them a seed and say

"I did it, and so can you."

I've thrown myself into recovery like it's my full-time job. In my opinion, there is no other way, especially at the beginning.

> "Never half-ass two things. Whole-ass one thing."
> – *Ron Swanson, Parks & Recreation*

I've chewed through the memoirs of countless alcoholics and joined as many online support groups as possible. I've hunted down my mentors and favourite authors and follow them everywhere on social media as though they're my daily bread. I try and give as much energy and attention to my sobriety as I did to my drinking and try and dedicate time each day to support others on the journey along with me. I treat recovery like going to the gym or working out: *you will never build stronger muscles if you don't use them.*

And I've found workout partners. Others just like myself on this road of recovery – some at 3 days sober and others at 300 days, or 30 years. Being inspired by, and inspiring others, has remedied the fault in my approach the first time around. I feel the absolute *opposite* of alone. I've been adopted into a massive family of warriors to learn from, share with, and support in both directions. It truly has become a family, and the fear of disappointing my family trumps any drink I could have.

Having a 24-7, round the clock lifeline to celebrate with and support, is in my opinion, better than any room you can sit in once or twice a week.

My best advice: *find your tribe and dance with them daily.*

Permission & Preparation: Lastly, (I know, this is such a long ramble) I found a method that works *for me.* Just like the same outfit doesn't look good on everyone, the varied paths and roads to recovery aren't designed for every vehicle. I had to find a method that makes sense *to me,* a system that just *clicks* – and in part, I found it through Annie Grace's *"This Naked Mind"* and her 30-Day Alcohol Experiment. I was able to transform my belief that *I wasn't allowed to drink* into whole-heartedly *not wanting to drink.* I turned all my unconscious cravings on their head and rationalized the shit out of them, calling them out as the liars they are, and demoting them below the growing list of everything I truly wanted. That, and Buddhism. Buddhism helps to fix everything, including your vision, so you can finally see again.

That list is filled with things I know without a doubt I want *more than any* drink.

This time around, I have given myself *permission* to drink, and in doing so put myself in the driver's seat. And now that I know I *can* have the drink if I chose to, it makes it *that much easier* to simply choose *not* to. We always want most what we can't have. The magic happened when I was learned (with some stumbling, practice, failure, and consistency) how easy it is to justify my way *out* of a craving, and it always comes back to asking myself the same question that kickstarted my newly sober life: *what do I want more?*

Did I want a drink *more* than I was willing to deal with the waves of getting tired, frustrated with myself, losing control and blacking out, to wake up flooded with regret and a hangover? Did I want a drink *more* than I wanted to make myself proud? Did I want a drink *more* than I was willing to abandon my accountability to myself, my family, my friends? Did I want a drink *more* than I was willing to be a hypocrite?

The answer is always a loud and confident *no*.

I had to unravel literally every belief I had (and didn't know I had) about alcohol to get to this point, and it's the most important work I've done. I meet every thought and every urge with the question: *Is what I'm thinking true? And how can I know if it's really, actually true, or just something I believe to be true?* The more I do this, the more surprised/overwhelmed I am to discover how many false truths about alcohol and drinking culture I carry with me.

My best advice: *know without a doubt your non-negotiables and ask yourself with every craving if you're willing to give into it more than you want what made you stop drinking in the first place.*

Sustainable Sobriety: I lied. I thought that was my last point. The glaring difference between last year's short-lived and unstable sobriety and this time around is that my first attempt *wasn't sustainable.* It was built on willpower which inevitably runs out. It was built on isolation and sacrifice, both of which bring depression and gut-churning feelings of going without. It was built using the same bricks I used to imprison myself in addiction, the same straw I built my rickety shack with before the Big Bad Wolf moved in. It was built on the wrong reasons, and because of that, *of course* it all collapsed in on itself. *Anything* could have huffed and puffed it down.

This time, I'm not going without or making a sacrifice – *I'm getting rid of alcohol.*

This time, I'm not alone – *I'm immersed and involved.*

This time, I'm not wishing for the best – *I'm demanding it, and making it happen.*

This time, I'm not doing it for the forgiveness of others – *I'm doing it for my own acceptance of myself.*

This time, I'm not just dipping my toes in – *I'm diving deep.*

This time, I'm reminding myself every single day, with every passing craving, *how badly I wanted my sobriety before I made it happen.*

And I'm more certain than ever before that I want to keep this feeling of being sober and in control *more* than any drink you could ever give me. I've turned the benefits of my sobriety into *a currency that I'm unwilling to spend,* especially on bottles that only leave me drowning in emotional debt.

This time around I'm not only saving all those emotional dollars, but I'm finally saving *myself.*

Until It Happens to You

APRIL 7, 2018

**"If I could define enlightenment briefly
I would say it is the quiet acceptance of what is."**
– Wayne Dyer

I remember with crystal clarity the day I sat down to write my first post on my blog, and it's one of the first entries in this book. It was titled *"How Did I Get Here"* and was a sad, desperately honest self-reflection and coming-to-terms with the *really real* reality of my addiction to alcohol. I was finally acknowledging, *but not yet accepting,* the reality I had been denying for so long, despite deep down inside knowing it to be painfully true.

Up to that day, it was easier to just keep suffering in impressive, oblivious denial.

To suffer because *I had imagined different.*

I suffered and stalled because I refused to accept that my life was unravelling and I was out of control, because addiction happens to other people – *until it happens to you.*

I suffered and stood on the outside of healing looking in since I couldn't accept

I had become so battered, because falling apart happens to other people *until it happens to you.*

I suffered and shamed myself for lacking the strength to resist my temptations, because weakness and dependence happens to other people – *until it happens to you.*

I suffered because I was clinging to my *imagined life* where troubles were few and far between and landed in other people's backyards, *not mine.*

Addiction was the thing of talk shows and documentaries, public health posters and high school social studies classes. It was something I walked past quickly and changed channels to elude; these were stories and warnings for other people who were out of control – *not me.*

I was floundering in flux between the *denial of my truth*, and the *quiet, shame-ridden half-acceptance* that arrived with every bottle added to the pile of empties staring me down behind closed doors. That *half-acceptance* was always there, showing up as the guilt-ridden sadness that came along with the first drink of the day and the beatdown defeat of each subsequent morning.

I was avoiding the truth and hoping it would, in turn, change the facts.

I was living like what Bill Waterson, the cartoonist behind Calvin & Hobbes, once said: *"It's not denial. I'm just selective about the reality I choose to accept."* And what I called my reality was nothing more than a carefully curated collection of only the most shiny and sparkling parts that matched what I had imagined my life was and would be like.

The more I resisted, the more things persisted.

And it was my resistance against admitting that my *reality* and my *imagined life didn't neatly line up that kept* me in place, stuck in the loop. I was effectively the hamster, and denial was my wheel. The longer I rejected and resisted the idea that all the truths of my addiction had indeed happened to me – *and not just everybody else* – the longer I was stuck there in constant conflict.

Rejecting the truth never changed my reality. It only held me in place and brought more pain.

I had to wrap my head around the idea that by accepting that I was an addict *didn't mean* that I liked it, chose it, *or* wanted it. The concept of *accepting something* for the longest time always felt as though I also had to *approve* of it, too. I spent a lot of unnecessary time on that wheel running in circles, because I was afraid that by *accepting the truth of my addiction* and its impact on my life and relationships *also meant* that I was somehow embracing and endorsing it.

I was wrong.

The first step of acceptance (and in turn, freedom) simply came down to me making room for my truth.

I didn't have to like it, but I did have to allow it.

I had to give myself *permission* to be the alcoholic I had become, as much as it conflicted with my imagined life. I needed to just let that reality be, to sit with it and *not take on any more shame* because of it. I had to remove the imaginary notion I had that only *other people* became alcoholics. I had to admit to the reality that I *was* one of those *other people*, and that it had indeed actually happened to me, and here I was.

This didn't take any of the pain away.

If anything, it brought more – but I *suffered* less.

I suffered less because I moved into a space where I had given myself *permission* to own the undeniable fact that I was addicted, and where I was finally able to start comparing what my *imaginary* life looked like, and what my *really real* life was actually made of. Giving myself *permission* to be broken and flawed and confused and addicted started the process of knocking my self-limiting imaginary life to its knees and began the unstitching of my dependence on alcohol.

My first impressions were underwhelming, after I finally gave myself permission to actually be the addict I had become, part and parcel with all that it meant.

I think I had it in my mind that *acceptance* was something that just happened, like a supernova exploding in one glorious *Ah-Ha!* moment. It doesn't. "Accept" is a verb and requires the ongoing practice of coming to terms with reality, as ugly and uncomfortable as it may be. As much as it conflicted with the fantasy world of who I imagined I was, I had to acknowledge that my addiction was as much a part of the *real me in that moment* as were my arms, my legs, and my deepest fears and desires.

I was lucky enough to also come to realize the impermanence of everything.

That just because in that moment it was my "really real reality", at one point it wasn't, and in the future, it didn't have to be, either. It was in this realization that the terrifying truth of my predicament became less terrifying because it meant it wasn't a life sentence.

It meant that it was curable.

I began unearthing a snake pit of realities I had long buried deep with denial. The pile of truths I had to start owning grew tall and towering, and I had to give myself *permission* to take responsibility for each and every one of them.

To claim them and sign my name to them.

You know, the things that I would *never* do, the things I would *never* say, and the situations I would *never* put myself in – *until I did them, said them, and found myself in.*

It was like arriving at a murder scene, with casualties from my imagined life laying lifeless everywhere.

This is where it would have been easy to stop or start backpedaling my way to the hamster wheel. To run back to the apron strings of my fantasy life, where I *wasn't* a dependent alcoholic, where I *hadn't* hurt the people closest to me, and where I half-heartedly lived a half-life day in and day out in the company of my meek half-acceptance.

I couldn't change what I refused to confront, and so, confront things I did because I wanted to change.

By admitting my truth, I was able to begin exploring solutions that up until that point had never felt intended for me. I was finally able to take the responsibility for my sobriety *seriously* – because that's what alcoholics need to do. The longer I remained convinced that my problem *wasn't as much of a problem as it was,* the longer I stood longing for healing, always looking at it from the outside in. I had to begin owning the solutions that were available to addicts like me – *because I was one.*

Because it had happened to me, and no amount of denial in the world could change that.

I had a long and littered past of failed attempts at sobriety, and I was beginning to see why. I could never seem to push past my first few sober days or hours, despite my burning desire for escape from the cycle. I would take a few timid steps into the scary and uncertain territory of *not drinking* only to find myself running back to where I started as quickly as I could every single time.

The further in I would go, the more apparent the severity of my predicament became.

I would find myself at the whims of cravings, and unable to overcome the demands of my addiction – but still I believed that surely, *I wasn't an alcoholic.* It was easier to abandon my attempts at getting rid of alcohol than it was to once and for all accept that I had no control over it anymore. I would try to *simply not drink,* but I kept tripping over the tricky symptoms of addiction. And since in my imaginary life, *I wasn't an addict,* I would repel and retreat, over and over again because I was unwilling to admit my truth. I bartered, I negotiated, I justified, I lied. I did anything I could to avoid stepping out of my imaginary comfort zone.

Until I came to accept that addiction was part of my *very real reality,* I denied all the symptoms because *they didn't apply to me.*

The truth that I was an addict who lacked the self-control to moderate and had at some point lost the ability to choose, was a terrifying truth I was unwilling to come to terms with for a very long time. And so, I kept suffering, because I was living in the constant conflict of *wanting* to stop drinking, not being *able* to stop drinking, and not being able to *admit* that this was my reality. I resisted accepting that this was indeed my truth – *that I was impossibly addicted, that it had indeed happened to me* – and I'd retreat back to my comfort zone and delusional, imaginary life where I wasn't *really* an alcoholic.

Except that I was.

> "Comfort zones are caskets where the living lay and
> practice being less than alive before the body dies."
> – *J. Warren Welch*

It was only in the decisive, brave acceptance of my truth, and giving myself *permission* to have *let it happen to me*, was I also able to begin exploring the options and solutions that were available for addicts.

Addicts like me.

It was in that slow, creaking approval that I allowed myself to face the symptoms of addiction head on, no longer afraid or shocked by them. I didn't have to like it, but I had to admit that what I was feeling was *what addiction feels like.* And because I was an addict, I needed to *deal with it,* instead of denying it and running away screaming "But this problem and these feelings don't belong to me!"

It meant dismantling my comfort zone to make room for my truth and all the challenges that came with it. It meant swallowing my pride, it meant brutal, painfully ugly honesty, and it meant freedom from the hamster wheel if I could step out of my imaginary life and into admission. It meant once and for all taking a long look in the steamed-up mirror of my ego and wiping it clean so I could finally see myself for who I was.

To begin overcoming my addiction successfully, I needed to accept it fully, because half-acceptance only allows for half-success.

In the beginning, overcoming my addiction seemed like an impossible feat – *until it happened to me.*

The idea of saying and putting the terrifying phrase *"I'm an alcoholic"* behind me seemed inconceivable – *until it happened to me.*

The prospect of not drinking in the face of ten thousand triggers seemed unthinkable – *until it happened to me.*

The idea of accepting how I allowed the unimaginable to happen to me seemed impossible – *until it very much happened to me.*

And that's what I'm discovering this beautiful, heartbreaking thing called life is all about. It can't be experienced from the window of your imaginary world because it happens in the mud, and in the rain, and in the sunny struggles of our *really real* world – *if you're willing to let it happen to you.*

Never The Tortoise, Always the Hare

APRIL 7, 2018

"Life is like riding a bicycle.
To keep your balance, you must keep moving."
– Albert Einstein

I wish momentum and motivation flowed as freely as wine used to around here. That we could top up our reserves to brimming fullness and just *keep going* as easily as the desire to begin possessed us.

Starting is easy, *persistence is an art*.

Me starting *anything* is basically like driving off the lot on New Car Day. Intoxicated by that leathery new car smell and the spotlessness of it all, I pull out of the dealership pretty sure I'm driving the Brad Pitt of cars even if it looks like Willem Dafoe hungover on a Monday morning.

It's shiny, it's new, *and I am Angelina Jolie.*

I'll look for reasons to drive it and excuses to use it. I'll go to places I never wanted to just so I can sink down behind the driver's wheel and discover all its shiny bells and whistles. The honeymoon lasts a few weeks, until I eventually stop noticing the fingerprints and dust. I stop treating it like a fragile new treasure and it becomes a tool instead of a trophy. It eventually stops being the *Brad Pitt of My Driveway* and slowly becomes just another car that needs washing, gas and maintenance.

The clock eventually strikes twelve and my magical carriage, without fail, turns back into the pumpkin it always was.

The early days of newness are sexy. The exhilaration is in the takeoff, knowing you are headed somewhere. My challenge is always how to stay interested when we're cruising through the air at 35,000 feet, forgetting the simple miracle that we're among the birds and above the clouds.

You can take off in stormy weather where everything is grey and depressing, and before you know it, you've transcended the rain. And it's there in that sky-high calm and comfort that you get used to the blue skies and sunshine.

But the storm is still there, right where you left it on the other side of your new high, but now, it's below you; behind you.

It's easy to settle in and forget about the chance of turbulence ahead until it rattles you awake; a jolting reminder that you're vulnerable and groundless. It's easy to love flying when it's smooth sailing. But what about when things get bumpy and the current you're riding is riddled with pockets of surprises just waiting to make you fall?

I am the *King of Incompletion*, and my kingdom is cluttered with half realized dreams. I'm the plane that drops from the sky when the turbulence hits, instead of flying headlong through it to smoother skies. I'm the boy on the bike that stops pedalling and falls, forgetting it was my momentum that got me going in the first place.

I am never the tortoise; I am always the hare.

I launch ideas and ambitions as though from slingshots hard and fast to the heavens, forgetting that at least on this planet, what goes up almost always comes down *(apart from gas prices and taxes)*. I relish in the excitement of those first powerful few minutes of flight, forgetting the inevitable arc that without a doubt always brings them back to earth.

I stare at the sunrise until I'm blind and end up missing the sunset.

This time I want to keep pedalling.

This time I want to temper the turbulence and feel the relief of finally flying on the other side.

This time I want to ride the inevitable but uncertain trajectory of my good intentions through to the end, from launch through to landing.

I want to keep moving, just above the clouds I broke through to get here in the first place, unafraid but aware that they're still there where I left them.

I'm tired of how the weight of something half-done feels twice as heavy.

I'm tired of living with the ghosts of my abandoned aspirations, shackled to their phantom potential, long dead but still haunting me.

I want to learn how to linger after the lustre dulls, and how to persist when I want to pull back.

I want to drive my desires every day like I just drove off the lot, instead of parking them when the new car smell fades.

I want to embrace how the flight is more than just the takeoff, but the landing and all the turbulence in between, too.

I want to finish what I've started, and for a change, *it isn't my 3rd bottle of wine.*

Giving up is the easiest thing in the world to do, and I've proven I can do it very well. For a change, I want to channel my strength to see things through. *To persist and persevere.* To come in for a landing more impressive than the launch. I want to leave my crown as *King of Incompletion* with all my half-done everythings, back in my half-life kingdom.

> "Well begun is half done."
> – *Aristotle*

I want to fly above the clouds as long as I can, but for once, finally get to where I wanted to go. Without turning around, and without the emergency landing or change of course. I want my impressive beginnings to stop getting deflated because of the slow leak in my momentum. I want to keep moving, *so I can get there.*

I want to finally *get there*, even though I know there's no real destination, so I can stop carrying the weight of all the things I start and never finish, that are twice as heavy and more uncomfortable than carrying something well begun, *and done.*

A Letter for Our Broken Hearts

APRIL 10, 2018

My dear, I know your heart is broken but you need to stop breaking it, too.

You are not what happened to you, and you are not what you have done. Your heart as it is, as it was, is more than enough; there is no need to wish it were different or for you to become the painful parts of your past.

Your heart is enough; it always was.

Broken hearts are remarkably reckless, and yours was in the path of someone else's hurt and misguided pain. Your heart was not broken out of spite or intention: your heart was broken by getting caught underfoot in the parade of someone else's heartache. You were never a target; your broken heart is collateral damage from someone else's sorrow.

Your heart was made with hinges, so that you can let in as much as you crave to let out. Don't let your broken heart rust them. Let them swing freely so your own hurt can leave you. Your heart was not made to only collect the suffering of everyone else, so your own anguish could have company.

Broken hearts cannot be healed in boxes or in darkness. Pull out all your shattered pieces without shame or suspicion and lay them all out in the sun like the stunning mosaic you've become.

Broken pieces have more facets and faces for the light to play on. They are more dazzling for being divided.

Your heart was broken by your own imagination, too. It was not created to withstand the unbearable weight of disappointment and unsatisfied expectations. We suffer when we imagine different than what is, breaking slowly while we wait for something that may not be on its way. The slow and subtle breakdown of your once hopeful, patient heart can cause more hurt than the pain of breaking beneath the gravity of swiftly falling.

My dear, hearts break by forgetting that all hearts are broken.

It's in the smallness of seeing our own hearts as *less than* that they crumble. Your broken heart does not mean that you've been undone, it means you've *become.*

We are not born in pieces; broken hearts happen naturally and necessarily because of, not in spite of, living and having loved.

Your broken heart is beautiful evidence that you have done both.

You are not what you've done. Your broken heart was already there when you broke it even more. We all inherit the pain of generations and harbour it in our habits and our health. It's no wonder your heart burst, holding heartaches that were never yours to own. You are not your addiction or your grief; that is only your heart trying to hold itself together while you learn how to help your broken heart keep beating.

Your heart is enough; it always was.

You are not the words you have heard or what has been said to you. The hurting hearts of others speak loudly so they can drown out their own shame-stricken distress. You can hear in the chorus of the broken-hearted notes that sound like mirrors, reflecting the instrument, not the audience. Hearts become broken when we turn someone else's serenade into a song we believe we need to play, too.

Your heart was meant to be a witness, not an echo.

Your heart did not break from being worn on your sleeve; it broke from beating for someone else. Do not lock it away in a tower of pent-up apologies, waiting to be given, or received. Wear it boldly in all its broken glory, more resilient and real than it ever was before. Broken hearts cannot mend in an unrequited void of wondering where you went wrong; they heal through accepting that they beat, and they broke as best they knew how.

What you believe broke your heart was never what broke your heart.

Your heart broke just as it was intended to, just as life breaks through a seed to grow into a tree.

Your broken heart does not mean that you've been undone, it means you've *become.*

Life In Detox

APRIL 12, 2018

**I didn't give the name of my blog much thought the
day I sat down to write for the first time.**

I was sad, I needed an outlet, and I had just come to finally admitting – and I mean
really *admitting-admitting* – that I was an alcoholic. I just needed a place to write
and get it all out somewhere that I could look back on one day.

To remind myself of where I never wanted to go back to.

We'll overlook the fact that *I did indeed go back there* eventually, because right now
– what matters is that *I'm here right now.* 15 months of stumbling and struggling
and scribbling and typing later, the name *Life in Detox* is apparently coming along
for the ride. At the time, it's how I referred to the idea of going to rehab, hung up
on the words that dropped like atomic bombs from my doctor's mouth: *You can't
do this on your own; you need a medically supervised detox. Because, well, seizures
and dying and shit.*

It's only been recently (the past few days) that I've really come to understand what
I mean/meant by *Life in Detox.*

Because it's so very much more than simply not drinking. It's so very much more
than getting the poison out of my bloodstream. It's so very much more than not
stopping at the liquor store every day no matter how hard my truck wants to
turn into the parking lot out of habit. And it's so very much more than meetings
and secretive online groups or following 10,000 sober torch bearers walking
the *Recovered Path* before me.

My life fell apart because of alcohol. *Not the other way around.*

My drinking didn't get to the point of award-winning addiction *because* my life
was crumbling, or my marriage was failing, or my business was floundering.

My life was crumbling, and my marriage was failing, and my business was
floundering *because of my drinking.* This is a truth I've spent a long time wrapping

my head around, because we are force fed the idea that *alcohol is the thing you need* when all these things *are* falling apart. That it's the cure for all our ailments.

It isn't. It never was, and it never ever will be. It's the *cause* of our ailments.

Alcohol is just one of the bigger, meaner piranhas in the pond.

I've been trying to swim, but it's crowded. The pond is full of hungry fish nipping at my toes, and it's overpopulated with distractions to keep me from reaching the other side. It's polluted with *things that hold me back and pull me down,* filled with all sorts of fish intended just to keep me in place. To keep me from swimming.

My at-arms-reach-at-all-times iPhone. Social Media. Facebook. Emails. Instagram. Notifications. The news. The *fake* news. My laptop, my iMac. Clickbait and data-gathering games designed to sell me more of what they think I want; to sell me more of what they *tell me* I want. Negative thoughts and false beliefs, sales flyers and billboards, shinier cars and *new and improved everythings.* Future yard sale items disguised as present-day solutions. Booze-infused marketing and Mommy Juice memes designed to convince me that I'm part of the majority, and as the majority, *this is what we do.*

We drink.

We drink to celebrate, and we drink to mourn. We drink when it's time to cope and we drink when it's time to dance. We drink when times are tough – and we drink to relish in the times when they aren't.

We drink to make all the other piranha bites hurt a little bit less.

And the piranhas are *everywhere.*

The longer I'm sober, the more sensitive I'm becoming to quite literally everything. I mean, if someone is breathing too heavily 3 blocks away, I need to find some Zen immediately or a sock to shove down their throat (not the most Zen solution, I'll admit). I've been getting very overwhelmed (understatement) by social media and the non-stop notifications on all the devices I'm glued to all day. Half the time I'm just scrolling while not even looking or reading (I call it the 'Scroll Hole'). We wait on our devices for the next notification to pop up. I learned yesterday that all these notifications, all those little red dots on your screen that tell you that something is waiting for you – *they all release dopamine.*

And if you know anything about addiction, *you know what dopamine can do:*

> "Dopamine is released after exercise, sex, anticipation of rewards, and when that reward is achieved. *The anticipation of the reward* is what actually triggers the good feeling that dopamine produces in your brain,

and you get another pleasure hit when you successfully achieve the goal. Furthermore, *dopamine is a learning chemical, which results in addiction.* It tells us what the source of the pleasure is, and then tells us *that is how we will get pleasure in the future.* Social media is a dopamine 'jackpot', says Delgado associate professor of psychology.»

– *via Quora by Natalie Engelbrecht, Psychotherapist, Researcher*

Hello Pavlov, meet dog.

I spent the last 20 years *chasing rewards* at the bottom of bottle after bottle, that were never even once remotely rewarding, and how many more years just trying to *unlearn* the dopamine trigger bell so I could once and for all stop salivating for wine every time a tough time (ding!) or a little stress (ding!) or a party (ding!) or 11 am (ding!) or a disappointment (ding! ding! ding!) would ring my bell.

This has been one of the biggest piranha's I've needed to catch, and though he's still in my pond, he's contained.

He can't bite me if I keep him caged.

Alcohol has been the big fish I needed to quarantine in my pond, so I get to all the other ones. It's the first and biggest step *towards a greater detox.* Towards a life where I'm swimming without constantly getting nipped. And my next big fish,

I'm discovering, is even more insidious than booze.

It's the global, all-encompassing blanket we are all neatly tucked beneath in the hopes that we'll all fall asleep: *social media.* It's with my bright white and freshly sober eyes I can finally see how it's taking as much or more from me as alcohol ever did.

Yesterday I sat myself down to make 3 very honest lists. One list was for what I want my life to be, one for what I *actually* do every day, and one for what I will begin doing & the lifestyle adjustments that I need to make. Nearly every row of "what I actually do every day" included *waste time on social media* and *reduce or remove social media* showed up as "what I need to *start* doing" if I want to realize my life how I want it to be.

I discovered that for the most part, what I'm doing every day in no way aligns with what I want my life to be like.

Nothing aligns because I'm sitting here salivating all day waiting for the damned bell to ring. Waiting for my reward to get tossed my way like a bone I've dreamt about all day, and I'm starving. Waiting for something to fill that "reward void" that getting rid of alcohol left gaping and hollow. Waiting for my life to come to me, instead of walking towards it.

Social media can be a wonderful thing if used correctly. But as an addict, I'll be first to raise my hand and confess that moderation isn't at the top of my resumé. Without social media, however, I wouldn't be sitting here in recovery without a hangover, and able to type these words. It's been through social media that I've found support, encouragement, inspiration and motivation. But like all things I dip my toes in, I end up canon-balling and make a splash by going *all in*. I so badly want to turn my *all-or-nothing* approach to everything into more of an *okay-maybe-a-little-bit-of-something* approach.

A taste, instead of always gorging on whatever is in front of me and wanting more.

So, I've turned off *all* the notifications. I've put all my devices into "Do Not Disturb" for 23:59 hours a day (seriously, my DND is set from 6 am until 5:59 am the next day). I've changed my email to only fetch messages when I ask it to, instead of them being pushed to me instantly. I've turned all the little red badges on my app icons off, so they aren't yelling at me for attention, to stop what I'm doing and distract myself with someone else's marketing or need to be noticed. I've started asking myself *"Why"* every time I reach for my phone or open a new tab in my browser. Most of the time, I become aware that it was only to distract myself from whatever I was doing, or to go looking for *"rewards"*. I've given myself an allowance for social media of 15 minutes in the morning, and again, 15 minutes at night.

You know, just so people don't think I died or something.

I'm identifying the apps and sites I waste the most time on and seeking out *real life alternatives.*

I'm learning that my *Life in Detox* is exactly that: detoxing *my life*, not only my bloodstream. It's coming to be aware of *what I truly want my life to be like*, and removing all the toxins that are keeping me from it. I'm learning to become conscious of what I'm doing, and whether it aligns with what I truly want, after all.

Most of the time, it doesn't. But I'm working on it.

I wanted to get rid of alcohol, because my life was as far as possible from what I wanted it to be like. And yet, here I am, still struggling, because *what I'm doing every day in no way aligns with where I want to go.* I want to walk East, but I'm facing West. I want to find peace, but I'm absorbed in noise. I want my days to be on my terms, but I'm allowing everything and everyone else to shape them. I want to focus, but I'm dropping everything at the ding of that bell. I want to be mindful, but it's so cluttered with distractions demanding my attention.

The assumed demand that we need to shift our attention from ourselves and our present moment to whatever is incoming is a toxin as horrible and as crippling as alcohol. Is steals you away from being present, which is the only place where your life actually happens. It doesn't happen in an app, or in the comments section of a thread on Facebook. It doesn't happen in your likes on Instagram or your upvotes on Quora or Reddit.

It's happening right now, while you are reading this. This is what you're giving your attention to.

This moment right now *is* your life.

I am starting to only give certain things my attention *when I choose to*. To say no, before I say yes. *To respect my own privacy* by stopping the incessant tapping on my shoulder for attention from iMessage or Facebook or any number of other sources that only keep taking and taking, under the guise of *giving*.

You know, exactly like alcohol used to.

I'm being selective of what I'm allowing in, and when.

I'm digitally detoxing my life, so that I can have one.

I want to find my dopamine in the trees and in the pages of books. I want my rewards to come from a place of my own creation, and a place from within myself – not the other way around. I want to start asking myself "why" more often, like every time I reach for my phone, or find myself whisked away by reward hooks outside of myself. *Why?* Why am I doing what I'm doing? And what is it I *do* want in my life, that I'm letting this help me avoid working towards?

It's a tricky one, digitally detoxing yourself. It's another addiction that's just as detrimental and sneaky as alcohol, and one that leaves you feeling just as depleted.

This is my life in detox.

One cunning poison at a time.

PART 6:

Emancipation

Transformation

APRIL 13, 2018

**Twenty-four years ago, I walked into a tattoo parlour in
London with absolutely no idea what I was going to get.**

All I knew is that my parents *really* didn't want me to get (another) one, so of course, *I had to get another one*. And there I stood with a binder in hand, flipping through the most cliche and cookie-cutter collection of tattoos, my 17-year-old mind trying to find one that would make me look worldly, deep and mysterious.

So of course, I got the Japanese Kanji for *"Transformation"*. Feel free to insert an eyeroll here. At least I really hoped that's what it meant, because that's how it was labelled in what should have been called their *Binder of Regretful Tattoos*. Looking back, I see it as equivalent to someone in Japan getting the English words *"French Fries"* inked on their forearm. This was before the days of smartphones and Siri (and apparently good taste in tattoos) and it was years later with sweet relief that a Japanese friend of mine confirmed that it *did indeed* say Transformation (or Change) which Google later confirmed a decade later (and that, of course, means it's true. Because, well, *Google).*

It was timely. I was at the awkwardly fumbling stage of growing into myself, and already diving my way to the depressive depths of stolen homemade wine from my parent's liquor cabinet every day. I'd dilute the remaining bottles with water so they *"wouldn't notice"* until company was over, all of them sitting around the kitchen table discussing how *that batch* didn't turn out so well (who was I kidding?) Meanwhile I sat sketching in notebooks and scribbling in journals, half pissed and alone in my bedroom, burning through packs of cigarettes that I'd smoke out the window, deluded into thinking my parents didn't know what was up.

You know, sort of like *the wine.* The gin. The vodka. That whatever I could get my hands on.

The only thing I was transforming into was an insomniac teenage alcoholic, addicted to caffeine pills (I could go through a bottle of *WakeUps* in a few days) with anorexia and devoid of self-worth, who once showed up hallucinating and sky high to gym class 4 hours into an acid trip. I was spending a lot of what we'll call *"inappropriate"* time with my English teacher, buying weed off the dude who taught math, dealing with the suicide of my close friend, and desperately trying to come to terms with my sexuality, and devastating and intimately dark family secrets that made me want nothing more than to be anywhere, *anywhere,* but where I was.

Miraculously my grades stayed top of the class *(especially in English - ha!)* and I graduated with honours, awkwardly accepting my certificate, freshly bleached and botched accidentally orange hair and all, in front of my parents, who I had just devastated in return, by moving out without any notice.

I just left.

My tattoo of course came along with me, worn like a battle flag on my forearm for twenty-three years; a permanent reminder of being 17 and desperate to change everything about myself and my life. Of feeling like if *I* didn't transform, nothing else ever would.

I fumbled my way through art school in Toronto (honestly, I barely went. I spent most days and nights drunk, high and hungover on our couch at the despair of my roommate) and moved homes and apartments no less than 10 times in as many years. I found a great gig at a trendy 24-hour cafe/club which fit perfectly with my continued insomnia and persistent drinking obsession; admittedly, I drank as much behind the bar as I served over it.

It was the holy grail of jobs for the addicted, downtrodden, and insomnia ridden.

At least until I voluntarily left after getting caught smoking weed (again) in the bathroom.

I moved once more, this time back to London. I kept chasing change and transformation as though it were a train that left without me; I was always two seconds too late for boarding and everyone was on their way except for me.

I changed jobs, partners, cars, houses, drugs of choice and varieties of cheap wine like they were underwear. I kept changing everything around me, and all that did was create a cyclone of perpetual insecurity, spinning like a top I had whirled all by myself. This drove my parents mad since I was raised by the generation of *The Stable & Responsible,* where any change was bad change, and risks were akin to a deadly sin.

I was raised to follow my heart, but only if it led me to the same spot every time. There was no room for wandering in the big picture; you got one pick from the bucket and that was your lot, and *if you didn't like it, you better learn to like it.* (End quote, *my dad,* almost every conversation ever until he died. I quoted him to his face many times in defence of whatever shit I had gotten myself into that we were arguing about that time). This obviously created conflict because *The Stable & Responsible* generation gave birth to the *Unstable & Reckless* generation, of which I was carrying the torch. Where their path looked drawn with a ruler, mine was more like a snake had a seizure in a sandpit.

I'm going to fast forward through the good times: finding love, getting married, getting promoted, buying my first luxury vehicle, buying my first home, the 24 Doritos-smelling paws of the 6 dogs I adopted, building my business and finally being able to afford the good wine and a weed dealer that delivered. I was on *The Today Show,* and *ABC World News with Diane Sawyer* followed me to Las Vegas to document while I helped the dreams of kids with cancer come to life.

I was soaring.

Sort of.

Finally, things were changing, including how when my drinking problem became a *"Drinking Problem"* (air-quotes emphasized) I noticed a lot of what I had to managed to build and gather started falling through my fingers.

Like I was living in a sandcastle and the tide was rolling in.

Drinking escalated, everything else receded. The more the tide rolled in, the more everything I had built started to roll out and get swept away.

My family and friends were dropping like flies, dying like a line of dominoes one after the next. My tattoos began piling up as fast as my regrets, with sleeves of quotes from the Dalai Lama to Rhonda Byrne, tall pines and the silhouettes of flying birds, mandalas and lotus buds. In the heart of them all, my transformation tattoo, now with an altar of ink around it showcasing all the things I was longing for.

Peace. Serenity. Calm. Balance.

Flight.

I wore them like S.O.S. messages written on a beach.

It was on a random, ridiculously drunken trip to New Orleans in 2016 (oh wait, it's the time I pissed myself) where I had a ginormous crow? Eagle? Falcon? 'Bird' tattooed on my upper arm. I was so drunk I would've let him tattoo profanities on my forehead. The bird's talons are clenched a couple inches from my transformation tattoo, as though he's seconds from plucking it like a field mouse for lunch.

I ended up loving it. It's the opposite of what screams "me" and it's nothing I would have picked out for myself. It's twice the size of what I wanted, and it's the perfect reflection of where I was at that time in my life. It's a hot mess, and so was I.

Especially considering I had no clue that just 3 months later I'd be flying to rehab.

And it was after rehab where I came home, transformed, at last. Well, at least for a little while (insert relapse story here). While my sobriety lasted, I was calm. I felt balanced and serene. And, I wanted more ink, starting with a cover-up of the now vintage transformation tattoo I had shared with my skin for 22 years. I wanted to let it go and pigeonhole it in one of my newly carved-out blocks of time, which will forever be known as *"before rehab"*, *"at rehab"*, and *"after rehab"*.

It's covered up to look like smoke and flames (trust me, it works with the whole sleeve though it sounds weird on its own) – unintentionally symbolic of my quest for change giving up and burning itself alive, or more poetically, maybe of it finally actualizing itself after all those years.

Transformation, transformed at last.

Sometimes, you have to leave things behind. Or at least cover them up, so you don't have to look at them *every day.*

Memories don't work like that, nor does trauma, depression or addiction, I've discovered. You'll always know they're there, just below the ink, still in your skin. I notice my *now-smoke-and-flames* transformation tattoo more now that it's covered than I ever did before. I forgot about it for years – *until it was gone,* having turned into something new.

I have days I wish I could uncover it; remorseful over wishing a time of my life away. And I have days where I admire the flames; grateful for the reminder of when I took things for granted and almost burnt it all down alongside all the smouldering bridges in my path.

I came to learn that I didn't want to change myself; *I only wanted to change how I was feeling.* I wanted the hollowness of grief to go away, the immobility of trauma to go away, to resurrect and make peace with my dead and to somehow transform all my ugly feelings so the confused, 17-year-old teenage me could finally rest. I tried to bury his battle flag, but I could always still hear it flap-flap-flapping behind the flames. I tried to drown his childhood trauma in red wine and cheap beer and bury his teen angst and disappointment beneath mountains of weed, partners and cigarettes.

If I couldn't transform, I could self-destruct.

It's the backwards nature of avoidance, that the deeper and more earnestly I tried to cover up what I really needed to transform, the more apparent and in my face things became. The more I tried to put my trauma to sleep, the more it would walk through my halls at night.

There was not enough ink in the world to cover up the transformation I needed to have.

The paradox is in how the *most* transformative step was coming to understand that in order to change, I had to stop *wanting to change*.

I know, sounds easy right? Good luck. Being okay with things *as they are,* as they happened, and as they haunt you is about as easy as swimming the English Channel. It's hard but it's not possible, lots of people have done it, plus it (apparently) feels damn good once you reach the other side. What I had to do was *transform all my unpleasant memories and disappointments into something useful and valuable; to carve something wonderful out of all the dead fallen trees* in my forest.

To let them be what they are, only more beautiful for having fell.

To transform not myself or my situation, but to change the way I looked at them.

For the longest time I felt as though I was stumbling about in a dark room, my hands sliding over empty walls in search of a light switch that was never there, never looking in my own pocket for the flashlight that was always with me.

I learned that my dad had been right all along. That *if I didn't like it, I had better learn to like it.* It's the only card any of us have to play with our unchangeable past, to find the treasure in the trash, or the flashlight in our pocket.

To channel my challenges into inspiration for writing and art, like little flashlights to tuck into other people's pockets.

To find a reason why I wouldn't wish things had happened any other way, so I can numb the pain with point of view, instead of the pouring of Pinot Grigio.

To transform *how* I was seeing, not *what I was seeing.*

To transform the crumbled bricks of my foundation into a sturdy staircase, *rising up* – instead of *covered* up.

The Ice Storm & The Melting

APRIL 15, 2018

I wasn't going to write today.

We've been hunkered down since yesterday morning, while a "potentially historic ice storm" has painted itself across the province like a thick, cold coat of varathane.

The power has been flickering on and off as much as my mood. There's something about a wicked gale that seriously makes me want to curl up with a bottle or 3 of wine to warm myself from the inside out; to paint myself as numb as I imagine all the feral cats feel on a stormy day like today.

I have always been a marionette to the weather.

It's not even the pretty kind of ice storm; where you wake up to a glistening wonderland of all the elements, where all the trees look like pieces of your grandma's best crystal, their branches clinking and tinkling against each other under the weight of their newfound beauty, the sun lighting everything up as though you're living inside a glass chandelier.

Nope.

It's the shitty kind of ice storm.

The kind where it's grey and frigid and the wind is gusting at 70 miles an hour.

The kind of storm where your premature patio furniture gets tossed around the yard and is only stopped in its tumbling tracks by all the downed trees and fallen branches that you've given up trying to count. It's the shitty kind of ice storm that just makes everything dangerous and damaged and crawls right inside you like a polar nightmare.

I wasn't going to write today. In between the brownouts and blackouts (power-related, not wine induced) I've had ten thousand thoughts about ten thousand things, and I feel as scattered as the birds out my window looking for shelter.

It's amazing when you realize that even *the weather* is a trigger to make you want to drink. It doesn't matter that I can rationalize the hell out of why I know *without a doubt* that *I don't actually want one* – but the ice has been pinging off my window all day like stones thrown by a desperate suitor, *and that suitor has wine.*

But ask me again, in three months when the sun is high and the pool is cool, and I'll likely tell you how the summer heat has fired up my sleeping thirst. Or how the rich colours of crisp October make me crave rum and cider; the flurries of winter calling for hot toddies and baths full of Bailey's Irish Cream or Cabernet Sauvignon.

Spring into summer through autumn and winter; the seasons will never disappoint in delivering reasons for *why I should have a drink.*

Even though *I don't want one.*

But, back to the ice storm.

It's addiction and recovery, *personified.*

It starts slow, a drizzle, some rain. Then it slowly gets darker, the temperature drops; the winds pick up and ice begins to build. Layer by layer and virtually unnoticeable, until it's grown thick and heavy, consuming everything in its path. What once was strong starts to break, branches begin to fall; everything becomes frozen in place.

Entombed.

Nothing is ever really the same, after an ice storm.

There's always some damage, and luckily, some things grow back. Sometimes, better things come to replace what was broken, and stronger trees are planted to replace the ones that fell. And, sometimes, when the ice storm passes and the grey gives way to better days, the beauty of it all is revealed *in the melting.*

When everything is slick and shining, lit up as though from the inside.

When light dissolves the ice and slowly everything comes back to life.

Where branches were broken, healing begins.

And it's from that great melt after the storm that it waters the earth like liquid lessons, never to be forgotten in the sweet thaw of sobriety.

You survey the damage, clean up what you can, and make peace with what you can't.

I wasn't going to write today.

But I felt another ice storm coming on.

I Don't Say Sorry Anymore

APRIL 16, 2018

My mom must be so disappointed, my dad must be rolling over in his grave, since my manners shot straight out the window and right down the drain.

I don't say *Sorry* anymore.

Sorry is too heavy for any heart to carry; burdened with sorrow and remorse.

If a word could round its back and hang its head, taking a small step backwards with a sigh of self-hatred, *Sorry* would be it. *Sorry* has nothing to do with what was said or what was done, and everything to do with what you have come to believe of yourself.

Sorry is nothing more than digging up the dead of your past, just so you can try and watch it die it all over again.

Sorry is just a tiny, small version of yourself that lives within, who spends her days drafting lists of your shortcomings and tallying regrets, who falls from your mouth in the shameful shape of a needless apology. *Sorry* gathers her shackles from your own expectations, so she can keep you small and saddled and stuck alongside her.

Addiction is a spiritual disease, independent of whatever it is you believe, whether it's God or Buddha, Jehovah or the Universe, addiction itself is *universal*. It's the desperate clinging to *things without* so you can fill up the void of *things within*, and it doesn't care if you're white, black or purple or where you call home; it carves out a hollow for all your *Sorrys* to thrive.

Sorry moves into your soul with a sort of dampness that turns it into a cave.

And she lives there, collecting your self-hatred like washed-up shells on a beach.

When I first stepped into recovery, I wore *Sorry* like my favourite suit of armour.

I thought it would protect me from all the truths I began throwing at like double-ended javelins, valiantly confessing that *"I'm sorry, I deserved that,"* and *"I'm sorry*

371

for all I've done." I wanted to apologize to everyone, including myself and my sorry state of affairs. I wanted to scream *Sorry!* From the rooftops like it was my rooster call that I was, at long last, *awake*, despite the crusty remorse from my drawn-out sleep, still dried up around my eyes.

My amends were inside out, and my apologies were flawed; the chinks in my armour of *Sorrys-strung-together* only left me feeling heavier and more exposed than before. For all the *Sorrys* I would offer to lighten my guilt-laden load, the more weighed down I became. The more I listed my faults and sat with my wrongs, *the less in love with myself* I felt.

It was as if every *Sorry!* reminded me of everything *wrong with myself*, that I was trying so badly to overcome, and showing everyone else in case they forgot, that

I wore my flaws like misspelled tattoos.

Where *Sorry!* chipped away at me, breaking me down into smaller, broken pieces of myself, *Thank You!* began to bind everything back together.

I stopped saying *Sorry* hoping to be redeemed and in some way undo all that was done. I stopped saying *Sorry* wishing all that I drank could somehow be undrunk.

I stopped asking for forgiveness, as though my sins could be bleached clean like stains from long ago spilled wine.

I stopped making myself small in the shadow of my good intentions.

And it was only when I began offering *my gratitude* instead of asking forgiveness that all the horrible awfuls I was dragging behind me started to fall away. It was then that I slowly stopped crumbling, and gradually began healing. Instead of *"I'm sorry for all the years I spent wasted and drunk, like the worst friend ever,"* I've learned to say, *"Thank you for being so patient while I was so lost and thank you for loving me unconditionally".* Rather than saying *"I'm sorry for all the times I cancelled our plans"* or *"I'm so sorry I'm late,"* I've began saying with sincerity, *"Thank you for understanding how my struggles made me isolate"* and *"Thank you so much for waiting for me while I was on my way."*

Sorry! makes you less, while *Thank You!* makes you more.

Where *Sorry!* stirs up negativity and guilt, causing a dark shadow of shame that requires a convoluted two-step to climb out of, *Thank You!* is brimming with appreciation and gratitude, building *both of you* up, instead of just knocking yourself down.

Thank You! has helped me shift how I think of myself and my addiction, and I get to remind people that *they're awesome*, instead of stirring up reasons *why I might suck*. It's proven to be one of my strongest supports while I learn to walk again in recovery. *Sorry!* on the other hand is a tiny, angry little lumberjack, wielding her axe at my shins always cutting me down, making me smaller, shorter, *less than;* always closer to the mud that I'm trying to grow out of.

I wanted to escape my addiction because I had run out of strength to wallow in my sea of *Sorrys* any longer.

And yet at first, I brought them with me.

I carried them in jars as though they were my treasured and watery penance, sloshing around and spilling themselves everywhere. It wasn't until I poured them out once and for all and filled them instead with gratitude and appreciation did all that I was carrying grow infinitely lighter.

I stopped asking people to place forgiveness in those jars and started asking them to remove some gratitude from them, instead.

I've turned my apologies inside out; all my *Sorry!'s* falling from the satchel of regret I strung for so long over my shoulder, giving space to fill it twice as quickly with positive, healing gems of gratitude.

Thank You! is made up of two parts – the *Thanker*, and the *You. I'm Sorry!* is as lonely as addiction – it's just *you,* and the awkward idleness of your apology, hanging in the air between wanting forgiveness and wanting to run.

Thank You gives, whereas *Sorry* only takes.

So, there is no room in my sobriety for *Sorrys* any longer because I don't say *Sorry* anymore. I spent far too long consumed in the sadness of addiction to keep offering pieces of it over and over again, like shallow sacrifices held up in hopeful trade for redemption.

And the first person I had to learn how to thank – was myself.

No longer lamenting what cannot be changed. No longer trying to absolve myself of guilt for having drank away days, nights and countless opportunities. No longer living like a lesser version of myself, somehow inferior and smaller, as though my addiction had shrunk me.

Living like that does not beg for an apology, *it begs for celebration.*

To *thank myself* for this second, third, tenth chance at living. To *thank myself for sobriety,* which has washed all the reasons for my *Sorrys* out to sea.

To *thank myself* for standing up against one of the strongest demons of addiction: the need to fill myself with reasons why I'm not good enough.

Sorry, *not sorry.*

Routine Maintenance

APRIL 18, 2018

I had an appointment with my eye doctor yesterday; routine maintenance, nothing serious (and the good news is I'm not blind, which would be a serious impediment to a photographer).

The last few days, for whatever reason, my cravings have been knocking at my door — you know, that Big Bad Wolf who has been trying to huff and puff and blow my house down for years. *He's been lurking.*

I've been confident in the craftsmanship of my new brick house; the kind he can't blow down anymore, held fast together with the glue of endless reasons why my sobriety is stronger than the feeble straw house of my addiction. But I wonder if he has a hidden key, stowed away so he can sneak in while I'm sleeping.

I guess it's time to change the locks. Or move.

That's the thing with things and stuff – they fall apart and need repair. They need paint jobs and oil changes, tune-ups and regularly scheduled maintenance. It's the certainty of impermanence that things will fall apart: houses, cars, bodies, *resilience.*

Time refuses to pass without taking souvenirs along her way.

If only I could keep my cup of self-will as full as I was able to keep my wine glass all the time; a little dipstick to measure by, ensuring my oil is topped up so things will keep running smoothly. So, I don't find myself stranded on the side of a road, smoke billowing and broke down. A gauge to measure my tire pressure so one doesn't fall flat, pulling me from the road and into the ditch. An alarm that sounds when my gas is low, so I know to pull over and fill up before I come to a sputtering stop.

And I do. *We all do.* We all have a messy box of memories and nightmares, goals and ideas that we can pour into our tanks to ensure we keep going. I have this blog and all my ramblings; myself turned inside out into words, spilling my secrets like snapshots I can flip through, as though they're an album of all my successes and struggles. So, I can always measure myself *now* and again against where I came from. All my at one time '*nows*' left on a shelf for a time when my *new now* needs a little jump start.

Like, *now.*

I'm not tempted, but I'm tired. I'm tired of boarding my doors against the Big Bad Wolf, of explaining over and again to myself the *life-and-death importance* of my sobriety like I'm explaining to a child why they need to chew their food.

So they don't choke. So they can be nourished instead of injured. So they can enjoy their meal and make it to dessert.

Sobriety feels a lot like driving an old car that's been parked for years; oxidized and rusty with all the gears seized up, badly needing maintenance and some highway miles to clear all the dust and cobwebs from the engine. A little wax, a little oil, a lot of rebuilding and cautious, gentle care and one day, it can drive like new again.

But it takes more than that.

It takes checking in. It takes topping up. It takes keeping your tires in balance and your levels in check. It takes routine maintenance to keep it fired up and flying down the highway like a beautifully restored piece of art. What was once written off as scrap on its way to the junkyard is now more impressive for its story of being restored.

Of being revived through the rust and resurrected through the rubble.

Self-care is not self-indulgence. Self-care is self-respect.

It's in that regular self-care, the *routine maintenance,* that can help ensure smooth sailing without ending up in a ditch or stuck on the side of the road. My uncle, dead of a heart attack in his 50's, had two prized classic cars – a '55 Chevy and a '67 Corvette. Both win awards to this day at car shows that my aunt still takes them to. If he had given himself the same attention he did those cars, he'd still be here today. He was also an alcoholic. Those cars were and continue to be cared for *because they're valuable and rare.*

Just like sobriety. Just like ourselves.

I think I've been driving as though I'll never run out of gas; as though the rebuilt machine of my *now-sober-life* is self-propelled, as if just getting it back on the road is enough. *It isn't.* I need to keep my oil can close, a spare jug of fuel in the trunk, and a toolbox on the passenger seat, and the driver's manual in the glovebox. Keeping it washed and waxed only keeps it pretty on the outside.

It's what's under the hood that counts.

You can't pour from an empty cup. Take care of yourself first.

Sometimes, that maintenance comes in the form of just resting and regrouping. Flipping through those old albums full of your *"whys"* and *"never agains"*, like you've pulled over at a rest top to just be idle for a while and let your engine cool off.

Sometimes, it's body work, smoothing out all your dings and dents. I've been finding my body shop at yoga and by eating healthy, plus the occasional tan (because, well, winter in Canada). I can't expect everything under the hood to work well if the hood itself is full of holes, rusted away from years of neglect, letting all the rain pour in and flood my engine.

Sometimes, it's checking my headlights, to ensure I can see where I'm headed; it's often found in the pages of books and the stories of others well on their road of recovery.

And sometimes, it's in the company: picking up strangers along the way so you aren't driving the long road alone. It's amazing what can be learned and shared by others on the same path as you – sometimes you are the one that picks up the hitchhiker, and sometimes you're the one that needs the ride.

So here I am, ready for a little maintenance; needing to ensure that my tank is full so I can keep on keeping on, with a polaroid of the rusted mess I used to be taped to my rear-view mirror.

I can't pick anyone up if I'm driving on empty, and it's a long walk alone if I stall.

There's no room in sobriety for complacency; it's the nail that will puncture your tires, leaving you flat and deflated, stranded on the side of the road. There's no room for assumptions that *now that you have, you always will,* or that the road ahead is straight as an arrow and not actually a dead end or a cul-de-sac.

Pull over when you need to, and pull out a map if you must, so you can keep sailing the sober highway full of pride for driving down the road that took *so much hard work to get back on.*

And when you hear the inevitable rattles, or the road gets bumpy and rough, it's often something that just a little routine maintenance can repair, and once again you'll be hanging out the window like a dog drunk on all the new scents and sensations of finally flying free.

The Riots

APRIL 20, 2018

"A riot is the language of the unheard"
– Martin Luther King, Jr.

I've loved writing and journaling for as long as I can remember. But it was fine art that captured my high school heart and dragged me away to art school, captivated by drawing and painting and creating.

Creating anything. As a child I was obsessed with my little Fisher Price magic set. The idea of making something real materialize out of nothing absolutely mesmerised me.

Years later, it didn't take long to realize that it's very hard to make a living by drawing and painting, not to mention it's even harder to excel (or even learn things) at school when you barely attend class. The only thing I was materializing was a proficiency for balancing drinks and drugs and the ongoing ability to stay awake for no less than 3 days in a row, fading in and out of blackouts while starving myself, inside and out. I later took to waiting tables and managing a beach bar; the perfect place for a budding alcoholic, still drawing, still trying to sculpt my feelings into something I could *actually see.*

I would explain that wine and weed were *"my most important art supplies".*

One of my healthier addictions has always been expressing myself artistically; if I was even remotely coordinated and had any scrap of coordination or rhythm, I'm certain I'd be a very drunk and washed-up musician, too. Whatever helps me get whatever is inside, out. Whatever helps me pluck on my own soul strings or those of others.

Whatever helps to distill the intangibility of emotions and ideas into something sensory, something that can be seen and felt deep beneath the surface of our fingertips.

Words. Lines. Colours. Shapes. Crescendos.

The subtle shading and attention to how light fades to dark.

I believe my alcohol addiction grew from a place of simply wanting to *quiet my mind*. To turn off all the screaming ideas and flashing lights that kept it lit up like Times Square, constantly bustling and buzzing and impossible to stop. Millions of thoughts would pass like tiny tourists, just anonymous little blurry streaks of inspiration in the bigger time lapse of my restless, creative brain.

Drinking became my barricade. Drinking became a way to turn all the tourists away and unplug all the lights for even just a little while. A way to dim the busy metropolis of my perpetually racing mind.

The more I drank, the more the dimming of my light became a bleak and rolling blackout until eventually, the entire city of my spirit simply went dark.

That's when the riots began.

That's when all the monsters crept from the alleyways, no longer afraid to be seen. That's when the darkness brought the demons, awake from their slumber like smoke slipping from dirty, lipstick-stained bottles. It was as though I had summoned them to grant me three wishes, having no idea what it was I was even asking for or wanting.

Wine became the genie I turned to, rubbing his belly in search of answers and begging for cures.

All it ever gave me were more demons, as if they were poured into my streets to chase all the other demons away.

It only made for a more crowded kind of hell.

It only made the riots louder, with more claws scratching at me as they tried to climb my towering walls, and the more of them there were, the more they blacked out the sky, obscuring the moon and whatever was left of the sun bouncing off it.

All the *"slowing of my thoughts"* I was unconsciously grasping for raised the barricades that stopped so much from pouring in, but in turn *they also stopped so much from pouring out.* Quarantined. Every drink, every binge, every bender, every bottle built them taller and taller until there was nothing left standing in the dark Times Square of my mind but myself and all the demons I was unwittingly trapped with.

I had successfully, and inadvertently, managed to smother my curiosity and my passion, as though when all the lights went out, the fire inside me did as well. All my creative motivation that was once thick and rich with ideas and inspiration became thin and diluted, until absolute indifference moved in.

All my demons gathered round to feast on what was left of my enthusiasm.

That's one of the saddest and sweeping side effects of addiction: *an overall indifference towards everything both inside and out.* Alcohol does not differentiate between what you love and what you're seeking to numb. It will inevitably inject your entire life with an apathetic anesthetic until you're in an overall state of simply *not caring.*

Except that somewhere deep down inside, you still do.

And I still did.

The childhood magician who was enamoured with creating something out of nothing was still inside me, but he was shaken up like a can of Coca-Cola, carbonated and under pressure and ready to explode. I had repressed ten billion bubbles of self-expression, and they were agitated and waiting to burst.

The riots raged inside me for decades like a drawn-out drunken war.

There are things you can quell and things you can quiet, but your youthful passions are not one of them. Whatever it is that makes you feel as though you're *in the right skin* will always be there, haunting you until the barricades come down.

Reminding you of the things you love because they in turn help you *love yourself.*

They're those feelings of indescribable, hungry sadness within that tell you that something is missing. It's that dark and heavy hollow inside you that weighs you down despite it being empty and unfulfilled. It's the things you say you'll do one day.

When you're sober, when you have more time.

When you finally have all your shit together again.

They're the things you once did and the times in your life that you come to use as landmarks, measuring how far your addiction has dragged you away from doing what truly makes you happy.

They're the good ole days. The days before the riots.

I never stopped being creative, I just stopped the flow from flowing. I never stopped having the ideas or the inspiration of things to draw or art to create or journals and stories I felt compelled to write; I just stopped drawing them and creating them. They were always still there, waiting, and my inaction is what caused the suffering, and it was my drinking that caused my inaction.

And it was that sad, predictable chain reaction that caused the riots.

I could write volumes on how so much of my life passed me by while I was cowering in dark alleyways, hiding from my demons during the riots, barely fighting for my own life. But one of the saddest chapters would be about all the years of unfulfilled ideas, that just piled up like never-inflated balloons, never taking flight, never feeling the satisfaction of *being full*. It would be the chapter that recounts the battle between my creativity and my addiction, and how my *"most important art supplies"* overtook their original purpose.

What was once a brush I used to accentuate my art became a blade that cut my desire to create into pieces, leaving it bleeding and lifeless like another casualty of war, with all the canvases piled up in useless shreds of fabric on the floor.

One of the most beautiful rewards of sobriety has been feeling creativity flow through me again since the barricades came down, as though the riots have ended, and the lights have slowly started to turn back on. It's seeing all the wreckage left behind as inspiration instead of remorse. It's knowing the riots ultimately gave me true appreciation of what I don't ever want to take for granted again and knowing that I can use all the ruins and debris as my *new favourite art supplies.*

Don't be afraid to start over. It's a new chance to rebuild what you want, this time.

Surviving the riots are how I finally got to hear once more the long-silenced voice of that little magician inside me, the one who doesn't need anything on the outside to create something beautiful from the inside.

It means I'm no longer weary of the dazzling lights of my inner Times Square, because to be lit up by them means *I'm alive, and I survived.*

Sleepwalking

APRIL 22, 2018

It's been a while now since I've found myself here in the quiet lamplight of 3 am.

I used to spend most of my time here, alone in the dark and soaking up the silence. Sobriety has given me plenty already, but among its most generous gifts has been giving me back something I lost years and years ago.

Sleep. Sweet, uninterrupted sleep.

The kind of sleep where you sink and fold into yourself, lost for hours in a shameless, sober blackout. The kind where you leave for a little while to wherever it is that still no one can explain. We've taken photos of pinwheel galaxies that are light years away and have photos of the earth taken from the dusty corners of our own universe, but we still can't see where we go when our eyelids are weary, and our brains turn off.

Or finally turn back on.

I woke up drenched in a cold, wet sweat, as though someone threw a bucket of watery awareness on me, the sheets stuck to me like a bad dream. I just needed to get up and dry out, *my middle-of-the-night metaphor for sobriety.* The uncertain blackness, the clammy discomfort, the *what-the-fuck-just-happened* moments of waking that cling to you like sweat-drenched bedding, trying to piece together where you've been and what you've done using the few mismatched pieces of what you *actually remember.*

I'll trade drenched and sober in the dark at 3 am for drunk and in denial at any hour of the day.

I love this hour of the night when ideas aren't shamed away. Imagination must be an insomniac, always wandering through our sleepy dreams and startling nightmares, painting scenes and ideas our waking brains couldn't handle or muster. She waits until you can't think her away, releasing the absurd and ingenious, like storm-crazed sparrows once you've fallen asleep, turning all the bits of your day they've collected into tidy nests in your dreams, hatching tiny little monsters that couldn't otherwise survive while you're awake.

Sleep and all that happens when our senses shut down is eerily similar to being drunk: *unconscious and abandoned in a world beyond our control, created from all the dark places deep inside us that only come out to play at night.* Maybe that's why I find this witching hour so provocative, caught in the throes between twilight and dawn, not lost to the ethers of sleep but also not exactly awake, either.

It's like being drunk without the drink.

> "To die, to sleep – to sleep, perchance to dream – ay, there's the rub, for in this sleep of death what dreams may come. "
> *– Hamlet*

Our poor brains. They never stop, not even in sleep. It's no wonder Hamlet craved that *dreamless sleep* with such distrust, as even in death there's no certainty of what might come. And so, we drink to usher on that *dreamlessness* like a half-alive kind of dying.

Like being awake at 3 am in the strange limbo between days.

Addiction was my personal purgatory, as though I was bound there alone in the dark. All the tiny monsters from my nightmares would cross over, blurring the lines between a waking hell and tormented, sleeping oblivion. I was never sure of which was worse as neither was better than the other; to be haunted and conscious or blacked out and dreading daylight.

Because drunkenness craves darkness.

It craves it so much that it creates it. But not the romantic *3 am sort of darkness,* like the kind that called me from my sleep tonight. It craves the indulgent, thick and intoxicating kind of darkness that spills like ink into clear waters; overtaking it, consuming it, *transforming it into darkness itself.* It creates the next-best-thing to the *dreamlessness* all addicts desire: a dead and numbing dullness, a sort of sensory blindness that leaves you sleepwalking through your life.

When I was drinking, I would wander in my sleep. I've been known to crawl into bed naked with house guests (sorry to all of you I've done this to) and to scour the kitchen cupboards to eat whatever I could find. I've left the carnage of half a dozen, half-eaten chocolate Easter bunnies all over the kitchen counter with only the ears eaten off each one. I've woke up with a mouthful of half-chewed cashews, nearly choking on my unconscious midnight snack. I'd wake up in places I know I didn't fall asleep/*pass out,* and I'd never have any recollection of how I got there, or why I was fully dressed when I know that I wasn't just hours before. The next morning I'd listen to the stories of my sleepwalking adventures from my unfortunate (though entertained) witnesses as though they were talking about someone else entirely.

I've been caught struggling with locks trying to leave the house, and Hubs hated our 6th floor apartment in New Orleans with windows that opened and had no screens, for fear in my sleep I'd be sure I could fly (I was once found by my friend in the middle of the night, naked and alone in the bathroom, dreaming I was a mosquito, hiding behind the shower curtain.) I've woken up *upside down and unclothed with my legs up the wall,* battered and bruised from somehow navigating my way to the other side of our old hoarder-esque storage room in what I can only imagine must have looked like Gollum traversing a junkyard blindly in the dark.

And even sober, I still sleep-eat. Just the other night I woke up halfway through eating 3 slices of banana bread in bed that I must have gone downstairs to *actually slice* and retrieve; it's terrifying to think I'm using knives when I'm not even awake. But that's what addiction and being drunk is like: running with scissors on slick, wet ice.

Even in sleep, I've always struggled to rest, always caught in the surreal space between being awake and dreaming.

Suspended somehow in the 3 am window *of being alive, where it's not quite twilight, and not quite dawn.*

Sleepwalking.

It's as though whatever remained of my sober mind would try and compensate at night for all the waste and loss of my drunken days, my reality becoming blurred to the point of being asleep while awake, and awake while asleep.

And that's how things end up in the inky, watery darkness of being drunk all the time. Your up becomes down and your down becomes up and it's forever 3 am and you're disoriented and sleepwalking through life in search of something, anything, to fill you up.

It's morning now.

I've made it to the other side of 3 am, the side where it slowly grows decisively brighter and where I'm not alone in the dark anymore, bookended between yesterday and tomorrow. I'm not upset that sleep was elusive, or that 3 am called me like an old friend so we could ride out the darkness together with sobering nostalgia.

I'd rather be awake through the night than still sleepwalking through my days.

Gasoline

APRIL 24, 2018

**It would appear that April showers have poured down with as
many triggers and cravings as raindrops from the sky.**

There's just something about the slow and easy melt of Spring that makes everything seem more loose, more flexible, more relaxed. Like the entire world has been holding its breath and is finally able to exhale. Just like me through the early days of sobriety, where everything felt stark and white and disinfected, now giving way to days where I'm reminded that *I still have a choice*. That the liquor store across the street hasn't moved despite my quarantine, and that all my wine glasses are still shuttered from view, unfulfilled and empty for months now, collecting dust and calling out to me. Out of sight and refusing to be forgotten.

It's in this damp awakening of everything around me that I'm reminded of summer days spent poolside, of late-night bonfires and the clink of glasses and crushing of tin cans.

Somehow all my fair-weather memories are kept in a bottle and defined by wine.

I had to talk myself down yesterday and the day before; finally free from winter's long detention, raking leaves in the yard and cleaning up the mess the snow kept so quietly hidden and held down. Just being outside and working, I could feel my body fire up, stirring a hunger I know I can't feed. At least not how I used to.

There is something about Spring that simply makes me want to drink.

A lot.

I wanted to sit back in my chair on the porch with a bottle of wine, rocking myself through the sunset as they do in every movie on sprawling covered porches in the old deep south, the sound of cicadas serenading the twilight. I wanted to watch the world go by, noticing less and less with every sip until darkness came, putting the day to rest to the magical, mystical dance of fireflies and sweet drunken bliss.

I wanted to wrap myself in a sweater just thick enough to keep the damp chill away, the kind of chill that comes with every spring evening, warming myself from within with each emptied glass of wine and the booze-fueled fire that flushes itself through me from the belly up as it hits.

Except that I didn't.

I didn't *really* want any of that.

I didn't want to find myself cleaning up the mess again.

I wanted the warmth without the wine, the reward without the regret. And so, *The Great Debate* began, standing in the middle of my yard with nothing but a rake in my hand.

I was triggered. That was obvious. I was standing in cravings much deeper than the piles of leaves I had gathered, and they were equally rotten; the only difference is my cravings wouldn't just decompose and rot themselves away. I couldn't just collect them and dump them behind the tall pines in my driveway or mulch them into tiny shreds of themselves to be absorbed back into the earth. My cravings weren't like brittle fall leaves that could just be swept away. They were invasive like weeds and needed to be dug up entirely or else they'd spread.

They'd spread everywhere in good time, choking out anything good in my garden.

I know because it's happened before.

The *Great Debate* always begins by replaying the inevitable chain of events, reminding myself of *The Pattern.* Just like the seasons tumble from one to the next,

I know my first drink will just make me sleepy, and the second will perk me up.

The third I'll be tipsy, then the fourth I'll be drunk. Then, it's fair game, and the winds will pick up and blow my freshly raked leaves all through the yard. I'll go three bottles in, and pass unwittingly into blackout, just to wake up tomorrow and see the mess I've made, strewn all over again.

I remind myself that I didn't come this far to only come this far.

And then, the ingenious thought that *maybe I'll just have one* arrives like clockwork, as though I've excelled at this in the past. It arrives like an *Ah-ha!* moment, as if I've just invented something that's existed forever and I'm claiming the stroke of brilliance as my own.

Except for my track record. My track record reminds me of all I need to know.

My one drink without fail has always turned into ten, then two bottles, then four, multiplying like wet little Gremlins in the rain. This is one of those rare times where the past serves me well, knowing better than to touch a hot stove because I've been burnt before.

Moderation for me is like the sample stand at Costco. I only need one little taste and without fail I'm buying the whole damn box in bulk.

When the patterns of my past aren't enough to douse the fires, I turn to my sloppy understanding of science and biology and start pulling out facts like I'm Bill Nye the Science Guy.

And it always comes down to gasoline.

> "Ethanol fuel is ethyl alcohol, the same type of alcohol found in alcoholic beverages, used as fuel. It is most often used as a motor fuel, mainly as a biofuel additive for gasoline."
> – *Wikipedia*

This is where I start to pull myself back to the sobering reality that I'm standing amid all these flames of cravings because *it was gasoline itself* that fueled this stupid fire in the first place.

I surely wouldn't pour water into the gas tank of my truck, so why would I pour gasoline *into* myself? If someone handed me a glass brimming full of ethanol, would I drink it? And what does it mean that I willingly did for so long, knowing I was sipping on slow death every day?

Finally, at long last, I summon my memories of *The Cycle*. The deceptive dichotomy of what I want, and what I'll get. This is often the nail in the casket that holds the lid down for one more day, keeping my zombie cravings contained. It's the moment where I force myself to look further than what I want *right now*, to the horizon and what *I'll receive* if I give in.

It's projecting myself to the destination I'll unavoidably arrive at if I keep driving down this familiar, bumpy road.

It takes breathing, at first. *To stop and see.* To see what I'm *really* craving because I know it isn't wine. It's the flush of relaxation, the quieting of my mind, and the *"reward"* at the end of my hard day's work. I want the immediate satisfaction but need to pause and place it on one side of a scale, weighing it against all the inevitable, heavy consequences that will arrive as surely as the sun tomorrow.

Am I willing to trade the few hours of being numb tonight for an entire day of regret tomorrow? Am I willing to quiet my mind with wine right now in exchange for all the noise I'll hear in the morning? Is it worth feeling nothing for a while, only to feel everything so very much more amplified later on? Am I willing to trade the ever-growing pride of my sober time for the certain shame of having to live with my weakness for having given in?

After all this time cleaning up the mess in my yard, am I willing to let the winds blow through and just throw it all around again?

I'm not.

I'm not willing to undo myself anymore. I'm not willing to be nothing more than a thirsty, leaking gas tank, always running on empty and coasting on fumes. I'm not willing to let the mess of winter lay rotting in my yard when I'm finally standing tall in this spring so full of potential.

I'm not willing to pour gasoline on all these piles of long-dead leaves that took so much work to clean up, leaving scars in my now nicely tidied lawn.

And it's in that fleeting and freeing moment of sober clarity that I'm reminded that what I'm craving isn't something that can be poured into me like gasoline, only feeding the fires I've been trying to put out. It's knowing I don't want to stand there *for always*, cleaning up the same messes over and over, day in and day out, at the whims of the wind.

It's knowing that after these damp days of spring that still carry bits of winter with her, that the summer I've been truly craving is on its way.

That my hard work and perseverance right now allow so very much more to grow.

Sometimes in recovery, you need to hold your own hand to remind yourself of how hot the stove really is. It's after those decisive little talks and winning the precarious and cunning *Great Debates* that you can sit back and enjoy all you've cleaned up, knowing it will be even more beautiful in the morning.

How To Feng Shui Your Freaking Life

APRIL 26, 2018

We were living in the old house when things started to fall apart.

At this point, it was mostly "just" business related. You know – finances and all those peripheral parts of my life that kept things well-oiled and sort of moving forward-ish. The type of things that ensured my daily booze allowance was accounted for. Customers were growing angry; bill collectors were ringing, and my drinking was escalating (who knew it could get worse?) All the while, my depression was swelling to suffocating proportions and my indifference was all-consuming. Both our bank accounts and my spirit were as empty as each and every mounting bottle of wine in my towering, disgraceful collection, waiting for the shame-filled recycling day when their deafening crash would wake the whole damned village.

It never *really* woke me up, though.

Not with the wakeup call I needed, anyway.

Our house was ancient; a 165-year-old dragon-stone beauty in a tiny, sleepy village of less than 300 people. I started wondering if it was haunted, desperately reaching for a way to explain the daisy chain of bad luck that had latched onto me.

Onto us.

I smudged the house with bundles of sage, in hopes of banishing whatever ghosts might be lingering in the hallways of our home. I started googling cures and remedies, charms to attract wealth and elaborate bronze elephants to usher happiness through my door, strategically placing mirrors to reflect all the bad juju back out and as far the fuck away from me as possible. I bought *just the right amount* of goldfish and placed them in *just the right spot*, I painted walls and furniture in varying shades of greens and blues and spent money I didn't have on pillows of just the right shape and texture, because, *well*, the internet told me to.

The internet promised me that Feng Shui would remedy all that was wrong in my life.

And all that was wrong *couldn't have been* because I was *making poor fucking choices.*

It wasn't because I was a self-absorbed booze hound, whose priorities were whacked, and whose direction was skewed. It wasn't because I was busy self-imploding, building a little internal bomb, just waiting to turn my whole life into shrapnel.

Nope.

It couldn't have been because of any of *that.* It had to be because my chairs were in the wrong place and my table corners were too sharp; my plants had wrong-shaped leaves and we were sleeping with our heads facing North instead of East.

I wasn't just *finally* suffering the myriad of consequences from decades of drunken poor judgement; I was simply *a bad decorator.* I even hired a Feng Shui guru (twice) to come and cure our home of all its evil chi and welcome some goodness back through our doors at long last.

Nothing changed, of course.

Nothing changed *because the bad energy was in me* – not the house.

I needed to Feng Shui *my freaking life*, not my corridors.

Things continued to go south for several more years – and here we are today. Hindsight is helping me see how ridiculous my earlier efforts actually were, but don't get me wrong. I do believe in Feng Shui and the energy of the universe and all that good stuff. But, back then, I hadn't yet arrived at the point of owning up to my mistakes or embracing my struggles. I was still blaming. Still projecting cause on things outside myself, for effects that I didn't like the taste of. I was still self-destructing. Still sinking lower into addiction and waiting for that inevitable-and-impossible-to-ignore *face-plant* onto the rocky depth of my new lower low, my new rock bottom, before I would finally admit that *the problem was in me,* not my circumstances or the house I was living in.

My circumstances were just a sloppy consequence of all my really, really bad, misguided drunken choices.

When I finally started *rearranging my heart and soul and all my priorities and fears,* all the *positive chi* I was earlier trying to reflect into my life through the hanging of Bagua mirrors and the perfect placement of lucky dragon figurines not surprisingly *finally* started to flow my way.

Because I needed to *rearrange myself.*

And so, I present to you my *Addict's 10 Step Guide to Feng Shui-ing*

Your Freaking Life:

An Addict's 10-Step Guide to Feng Shui-ing Your Freaking Life

Step 1: Know Your Intention: The first step towards creating good Feng Shui is understanding the goal you are aiming for. This is called *"Knowing Your Intention."* Do you want better relationships, better health, a smoother career path, or just maybe *freedom from feeling 'stuck'* and like your life *isn't* wildly spinning out of control?

Well, um, yes? *Of course, I do!* Can I also add 'stop drinking the entire liquor store every day' to that list of intentions, too? No one starts reaching for voodoo or Feng Shui cures until all those good things in your life have started to suffer. When your addiction outgrows your goals and control, it's probably a good time to revisit not only what your intentions actually are, but if what you're doing every day is in any way aligned with getting where you want to go. For possibly the first time in my life, I had to be crystal clear and brutally honest about what my life had become – and what I wanted my life to look like. I couldn't do that without admitting – and owning – how shitty things had grown in all those departments – because of *choices I made.* So, I set my intention to grow bigger than my addiction, to make better choices, and to make sure that those choices were in line with my goals.

My intention was sobriety, and to feel alive and in control again.

Sounds simple, right? Ha.

Now I had to start walking the talk if I wanted this voodoo to work.

Step 2: Eliminate the Clutter: Wouldn't it be great if it was as easy as putting all your excess emotional baggage into totes and cardboard boxes, neatly labelled *Yard Sale* because they no longer serve you? Well, that's essentially what I needed to do.

I had to collect all the things that were no longer adding to my life, that were tripping me up, and that I no longer had use for – and start getting rid of them.

It's easy to gather lamps and tchotchkes and all that collects dust from the shelves and closets of our home, but it's another story to do the same with all the skeletons we've been *drinking to forget.*

Clutter isn't just the crap in your closets. It's the noise in our heads. It's the horrible food we put into our bodies, it's the negative self-talk and the whirlpools of shame that suck us down to the bottom of a bottle. Clearing it out is not for the faint of heart, but you can't move forward when you're trying to carry things that are too heavy to hold. Journal. Say mantras every day. Meditate. Read books on self-worth and self-improvement. Say *"I love you"* to yourself in every mirror you see.

Addiction is full of self-loathing, so start learning how to *self-love* instead. I had to dig deep to unearth my old limiting patterns and beliefs that were keeping me stuck. *I had to challenge myself to find out what it was I wanted in life, and then gather the courage and strength to know that I was worth all of it and more.*

There were tears. There was a *shitload* of digging. But I had to identify all the emotional clutter that was causing my pain, and in turn made me turn to drinking to try and make that pain and discomfort go away before I could venture onward to truly *living* my intentions.

Step 3: Keep the Lid Down: In Feng Shui, open toilet lids are more than just another reason to yell at your husband. They're akin to sewers, that suck everything down the drain – good or bad, they don't care. The idea is that good energy and money is sucked away from you when you leave the lid up. So, keep 'em closed, kids.

So how do you keep the figurative *toilet seat of your life* in the down position? Identifying patterns, people and things that drain you emotionally, physically and mentally. For me, that was obviously the booze, but it also involved figuring out what was *toxic* in my life: the energy suckers. As they say, *"water seeks its own level"* so my life was vibrating at the same frequency of what, and who, I was surrounding myself with. And that was a damned low vibration, let me tell you. It's amazing how we can waste away our days by doing practically nothing, and feeling over-busy, over-stressed, and underwhelmed while doing it.

I had to start closing the lid on everything that was just *taking* from, and not *adding to*, my life. I had to start creating boundaries: for others, and especially myself. I had to start taking charge of the *time suckers* (social media, television, getting shit-faced every night) and ensure the lid stayed down to keep all my *energy suckers* at bay, too, which are the things that are *mentally* draining and would always drive me to drink. Too many commitments, negative people and unfinished projects all had to go down the drain and stay there.

Lid, *closed.*

Step 4: Balance, Balance, Balance! It's good *Feng Shuetiquette* (I just made that up) to always have two night tables, or pieces of furniture, on either side of your bed. You know, to encourage couplehood, healthy relationships, and general feelings of being grounded and balanced. It creates deeper and more restful sleeps, and deeper and more honest relationships.

If there is one thing my life was missing, it was *balance*. My life felt as balanced as a hungover, half-in-the-bag-by-noon hot mess trying to walk a tightrope in a windstorm with no experience or safety net. Wobbly and about to plummet like a lead balloon would be a generous understatement. It's not only that I was trying to carry too much, but every choice I was making was working *against* me. Add to that an unhealthy *allergy to moderation* and I was way too much *this* and not enough *that* with quite literally everything in my life. Everything was all or nothing, and it usually ended up as *all*, with just *a little bit more* for good measure. I was *all drinking* and no activity, all junk food and no real food, all noise and no silence, all in or all out. There was no mindfulness, no presence, no peace and *definitely* no calm. I was a spastic squirrel on speed in the middle of a freeway, always anywhere and everywhere – but *here*.

In literal Feng Shui, I *was* that lopsided bed with only one lonely night table. Yoga, meditation, a healthy vegan diet, Buddhist Dharma books and quiet introspection; I first had a taste, then I ate them all up. That whole classic "peace out" hippy-Zen-vibe that all of the above conjures up is for good reason: *because it works.* Identify the areas of your life that are either extreme or completely absent and start with those. Cut some things back while you add new things in. Find a recipe for your day that helps you bring your life back into balance emotionally, spiritually, mentally and physically.

Whatever it is, find the matching 'night tables' that work for you, and help to keep you grounded.

Step 5: Don't Work with Your Back to The Door: The rules of Feng Shui suggest that working with your back to a door puts you in a compromising position, even if you don't realize it in the moment. If you reposition your desk and work *facing* a door, you may be surprised to feel how much more powerful that position actually is. Essentially, put yourself in a position where no one can sneak up on you.

If I were a desk, this step would be so much simpler. But, alas, a desk I am not – so I had to start identifying all the situations that were putting me into compromising positions. And the most compromising position in recovery is one where you are tempted, where your back is to the figurative door and out of nowhere the cravings and triggers pop up and over your shoulder and scare the shit out of you with a big *"Surprise! I'm here!"*

This takes planning and keeping your eyes looking forward and your back to the wall. If we are going out – I plan in advance what non-alcoholic drinks I'm going to have. If friends are coming over – I disclose ahead of time that I'm not drinking and that it's a done deal, establishing the precedent beforehand leaves far less margin for impulsive errors. Make your decisions *in advance* when you can, so you don't waver and give in on the spot, because old comfortable patterns will make you say *yes* when you want to say *no*. By failing to prepare, you're preparing to fail, as cliché as that sounds, and is.

Keep your eye on the door and treat it like a game of Whack-A-Mole. You know the cravings and temptations are going to pop up, so be ready for them when they do and *clobber the heck out of them every single time.*

Step 6: Go with The Flow (and drink lots of water): Most of us are drawn to things like water, plants and animals naturally – because they awaken all that juicy good energy in us. They're nurturing and nourishing, and help energy to keep flowing, where otherwise bad energy can grow stagnant and settle in. Plants are a wood element, helping you to open up and expand, and encouraging flexibility and strengthening your intuition. The term Feng Shui literally means *"Wind & Water"*, with the water element bringing renewal, purity, freshness and a sense of *flow and abundance* to your life, often introduced through the colour blue, mirrors and properly placed water features.

First of all, I'm going to start with the obvious: DRINK. ALL. THE. WATER. This cannot be overstated. I still struggle with this every day, but speaking of plants and water – you know how your house plants start to wilt and dry up and slowly die and look offensively angry and disappointed with you? Ya, that. Well, *you are basically just a houseplant with more complicated emotions.* You *need* water to thrive. Pouring wine on a plant doesn't work (trust me, I've tried, accidentally.) I've been so used to having a wine glass glued to my hand (hello, dehydrating diuretic) so it's been a transition having a water bottle full of Liquid Life there, instead. But it's helped more than I can say, from flushing out my backlog of poisons and toxins to giving me the life-giving energy that water is bursting with. Plus, my skin looks great. Win.

Next, get out into nature. There is truly nothing that sunshine, sand and surf can't fix; it's a natural healer and throughout recovery there is a tonne of healing required both inside and out. Addiction makes us isolate, whether we intend to or not, so stepping back into the natural flow of the world around us is one of the best ways to start flowing again. Personally, I spent way to long "stuck" in addiction, like water building pressure behind a dam, refusing to just let things *be as they are,* and trying to control everything – and failing miserably. In trying to control things less, I'm finally learning to just go with the flow, more.

And holy hell, literally *everything* is so very much easier.

Step 7: Fix What's Broken: Broken things have no place in your home – and your home is a mirror of *you*. Broken items are the epitome of negative energy, and ideally you want to replace, repair or get rid of broken items as soon as possible.

If you can't fix things, *let them go.* Don't allow things that need repair to linger or pile up, since that only amplifies negative energy and prevents good *new* things from coming into your life. This cure allows you to release your frustrations and anxieties and smooths your life path.

I wish they made a superglue for life and relationships; something that pieces things back together and replaces all the broken parts. But there isn't, so we must go about it the hard, and surprisingly empowering, way, which is through *demonstrating our changed behaviour.* Apologies are lovely and absolutely necessary, but words can catch and be lost to the wind and end up spread too thin, whereas *our actions* are what can seal the deal. It shows that we're committed to our recovery, that we're making amends with our past and wrong-doings and doing our *absolute best* now that we know better.

There's no use beating yourself up here. Leave the shame where it belongs: in the past. It's amazing how quickly things begin to improve when everyone around you begins to see you walking the talk (and there's no room for zealots here; so just do your thing). What can't be fixed, release it, and commend yourself for having tried. Nothing goes back together exactly how it was before. Sometimes things get stronger, and sometimes the pieces never fit back together the same way.

And that's okay.

Let go of what can't be fixed and make room for better things to take their place.

Step 8: Wind Chimes for The Win: According to the rules of Feng Shui, you can encourage helpful people into your life by hanging a pleasant-sounding wind chime. The sound of a metal wind chime hung in the right-front area of your home, office, or bedroom activates more people to *help you* and gets you more help from the people who are already at your side.

This, I believe, is one the most important steps in *Feng Shui-ing Your Freaking Life.* Because especially in the early days of recovery, we're still dragging our secrecy and shame along with us like a ball and chain. It follows us everywhere, and we don't want anyone to know about it. So, we pick it up and carry it beneath our coats, we tuck it into the corners of our purses and bags, and we fling it over our shoulder like the shame-filled weight of the world. Don't be Atlas. Eventually (thankfully) we realize that it *isn't* something we can do *alone.* As isolating and individual as addiction becomes, recovery needs to be the inside-out version of it – meaning *find your tribe.*

My early days of recovery, I was certain there was no one whose life was as messed up as mine. There was no one who needed to drink 3 or 4 bottles of wine a day, *every day,* like I did. There was no one who was struggling like I was – because there was obviously something wrong with *me* because I simply couldn't just *stop.*

And I could *not* have been more wrong.

Taking myself down from my isolated pedestal of addiction I found what I was going through was incredibly common and normal, and that there were so many other people in far worse positions who are now thriving without alcohol. I discovered that my addiction caused far more near-sightedness and self-absorption than I had ever imagined.

I wasn't alone.

And now, I was inspired. There is priceless value in supporting others through your journey, and it always, *always* returns ten-fold. Source out online groups or in-person meetings that click with your vibe – whatever works for you, *work it.* I favour online closed communities like This Naked Mind and Club Soda, where it's like a round-the-clock room I can pop into whenever I need support or accountability, or have the time to offer that to others. It's as addictive as the drugs we used to need like oxygen, and stronger medicine than anything a doctor could prescribe.

Next – surround yourself with people who support your recovery, are genuinely thrilled for you, and want nothing but your *wild and crazy sober success.* There is absolutely no room for any type of other kind of "friend" or company in the early days of recovery. Never forget that crushing this sober thing is more important than anything right now, because without it, you'll lose everything – including a lot of your relationships. So, focus on the ones that are nurturing and nourishing, and run like hell when you sense that someone isn't respecting your *life-and-death* need to get sober.

Step 9: Do What Feels Right: The magical part of all the many Feng Shui rules are that there is only truly *one real* rule. And it's the best cure of them all. *Do what feels right.* If it doesn't feel right, don't do it. It's as simple as that. Go with your gut, follow your intuition, call it what you may – but what it comes down to is ensuring *what* you are doing is *the next right thing.*

This applies in the real, physical world too, when you just feel like the couch is in the right place, or that a room feels good to be in and is easy to walk through. It's ensuring there is *flow* and few obstructions, that the overall feeling is calming and peaceful, and that the energy of the room *vibrates with what you want to experience in it.* In the world of recovery, it's all about listening to your body and your needs. It's about pausing, and sometimes stopping. It's about learning how to love your new, healthy body and all that it needs to continue serving you. Can we give a huge thank you to our ever-forgiving bodies? After all we've put them through, they're still all rooting for us.

When I was in active addiction, I just did *whatever* made me feel better (and eventually much worse) *whenever* I wanted. I would always take the shortest, fastest route to those cozy feelings of comfort, and eventually, blackout and the inevitable death-defying hangover. Addiction causes spontaneity, poor judgement, lack of forethought and the convenient oversight of consequences. Recovery and sobriety? It requires the opposite. It requires a *constant* commitment to Step 1 of *Feng Shui-ing Your Freaking Life: Know Your Intention*. If what you're about to do, or what you're thinking or feeling doesn't align with that intention – don't do it. If ten thousand butterflies light up in your gut when you think – and you will – that you can moderate or *just have one,* it means that your body disagrees. It's not agreeing with you because it knows better. It *knows* your track record and it *knows* the consequences. Listen to your body and listen to your heart.

They'll never lie to you the way that alcohol always did.

Step 10: Rinse & Repeat: There's no off switch. There's no do-it-and-done when Feng Shui-ing your life. It isn't a 2 in 1 shampoo and conditioner you can toss in and wash all the dirt away, leaving everything shiny, bouncy, clean and smelling like a country breeze. It takes work, it takes repetition, and it takes commitment to exorcising your life of negativity and welcoming nothing but goodness back in.

And there's so very much goodness.

Be gentle with yourself, and introduce these changes and cures slowly but deliberately, with every ounce and then some of your entire being. Give yourself the same chance at renewal you'd want for your best friend – and be your own best friend, for what will most likely be the first time ever.

And *just wait.*

Just *wait* until you can sit back and feel the changes as everything starts to flow through your halls again. Just wait until everything feels lighter, no longer weighed down between all the clutter and dust, when everything stops flowing down your drains, and the good stuff decides to stay and hang out for a while.

"Arranging a home to hold happiness in place is the primary goal of Feng Shui."
– *Terah Kathryn Collins*

Welcome home.

All My Hungry Ghosts

APRIL 28, 2018

"A man takes a drink, the drink takes a drink, then the drink takes the man."
– Confucius

The word "alcohol" is said to come from the Arabic term "al-khul" which literally means "Body Eating Spirit". It's the source of why many drinks are called "spirits", and also, it's the origin of the English word "ghoul", which is an evil spirit or phantom that robs graves and feeds on dead bodies. The current Arabic word for alcohol (ethanol) is الغول or *al-ġawl* – properly meaning "spirit" or "demon".

Just let that sink in for a second.

There will always be a divide in the timeline of my life. Before drinking, while I was drinking, and wherever I am now, in recovery. Not as much like distinct chapters in a book, but more like actors on a tv show, where they swap out someone new to play the role of the exact same character.

They look alike, but they're still so very different.

Without sounding over dramatic (who, me?) I look back on *Drinking Shawn* like an entirely different person; a man possessed and obsessed, pushed down and out by everything he was pouring into himself. It's like watching a slow, sinking car that somehow found itself in the middle of a lake. It doesn't sink all at once. It just gradually fills with more and more water, until eventually, it's consumed and just disappears into the dark abyss below.

Gone, but still there.

Rotting.

And there were casualties. Parts of me that never made it out alive and parts of me that weren't strong enough to swim back to the surface, tangled forever in time beneath the unbearable weight of my addiction. They're still there, in the murky depths, like an underwater homage to when my life drove straight off the road and into the lake.

As though I wasn't driving at all.

I became an unwitting passenger before I got locked in the trunk. I traded my keys for just *one more drink*, for just a little more numbness, for someone else to *please drive for me* because I couldn't stand to stare at the road ahead any longer.

I contorted myself into shapes and positions I didn't think possible, just to *escape myself* for a little while in whatever blackness I could get in trade from all my hungry ghosts.

They stood there by the open trunk while I willingly crawled right in and let them drive.

And they lined up to crawl inside *me* with their big bellies and tiny throats, their miniature mouths never able to take enough in to fill themselves up. Their mouths the size of a needle's eye and their stomachs the size of a mountain, always hungry, always wanting more, all my *hungry ghosts* just nibbling away at me and everything I offered up to try and keep them satisfied.

I was already dead; a feast for the ghouls I poured down my throat every day.

The ghouls that feed on the bodies of the dead, and that was me.

Alive, but not. Living, but dead.

And they could smell it.

They could smell *me.*

They lined up, one by one, to swim in my wine glass and dive down my throat to the pit of my stomach where my sorrows were stowed.

They lined up for their feast like vultures above, circling and waiting for me to collapse, eaten away from the inside out, still pouring thirsty demons to my depths, hoping to feed all the hungry ghosts inside.

And that's what Hell feels like.

Forever feeling *unsatisfied.* Feeling *bottomless,* like an echo that grows weaker until it disappears into absolute, infinite nothingness.

Again, and again, and again.

Consumed.

Hell is when all your *hungry ghosts* stop trying to fill themselves from flasks full of spirits and glasses of ghouls, and they start to feed on *you,* instead.

I didn't turn to drinking intentionally.

I didn't consciously fill myself with evil spirits and surrender my life to an unquenchable thirst. I didn't decide one day that I preferred to die slowly, eaten alive from the inside out. I didn't even notice that I was sinking, or that I was locked in the trunk of a car I was no longer driving until the water began pouring in and I was well on my way down, far below the surface, beneath the unbearable pressure with no way out that I could see.

All I ever wanted was to feed my hungry ghosts.

To keep them quiet, so I could sleep.

And yet that's where I ended up, at the bottom of the lake like a sunken, sad version of myself, warped and distorted in a way only things underwater can become. Haunted and possessed by the very *spirits* I summoned to spook away the ghosts that lived inside me.

Escape has been a slow process; a gradual exorcism of one demon at a time. It was finding morsels of just the right size that I could feed to the ghosts bit by bit, and finally appease them with what they had been craving all along: *closure and acceptance.*

All my years of trying to drown them away only filled me with more spirits to expel.

And they have left me, one by one, in between the lines of letters written to my dead, finally saying all the things that were left unsaid. They have left me in the space between myself and the mirror, finally learning how to look myself straight in the eyes, again. They have left between my fingertips and loosening grip on everything I clung to and tried to hold. They've fallen from my hands along with all the guilt and remorse that I carried far too long.

> "Monsters are real, and ghosts are real too.
> They live inside us, and sometimes, they win."
> – Stephen King

If Hell is eternity spent trying to fill an insatiable and bottomless void, then *sobriety* is the chance to finally fill yourself up and be full.

To no longer allow yourself to be *eaten alive* from the inside out.

To swim back to the surface, wiser and lighter than ever before, no longer weighed down by so many demons disguised as drinks.

To finally fill the space that all the hungry ghosts have left behind.

To have the courage to no longer consume what consumes you.

Branches & Vines

MAY 2, 2018

**I'm finding it harder to find the time to write these last couple weeks,
with spring having sprung and wedding season upon us.**

As a wedding photographer, every day begins to feel like Black Friday in a mall about 30 minutes from closing time, starting now through until the end of November.

That's the thing with time – it isn't simply laying around, waiting to be found. In each moment, we have all the time we will ever have, until the next moment arrives.

So, it's about choosing, not finding.

We all have the same amount of time in the day as Beyoncé.

I love the feeling I get when I click the publish button on this blog; like I've raised a small little bird made up of my thoughts and curiosities and set it free to fly from the nest at last. I always feel like I have more *space* after I'm done writing, when all that's cluttered in my head gets translated onto the screen and the page, making room for more to fall in their place like a never-ending game of mental, emotional Tetris.

I'm always trying to align my thoughts and beliefs, so they somehow fit together, and in turn, disappear and leave me, acknowledged, named, and free from captivity.

I love the therapy of writing, but I really love the rush of the publish button. Of setting whatever I wrote free, like each bit of writing is time spent confessing my transgressions to the page and in turn, the rest of the world. I get a sense of lightness and freedom each time all the thoughts I've been holding in get a chance to come out and speak for themselves. We are creatures motivated by rewards, and it's that bait and return that keeps us hooked. Hooked on eating, on writing, on the gym, on drinking and hooked on the drugs, eating disorders, and senseless self-abuse that we've convinced ourselves feels good.

It's always about the reward and so very rarely about the process.

We always want the fruit with little love reserved for the vine that made it possible.

When I decided to stop drinking, I was motivated by what felt like the hidden riches of a kingdom everyone else was enjoying finally, one day, being mine as well. I was motivated by the results that were promised: better health, clarity of mind, more money, less calories, the ability to drive when I needed to and the miracle of waking up guilt-free, rested, and no longer drenched in regret and missing pieces of my yesterday. Of long-awaited apologies, given and received.

And yes, of course, these are just a few of the very real benefits that have generously washed over my sober life.

But the one I didn't anticipate, and I absolutely love the most, is what I'm learning and who I'm meeting in the process, from whole-hearted strangers in recovery on the other side of the globe, to getting reacquainted with my true self at long last. Without sobriety, all those benefits – the fruit – could never grow. Without sobriety in this very moment, I'd still be dying in bed and nursing a harrowing hangover, or awake at all hours of the night, sleepless and trying to sort out all the drunken voices in my head. All those fruits – the rewards – would be nothing without the vine.

They can't grow without something to grow from.

Rushing results and being impatient for rewards only creates anxiety about the future. It creates restlessness and makes you question the process, your ability, and your intentions. *What am I doing wrong? Why is this taking so long? Why haven't I lost ten pounds when I was drinking my weight in wine every night?* Or thoughts like *I've spent two weeks sober, and my energy is still low* and things like *Why am I still so cranky and short-tempered, I haven't had a drink in weeks!*

We always want it all and so often aren't willing to nurture and care for the process that yields the rewards, that with patience and care, will certainly arrive in due time. If all these things were fruits that grew on trees, you'd water and feed the plant to ensure the sweetest crop and eventual harvest. You'd enjoy the shade it provides in the meantime. And you'd be patient knowing the more care you give the plant, the better your yield will one day be.

Without a healthy plant, there will never be delicious fruit to enjoy.

You know how when you bake something, it always tastes sweeter than something store-bought? And you've heard the old adage that when you chop your own wood, it'll warm you twice?

That's how sobriety works, too.

Some of the most wonderful and unexpected rewards are ones I have stumbled across while feeling my way through the thick of recovery because *the real perks are in the process.* They're in the day-to-day mustering of strengths I didn't know I had and the quiet personal moments of triumph when I overcome a craving or outthink a trigger that seemingly fell from the sky. They're in the out-of-the-blue moments where I remember that I haven't had a drink in months, or the times when I notice that what once would have made me sick with anxiety breezed past me like no big thing.

It's in the process of holding hands with my ghosts and making peace with my past and getting to know the new brightness that is slowly creeping through and lighting up my days. It's been through the process of *nourishing and celebrating my sobriety every day* that I'm in turn helping the original rewards I set out to claim as my own, to *grow.*

For once in my life, my actions are not simply feeding my desires for *this result or that reward. My actions are focused on continuing* to cultivate my sobriety in this moment – and this moment of sobriety is the vine that all the branches and fruits eventually come from.

If I stopped taking care of my sobriety and giving gentle attention to my struggles, I'd miss out on the opportunity *to ask myself questions.* I'd miss the chance to try and understand why I was compelled to drink at the first sign of discomfort or unsavoury feelings, and I'd miss the priceless and unexpected benefits of coming to know myself, vulnerability, shame and all. If I kept rushing headlong with impatience for the rewards that aren't mine just yet, I'd only end up questioning what the hell I was doing wrong instead of seeing it as an opportunity to pause and appreciate that *delays are actually gifts.*

Delays give you the chance to take it all in. You can sit angry and stewing in your car in the heart of a traffic jam, or you can, for what will likely be the first time ever, see it as an opportunity to notice what you normally fly past at a hundred miles an hour.

The destination will always be there. The chance to breathe and take in the journey and all its hidden lessons as you go along won't be.

> "The mill cannot grind with water that is past."
> – *Anon, 17th century*

So be patient and embrace the process as a reward in and of itself, because without it the fruits you're waiting for will never, ever grow. Find a way to be honestly and gratefully fulfilled by the journey itself, and not what you'll receive when you get where it is you think you're heading.

Because you're already there.

So, it's fair to say I'll be writing a little bit less these days as I soberly dive forward into wedding season and my work – but I'll still be here, watering my vines every day and growing more fruit to write about. And, even though hitting that publish button on this blog sets my belly aflutter, it's in the process of *getting it all out* that I grow. It's in all the living that happens *in between the lines and the words* that I unearth my ideas of what I feel is worth writing about and setting free.

Because there is no arriving.

There is only a series of moments and steps, and if you can learn to see each as a destination unto itself, then you have already arrived, *and the fruit is already yours.*

Courageous Love

MAY 14, 2018

I never end up writing about what I think I'm sitting down to write about.

My ego shows me the chair, but my heart usually has a different agenda. There's always a kind of deception between my hands and intentions, which in a nutshell is exactly how I ended up here. *Recovery is quirky like that.*

Most people celebrate having *done* something; addicts celebrate what it is we *haven't* done.

I wanted to write and share my growing list of *100 Reasons to Quit Drinking*, and one day, I will. But this morning, waking to my 100th day sober, there was just one thing on that list that kept pushing its way to the front of the line screaming *Pick me! Pick me!* and so, here we are. Of all the 100 (and easily more) reasons to not drink that I've collected, this little gem is the *piece de resistance* in the new, sparkly crown of my sobriety.

Courageous Love.

One of the most regretful parts of addiction is that it numbs your ability *to love.*

Anything. Anyone. Everything.

Yourself.

I used to refer to booze as Liquid Courage – and it's absolutely anything *but* that. There was nothing courageous about drinking myself to oblivion. I was cowardly, numbing myself each day as a way of eluding the truth. There was nothing brave about my tolerance. Being able to easily drink anyone under the table (including myself) is foolish, not fearless. There was nothing gallant or valiant in poisoning myself bit by bit and bottle by bottle, aware of the slow death I couldn't live without. Killing myself from the inside out was pitiful, and nothing to be proud of.

Referring to alcohol as Liquid Courage does a disservice to those who are truly courageous.

Courage is having strength in the face of pain and struggle. And the more I drank, the less strength I was able to muster. The more I drank, the more I summoned situations that brought me – and everyone around me – nothing but pain. The more I drank, the less courageous I became, and the less courageous I became, the less I was able to love – myself and everyone around me.

> "Fear and courage are brothers."
> – *Proverb*

What *is* courageous though, is feeling fear and still choosing to act. Courage is following your heart. Courage is persevering in the face of adversity. Courage is standing up for what is right. Courage is letting go of the familiar. Courage is suffering with dignity and faith.

Courage is being sober when all you want is to be is wasted. Oblivious. Asleep.

Courage is *acceptance* when all you want is *to forget*.

Courage is *loving* when all you want *is to run*.

And I ran.

With every drink, with every bottle, I ran like the Cowardly Lion in the face of all my Flying Monkeys: my responsibilities, my desires, my fears and my hopeless *disability* to truly love. It's impossible to feel love when you're so drunk you can't feel anything at all. I ran to what I thought would give me pleasure and escape, but instead it only ever gave me disappointment. I ran to fill myself with what I called courage, but I only ended up full of cowardice. I didn't yet know the one thing I was searching for, was my *pride*.

I believe addicts have the biggest of hearts, and they are the most easily broken.

It was my *desire* to love and be loved, to love *myself*, and to somehow *be better than I was* that perpetuated my drinking to the point of hopeless dependency and despair. It's because of our big hearts that long to feel full that we try and silence the hollow and endless echo with drinking and drugs. It's because our big hearts are *too full of feelings* that we turn to anesthetics outside ourselves to numb what we do not know how to accept, understand, or embrace.

It's because we feel everything so loudly that we try and quiet the riots in our heart.

It's because our big addict's heart is longing for courageous love, and to love courageously, that we shutter them away in liquor cabinets deep inside our half-dead chests because we are afraid that we don't know what to do with them.

We stay drunk and saddled to what's familiar, thinking the fear and the failure can't find us. We hide our cold feet in boots so heavy we become stuck in one place.

And it was in an anxious, brave moment of decisive self-love that I rallied the *courage* to *free myself from the familiar*, once and for all allowing all the pain and anguish to pour through me, no longer dulled and drunk – so that I could courageously love and *allow myself to be loved.*

As is.

Choosing to get sober was understanding that there would be tender parts that would need healing, and allowing myself to love myself enough to feel them and forgive myself so I could in turn love others with the fierce honesty they deserve. Getting rid of alcohol was the first step in acknowledging that my heart was not inherently flawed after all, but instead, it was bursting.

For quite possibly the first time ever, I gathered enough courage to swallow my fears and insecurities instead of another drink.

I was so tired of never having enough of what I no longer wanted – and it took courageous self-love that I didn't even know I had to sweat it out and push through so I could finally allow myself to have what it was I truly wanted all along: *freedom from feeling powerless.*

Here is the most important thing I have learned in my sobriety:

When you want to run, *stay*. When you want to hide, *open up.* When you want to give up, *go a little further.*

That right there is courage, and it's the most important ingredient in this wild recipe of sobriety. It takes courage to admit you have shrunk in the shadow of your addiction. It takes courage to allow yourself to feel all the feels. It takes courage to own your story, and it takes courage to reject the assumed shame that comes tied to it with the same ferocity as you once used to repel reality.

It takes courage to learn how to love yourself enough to stop undoing yourself.

Amelia Earheart put it most perfectly, and I'll close with this:

> *"Courage is the price that life exacts for granting peace."*

"When you want to run, stay. When you want to hide, open up. When you want to give up, go a little further."

– SHAWN VAN DAELE, LIFE IN DETOX

You're Going to Want to Give Up

MAY 18, 2018

You're going to want to give up.

I know I did.

I still do, some days.

But the prize is in the perseverance. The enduring.

The carrying on.

You'll believe you can't tolerate it anymore. Your life. Your addiction.

Your losses and your mistakes.

Your immutable past.

The task of pushing what feels like an unbearable weight up an endless hill.

The fear of failing. Of fumbling. Of falling.

Again.

You'll doubt your strength to bear the pain of pushing through, and your sorrows will try and tether you to the toxic refuge where you've lingered longer than you were meant to. It will call you by name and promise you what it can't ever deliver, but what you so badly want and so very much deserve.

It will show you escape, but you'll only end up ensnared.

Again.

You're going to want to give up.

You'll try and wish away your feelings. You will want to numb them and extinguish your light, if only for a little while. You'll long for the black anonymity of isolation and the false freedom from your feelings that you think it will bring. You'll want to crawl back to the comforting darkness you fought so hard to free yourself from.

You'll want to release the reigns and let your fear drive, just like you always have. The same fear that drove you to that dark place in the first place. The same fear that kept you there, and the same fear that *terrified you enough to leave* so you could try and save your soul.

Please persist. Endure. *Carry on.*

Stay.

For once in your life, *please stay.*

Stay through the pain and stay through the waves of apprehension. Stay through the uncertainty and stay through the unyielding pull to run, to numb, and to avoid like you always have. *Stay through it all.* Stay through the heartbreak, the anxiety, the grief, the doubt and stay through the slow and marvellous process of *healing.*

Stay through it, so you can grow through it.

Just for today. Just for tonight.

Stay.

You're going to want to give up.

You're going to lie and tell yourself that things will be different this time around. That you're bigger than your patterns and better than your habits. You'll want to run back to the good old days, that you know deep inside weren't really that good after all. It's those good old days that ultimately drove you to despair, fuelled by gallons of anxiety and days full of doubt.

You're going to sift through your wishes and neglected desires, searching for your long-lost lust for life, only finding a *longing for belonging.* You're going to try and convince yourself that it's all too big, too beautiful, and too promising *to be yours.*

You're going to try and convince yourself that continuing to break your own heart is easier than finally gathering the courage to *mend it.*

You're going to forget that just because *you always have* doesn't mean you *always have to.*

You're going to forget that your heartbeat hard enough to push your *desire to change* to the top of your pile of all that you're pining for. You're going to forget that before you started you would have done anything to be where you are right now.

And still, you will want to run.

Please persist. Endure. *Carry on.*

Stay.

For once in your life, *please stay.*

Stay, because you're going to believe that since you don't know how, you never will, and that just because it's hard, it always will be. You'll forget how you've learned things like languages and speech, or how to walk or build houses or swim or create art. You'll forget how you've grown to master things you once didn't even know the name of, and you'll forget that what you're going through now is *no different* from everything you've learned and now take for granted.

You'll forget that this too will be easy one day, but only if you hold out and hold on.

Only if you stay.

Only if you silence the judge inside you.

Only if you give yourself permission to *not know everything and* allow yourself to stumble so you can learn how to pick yourself up.

Again, and again, *and again.*

You're going to want to give up.

You're going to feel the heat like your hand touching fire, and you're going to want to pull it back to what's dangerously familiar. But for once, you need to let yourself feel the burn. You need to endure what you don't believe you can tolerate because the only way to get where you want and need to be – is *through.*

So, stay with the pain. Stay with the sorrow. Stay with the uncertainty so you can come to call them by name and in turn, take their power away.

Stay so you can prove them all wrong.

Stay so you can say you didn't give up when persevering was painful.

Stay because you know it's worth it.

Stay because you deserve better.

Stay, *because aren't you tired of running?*

Dust

MAY 23, 2018

"I will show you fear in a handful of dust"
– T.S. Eliot

I keep sitting down to write and stopping myself halfway through.

I pour out paragraphs of what I *think* wants out, of what I *think* you might want to read, and I keep stalling before I get to where I *thought* I was going. I have no less than a dozen bottled-up drafts sitting unpublished on my blog, collecting digital dust on the shelf.

I haven't been listening to myself.

I haven't been taking my own advice.

I haven't been writing as though no one would ever read what I was spewing through my fingers and onto the screen, which is the little trick I try and use to outsmart myself so that I stay honest, vulnerable, and able to write from my heart instead of my head.

That stupid, damned head.

It's the same stupid, damned head that got me into trouble in the first place, from too much thinking which always led to too much drinking.

Way too much drinking.

My thoughts always turn into this chain of little red wagons full of suffering, some full of the future, and others, the past, and I willingly towed them around everywhere I went for far too long.

They only grew heavier and harder to pull.

Thinking is exhausting, especially when you're dragging your swollen, heavyweight ego behind you all the time.

And he always hops on for the ride.

I've been in a bit of a (read: very) crusty mood the last few days, brought on by a sobering cocktail of bad sleep, bad diet, bad finances and a bad self-image strong enough to stir up a scarily familiar, intense desire to *drink*.

I won't.

I can't.

I know better.

This is a rare situation where thinking actually serves me. I've arrived at a glorious point in my sobriety where just one quick glance at my track record is enough to turn me off and set me right again, like one of those inflatable clowns that tip over but always pop back up.

Ready for another beating.

It's taken years to inflate myself enough so that I don't just stay there, knocked over and deflated, waiting for something or someone to blow me back up again. Yet still, the romance is there like a dog-eared storybook filled with the magical lies of a children's fairy tale, and I'm the damsel in distress and a drink is my Knight in Shining Armour. It's easy to cast yourself as the victim who needs to be rescued, forgetting that you're the one who locked yourself in the tower to begin with. It's easy to wallow alone inside yourself, in some empty room that still somehow feels overcrowded and stuffed with all the things you think you're missing and everything you feel you've lost.

Suffering.

Suffering, because you're clinging to the past and grasping at the future, trying to freeze the ephemeral and capture the fleeting.

Suffering, because you're trying to control the uncontrollable.

Suffering, because you've fallen for the fairy tale.

Suffering, because you're *trying.*

Trying so hard to force things.

I catch myself trying to make water flow upstream and forcing square pegs into round holes, and every time I'm left exhausted and frustrated in a heap in the corner, no good to others or myself. That's how I ended up in the messy predicament I did, after all: addicted and knee-deep in dust. It left me choking on mouthfuls of all my past regrets and pleasures, tripping over all my insecurities around the future, all of them swarming at my feet like ten thousand dusty, red-eyed mice.

Dust is just tiny little pieces of things that once were, because everything always leaves something behind.

All that dust builds and collects, and over time, only ruins whatever is beneath where it settled. That is, unless you keep sweeping. Unless you keep moving. Unless you keep all you value shiny, polished and clean – sobriety included. It takes being engaged and not allowing the past to cover everything like stale sheets draped over furniture in some locked-away room, crammed full of all that you're hoarding and want to keep but have no use for anymore.

All that you're struggling to hold on to.

All that you can't let go.

Struggling and suffering are verbs.

They require *action*, and for so very long I always assumed they were things *that happened to me*, when in fact, they were circumstances I brought on myself. I always knew they were, but I struggled to admit it. I refused to own it. Just like my addiction, I excused the cause of everything *wrong with my life* as far away from myself as possible, always ready to justify my next bottle of wine with any number of things from my ten-mile-long list of *Reasons I Deserve a Drink*.

I refused to admit that my world was covered in dust *because I failed to keep dusting*. I chalked it up to the delusion that the world was simply an overly desolate and dusty place.

And, sometimes, it is.

I refused to admit that life felt hard because I was making it hard, and I was making it hard by wanting and trying to force things. I kept imagining different than what was and kept coming up disappointed.

I was making it hard by wishing everything and everyone else had the capacity to stand as still and stuck in time as I was.

Covered in dust.

I'm pretty sure that I've been in a bad mood the last few days because my imagination isn't lining up with my reality, again. That I'm resisting just feeling what I'm feeling. That it's okay to have bad days. That it's okay to let my cravings come and go, and to call them out for the little liars that they are.

That I'm allowed to rest.

Losing Control

MAY 24, 2018

**"Surrender is not the best way to live; it is the only way to live.
Nothing else works."**
– Rick Warren

If there is one thing that drives me to want to drink, it's *technical problems –* and money problems, and relationship problems, weeds in my garden, business problems, and concerns over North Korea and Armageddon and all that other stuff.

Downed internet, wonky website plugins that refuse to work and that moment when the control you have over things is handed over to anonymous nameless customer support reps somewhere out there in the ever-sprawling inter-webs.

Because, well, *control.*

I wish it ended there, somewhere in the binary land inside my computer or contained to things I can hold and place my hands on, instead of spilling from an immeasurable internal struggle inside myself where I feel obligated to control *everything.*

People. Situations. My circumstances.

The future.

My garden.

My addiction grew the way an invasive weed grows through your garden, choking out the good stuff and creeping through your lawn, well past your neighbour's yard, somehow finding a way to push through bricks and concrete, showing up everywhere and overtaking everything.

I tried ripping it out. I poured poison onto it and into myself. At times I even believed I had at long last got ahead of it and that I had stopped it from spreading.

But the roots were still there.

The roots that it all stemmed from were still thriving, deep below the dirt, just looking for a crevice to grow through. And the only way I could get to them was to *dig deep.*

I'm still digging.

I know now that it was my fear of feeling uncomfortable that perpetuated my addiction, and it was feeling out of control that constantly kept me in a state of perpetual discomfort. It was from that feeling of *dis-ease* that I quarantined myself in my horribly uncomfortable comfort zone: drunk, disappointing everyone including myself, and wildly out of control because of wanting to *be* in control.

It's just one more glaring example of how alcohol gave me *exactly the opposite* of what it promised and what I wanted.

What I *needed.*

What I actually needed was to somehow learn that the only thing that my subtle but persistent *addiction to trying to control everything* could guarantee was a lifetime of frustration.

To learn that the only place *control* exists is in our own minds, locked in a room with the future, like two angry, insecure roommates stuck together forever in disagreement, throwing pots and pans at each other and smashing wine glasses off the walls. It was a never-ending rollercoaster ride that never stopped to let me off or others on and left me sick to my stomach with every gut-wrenching plummet from a never-long-enough fleeting high.

There are two kinds of people on a rollercoaster: the ones with their arms in the air and thrilling howls of freedom erupting from gigantic smiles on their faces, and the ones gripped with fear and a mouthful of vomit.

I was the latter.

I refused to simply go with the curves and bends, the slow exhilarating climbs and inevitable, terrifying falls. It was impossible to enjoy the ride because I always needed to know what was coming next, always waiting on short-lived moments of security while dreading the certain rush of inescapably and fearfully, uncontrollably plummeting.

There was no *riding* the rollercoaster.

I was imprisoned on it.

I wasn't born like that. There is no innate desire to predict and control the future, which is why children can be so inspiring and fearlessly carefree. We aren't born fighting the flow of things or filled with anxiety or frustrated by unpredictability, needing to numb ourselves so we can make reality feel less real.

We don't arrive in pieces, torn apart because we are struggling to hold ourselves together in a world that feels determined to divide us.

But we do arrive afraid to fall.

Falling and loud noises are the only two fears we are born with (according to science), and it's that fear of falling – the valleys after the peaks, the gravity after the high – that we carry with us headlong into our lives, and eventually, our addictions.

I spent so very long trying to stop everything around me from making me fall, instead of trying to control myself so that I didn't. I spent so very long trying to keep my garden perfectly and meticulously weed-free.

It wasn't until my first feeble and fearful steps into sobriety that I came at long last to understand and embrace the certainty of all of life's peaks and valleys, and to accept that we have been *born* on the rollercoaster, which doesn't ever stop until the fateful day that our bodies finally do. All my drunken days and decades were just sad attempts at ushering that end as quickly as possible, fighting the truth that the ride actually *was* my life, and that I never had, or would ever have, control.

It wasn't until this point that I came to understand and embrace the beautiful truth that *there will be weeds* and that weeds are only *plants growing where you don't want them.* I finally came to understand that we only ever have two options: to give in to our fear and anxiety, or to surrender to the great mystery with courage.

To accept that the only control we will ever have is in choosing how we are going to respond to the ride.

And trust me, the ride is so much more enjoyable with your hands in the air and without a winery in your stomach.

You've Been Warned

MAY 25, 2018

"It does not matter how slow you go as long as you do not stop."
– Confucius

I've spent the last week at absolute odds with myself.

Idle. Miserable. Cranky. Irritable. Exhausted.

Numb.

I had been chalking it up to the bad and broken sleep I've been having lately after the glorious run of deep, restful slumber that I swear is one of the most prestigious and desirable prizes of sobriety. While I was drinking (read: guzzling) four bottles of wine a day, I would sleepwalk through my days, and stir myself crazy through the nights.

I called it insomnia, *the curse of a creative mind*, when in fact it was just the daily clockwork of my 3 am withdrawal as the dopamine in my brain plunged to dreamless depths and ripped me to alarming, depressing consciousness. I'd wake up to whatever the opposite of euphoria is. I'd wake up, on the dot, at 3 am every night in a sweaty pool of my deepest regrets, wondering *what the fuck was wrong with me.*

Sobriety changed all that.

Instead of the chemicals in my brain smashing wildly against each other like angry, raging tidal waves on rocks, they now sort of lap gently back and forth in a gentle circadian rhythm.

I probably should have worn galoshes this week since I've spent it knee-deep wading through cravings and mood swings as murky as my disposition. I've been feeling out of control, which is a terrifying place to be for someone who has struggled so hard to regain even the smallest scrap of sanity after decades of addiction. I've been short-fused and irritable (sorry, Hubs) and without a drop of alcohol crossing my lips for four months I feel as though my veins are demanding it *or else.*

I've been hostile, mostly to myself.

The once quiet refuge in my finally calmed mind has apparently hosted a great big high school reunion and all the savage voices that beat me down for so long are back, louder and fatter than ever before. All the bullies in my brain that pushed me through the dark corridors of my thoughts for decades have returned, and I've been feeling powerless to push back, like all the clocks have wound themselves backwards and I've somehow lost all I've learned.

My mind has filled with fog, and I've been struggling to get the simplest of ideas out of my head and onto the page. Sometimes, simple sentences have been hard. I've been feeling like an absolutely different person from who I was only last week, like I've been washed away by a surprising tsunami in the middle of an otherwise perfectly peaceful stroll on the beach.

This is what PAWS feels like.

Post-acute withdrawal syndrome.

I was pretty sure I was losing my mind, and that all the hard work I'd invested into reclaiming my life was on the precipice of being forfeited. Thoughts of just numbing my discomfort in a bottle or four of glory has seemed far too tempting, and the taste of relapse has been lingering on my tongue.

Anything to make these feelings go away.

It wasn't until yesterday when I came across a post on Facebook (thank you, Belinda) that felt as though someone ran up to me at the reunion to let me know I'd been wearing the wrong name tag all along. That the bullies that returned were beating up the old me, who didn't know any better. That I was being pushed down the corridor by old patterns and habits I didn't own anymore. That I wasn't losing my mind or my sobriety, after all.

That this is part of the process.

That this too, shall pass.

The thing with PAWS is that it comes out of nowhere, for no palpable reason, without trigger, and without cause. And when it does arrive (and it *will* arrive – you've been warned) it rolls in like a tsunami you didn't even see coming.

It brings with it all the dark creatures from the depths you thought you left behind. It transcends time and space, because suddenly, you feel as though you're back where you started like the dice worked against you in a slippery game of Snakes & Ladders. PAWS is very much a psychological condition, so it disguises itself in the chatter of your mind with voices you recognize and in turn, accept.

It feels familiar.

The depression, the cravings, the anxiety and exhaustion. It feels like the first day not using, all over again, but without any physical symptoms you can check off on a list to diagnose what's wrong with you. It feels like a good excuse to go to the liquor store, to make it all go away, just like you used to.

It feels like you're losing grip.

I'm learning that the answer to PAWS is in the name itself. Pause. Wait.

Let this pass.

Stay.

The moment I recognized that what I was feeling wasn't actually *me*, and that I didn't have to believe the thoughts I was having helped immediately to put some of the symptoms to rest. Knowing that they too would wash away the same way they washed in helped to make what I was feeling a little more bearable.

Okay, at least I'm not going crazy.

Then, there's something oddly comforting in being able to label what you're feeling. To give it a name. To take the scary uncertainty of what is happening to you and tuck it neatly into a box. To minimize the fear that you're falling apart again, and maximize the truth that this is an often experienced but seldom discussed reality of recovery.

The adventure of getting sober is much like following the Yellow Brick Road. It's dazzling, with promises of all you are hoping for, just waiting for you at the other end. It begins at the end of a destructive storm where you yourself have been the tornado in your own and other people's lives. You land, staring at the witch that's haunted you, once and for all defeated and shrinking beneath the weight of your own arrival, and you're greeted by swarms of friendly folk who want to help you on your way.

The freedom you're seeking takes strength and resolve, and the Emerald City you're wanting to reach is just a façade, so you have something to aim for – because it's in the journey itself that the growth occurs.

If getting sober is anything like a trip through Oz, then PAWS is the Dark Forest, full of angry trees throwing all the rotten apples of your past at you.

And, just like Dorothy and her friends discover – they had the strength and power to get where and what they wanted all along if they had only looked inside themselves.

I know, it sounds so cliché.

But when PAWS hits (and it will) you'll feel as though ten thousand flying monkeys have stolen you away. You'll feel as though you're deliriously drunk in a field of opium-powdered poppies, so close to where you've been headed, but somehow frozen and in a sudden, shocking nightmare.

You'll feel as though the Wicked Witch is back.

But if you wait and keep walking, if you dodge all the rotten apples and stay close to those who have helped you on your way, you'll reach the other side.

Even Dark Forests can't sprawl on forever.

Tsunamis can't keep breaking with surprising, mountainous force. And you need to remember that *you can't ever unlearn what you already know.* So, it turns out I'm not losing my mind after all. It turns out that the last week of misery and miserableness have a somewhat logical, almost scientific explanation.

That it was just a Dark Forest, not a dark world.

Here's what you need to know about PAWS, because if you're braced and prepared for it, you won't get swept away by the tsunami, or lost in the

Dark Forest:

- Though many, many people experience PAWS, it is not an official medical diagnosis (yet)

- PAWS is difficult to measure and is more like a mental health condition than a physical illness, like the flu

- Post-Acute Withdrawal Syndrome lasts up to two years

- Episodes last for several days, but over time, the span between episodes can grow further apart, and the episodes themselves should become shorter

- It's important to discuss PAWS before it occurs with your loved ones and those you spend time with, so they can help you recognize it when it's occurring

- **PAWS is a dangerous trigger for relapse.** Being prepared and knowing that it should be a short-lived, passing series of strong emotions and negative thoughts is your best defence against relapse when it happens

- Common symptoms of PAWS include mood swings, anxiety, irritability, tiredness, low energy, low enthusiasm, poor concentration, disturbed sleep, hostility and aggression, anxiety, feelings of panic or fear, depression, fatigue, trouble concentrating, lack of interest in sex, memory problems and heightened sensitivity to stress, and an overall numbness or inability to experience pleasure (have I had PAWS my entire life?)

It would be wonderful if I could tell you that the road to sobriety was a neat and tidy straight line. That the pink cloud lasts forever. That by the courageous steps of getting rid of alcohol all the waves of negative self-talk will disappear, and the wicked witch will stay shrivelled up beneath your house.

But it isn't.

It's a winding and wonderful Yellow Brick Road, full of adventure and learning, self-discovery and surprising friends you'll meet along the way. There will be dark times. There will be scary times. There will be times when you aren't sure you'll ever make it, and that your ruby slippers are nothing but cheap knockoffs.

And there will, most likely, be a Dark Forest or two you will need to pass through to reach that sunny open field once again on the other side – so you can find your way home.

So, keep going. Learn to recognize the symptoms of PAWS, and when they start to wash over you, pause while they pass. And I promise you, they *will* pass.

You're still as strong and sober as you ever were, it's just your chemistry that is catching up with you.

When Things Go Away

JUNE 22, 2018

The other day, our tree fell down.

Not just any tree.

The tree.

It was the Bette Davis of trees: bold, unsympathetic, beautiful, revered, iconic. It defined our yard and graced us and many others with its unique shade and beauty for decades; perhaps more. It wrapped its arms around our patio, and we decorated it with twinkle lights and Edison bulbs, so we could soak in the hot tub beneath her massive, gnarly moss-covered branches and the sparkle of our manmade sky.

Until the storm.

The storm took her down. Not in one fell swoop, but in pieces and parts, one heavy limb at a time, until what was left standing was just one precarious massive trunk, ready to come down and take out our house, hot tub and all. It was a delicate race against time and the elements to keep it standing until the storm passed, the winds calmed, and daylight came with a team of professionals to haul her away, leaving a gaping, naked void where she once stood.

Our yard would never be the same. Walking out the back door became blinding; where there was once cool shade, we now had to shield our eyes against the sun. Where I would look up to watch the robins build their nests and feed their young,

I could now just see them flying over and away.

Gone.

It's how I felt in the early days of sobriety: blinded. Shocked. Sad. As though there was a massive void and something *huge* was missing from my life. Where I had always ran to (what I thought was) comfort, there was now *nothing*.

Nothing but debris scattered all over the yard, left behind from when it all came crashing down in bits and pieces, some heavier than others, nearly taking down my whole house, my marriage, my friendships, my business, my sense of safety and my weak grasp on sanity. It wasn't until later in recovery that I came to admit that alcohol never gave me one bit of lasting comfort; it only helped to create and perpetuate thoughts and situations for me to seek comfort and asylum *from*.

Drinking was never the escape I thought it was, it was the wolf in sheep's clothing that dazzled me with its warmth only to bite me when I turned away.

Drinking was that tree in my backyard: alluringly beautiful, stunning to behold, but rotten on the inside and ready to come crashing down at any moment in the slightest of storms.

I think it's human nature, *when things go away,* to sink ourselves into the void they leave behind.

Loved ones, pets, jobs, routines, your favourite restaurant, your favourite drug or the drink you always reach for when the clock hits the same hour every day – when these things are uprooted, we're left standing there blinded and lost.

Because we can't imagine life without it.

Because we weren't prepared.

Because our fear is bigger than our ability to let go and move on.

I stood there on the first day after they hauled away what I believed defined our landscape, heartbroken and disappointed. I loved our yard less, somehow. I thought our house would never be the same, that our nights in the hot tub under the sparkle of string lights would be wasted and stale. The same way I stood there at noon on my first day sober, imagining my life barren and dull without a drink in my hand and intoxicating weakness in my drunken knees.

It felt like nothing would ever, ever be the same again.

I expected worse, naturally. Because that's what we do. We anticipate all the things we'll go without now that the constant we've always expected to be there has gone away. We list our losses like leaves on the branches that no longer stretch over my yard, too innumerable to count, because we believe *they were everything and we defined our happiness by them.*

Automatic negative thoughts come parading to you, filling your mind and trampling your soul like a festival in a field.

Camping sober will be impossible. I can never go camping again. So much for going to concerts, the fun is gone if I can't get drunk. How in the world am I going to lay by the pool or go to the beach without a cooler of chilled wine and case of backup beer? What am I supposed to do when I get home from work? I don't think I can go to restaurants anymore. And oh no – what about flying and airports?

We give in to the fear that now that it's gone, part of our joy – part of ourselves – has gone with it.

It wasn't until I sank myself into what was left behind last night, instead of allowing myself to be caught up in the void of what's gone for a change. It was then that I came to realize that now that the tree is gone, I can sit back and look up – and see the stars.

The real stars.

Not the strings of store-bought lights we strung up in our tree to imitate the sparkle of galaxies and constellations, since its branches were too wide and too vast to offer anything but darkness in an already dark night.

I sat in the hot tub in silence staring up. The big dipper. Orion. Saturn. The North star. They were all there, winking at me from lightyears away, as though they were all saying in unison: *"Ok, do you get it, now?"*

It was very much the same when things finally clicked after my last drink of wine. What I had been defining myself with for decades was now gone, and I was spiralling into a hole of *poor-me's* and *what-if's*, not yet realizing how much beauty all my drinking had been blocking from my life. Just like how the tree I believed I needed to have a yard worthy of enjoying had been blocking the true beauty overhead, every empty bottle before me had been piling up and obscuring the incredible, breathtaking view of my wildly amazing sober life, just on the other side.

I've been given a clean slate.

I've been given the opportunity to create whatever I want now that the tree is gone. Perhaps a new deck, a pergola with flowering vines, an outdoor kitchen, or a place to curl up outside by a fire and just be mesmerized by the stars that have always been there, just waiting to be seen.

And the same thing happened when my addiction came crashing down on me, leaving me blinded and lost, stuck in the void of wondering *"what now"* and *"how can I go on without this?"* When the shady false comfort I kept running to by drinking myself to indifference every day when things got too bright and blinding went away, I was finally able to stand in the sun.

I was finally able to see – *and begin creating again* – the beautiful life I not only always had but have always deserved. I've come to embrace the perfect impermanence of our world and the short time we are given to enjoy it.

I've come to appreciate that sometimes *when things go away,* they open up views and vistas you never imagined possible because you've grown too rooted to the familiar.

And I've come to *expect better things to arrive* in place of what's gone, instead of dwelling on the void they've left behind.

Just look up.

The stars have always been there.

The Worst Thing I've Ever Done

AUGUST 3, 2018

Today is the last day of my vacation.

I'm wrapping up five serenely sober days in Calgary, a welcome reprieve before wedding season erupts in full force and starts absorbing my time like a super sponge. I've sat myself down and started writing a few different pieces, but I couldn't seem to wrap any of them up despite one of my goals for this vacation being to write, write, write. Instead, I've relaxed. I've thought. I've wasted my time on Instagram (still working on that digital detox) and I've drank beyond my healthy share of coffee and virgin caesar's. I've been surrounded by temptation and booze and pubs and bars and *not even one desire to drink* (can I get a Hallelujah?) I've sat at the kitchen island with friends who were sharing a growler of fancy beer that's been aged in gin barrels for months and have been offered mimosas with breakfast at restaurants and walked past what feels like four hundred liquor stores in the span of two short city blocks.

For the last two years, I've been hesitant to come back here.

Because the last time I was here *I did the worst thing I've ever done.*

I've referred to it as the *Horrible Awful* and that's exactly what it was. I was knee-deep in addiction and things at home with Hubs were disintegrating in direct proportion to my drinking and fumbling attempts at escaping my reality. I searched for it at the bottom of bottles and the oblivion of blackouts, collecting anything that meant something to me like delicate eggs in the most depraved and drunken Easter Egg Hunt imaginable, placing them all in one basket and just waiting – *almost wishing* – for the moment when I would finally lose grip and watch it all collapse and in turn, fall apart.

If my life were the story of Humpty Dumpty, I was waiting with a bag of popcorn for his Great Fall from the wall.

I was in the final epic throws of self-destruction and spent my days eluding reality. Instead of dealing with the hundreds of hot messes I'd made, I just kept making more and trying to hide them as best I could as if I thought I could hide a pile of shit by shitting on top of it.

I booked a quick trip to Calgary for what my addict's brain considered a healthy alternative to facing my sorrows and concerns and talking things out with Hubs.

The escape I thought I was finding in my four bottles of wine a day wasn't cutting it anymore. The drugs weren't working, the wine felt diluted, and nothing was numbing me enough anymore, so naturally, leaving for even just a little while seemed like the only door I had left to try.

When the poison stopped working and reality was again beginning to feel too real and my parade of failures were catching up to my stumbling excuse for escape, I had to somehow escape further.

Across the country.

As far from my failures as possible.

Somewhere all the reminders of my inadequacies couldn't find me.

Somewhere that my reality wasn't so real.

You can't face your fears or talk through your troubles if you leave them behind and leave, for a while. *Right?*

Wrong.

The problem being, you can't hide from your problems on an airplane or in a new city, or in the clink of ice cubes in triple gin & tonics in a hotel lobby. *I myself was the suitcase* and my problems were forever packed inside me, ready to board and follow me anywhere I went. And of course, *they did.*

I drank my face off at the airport, I drank my face off on the plane, and I ensured a bottle of wine was in my room upon arrival so I could top up whatever I metabolized on the cab ride to the hotel. In all honesty, the week I was away is hazy as best; the altitude only amplified my avoidance and my addiction, giving me what felt like a judgment-free pass to stay as deliriously drunk as possible.

And, *I did.*

In a skewed and spontaneous moment of absolute disregard for quite literally everything and everyone in my life, including myself, I hopped on the booze bus to Wherever-The-Fuck-Because-I-Didn't-Care. The most insidious effect of alcohol is that it fuels self-destruction, the same way ethanol fuels a car. I had poured so much into myself that I was overflowing and well on my way to figuratively plummeting fast and hard off whatever cliff I could find, when what I *should* have been doing was taking myself in for a long past due tune-up of *routine maintenance* and a chance for my engine to cool down.

Instead, I betrayed Hubs, myself, our marriage, all my ethics and moral standards, and the final threads of whatever was holding it all together in my mind. I'll let you read between the lines here, but it wasn't the *act* of what happened but *what it meant* that matters.

Over time, alcohol convinces you that you're worthless.

As simple as that. No sugar coating, nothing fluffy, just plain old stripped-down *worthlessness* with an ample side of disregard for everyone around you. As much as alcohol turns you into a selfish, twisted and self-absorbed Gollum-esque version of yourself, it also delivers an undefinable feeling of disgust and self-loathing. On one hand, you are obsessed with yourself and your situation, and on the other you are collecting and creating as much pain as possible so you can keep trying to endure it.

It becomes a sloppy game of trying to balance your obsession with yourself, and at the same time, your self-hatred.

It becomes a sloppy and hurtful self-deprecating game of trying to build things up just so you can tear them down.

Alcohol turned me into both the sadist and the masochist, doling out hurt as much as I loved wallowing in it. Addiction split me down the middle and left me and everything around me in pieces.

It's easy to blame the alcohol – *and I did and still do.*

Because I know I have a good, though troubled heart.

I know the peaks and valleys of all my intentions, and now through the less-smudged window of sobriety I can see in hindsight the sabotage I was doing to myself and everything and everyone around me.

Alcohol just deadened my feelings, so everything hurt a little less; until I realized that I was the only one who was numb, and *everyone else* was feeling the impact of my actions with fierce and crystal-clear honesty. Drinking just fast-tracked my downward spiral to that dark and lonely place where I kept all my hurts hidden, waiting for me to realize that I never actually had a drinking problem – I had a reality problem.

I eventually returned home; where I subsequently lied (because that's what alcoholics do) until the truth surfaced (because that's what truth does). Hubs and

I balanced on the precipice of absolute implosion; it took reaching this extremely new lower low for me to admit that if my drinking weren't as award-winningly-impressive what *had happened* never would have happened. That *The Worst Thing I've Ever Done* award would still be pinned to something vanilla and laughable instead of the top rung of the 10 Commandments ladder.

I've spent the last two years defining myself, and being defined, by what went down in Calgary that fateful day when my soul was as frigid and reckless as the winds whipping down the Rocky Mountains. I've spent the last two years associating Calgary with the *Horrible Awful,* and my addiction with the cause behind all of it.

I've been defined – and have been defining myself – by the worst thing I've ever done.

I've spent the last two years as torn as the pieces alcohol ripped me into; desperate with regret for what I put Hubs through and everything that happened, yet still grateful that it happened – because it was the impact of hitting that cold rock bottom that finally woke me up. The last two years I've avoided even *talking* about Calgary or thinking of visiting, certain that the ghosts of my 2016 breakdown would be waiting for me.

For us.

But I'm here. And this time I didn't pack the self-hatred, the self-loathing, the self-destruction or the damaged, heartbroken shame that followed me last time.

There wasn't room for it this time around, since I've filled myself with forgiveness and sobriety and a painfully beautiful and raw understanding that what is, is.

And what was, was. And that what is, is enough. That *I'm* enough, and the imperfections of my life and love and career and ideas are curiously perfect in themselves. That by tearing everything down I would never uncover a hidden treasure, but instead be left with nothing – and everyone around me would only be left dodging the rubble and shrapnel as I flew through like a wrecking ball.

Returning to Calgary has felt a little like a trip to the cemetery, giving my regards to one of the most life changing and tumultuous times of my life. Putting to rest a Polaroid of my past that was just that – a snapshot, a moment in time – and not a high-definition live stream of who I am.

The Worst Thing I've Ever Done is possibly one of the *best things* that has ever happened to me. I know Hubs and his huge heart struggle to see it like that, because what I did – I did to us. But *The Horrible Awful* was the solid (though incredibly painful) foundation that I've been able to build my sobriety on, always there at the bottom of where I've climbed out of as a shadowy and dangerous reminder of how far I have to fall if I ever start drinking again.

Of how much I have to lose, and how irreplaceable and priceless it all is.

I found my rock bottom at the bottom of the Rocky Mountains.

So, *thank you,* Calgary.

You're so much more beautiful, finally untethered from my memories as the place where I did *The Worst Thing I've Ever Done* and instead, reframed as the *Ground Zero* of the *Beginning of My Recovery.*

PART 7:

Aftermath

Did you really think there wouldn't be one?
This is no fairy tale.

From The Belly of The Beast

FEBRUARY 5, 2019

It was dark inside the wolf.

You know, the one that came banging at my door every day. The one disguised as a bottle where I could climb deep down inside, cleverly protected by thick walls of foggy glass, down to where my troubles and truths couldn't find me, floating in a septic sea of red wine and denial. The Big Bad Wolf that promised me warmth, wrapped in his arms and the soft security of his blankets of fur, just to tangle me up and draw me in.

The one that refused to stop huffing, and puffing, and trying to blow my house down.

The one that gobbled me up and kept me there, stuck in its belly for so long, shackled and addicted.

I waited for someone to come pluck me from the darkness, to drop a rope for me to climb out, but no one ever did.

Or, when they did, I was too afraid to leave.

I waited for someone to notice I was missing, but my moment of awakening (read: finally getting tired of my own bullshit) came years and years after everyone else realized I was long gone. Written off. Excused. Another casualty of changelessness.

Well, you know Shawn.

No one truly believed I was capable of change. Not even me. Not like this, anyways.

Not with wine.

Where some people paired fine wines with entrees – a crisp chardonnay with a buttery lobster tail, perhaps – I had graduated to everyone just pairing me with wine, and basically, anything and everything you can drink.

Good day? *Shawn's drinking.*

Bad day? *Shawn's drinking.*

Half asleep? *Shawn's drinking.*

Tuesday, 10 am? *Shawn's drinking.*

Celebrations, travesties, dramas and dilemmas – every situation somehow paired perfectly with wine, and me.

If I weren't drunk, I'd be hungover, and if I didn't have a hangover yet, I was working on one as if outdoing every other viciously painful morning along with the misplaced memories of the evening before was my full-time job. If just stayed drunk, it's impossible to actually *have* a hangover, right? That's alcoholic logic, right there.

I woke up one year ago this morning, barely able to keep myself from drowning in the caustic acid of the alcoholic pit I was trapped in again (which for the record smelled more of sour, rotten decomposition than the sweet nothings that had originally lured me in). All those candy-coated lies the Big Bad Wolf fed me so I'd step into its salivating mouth day after day and night after night were just that: coated and colourful, disguising the bitter truth of its offensive flavour and even more unpleasant after-effects.

It smelled like something breaking down, and that something was me.

I had spent so long treading there in the belly of the beast that I was beginning to forget what daylight felt like.

It was easier to keep my eyes closed to the blackness than to try and hold them open, just *pretending* there was light.

Pretending there was something new to see, and not the same-old-same-old cycle of *man takes a drink then the drink takes the man.* I had collapsed to that point of tiredness – with myself, more than anything – that even my eyelids had given up.

One more way to keep the darkness in.

One more way to punish myself for all my unforgivables.

One more way to deny myself the truth that I – just as much as anyone else – deserved that sunshine, too.

It was easier to sink into darkness than claw myself out to the light.

Standing here one year later, the grass has filled in over the grave.

I still catch myself looking over my shoulder knowing the wolf's progeny are out there, just as cunning, just as thirsty, just as desperate to devour me as ever. Like shadowy, small figures standing at the edge of a funeral, cloaked in the shade of mysterious black umbrellas, they're still there. Watching. Waiting for me to falter because the world has not changed.

But I have.

Oh boy, have I changed.

I'm not going to feed you sugar-coated sweet nothings, or sprinkle my story with sunshine and rainbows, cleverly curating my recovery to sound like I now live in a land of bouncy Care Bears and sparkling unicorns. And even if I did, take note: Care Bears and unicorns still shit like the rest of us, and if you aren't being mindful, you can bet you're going to step right in it.

I'm also not going to apologize for having taken 8 months off from writing, but I will thank you all for your kind words and patience, your letters and comments, your encouragement and concern. I've grown increasingly unapologetic in my sobriety – but don't confuse this with heartless disregard for others. That's a skin I thankfully shed as I outgrew the small, unworthy shell I kept myself in for so long, saddled to addiction and four bottles of wine a day. But I do promise to write more. I have 8 months' worth of words hoarded up in a mountain of anecdotes and drafts that are begging to get out, to spill themselves upon, more polished on the page, and to take root somewhere, hopefully, in someone else's sobriety.

I will share them all here slowly, eventually, because that is how things happened.

Please also don't confuse my recovery with visions of me bouncing out of a cake, suddenly sober and celebrating life, streamers, confetti and all.

It was more of a slow, creaking, sloppy rebirth, slick with globs of icing and chunks of cake stuck in my hair, more than once.

It wasn't pretty, but damn it tasted sweet as I chewed my way out.

I won't fill your screen with *101 Ways My Life Has Improved Since I Gave Up Alcohol* because the internet is lousy with those already. But what I will tell you, is that it happens.

That moment where it just *clicks*.

It happens.

That glorious moment, followed by another and another – when you're finally willing to stay through the tough stuff because for once in your life, you aren't afraid to admit *that you're worth it*.

You are no longer afraid of *staying*.

You're worth the reward. The pride. The sweet, unspeakable, beyond-words-sort-of-inner-peace that comes with having survived, having escaped, having persevered, having toughed it out when it would have been easier (oh, so much easier) to have simply given up.

You're worth allowing yourself to enjoy quiet, painless mornings.

You're worth a lighter load to carry.

You're worth knowing that you are allowed to feel good.

You're worth the indescribable liberty that comes with no longer being the puppet dangling from strings tied to a bottle.

It happens when you at long last realize that you are thirsty for things you can't drink.

And it's in that moment of unapologetically claiming responsibility for your own life that your flight from the belly of the beast can begin. Until then, you're only surfing on *maybes* and exhaustible willpower, making one more bumpy trip around the sun, arriving back where you started every time.

Hungover. Tired.

Sticky with shame.

Honey, you have to love yourself sober.

So here I am, one year later, *one year sober,* one year older and light years wiser, standing over the grave of the Big Bad Wolf I narrowly escaped from. I'm not a fool – I know he's only sleeping, though buried deep underground. Some days I can still hear his growling, his huffing and puffing blowing through my halls like familiar ghosts of a hunger long dead but unforgettable. I can still smell him.

Some things never truly die, but the way we remember them changes.

I'm strangely grateful for the echoes of that hunger because hunger and thirst remind us that we are still alive.

What I hear when those whispers whip past my ears and over my scars sounds different now, twelve months sober, twelve months stronger. And it's what – and how – I hear now when the wolf eventually comes banging at my door again that I hope to share with you here.

"I know now I was thirsty for
things you can't drink."

– SHAWN VAN DAELE, LIFE IN DETOX

One Weirdo Closer

FEBRUARY 6, 2019

**I'm "supposed" to be more concerned with admitting that
I've had a tonne of partners in my life – but that whole
"shame thing" got old the moment I got sober.**

Moderation – of anything – has never been my forté.

I was young, confused, tormented, experimental, melancholy (and maybe a little bit slutty). You know, a typical teenager/early-twenty-something in the late 1990s who just left the small town for the big city.

I fell into what I thought was love easily.

I see now that what I was falling into wasn't even close to love, resembling more of a waterbed of approval I would sink into over and over again, riding the waves until it settled, predictably, into boring, self-conscious, insecure stillness.

And I'd be lying there alone.

Again.

I fell in love with what I thought was being seen. The only thing I was being seen as, however, was available. And being seen as available is about as unflattering as it gets. I may as well have been a marked down dishtowel in the checkout aisle that you impulse buy since you know you'll use it, but it in no way means it's something you want or need or have any intention of treasuring for the long term.

Every time, when I sensed the attention waning or the addictive sparkle of being needed start to fade, I would leave.

I have a lot of experience with leaving.

Escaping. Running. Hiding. Ghosting.

Gone.

I see the pattern now.

I can see the fear, and I can see how leaving relationships and escaping reality via bottles and bongs are more alike than they are different; they are all just varied paths to the very same end – avoiding pain at any cost.

By being the one who leaves, you can't be the one who gets left.

Each time, I would chalk up another failed relationship (friendship, job, opportunity, you name it) as being "one weirdo closer" to the real thing.

End quote.

I always bailed before I could get burned, then wrote it off as though I had narrowly escaped entrapment by a psychopath or something similar – anything to help me lick my wounds (read: justify my fear-based reaction as having been absolutely necessary) and take the onus off myself (read: project the blame anywhere and on anyone but myself).

Drinking naturally fit perfectly with my pattern: escapism comes in many sexy shapes and sizes, not to mention flavours and varieties of grapes.

The most dangerous thing about fear is that it's *liquid*.

It seeps.

It finds all your nooks and crannies, all the tight crevices you fight to hold closed, and it gets inside. And just like water, it flows to your lowest point and gathers. Souls were, unfortunately, not made waterproof.

Fast-forward 20 years and here I am, still struggling with *staying* – but now, with opportunities and situations rather than relationships for a change. Perhaps its residual dampness left behind from 40-odd years spent underwater, but I recognize it now, no longer obscured and warped in the way things bend below the surface.

No longer viewed through *merlot-coloured glasses*.

I'm still working on calling myself out when I see the pattern re-emerging.

"You're doing it again."

It happens, unfailingly, when I get *close*. Close to success, close to realizing a goal, close to being vulnerable and exposing my underbelly where I can be hurt the fastest and the most. Close to actualizing a dream, or close to being uncomfortable, suspended in some uneasy space between feeling out of control and the reassuring emergency exit door. Close to possibly falling but shedding my wings before ever giving flying a chance.

And then I place whatever I've abandoned into the greedy hands of *The Future*, who never hands things back. I set things aside, I avoid and procrastinate, and I will 'finish that later' – forgetting that what I do now is what I need to deal with down the road. I give them up the same way I gave up perfectly good people and perfectly good circumstances – that this just *wasn't the one*.

This just wasn't the right time.

It will happen when it's supposed to.

I'm just 'one weirdo closer' to the real thing.

Again.

It's that deeply rooted, waterlogged fear of "But what if they don't like me?" and "What if I fail?" The grasping for approval, still there after all these years, swishing and swooshing beneath me like the same old waterbed with the same old apprehensive anxiety making me seasick. And so, I lay there until it settles, until the waves calm, until it's safe to climb off and walk away.

Except I don't walk to the liquor store, anymore.

At least there's that.

That emergency exit has been permanently boarded up for more than a year now, heavily graffitied with afterthoughts of whether my addiction was the chicken or the egg – the cause or the effect of so many of my insecurities (but we all know it was a bit of both).

This past year has been without a doubt, the best year of my life.

I don't have much money in the bank, my name in lights, or a quaint cottage on the lake. But I feel as though I've won the lottery. That's the curious thing about sobriety – the more you remove, the more you gain.

The space that becomes available when you take drinking out of the equation is incredible. Sobriety acts like a sump pump slowly helping to drain away all that watery fear that has collected at your rock bottom, all the damp insecurity that saturates your confidence. Now that I'm sober, I'm properly on my way to fully drying up once and for all, because once you've fixed the source of the flood, you can start working on the damage it's left behind.

I've dried up, and I've opened up.

I've become a teacher – like a real-life, stand in front of a classroom teacher. I've taken up new hobbies, sourdough bread baking is my new and much healthier addiction – and yes, I know there's a Jesus joke in there somewhere about multiplying loaves and turning water into wine, but maybe the other way around this time. I go outside. I meet up with friends. I stay in touch with family. I wake early and read, write, and meditate. I keep my promises and my appointments.

I do all this, and yet there's still so much work and repair still left to be done. The storms left a lot of damage.

But that's okay.

Because now I'm one day closer.

One more drink I haven't drank, closer.

One more moment of staying when I want to run, closer.

Closer to knowing in my bones that growing *closer to myself* is where I have always wanted to be heading. Closer to truly understanding that every moment and experience can only take on the meaning that I give to it.

Closer to knowing that success is measured by how easily and peacefully I sleep at night.

Closer to appreciating how the weight of taking a chance and *staying* through what makes me uncomfortable is infinitely lighter than the weight of things avoided, undone, and unsaid.

I'm no longer one weirdo closer, because I know that the approval and attention I was seeking can't be poured into me. It can only grow from *inside* myself, in all that glorious new space that has opened up since I've dried up, gently watered with self-awareness and self-care, instead of flooded beneath waterfalls of fear.

Learning To Let Go

FEBRUARY 11, 2019

**Letting go does not happen in a glorious supernova,
like some cosmic severing from what was.**

Letting go happens in *inches*. It happens in small, solid steps toward your ghosts.

It happens quietly in wordless prayers and whispers.

To let go is to let be.

It has driven me to near madness, trying to understand how to "let it go" – the holy grail of recovery and growth, fed to me in the pages of self-development books and blogs. It's always the secret ingredient of success stories, without ever telling me where to find this elusive "let-go-ability" or what to do so I could, at long last, let go too.

I've longed to let my dead rest in peace, to make the past sit still.

I've wanted to let those things I did - or oftentimes worse, the things I didn't do – fade to blackness and forgetfulness, to turn into myths as though there were a chance that maybe they didn't happen after all. The things I've said, or definitely worse, the things I didn't say, to be unspoken or confessed.

To be released from gravity and history and lifted from me.

"You need to let it go."

Famous words that are usually offered by hoarders of their own regrets, Professional Projectors of Advice who don't even know themselves how to follow their own suggestions. "Just let it go," as though I could stuff all my sorrows into a balloon and send them off to the sky to be dealt with by the clouds.

You can't simply let go of decades or years, of fleeting moments that have lived on for undying eternities, lined up like headstones in a cemetery of everything you've ever said or done, forever corner stoned to revisit, over and over again.

I always thought that letting go meant *forgetting.*

Burying.

Erasing.

Dissolving.

But letting go is the opposite of all of that.

It is about connecting. Resurrecting. Honouring. Allowing. Transforming.

Letting *be.*

It's about letting go of the *desire to change the unchangeable.* It's about letting go of myths to make space for the truth of what happened or is happening. Of learning the language of your pain so you can sit with it, comfort it, and accept it.

As it is.

As it was.

Without wishing it were different.

Letting go is not a quick unclenching of events or feelings that you are clinging to, but rather letting go of the suffering that is created by *trying to change them.*

Letting go is allowing those events or feelings to be as they are, and to allow them to become solid. To become real. To let your dead have died, to let your words have been spoken, to let your deeds have been done.

Letting go is finally signing your name as the witness to unchangeable facts.

Letting go, paradoxically, is the same as *owning.* Instead of *getting rid* of what you perceive to be holding you back and holding you down – you learn to *own* it.

To take it. To accept it. To carry it, and to comfort it. To accept our own history and coming to see it as having served its purpose.

This is how to let be.

And it happens in inches.

It happens by sitting with your stories, replaying them without guilt or shame, or the desire to rewrite history or the present moment.

Over, and over, and over again.

It happens in the slow, creaky release of *should-haves and wishes,* and it happens in quiet, liberating moments of honesty.

There is no such thing as forgetting.

But you can learn how to remember differently. You can learn how to change how you see. You can learn how to see the past with purpose, regardless of how tempting it is to wish things had played out differently.

I am here to remind you that *they did not.*

When I set out to get sober, I wish someone had told me that *not drinking* was the easy part. That understanding how to *let go* of all that drove me to numb and to run was the real issue, and that my addiction was to escaping reality – not wine.

And it is *that* addiction – wishing we could traverse time and space and undo what's been done, to change the facts and in turn, our pain – that causes our suffering. It is our addiction to not allowing things to just *be* that keeps our wine glasses full and our hearts heavy.

For better or worse, what's done is done. As solid as the earth beneath your feet, the past is unchanging and unchangeable, no matter the earthquakes, no matter much is drifts and shifts over time. This moment right now is exactly how it is – and now, it too is gone.

As is this one.

And this one.

And this one, too.

You can't un-read what you've just read any more than you can un-spend the time you've sat here reading this. Every moment in your past, every death, every loss and misdeed, every celebration, every hangover, every misspoken slur and slip are no different than the moments you have spent here.

Unchangeable.

A butterfly spends up to three weeks in the chrysalis stage, while its wings are forming. Once it emerges, it has the ability to fly. And it does, taking flight – and freedom with it – leaving her cocoon behind.

She doesn't try to climb back in.

She doesn't try change its shape or the truth that its where she came from. If she tried to carry it with her, she would never leave the ground.

And so, she lets it go and leaves it behind, knowing it has served its purpose.

And she soars.

I'm Still Here

MAY 22, 2020

We've just fast-forwarded 15 months.

In the last 6 months alone, I've lost my house, my husband, my best friend, all my belongings, my career and *all* my income, and even *more* of my eyesight – glaucoma is a beast. But don't worry, this isn't a sad story, it's one of hope, acceptance, and a *whole lot* of patience.

In the midst of all this chaos – both mine and that of everyone on this planet with the lovely, surprising Covid pandemic – I have had to learn to be forgiving. I've had to learn patience, acceptance, and the ever-being-refined art of Letting Go.

It's something I need to practice not only daily but minute by minute, as it seems anything I'm trying to hold onto keeps somehow slipping through my hands.

And it's been in this daily holding on and letting go, holding on and letting go, that I'm learning the letting go is much less painful than the holding on.

In the short span of 5 years beginning in 2007, I lost the entire paternal side of my family, not to mention too many friends to suicide or overdose than I care to count. Gone. In the blink of an eye, and at the same time, drawn out over the longest 5 years of my life – which I'm still drawing out every day, 13 years later. Then, I somehow garnered the adoration of the planet and gained global notoriety for being that guy who makes sick kids' dreams come true with the Drawing Hope Project. Following this, I was catapulted once again into, this time undesirable, notoriety for – by request – creating a wedding photo that incited the anger and ruthless witch hunt narrow-mindedness of the entire globe. That was fun, the death threats, and everything.

I was ripped from a pit to a pinnacle, then kicked back down with the unbelievable force of ten thousand steel-toed boots, and somehow asked to figure it all out: this small-town boy who never actually even truly graduated from university. I was in spotlights I didn't ask for, and my intentions turned into prayers I had no power or understanding of how to answer.

This threw me into a spiral - one that led to an all-encompassing alcohol addiction as a result of not knowing how to deal with all the loss - and gain - that was occurring in my life.

Honestly, all I wanted to do was make some people happy.

There were too many parts of me I hated, and too many I wished to love.

And, I had no idea or instruction on how to deal with any of it.

Then, well of course the Drawing Hope Project led to tens of thousands of people turning to me – who knew/knows nothing – to help them unleash their own demons that turned them to drinking.

Meanwhile, I still had hundreds of demons on my own back.

I am learning I crave silence more than celebrity.

Every time I'm close to celebrity, I run. Maybe it's because I don't feel as though I'm good enough, but also, maybe it's because I really just value silence.

Maybe it's because I'm still trying to understand myself and this entire catastrophe.

I am learning to forgive myself for wishing things were different than how they are.

Every day.

Bear with me here, the good part is coming. I promise.

Fast forward years later, past the ugly parts of my marriage still referred to as *The Horrible Awful* that sowed the seeds for its ultimate dissolution this past November, 1 day after our 10-year wedding anniversary (but 18 years together as a couple)

I'll skim over the medical, past that part last October where I somehow managed to anger the entire planet and received everything from death threats to hate mail because of *one* innocent wedding photo - to bring us back to where we are today, where I've been sitting in my yard watching what I didn't even know was left of the foundation beneath my feet crumble away.

Somehow, trust me - *there is always more to lose.*

Rock bottom is being held up by something, and if you aren't careful - it will claw you down into it.

But I digress – I said this wasn't going to be a sad story, and I promise you it isn't.

Because I'm still here.

That is the point.

Through it all - which I know "my all" is just a sliver of the awfulness so many go through on a daily basis; but to ME, it's big. And I *am* still here. Through the pandemic, through being loved *and* hated by the entire world, through losing half of my family, my husband, my identity and everything I identified myself as. And so much more I don't have the liberty to discuss, just yet, but trust me – there's a lot of loss. There's a lot of trying to absorb it, and simply try to make sense of, it all.

I'm still here.

Perhaps it's partly because of grace and providence, but perhaps it's also partly because of knowing – always – that at this moment, *I am okay.* Right now, this moment, pandemic or no pandemic, global hatred or adoration, expectations or lost loves and friends – right now, *I'm still here.*

It's almost as though I had spent years putting this intricate jigsaw puzzle together, mixed with beautiful shapes and colours and I was almost getting to understand that final art that I was creating. Then, someone came and flipped the table, and all my pieces went flying into ten thousand new and confusing shapes.

Yet I am still – somehow – yearning to put it back together.

That's life. *Yearning.* Despite it all.

It's also coming to understand and appreciate that not everything ends like you'd hope it would. And – here's the key – being okay with that.

I don't think I'll ever get tired of wanting to know what that final puzzle looks like, once it's together. If it ever is or will be. This doesn't break us. Pandemics don't break us. Divorce doesn't break us. Loss doesn't break us.

Our attitudes break us.

Fear breaks us.

Among some scary health conditions that are manageable but terrifying, my nearly two-decade marriage fell apart. It's awful and sad, but it happens.

I could feed these fears, or I could use it them as fertilizer to start growing new things.

I could let this break me, or I could (and am) using it to understand *who* is good for me, plus *why,* and *how* I can be good for them in return.

I could let the totality of my entire world crumbling and being disassembled – emotionally, financially, and realistically – break me into pieces. Or I could use those pieces to rebuild what I always wanted and was too afraid to ask for or build for myself.

This whole pandemic, the lockdown and breakdown – it can be a chance for me to whip up wonderful conspiracy theories and stories of lack, or I can see it as a chance for me to finally being handed what I've asked for.

A break.

A rest.

A time to breathe.

A time to regroup.

This could not have come at a better time for me, and I hope that you're using this time the same for yourself.

And if you're not, *that's okay too.*

Because you're still here.

Heartbreak is hard. Loss is hard. Letting go is hard.

I'm fairly certain that there aren't many parts of this life that are *not* hard.

And I think that's the point.

To find your soft spots.

To find the spots that ache when you touch them.

That cry when you come close.

To find those places and to give all your attention to them.

This pandemic has been a gift, for me. I'm one of the lucky ones, that so far, has been left untouched by illness or death – my own or others. Many haven't been as lucky. I try, always, to keep perspective and my eyes wide open.

This breath of air has been what I've personally needed, to navigate what I found growing rampant through my life from seeds I didn't notice were planted nearly a decade ago, and likely longer. This is our chance to quietly – or loudly – accept or decide to refuse what we are being faced with in these lives we ourselves have created.

So yes. It's been a very hard six months. And I'm leaving out 98% of the details, for the record.

Because oh boy, *is there more.*

But what I'm hoping to have got across in this long, very past due ramble - is this:

You are still here.

I'm still here.

And, if all goes well, we will be here tomorrow, too.

So, step back. Remember that it's all *no big deal.*

Remember that you've been through (and likely will go through) much, much worse than what you think you're going through right now.

This is easy.

Repotted

MAY 22, 2020

**Sometime last fall, I bought one of those cute little
money trees at the local grocery store.**

His trunk was all twisted and braided, with maybe 6 or 7 very sad looking leaves
total springing from the entire plant. He wasn't well.

What can I say, I have a thing for underdogs.

I've taken good care of this guy (who for some reason I've never named, and I
tend to name everything) and he's slowly been growing into himself, a canopy
of leaves now springing proudly above his knotted little trunk. It was roughly at
the same time that I bought him and brought him home that my home itself felt
twisted and full of struggle, my marriage as tangled as this money tree's sad little
stem, and as sparse as its leaves that were vying for sunlight, love, and attention.

In retrospect, I can see the pathetic fallacy in action.

We also attract our vibe – *never forget that.*

So long story short, whether this little plant picked me, or I picked him, it was
evident I wanted to fix him. To make him better. To make him strong. To help
him grow, to flourish, to reach higher and wider and sink his roots in deep to find
nourishment.

I wanted to give him what I couldn't, and hadn't been, giving myself.

And so, it's been over the past several months that I've tended to him daily,
pruning away leaves that aren't serving him to allow others that are to grow. I feed
him music and daylight, water him well, and ensure I turn him regularly, so he
grows steady and true, well-balanced, and not too far one way, or too far the other.

If you read the piece, *I'm Still Here*, you'll know that I recently separated, moved,
sold my marital home, and am starting with a scary, fresh clean slate – *again*. I've

been working at giving myself the same attention I have been giving this plant, watching it thrive with *small efforts, repeated daily.*

Watching it come back from what was otherwise an inevitably sad and lonely fate.

And guess what?

It's true what they say – we are all just houseplants with more complicated emotions.

I'm growing too.

I'm recovering.

I'm healing and sinking my roots in deep, finding pockets of nourishment deep within myself that are satisfying both my soul and the body I carry it around in – because I refuse to shrivel up.

About two weeks ago, I noticed my little plant was becoming sluggish and his leaves were more pale than normal. Something was off, and I'm pretty sure it wasn't because I was making him listen to Lady Gaga's *Chromatica* album on repeat for days on end.

I've learned his musical tastes are as diverse as mine.

And then it dawned on me that I had never repotted him, and he was root-bound. He had outgrown his little pot and was in dire need of claiming his space. He needed to stretch out, to relax, to give his roots a chance to breathe. He needed to leave his old pot behind because it wasn't serving him anymore. It was holding him back, and in turn, making him sick.

And this is what we all do.

We stay stuck in our old pots too long, until our situations become dire, and we make drastic, terrifying changes in these scary last ditch attempts to save ourselves. We allow ourselves to become root-bound because it's easier to stay where things are familiar than face the growing pains and risks of moving on.

We would rather struggle to survive than deal with the discomfort of repotting ourselves.

This past March, I finally repotted myself.

And, as each day goes by, it becomes easier to breathe. Easier to treat myself better. Easier to find the sunlight.

Easier to see myself growing, twisted trunk or not.

And though at first, I longed for the familiarity I had left behind – my old pot, my old home, my old life – it's now many long days later that I can look back and see how sick that old pot was making me. Regardless of my years of being sober, my years of recovery, my years of inner work I've been doing to try and figure myself out, and all the years my roots felt twisted and tangled and tight, I still found myself sick in the soul.

Sometimes, our environments are as toxic as our habits and thoughts, and they are codependent on one another.

The thoughts lead you to believe you belong there, in a pot you long ago outgrew. That though the soil has been tapped and there's nothing left to feed on, this is where you belong. Despite all the nutrients that help you grow being long depleted, you're still trying to force growth in a tired and dried up place.

And then there's the worst and most toxic thought of all – that you *deserve* it.

I'm lucky and grateful and partly ashamed that I was pushed out of my old pot, that as the universe tends to do, it got fed up with waiting for me to admit what I already knew, so it shuffled my life around for me so I could find a new home to sink my roots into.

So, I could find the nourishment I'd long been needing and missing.

So, I could be in a better place to heal myself, just like I helped to heal my little money tree.

> *"If you don't like where you are, move.*
> *You are not a tree."*
> - Jim Rohn

What Love Is Not

JUNE 14, 2020

**If nothing else, the Covid-19 pandemic has given me more
than enough time to think about a lot of things.**

Like how it's so much harder to pinpoint and explain that moment in time when you finally fell out of love. It's much easier to describe the when and the how and why you fell *in* it — but *out*? Now that's an entirely different story, and a tough one to tell at that.

Because all you can remember is what you wish you could forget.

Because to understand what love *is*, you must first learn what love is *not*.

Falling in love can happen instantly, like a supernova that bursts inside you – this bright light that finds its way into all the hollow empty spaces rattling against your core, somewhere deep within you. Falling in love can also be a slow burn that smoulders and cracks like a bonfire ready to erupt into a fury of flames.

But falling *out* of love almost *always* takes time.

Falling out of love happens in inches and small steps that all add up to a long walk *away*.

Falling *out* of love is much less like falling, and more like stumbling and staggering. The ending of a relationship looks an awful lot like the end of a night of heavy drinking: everything becomes blurred and slurred and misunderstood, suddenly underlined by false-courage and brutal honesty, and almost always, *always*, followed by regret.

And just like alcohol is full of false promises of comfort and relief, so too is love.

False promises that we make to ourselves.

That this person, or this place, or this thing, or this job will finally make us feel whole. That it will give us substance to replace all the stuffing and straw that we've filled ourselves with in a sad attempt at feeling complete.

That maybe this…maybe *this* will finally make us feel okay.

And that, my friends, is what love *is not*.

Love is not a substitute for dealing with your demons.

Love is not a distraction that gives reason to stop looking yourself in the eye.

Love is not just fresh straw and stuffing to replace the false fullness you have spent years and decades filling yourself with.

Love *is* being called out when your stuffing is showing.

Love *is* being reminded that you aren't the only scarecrow out there.

Love *is* having the courage to admit when we act in ways that love *is not*.

Love is changing our behaviour – not in the hope of reciprocated love, but love is changing ourselves, for ourselves – and in turn, for the benefit of all mankind.

Our world is so small, and so divided, and so horribly stumbling *out* of love lately. Demonstrations of what love is *not* are everywhere, and I hope more people begin to understand that to demand love in the world, we first need to begin with love within ourselves.

For ourselves.

Love is not *hoping* that others will change to fit your mangled form and opinions.

Love is not *hoping* that by agreeing to disagree we can happily carry on, still divided (my marriage was like that near the end. Trust me – it doesn't work.)

Love, simply put, is not *hope*.

Love is *doing.*

Love is *admitting.*

Love is *realizing* we always have more to learn.

And then learning it.

Love is *educating ourselves* – about our differences and diversity, in our relationships, our homes, our workplaces and our entire world.

Love is *understanding* that those differences are what truly fill us up and make us whole; all separate pieces of a much larger, stunningly beautiful puzzle that yes will take time and work to put together – but what a masterpiece it will be.

Love is *recognizing* that the torment we hold within our hollow shells becomes amplified and infects – and affects – the *entire world*.

Love is not *hoping* for change.

Love is changing.

I truly hope we can mend this world's big broken heart – but I also truly hope that we all begin to see that it starts by mending our own. I've been working at removing all the straw and nonsense that I've been carrying around inside me, and replacing it with knowledge, and patience, humility, empathy and forgiveness.

Forgiveness for myself, for others, and for this entire world that has stumbled so deeply out of love with itself.

Unsubscribe

FEBRUARY 2, 2023

Oh look – nearly 3 years have passed since my last entry.

Well, who am I joking?

I'm sure a lot of you thought I was dead.

And in all honesty, in a less literal way, I basically was.

For far too long. It *has* nearly been 3 years since my last words here.

A lot can happen in three years.

Don't get me wrong, though. So many wonderful things have happened during my radio silence, and I'm sure I'll ramble on as I go, as those hidden little paths in the woods I'm walking through try to sneak past me, and I unwittingly follow them anyhow, never knowing where they're going to lead me.

And without fail, I usually end up at surprising, otherwise overlooked, beautiful spaces.

Though sometimes I also find dead-ends and scary cliffs I come too-close-to-comfort at plummeting over in my constant distraction with so many things that aren't worth being distracted by.

But I digress, which is sort of my thing. (**Spoiler alert:** I'm happy. Like, *really* happy. That's the tl;dr version of everything to come below and in future posts - be forewarned, I have a lot to say and an entirely new trajectory for my writing.)

Once again, I find myself unpacking all the things I'd tucked away and put in storage to be either forgotten, ignored, or dealt with 'later' – despite convincing myself I really *had* faced these demons, did the wash, and cleaned up my messes.

I really, honestly *did* think those things.

I just forgot to take out the trash.

That was the problem – I stored them.

I didn't *get rid of them.*

Or, maybe, I didn't tie up some loose ends that were too scary to invite out - you know, the deep-rooted stuff that all the *other* deep-rooted stuff stemmed off – and repeat. Or, I didn't tie the garbage bags up tight enough and all that *stuff* spilled back out, all over my floor.

That stuff.

Those flapping little frayed bits on the big, long web of your life; the broken parts, the excess, the snags on your favourite winter sweater.

That's not what I'm writing about today, but it's worth noting that despite having it all either fall at my feet (though earned, if you asked me) – celebrity of sorts, a grateful audience, deep satisfaction in my work – it turned out, it was never the *attention* I was seeking. It was never fame. It was never money.

It was validation.

How does that Marlon Brando quote from *On the Waterfront* go? You know the one where he was being controlled by this big mob boss before he himself became the mob boss in *The Godfather*?

<blockquote>"I coulda been a contender!"</blockquote>

And that right there, is what I've been doing. You know how when there's something that smells off in your house? Like, '*Where is that smell coming from?*''

The fridge? Those old lemons in the bowl by the stove? Did I forget I throw out shrimp tails in the garbage 3 days ago? Did Cruella (our new Chinese Crested pup) take a poop somewhere behind the couch?

You focus. You find it.

You clean it up.

Because you can't live in a house that smells like that. So, what's so different?

Why do we treat our homes so different from the only home we really have?

Our bodies. Our minds. Our souls. Our environment.

Our thoughts.

Maybe even more importantly – our actions, and our words.

To others, *and ourselves.*

It's easy for me talk about all this – but *how* did I go about this?

Or more accurately – *how* am I going about this?

What did I unpack? How did I find *that smell* in my house?

Not to disappoint you after trailing you along this far, but I honestly *wish I knew.*

But, I'll do my best.

All I can talk about (*and I can talk*) is *what I've done.*

This entire book is a ramble about what I've done – and to be completely honest, in re-reading them all while compiling this, thing – whatever you want to call it – I can't help but see all the parallels to other people, other places, other times, other situations – *other smells* – if you'd just swap out one word for another:

Drinking?

Replace it with eating disorder.

Replace it with gambling.

Replace it with depression.

Replace it with negative self-talk.

Replace it with procrastination.

Replace it with self-induced-anxiety, self-abuse, social withdrawal, abusive, toxic relationships - the list goes on.

Make this post and this book your own. Swap a word here or there as needed, and hopefully it'll in turn help you find that smell that's filling up your house.

I'm not going to go on at length here (really, Shawn?) because I already have, but now that I have momentum, I have a lot to talk about (finally, again.)

I honestly just woke up tired.

Who doesn't, right?

I know you can identify with this: I woke up *tired* in a way I couldn't put into words. The *'I can't get out of bed'* sort of tired. But for days on end.

Months.

Again.

Despite, once again, seemingly having the entire world at my feet (I'm a cat like that, and somehow always land on my feet – disregard all the bumps, breaks, scars and injuries incurred on the way down, though – at least they all come with very good stories). I became a very much high-functioning-self-imploding-self-abusive-robot.

And I wasn't paying any real important attention to *anything that mattered.*

Since my separation and divorce from Hubs, I managed to not only survive the pandemic but found the love of my life, my best friend and now husband, Darrell – in insolation – on Instagram. I crushed the pandemic – *somehow, I thrived.*

We rebuilt my life together, got married, and are quite delightfully living happily ever after, bumps, scrapes and all. My careers collapsed, my life was turned upside down mid-pandemic in ways I never thought possible, or that ever even crossed my mind as a possibility. My finances were/are devastated as a result, and that's a post for another day.

I had every reason in the world to give up, even though I had everything I wanted, everything I needed, and the best partner you could ask for.

But, I was *still tired.*

I was done. Or at least, I should've been - despite everything.

Full disclaimer, again: I am happy.

Perhaps more alive than I've felt in a really, really, *really* long time.

You know all the emails you get every day? The subscriptions; the newsletters, the marketing – all the *noise*? It's the stuff that fills your inbox and sways your thinking. It manipulates you to buy things you don't need, to click links you don't need to click, to lose yourself in a scroll-hole of wasted moments-in-time when you could otherwise be living your *actual* life. And we contribute to the noise. Never forget whatever you put out gets absorbed by everyone who follows you, loves you, whoever likes and comments on your posts and reels, your stories, the news and links you share – that all becomes part of other people's day. You are your own newsfeed, and it's up to you what content you choose to believe in and share, not to mention send forth into the universe where it will become part of everyone who sees its life, day, brain, thoughts, and feelings.

Pay attention to your words and actions. You aren't only contributing, but you're absorbing it in the other direction.

I'm not saying social media is a toxic wasteland (it often is), but used responsibly, safely and with compassion, it's the most powerful tool that has ever been introduced in modern times. It can do as much damage as a nuclear bomb – or used properly and in the right hands with the proper intentions, it can be a blessing.

You can find good in something as personally impactful to every person as the Covid pandemic, like I somehow managed to miraculously thrive during it.

But, the more subversive subscriptions that fill up our inboxes, lives, and cause all those *smells in your life* come in a lot sneakier ways:

- Social Media (to excess) *see above

- Drama

- Stress

- Self-or-other-induced anxiety

- Worrying

- Procrastination

- Passive-Aggressiveness

- Narcissism

- Lies

- Yelling

- Blame

- Anger

- Resentment

- Hatred

- Guilt

- Shame

- Negative self-talk

That's the short list.

I started by unsubscribing to a lot of these, by choice – as I noticed myself *engaging* in them. I am sure a professional would recommend making a list of all the things and ways you do this (we all do, don't beat yourself up) and tasking them. I am no professional.

But we're human. We know what we ***should*** do.

We just…don't.

But in whatever way works for you - name them. Make them real. Invite them out. Acknowledge how you engage - and participate - in these things in ways you don't even know you do (we all do).

You *have to make them real. You have to confess to yourself that you do this.*

Because we all do.

You *have* to start *noticing* when you're knee-deep in it. When you're usually already too far down and you're covered in it – when you're filled with the noise.

And you'll know. Because once you start noticing it, you'll recognize it in your body, your thoughts, your words, your actions, behaviours, patterns, and all the ways you (we) all reinforce it.

Every. Single. Day.

Then, no different from that cluttered inbox, from the garbage you forgot to take out, from the rotting lemons on your countertop – you get rid of them.

Unsubscribe.

Just STOP.

Tell yourself you're done. Tell yourself that you no longer subscribe to this, and you *definitely* no longer engage in it - or worse - own it. Then do some of the things that you DO subscribe to. Things that support your peace of mind, your health, and your well-being – no matter what that looks like to you.

Here's *what I DO subscribe to* these days. Anything on this list can take all my energy, with my full blessing, and I fully engage with them to whatever capacity I am capable of *that day*:

- Passion

- Honesty

- Listening

- Patience

- Positive thinking

- Self-reflection

- True friends and family

- Talents

- Strengths

- Creativity of all sorts

- Generosity

- Compassion

- Simple things

- Minimalism

- Good homecooked real food

- Slowing down

- Personal health of all kinds

- *Love*

Sounds easy, right?

It's not - but in another way – it actually sort of *really, really* is.

Like any mindfulness practice, this is just noting.

Noticing.

Paying attention.

And honey, I'm not talking paying attention to everything around you. I'm talking about paying attention to *what you let in.*

And, in turn, what *you're* putting out.

Just start *paying attention* and taking out the trash, whether it looks like that rotting garbage, the cluttered inbox, the boxes of things in your basement you'll never need nor use, and all those awful habits you beat yourself up for every day.

Find *one thing* that makes you excited to wake up. It may be something as simple as buying yourself a tiny miniature teacup rose plant that needs you and pays you back by smelling so sweet, filling your house with something that smells a lot better than 3-day-old shrimp tails.

Start with that.

And let's face it - we are all addicts, in our own special way.

Just try and get addicted to things that nourish you, instead of depleting you. Replace actions, words and thoughts as you catch them. Just note them as they start passing through (and taking hold) of you. Notice the things you really wish weren't part of your life anymore, and just unsubscribe, as hard as it is. Stop participating.

My best friend introduced me to the *Golden Question*, and I toss it back to her on occasion, and it's transformative. I'm sure that I'm going to massacre the proper phrasing of this, but I know you'll get it.

So, I'm going to leave you with this, for now"

> **"If you woke up tomorrow, and everything was better, what would have changed?"**

Sleep well tonight. Tomorrow is a new day.

Pay attention.

Unsubscribe from the noise.

What's Your Word?

FEBRUARY 6, 2023

While watching the breathtakingly heartbreaking film 'Spoiler Alert' the other day, I was struck by *one question* that one character asked another.

What's your word?

At first glance it doesn't look like much of a question, but here's the actual question behind the question: *if you can only pick **one word** to describe your life thus far, or overall, for your entire life until you die – what would it be? And to make things more complicated: Why?*

No phrases. No sentences.

Just. One. Word

Admittedly, I couldn't stop thinking about this, jotting down words that came to me over the next few days. Being a word geek, I came up with a not-surprisingly *very* long list. But I didn't want to just settle on one random word and in turn, try to give it meaning somehow.

No – I wanted to figure out *the* word.

I settled on: ***surprising.***

sur-pri-sing

adjective

1. Causing surprise; unexpected: "a surprising sequence of events"

verb

Gerund or present participle: surprising
1. (of something unexpected) cause (someone) to feel mild astonishment or shock.

Don't worry. I had to look up what 'gerund' meant, too. It's a form of grammar that is derived from a verb but that functions as a noun, in English ending in *-ing*, e.g., *asking* in *do you mind my asking you?* #TheMoreYouKnow.

Before I chose this *surprising-in-itself* word, I toyed with other words like perseverance, guided, opportunity, lucky, learning, generous, gratitude, patient, creative, random, adventure, and of course - rollercoaster. The list goes on and I *really* would love for you to do the same exploration and find *your* word.

I promise you'll enjoy the process.

It's sometimes hard to remember other people have different stories, as unique and often troubled, challenging, joy-filled, and *surprising*, as your own; unlike my blog, it's hard to gather the 'words' of everyone who is reading this book right now. It would be amazing to see your words, and in turn, help give context to – and perspective on – the vast and varied kaleidoscope of people, lives, personalities, cultures, traditions, hardships, successes and stories that we all take for granted that *other people* see or define their lives as.

I think the element of *surprise* is the best and most thrilling part of being alive. It's also sometimes *really inconvenient* – and yes – a lot of things are. But they don't have to be if you are able to step back and see it with a different perspective, in context with the bigger, endless web of your life. There's usually another reason those surprises pop up in your life. By definition, they also pop up at the most curious of times. I always strive to turn every situation upside-down and look at it from another, more empathic – towards myself, the situation, and all parties involved – perspective.

That's easier than standing on my head, though if this is one of your hidden skills, by all means, stand on your head and mull things over on occasion. You'll be so distracted by the fact you're now seeing the world upside down that you may pause long enough to find a new way of looking at a situation, once all the blood rushes to your head).

Here you are, minding your own business, being all busy like we are all so very good at doing, and out of the blue, along comes life and knocks you flat off your feet.

Usually with a sharp smack to the head.

To wake you up.

It's not always bad – and I really mean that. The *unexpected* is what gives life meaning, direction, cause, purpose, excitement.

Joy.

Some of the best, most thrilling times of my life have arrived not only through struggle but as a result of the universe delivering me exactly what I needed – but also, what I usually wasn't paying attention to. Like how I found my husband on Instagram of all places (well, he found me) after I had *promised myself* I did not want a relationship. Yet here we are, and I wouldn't change a thing. (PS: He got my attention by telling me my dogs were cute). This has been one of the best surprises of my life to date.

Not unlike the human body, if you don't take care of it, it'll take matters into its own hands, and you'll have no other choice *but* to take care of it. To pay attention. To deal with it.

To confess you have work to do.

Life does the exact same thing. Humans, by nature, usually don't pick up on subtleties – especially when they're coming in the form of signs and accidents, total redirections in your life, tragedy, illness, birth, death, winning, thriving *and failing*. We're all busy, right? Especially when something comes along that I don't want to deal with – it's amazing how quickly I can bullshit my long list of justifications into a steaming pile of excuses.

The trick, I'm learning, is in the *paying attention* when I catch myself doing it.

Calling myself out for doing it *again*.

When you were planning on something entirely different in your life (you know, because life always happens when you're busy making other plans), it's easy to *not* pay attention to the little cues we're given every day. Or what is more likely, to just put off doing the work, ignoring it, and adding it to the likely towering and teetering mountain of all your procrastinations.

Procrastinations, because you feel you don't have the time, you don't have the strength, or you're simply just too damned afraid of doing it. Or, also very likely – you're just *tired*.

I personally have a deep-rooted fear of failure (insert facepalm here). I admit this,

I struggle with it constantly, and I know that it has prevented me countless times from succeeding, from excelling, from thriving, and most importantly, from reaching goals and aspirations I still hold dear in my soul that I know would only bring me pure joy. At least in the having finally accomplished it – no matter what timeline I did it on.

I struggle with this. Every. Single. Day

So, back to what 'surprising' means to me.

I slept on it. I mulled it over. Because it's who I am – I made lists.

Whatever/however your process is, just go with it. You may already know without having to think about it, but if you're anything like me, you have to look at every possible option and weigh which ones make the most sense, even though it's often the more difficult one to explain.

But it feels right.

The English language has no lack of words to choose from. Find yours.

Never in a million years could have planned the life I've led, so far. I never would have imagined I'd be featured on *The Today Show* or *ABC World News with Diane Sawyer*, that I'd be held at gunpoint in the middle of the night by the leader of a biker gang, on the 3rd floor of a 24-hour bar I worked at in Toronto, held hostage alongside the owner whose sister was a police officer, or that I'd also be receiving death threats from keyboard warriors, sent from every corner of the globe, for creating *one* innocent wedding photo. I had no clue I was going to become a professional photographer for 14 years of my life, a professor teaching 3rd year Advanced Photoshop, a Creative Director, or an author.

I went to feakin' ***art school***, for Christ's sake, to study drawing and painting.

None of that was ever on my radar. It all showed up as a glorious surprise, followed by another, and another, and another.

That very big chapter of my life was one of the most surprising and rewarding chapters – up until now. There's no way I would have embarked on that journey if I had planned for it. And, in turn, it has opened the gates to so many other delightful surprises in this supernova of coincidences and connections, all intertwined and giving me life and purpose

I never could have planned that I'd trip and fall and break my collarbone, and struggle to rebuild my entire world and career in the shadow of a divorce, relocating homes – for the 19th time in my life (I know, I know – I'm a nomad), finding the love of my life when I definitely was not looking when all I was looking for was *balance*, or ending up married in my favourite, most homey-home-that-feels-like-home yet, with my best friend who sometimes pushes me to my limits, and who I also push to his. All these struggles pushed me to finding new work to make ends meet, and I've met some of the most wonderful people I would likely never have met otherwise. In hindsight, it was exactly what I needed for a revived sense of purpose.

Not surprisingly, embracing all of this *and leaning in* to surprises when they arrive helps me extraordinarily at being *less tired.*

It gives me life.

Plus, the words of praise I occasionally get in my work now hits on that *dopamine* hit / need for approval / love language that guides a lot of my life.

I never would have predicted losing so many loved ones in such a short period of time – from illness, suicide, struggle, losing touch, and so many countless, often unavoidable, other causes. These are the hardest surprises to come to terms with and find meaning in. Grief is a tough one, and we all process it differently, in our own time, in our own way. Sometimes, some of us never do.

What's important is that you *do* process it and come to find meaning in it, no matter how long that takes, or how you do it.

All that sudden loss gave me a newfound appreciation for those close to me: my family and my friends most notably, and it continues to bring me closer to life's most meaningful purpose.

To love and be loved in return.

Actually, to *allow* myself to love, and be loved in return.

So, to wrap things up, because I could go on for days about the millions of times life has surprised me in the most wonderful ways, if I just pause long enough to see the triumph in the struggle, without these surprises – life would be horribly depressing, boring, and senseless.

Surprises are an opportunity to find beautiful purpose when it's usually dressed up as a clown - and a lot of the time, that clown is more terrifying than funny.

Surprises are a chance to put *yourself* into the bigger picture of how intertwined we all are, and in that sense of purpose, it gives you the opportunity to recognize how many wonderful reasons to be alive we are always being offered, and an opportunity to give back.

To be a delightful surprise in someone else's life.

I hope the rest of my life never ceases continuing to surprise me.

Where Do You Keep Your Dreams?

You know.

The ones that won't leave you alone, like a nagging dirty-faced little kid tugging at your pant leg.

The ones that sit in the seat of your throat, that little hollow part where it meets the rest of your heavy, clumsy body.

The body that's been putting them off, busy doing *other things*.

Important things.

Things that don't matter.

At all.

Maybe they're the dreams that you can't stop thinking about, for days, weeks… *decades*. The kind of dreams that keep you getting out of bed in the morning, delusionally believing that you'll get there one day.

Even though your habits never change, day-in-and-day-out, and you're busy watching tv just waiting for them to come to you, knock on your door and ask for a cup of tea.

If you're anything like me – *and if you're here, I have a terrifying feeling that you might be* – you'll understand the feeling that you're somehow running out of room to keep them all.

The attic is full.

The basement is a crime scene.

The closets…well, don't even get me started on the closets.

And all those skeletons.

It's exhausting, dragging them everywhere with you, as though you've put on 200 pounds of extra baggage, all tucked in and under every crevice of your being because you're too afraid of losing them.

Or worse, forgetting about them.

But for some reason, they're important.

If only to you.

The term 'important' is a tough one; so relative, so subjective. But the essence of the word is:

im-por-tant

adjective

1. Of great significance or value, likely to have a profound effect on success, survival, or well-being.

And there we go.

Dreams are *important*. So, in turn, they're likely to have a profound effect on our well-being (we may or may not get into what it means to have a *profound effect* later, or maybe we won't. But what we *don't do* is usually even *more profound* than what we actually *do.*

What we *don't do* tells us more about ourselves than we can ever be told or taught, and if we pause long enough to take an inventory of those traffic jams in our life, we'll learn more than we'll honestly ever want to know.

Because we already know what they're going to tell us.

So why am I over here just talking about them and putting on the kettle every day and saving them a seat at my table, when I didn't even give them my address?

Oh right, I'm too busy tripping over all of them that I have hidden everywhere I look; in everything I do – *and don't do* – and frankly, they're starting to get in the way – the skeletons are stacked to the ceiling and the doors are shut tight for fear they'll all tumble out.

Plus, they all still live here.

Up until now, I've always struggled with dissecting my dreams (and just so we're all on the same page and talking about the same thing, I'm not talking about those bizarre and unexplainable storylines that visit you while you're thankfully unconscious, like strung-out little messengers that speak an entirely foreign language; the sly bits and pieces that creep from your *Dream Box* every night, from your stash of scraps of the day left behind you). I'm talking about our aspirations, our goals, our **Big Dreams. Our Important Dreams.** *With capitals.*

Where was I? Right.

I've always struggled with dissecting my Dreams (see? capitals) into manageable little bits that are more easily swallowed, more easily digested, and processed – but I'm not a biologist or whomever it is that specializes in digestion. A Gastritician? Stomachetitist? anyways...) into manageable, digestible morsels that taste better than devouring the whole plate at once.

Food tastes better when you eat it slowly.

And Dreams are no different.

But, the first step is dragging them up from the basement, one at a time – in your own time – and *staring them in the eye, asking them why and how they're here.* (Plot hole: skeletons don't have eyes.) Learn their language, understand why we've kept them tucked away so long, and ask *yourself* why you've been dragging them (and yourself) around for a tour of your everyday nonsense, until you're *finally ready* to *maybe* take a stab at *possibly failing.*

Trying though?

Trying is a *much better feeling* than *never trying.*

Trying, with a capital, is *Important.*

So, *Try.*

Try, for maybe the first time in your life – or at least recently.

Try, because it's far more glorious to be failing at it than letting it drag you down, day in and day out.

Try, because it's Important.

Try, honestly – simply Try because you know that you're lying to yourself if you said you didn't want to.

Try, because you know what?

Maybe you'll succeed.

Maybe you'll *thrive*.

Maybe the entire chaotic trajectory of your life will change, suddenly fuelled by a sense of purpose, a sense of accomplishment – a sense of simply put – *I did it.*

I Tried, and I Did It.

So, here's hoping, for a change, I can do better at taking my *own* advice.

Write the book.

Take the course. Go to the gym. Put down the drink. Stop the negative self-talk. Go to Tibet and climb a mountain. Go deep sea diving in the Galápagos Islands (they'll be, and almost are, extinct, so you should probably get on that – though our human interaction is honestly the *actual* problem). Do the scary things. Make the phone call. Put yourself out there. Dress better – so you'll feel better. Shower in the morning. Make the bed. Buy the thing (but don't in case shopping happens to be your personal addiction or struggle).

Lean in, just a little bit.

Possibly the scariest yet – *have the conversation.*

The one that *you know* is sitting there in that hollow of your throat, waiting to be released into the heart of the person you've been holding it for. No matter how possibly uncomfortable it may be; honesty and release are far healthier than poisoning yourself by keeping it in.

Just try.

Stop keeping your Dreams in storage. Clear out the attic. Disassemble the skeletons into manageable bones you can study and put back together correctly, just how they were supposed to be when they were, once upon a day, a *Real Boy* (have I mentioned that I'm slightly obsessed with the *real* meaning and story behind Pinocchio? Stay tuned for a piece about this soon. It will be dark. You've been warned.)

And that is all.

I promise, to you, and more importantly, *to myself,* to Try.

I promise to stop keeping my Dreams to myself.

I promise that I will, but you have to promise, too.

Deal?

Also – eat slowly.

Cracks in the Sidewalk

FEBRUARY 20, 2023

I used to think I was a "Recovery Blogger".

A person who rambled on about *not drinking*.

About addictions.

But then I realized, that's not *at all* what it's about, or what I know.

Like, *not even close.*

I realized that beneath that – there's something *more*.

Something that connects us all (sadly).

Some innate *fault* in our common human nature (or in reality, the world we live in) – and it's that common thread that ties us all together, despite our differences, our borders, our habits, our incomes, our health or sickness or childhoods or successes or our failures; despite our races, our skin tones, sexual preferences, careers – *you get the idea.*

We all struggle. No matter *who we are.*

I think my writing is more about our *common struggles.*

It's more about *being human.*

It's about *trying to be alive.*

Trying to *stay alive.*

To feel alive.

To find a place where you feel safe and like you belong; a place that gives you a *real sense of purpose and connection,* which helps to give purpose and meaning to our struggles, and a place that helps us all realize that *there's nothing weird or wrong with ourselves, because we all share this feeling.*

Whether some people like to admit, or not.

It's not about not drinking, or all the baggage of mistakes (that I am getting *so* much better at unpacking and never dragging along with me – but I *did* make a deal with them all, that I would share their stories one at a time, over time, in hopes that in their unpacking and release someone else somewhere might find a little piece that fits them just right, tries it on, and maybe finally feels *seen.*) And that is this book that you're holding in your hands right now.

That is the culmination of that promise I made to all my baggage, all my stories, and everything I've learned up until now.

That *trying to feel alive and trying to be alive* looks very, very different to each of us.

After all, how many of us wear the same prescription of eyeglasses? How many of us are so alike that a shared, new perspective can put it all *into* perspective? How rare is it that you can borrow someone's else's glasses and by sheer luck and chance, everything somehow comes into crystal clear focus?

The world doesn't work like that (thankfully – because it would also be horribly boring).

It's about being that *little airborne seed,* that breaks away and catches itself in the wind, tumbling along some crooked, broken sidewalk in some small dusty town, and by providence and luck (and a hell of a lot of fate) it happens to rain, just as it thinks it's doomed forever, falling into that dark and ugly crack in the sidewalk that has put more mothers than we could ever count into wheelchairs because of broken backs caused by angry, resentful (or oblivious) children, and turns into this miraculous little flower, or weed, or most importantly – *happy little bit of life* – thriving *exactly where it shouldn't.*

That's what it's about.

What this is all about.

It's about that flight to the crack in the sidewalk.

The waiting for the rain. The terror of facing the end straight in the eye; of that swift fall into *exactly* what you were trying to avoid. And, hopefully, the subsequent rain that washes it all away, somehow, and gives you a chance at being brought back to life again.

It's about finding a place to grow.

A place where you feel you *belong.*

A place where you can be more than *just a seed in the wind* and be a little piece of life surprising you where you'd expect there to be none.

So that is all. Short and sweet. Nearly 500 pages later.

Cracks in the sidewalk aren't all there to trip us up.

Sometimes they're there to offer us a place to rest, a place to regroup, a place to wait for the rain so we can grow into something we weren't ever sure we'd become, giving purpose to our directionless and haphazard tossing about for so long, riding winds we had no control over.

And hopefully, in the end, we're able to bring a little joy to others, in return.

And then – *then* you can finally *grow.*

With very big love, now and always,

xoxo Shawn.

The End.

Just joking.

PART 8:

Retreat: The B-Sides

You could just stop reading here if you want.

But what follows are resurrected pieces that were written on a private writing retreat in February 2019, while I holed myself up in a tiny little cottage in Washago, Ontario.

Long lost and stashed away in my journals
– until now.

You can think of them as 'extras' but to me, they're pieces of the puzzle that best fit in here.

At this pseudo-ending.

That isn't an ending at all, but another new beginning.

Scars & The Pause

Getting sober has been one of the most terrifying, wonderful, surprising and exhausting adventures of my life. It's been a very long and winding road out of a very dark forest with more flying monkeys than I care to mention. And as varied as our reasons for drinking are, so are the paths we each take to claw ourselves out of the rubble.

But all our escapes start in the very same spot.

Ground zero.

Finally growing sick of our own bullshit.

For me, it took watching every last thing I cared about start turning to ash before my eyes, burnt down by fires I had set myself. It took finally recognizing the storyline I'd been telling myself – for years and years and years – and it took finally learning how to stop pouring fuel on those fires.

For you, maybe it's heartbreak or losing your home. Maybe it's jail or killing someone in a head-on collision while you're flying blind and drunk down a highway. Maybe it's liver failure, losing your kids, or finally growing tired of feeling like absolute shit every day.

Have you asked yourself yet, what *exactly* is it going to take?

To explain how I finally got sober, you first need to understand how I came to realize, *and admit*, that I was, indeed, a drunk.

It wasn't enough to bear the shame of the devastating crash of the recycling bin every week, overflowing with nearly 30 bottles of wine that I could never bring myself to return the normal way for a refund on their deposits because the uncomfortable eye-to-eye contact with anyone in the shadow of my mountain of empties was too close to admitting the savage honesty of the truth of my addiction. Leaving them anonymously for city workers to collect in my absence was closer to my delusion that *there wasn't really a problem at all.*

It wasn't enough to fail miserably at coping each and every morning with the razors of regret that sliced through my veins.

It wasn't enough to be so intoxicated the night my dad died that I forfeited my opportunity to say goodbye, as I needed to wait for my friends who were on route to arrive before they could drive me as fast as possible in fog thicker than pea soup, cutting through the jet-black darkness at 10 pm. I arrived ten minutes too late.

To say goodbye and so many other things.

It wasn't enough to start collecting bad business reviews online and watch what I had built with Hubs start crashing to the ground week after week, and day after day.

Imploding.

It wasn't enough to be riding a downward spiral with such velocity that everything around me seemed blurred and impersonal.

None of it seemed to ever be enough to peel back the guise I had draped over all of it, casting every disappointment, every crumb of self-destruction, as simply *how things were.*

It was as though my entire life fit in a bathtub, and I was mesmerized by watching it all get sucked down the drain. Almost as though I was outside of myself, displaced, watching it all go down like a car crash you can't turn your eyes away from.

Destruction can be fascinating to observe.

No, none of it had the strength to rise up enough to deliver the unforgettable (and necessary) slap across the soul I needed to once and for all step back into myself and choose to stop the drain from draining

To try and salvage what was left and use the rubble of what remained as a new foundation – for something, *anything,* other than one more way of heading downward to a deeper and darker rock bottom.

It took infidelity and the worst kind of dishonesty, and it happened the day I somehow managed to pull the earth out from beneath my very own feet.

It took one bottle of wine in a distant hotel room, the stars so aligning that it delivered to me *every last ingredient* I needed to concoct the ultimate and perfect bomb so I could finally blow up my entire life – and the lives of the those around me.

Everything, except the strength of character and clarity of mind to make better decisions.

It wasn't made of metal and nails – oh no. The shrapnel from this type of bomb is well-lubricated with liquor and disregard so it can seep right through your skin and straight to the core of your being. It's the kind of pervasive blast that only an addict can deliver.

The kind that leaves scars on the inside.

It was never my intention to hurt anyone, and I am certain that applies to almost every living person, even the worst addicts out there. We have an innate goodness – it's just that sometimes…sometimes we forget.

Alcohol made me forget a lot of things, not simply the events of the evening before.

It made me forget the innate goodness we are all born with.

It made me forget that there's more than just what we remember the past as and our imaginations of the future. There is also an irreplaceable and limitless space we can all tap into *right now* that has the proven power to pluck you straight out of the loop of your storyline.

It made me forget that nothing is certain, and nothing ever will be.

It made me forget that the imaginary world inside my head looked nothing like what was actually, *really real*, on the outside.

It made me forget that nothing is static, and all of my self-induced misery I kept pouring into myself every day was all in a sad and vain attempt to have some semblance of control.

Of something.

Of anything.

It made me forget that the only thing we have control over is how we react to what we have no control over.

Which is *everything*.

And that's where the unquenchable thirst comes from – our need to swaddle ourselves in some form of security, some kind of numbness, because we can't stand feeling out of control. We can't come to terms with the idea that just maybe *nothing is a big deal, after all* – including ourselves.

And it's not really about forgetting.

Let's be honest. We don't really forget. We're just too busy self-destructing to care.

We take it all for granted.

I finally came to admit I was a drunk when I shattered Hub's heart so loudly it deafened me and left permanent ringing in his ears. For the first time in too long, something resonated louder than my own sirens that were blaring inside me.

It took waking up to the reality that *it wasn't all about me.*

That's the thing with addicts – we're not only addicted to using – whatever your poison of choice is – but we're addicted to an *idea* of ourselves, and we're also addicted to defending it. We're addicted to being self-absorbed, while hating everything about ourselves at the same time. Our addictions are never *truly* to things you can drink, or stuff you can smoke – *it's always to our idea of how things should be.*

I finally realized that I was thirsty for something I couldn't drink.

And the harder we try to materialize – *and freeze* – that impossible ideal of the way things *should* be, the more unlike that things become. It's like pedalling a bicycle backwards and wondering why you're so exhausted despite not actually ever going *anywhere except backwards.*

So, we drink.

We smoke, we snort, we shoot up, we shop, we have sex with strangers, we gamble, we lose ourselves in eating disorders, and we binge watch mindless nonsense just to distract ourselves from even getting *close* to looking inside at all our scars that need tending. We keep ourselves busy to prevent us from looking *outside* to all the scars we have *caused.* We act as though we are *choosing* to be the way we are, instead of admitting that it's *our patterns and automatic reactions* that have shaped, and continue to shape, our reality – which we simply refuse to believe.

On the surface, it looks as though we *choose* to pour the wine, we *choose* to have just one more, we *choose* to inhale oblivion as deeply as we can.

But our actions are rarely the result of our choices.

The same way a path in the woods is beaten down and the earth is scarred from the same pounding of footsteps, our patterns scar our behaviours. Without pausing and without conscious, sober choice, we simply repeat the same self-destructive actions, regardless of how we get the same unsavoury results *every damn time.*

Our emotional scars are our most valuable roadmap to sobriety.

They show us where all the hurts got in.

481

They point to where we need look, to work, to listen, and to what we need to *let be*.

They give us our *personal homework*, which is ours and only ours, and unlike anyone else's. And the only way to learn from these lessons is to *study them*.

To get close.

To lean into them and learn their language, so you can finally read them a bedtime story and at long last put them to sleep. To know their language, so you can negotiate with all the monsters under your bed and come to see *you were the monster under other people's beds, too*.

These are the places where we need to start, as it's only through getting to know them and comforting them that we come to finally *"get it"* so we can pass all the pop-up quizzes on the winding labyrinth of our path.

So, look to your scars, if you have your eyes set on being sober, or healthier, or just happier to wake up every morning. Whatever your reason, they are part of you because they are your tools for learning how to heal.

They're the doors you need to walk through, one at a time, closing each behind you as you go.

It sounds so easy on paper, and yet in practice, even getting started seems impossible – just like what everything else feels like to an alcoholic.

Everything else *other* than drinking yourself under the table each day, of course.

How do you even start to identify your soft spots, the tender places that flare up and drive you to drink? Where is the 100 Proof version of the manual for *How to Finally Start Healing Yourself*, that gets to the point faster than yourself on your way to blackout on any day of the week?

Well, there isn't one.

All we have, and all we will *ever* have, is what I like to call *The Pause*.

And it's through learning how to pause – to stop pressing all the buttons and fast-forwarding and rewinding our wishes and fears, looping and repeating our diaries of remorse and zooming in on our insecurities – that we can finally step back and see a clear picture of what *actually* is.

Pause before you spend your money, your time, and your words.

Pause before you pour a drink or your heart out, and learn to pause before you believe what you read, what you're told, and especially what you're thinking.

Learn to pause, always, just long enough to remember that you always have a choice.

It was ultimately through learning how to pause that I was able to interrupt my irresponsible, ignorant, impulsive autopilot. It was how I learned to *not* stop at the liquor store on my way home, and how I learned to begin questioning the truth of all the clutter in my heart and soul. It was through pausing that I came to lean in close enough to the *really real me* and finally hear what he'd been asking for all along.

How can you hear what it is you need *now* when you're so busy blasting re-runs of your favourite highlight reel of regrets? How can you squint tightly enough to finally see in focus where you're standing, while you're so busy fast-forwarding to imaginary future nightmares?

You need to pause the non-stop dialogue and chatter in your head so you can hear what it is your scars are asking for, without the narrative, for a change.

Without the judge inside you telling you that you're stupid or weak, or that you don't deserve to be happy, or sober, or that your partner could do better than you and why don't you just off yourself already and do everyone a favour, or that you'll never get sober because you're a failure and even your dog doesn't like you, and while we're at it here's a list of all the ways your best intentions will once again fall apart in a heaping, steaming pile at your pathetic feet.

Or, maybe your narrative sounds more like the panel of *American Idol*, with a panel of professional judges critiquing everyone and everything *but themselves.*

That is the noise that needs to stop.

That noise is the knife that cuts open your scars and never lets them heal.

That's the noise that bubbles up in your Prosecco and then ferments all the sorrows bottled up inside you.

It's *that noise* that keeps you stuck and all your scars weeping and sore.

You could simply not drink, after all.

Right?

There's tens of thousands of books and apps on the subject that will most likely get you there, if you're diligent and packing willpower. You can just *not pour the next drink down your throat* and pour it down the sink instead. You can cut out your addiction like a cancerous piece of flesh, so you don't have to look at it anymore – but under your skin, it's still spreading.

The sickness is still there.

But if you're here and you're reading this, chances are you haven't excelled too greatly at simply *not drinking*. Or perhaps you have (go you!) and these words are finding you as a timely reminder of why you've made the better choices to pay attention to your life and scars and all the work we all need to do.

I'm here to remind you that drinking is *not your problem*.

Yes, it's likely the *cause* of **most** of your problems – but drinking isn't the problem you need to remedy so you can heal, and in turn, *stop* feeling like you *need* to drink.

Simply *not drinking* is no different than taking Tylenol for a nail in your head.

Until the nail comes out, no matter how numb you try and keep yourself, the injury and pain will always be there.

And it will get infected.

Getting sober requires a level of personal honesty I never imagined was possible, and it only became possible when I learned how to pause long enough to start seeing all the nails in my head, instead of keeping myself constantly busy trying to find more painkillers to numb the pain.

Hitting The Floor

**"Something very beautiful happens to people when their world
has fallen apart: a humility, a nobility, a higher intelligence
emerges at just the point when our knees hit the floor."**
– Marianne Williamson

For as fragmented as my memories are spanning my two-decade-long-day-drinking-career, none are more solid and crystal clear than the day I hit my lowest rock bottom.

The day of impact.

I know that I've come to accept the events that took place – *and have forgiven myself for them, too* – since my stomach no longer backflips when I turn my mind to it.

The reality that I am sitting here today writing this book is evidence of how I've managed to turn *the worst day of my life* into something that can, I hope, help others.

It's magical alchemy at work again, transforming shit into shamrocks.

I didn't hit rock bottom in the classic cartoon falling from the sky sort of *splat*, where you know there's a piano landing on your head three seconds later, followed by whirling lines and dizzy little yellow birds.

Oh no.

I sort of banged and bounced off boulders jutting from the pit I had dug myself, rebounding off all the sharp-edged consequences I had built into my own grave.

And *then* I sort of came to a flesh-burning face plant where I skid until I landed smack into quicksand and stopped, *but didn't stop sinking.*

It was, without question, one of my least graceful moments.

Looking back, I see that I *needed* to crash with such force because the gentle taps on my shoulder from my exhausted conscience were going ignored. It's almost as though something long dead inside me was resurrected at the very moment my face hit the floor, knocking it awake from its slumber only to realize, it too, was as trapped as much I was.

Except it was trapped *inside me.*

Sometimes it's only when our nightmares come to life that we're able to remember our sleeping dreams. Sometimes it takes the monsters under our bed to climb right under the sheets with us before we're able to see how haunted we really are.

The exact circumstances around my epic fall from grace are irrelevant – what's important is *what happened next.*

I cracked open.

Not enough to let all my demons escape, but just enough to smell how rotten I'd become, holding them all inside me for so long, pickled with wine and denial.

What no one tells you, is that rock bottom is made up of mirrors.

I was forced to stare into the heart of my *inability to control myself* and made to see myself for *what* I truly was – a fractured, bruised, and now seemingly broken shadow of *somebody I used to know.* I saw myself through the blood and the bruises – but that didn't mean I *recognized myself.*

I was suddenly surrounded by reflections of my every action, and no matter where I turned it was impossible to avoid meeting the truth of my very sad, very scary reality.

The only thing that felt solid was the ground of this new lower low beneath my feet, while everything around me was shifting and moving, reminding me not only of my surroundings, but of my *company.*

My lack of company.

I was alone; nobody was coming to save me, and I was stuck having to stare at all the discarded facets and fragments of myself I'd tried so hard and so long to avoid – and there was no avoiding them now.

It's almost as though at the moment of impact, when it felt as though my whole world was rushing up and away from me in a dizzying blur, all the veils were lifted and the sharp reflection of my reality was revealed; smoke, fractured mirrors, and all.

My magic act and all its illusions were over.

Navigating my way through the disorienting realm of rock bottom felt, to say the least, next to impossible.

Next to impossible – *but necessary.*

Staying there, thankfully, was not an option.

Funny things start to go through your mind while you're falling, after you've pulled the ground out from beneath your own feet. All the times you ignored your better judgement replaying missed opportunities on loop; all your loose ends flapping around you just out of reach; and every dreaded future nightmare firing up in an angry inferno of ten thousand possible, devastating outcomes.

It's like how they say your life flashes before your eyes in the moments before imminent death or injury – *except it was sort of in reverse.*

All the life you didn't live, all the memories you wish you could forget, every lie and misdeed all come rushing to greet you and start prying the demons free from the broken shell you've become.

Instead of life re*playing* before my eyes, it was *rewinding,* unravelling, and unstitching itself into a mountain of tangled threads at my feet, reminding me of how much life I'd avoided, how much life I had *wasted* – my own, and the lives of others. There was so much of it the floor became covered and it all began clawing, crawling and creeping its way up the walls.

I was no longer just stuck at rock bottom; I was drowning in consequences.

Another thing that no one tells you is that rock bottom isn't a place you *enter* – it's a place that enters *you.*

It's suddenly feeling not unlike the pit of your stomach feeling bottomless, and all your limbs turn numb in the same way you wake from sleeping and your arms are paralyzed.

Frozen and lifeless, no longer responding, and seemingly possessed by forces you can't control, somehow attached to you, but suddenly refusing to listen.

But you know they're *still there.*

I became a fly on the wrong side of a moving car window. Trapped, though able to see clearly where I wanted to be.

Shrinking behind me.

Further, further, far down the lines leading to the horizon that was pulling it away from me until it became nothing but an indistinguishable fleck on the horizon of my past – a place you long to be but can never go back to.

Back where I used to be when I was flying, when I was free.

Back before I fell.

And now, I was stuck, imprisoned by my own faulty navigation, and being taken somewhere I didn't want to go but I flew myself into, watching the entire world as I knew it disappear in front from me.

Forever.

This wasn't just a wake-up call. It was an ultimatum from the Universe. I was being deported from all I had taken for granted and transplanted into a backwards Oublier where instead of being left *to be forgotten, I was being held so I had no choice but to remember.*

I was being left with nothing other than the shaky ground beneath my feet, and I had no choice but to stay there until I stopped viewing it as *the floor* that caused my fall to stop and begin seeing it as the *foundation* on which I needed to rebuild, instead.

I was being held to remember everything that was at stake.

I was being held to remember everything I'd already lost.

I was being held *to remember myself again.*

All along, I had been tossing what I couldn't accept into what I thought was a bottomless well, where my troubles and aversions would magically disappear into the depths. What I didn't know is that they would all be there waiting for me when I threw myself, my life, and the rest of my disowned parts down it, too.

So that's where I started – at the beginning of another end, building a new foundation from all the pieces of myself I had tried – by intent or accident – to throw away.

Pieces I could never be rid of because those pieces *were* me, and now I needed to learn how to accept and use them to build my own escape.

Falling so completely and painfully was a gift.

It delivered me to exactly where I needed to land, shattered, so I could start over again, with all the missing pieces that had left me feeling hollow and flawed.

Pieces that I was responsible for trying to hide and deny, tossing them willfully into neglect, down the very same well made up of mirror that I didn't imagine I, myself, going down as well with such violent force to be reunited with them.

Out of sight does not mean out of soul.

They were the same *limbs* of myself that I'd now need to learn how to use as *tools*, so I could stack them up, one by one on the very same floor that stopped me dead in my tracks. Stopping me not quite enough to kill me, but definitely stopping me *more* than enough to wake myself up into a startlingly, painful new awareness.

Thank heavens for karmic gravity.

The Perfect Conditions

I spend/waste a lot of time *not doing things* because it's just *not quite the perfect conditions.*

Responding to work emails. Yard work. Laundry.

Getting sober.

Writing this book.

It's our tendency to criticize and compare – people, things, events, music, food, circumstances. It's rare that we ever accept something simply *as is.* We are constantly judging and diminishing *what actually is* and imagining any number of alternate realties – other than this one.

We call it *waiting,* when in fact, it's *avoiding.*

By waiting until Monday, until you're more rested, until you have less going on, until you get home, until you have more money, more time, more patience, less fat, less stress, less to do or less to worry about – we put off whatever discomforts we hold aversions to and will do anything to avoid.

Anything that isn't *just how we like it.*

Anything that makes us feel *uncomfortable.*

I put off even *trying* to get sober for decades, with as many excuses as days that passed while I just sat there on the sidelines, avoiding feeling all the feels of what I *knew* I had to go through.

Here's the thing.

The conditions will never be perfect.

It's our job to make it work anyways, and it's our job *to do the work.*

The time is going to pass regardless, so you may as well just start *now.*

I wish I had given myself that advice 20 years ago.

490

Or honestly just *listened to it* when others gave it to me over and over *and over* again over the years. As they say, the best time to plant a tree is ten years ago, and the next best time is now.

I still find myself constantly trying to curate the *perfect conditions* for everything from writing to maintaining my sobriety. When I opted to *stop* saying that I was a writer (who wasn't doing any actual writing) until I made the commitment to start writing more regularly, the first thing I found myself doing was shopping for desks, and chairs, and lamps, and candles. I caught myself spending an entire day sourcing furniture and building the *Mecca of Writing Nooks,* complete with a freshly downloaded screensaver of casually swimming koi for my computer that was just sitting there *waiting to be used.*

If I'd just spent that day writing instead, I'd have more to show and be proud of than just a pretty desk and blank white screen with its flashing cursor taunting me.

The exact same thing happened (I say *happened,* as though it wasn't my own doing) while I was getting ready to come to this cottage to write.

I spent/wasted two days fussing over what to bring, preparing food, packing and repacking, making lists and shopping for things I've yet to even unpack and know I'm not even going to use.

Two days of expertly avoiding the reality that all I *really* needed to do *was write.*

And since my deeply rooted fear of failure (and success) was stirring at the prospect of having to *buckle down and actually write if I wanted to call myself a writer,* it stepped right up to help distract me and avoid those painful, uncomfortable feelings of *doing what scares me.*

Getting sober was no different.

I'd wait to maybe try and quit drinking (or smoking, or eating properly, or spending less, or going to the gym – you do you to make all of this blog uniquely *yours* – the lessons are the same no matter where you come from) until after this weekend, because company was coming. I'd wait to maybe try and quit drinking until tomorrow, because I'd already been drinking for 5 hours and it was only 4pm, so rather than stop *now* I may as well just wait and start *tomorrow,* instead.

Truth is, I was just scared shitless of the unknown.

I would rather carry the burden of *not even having started* instead of facing the inevitable and having to deal with it.

Of having to maybe be *uncomfortable.*

Of having to feel my way through it alone in the dark.

Of admitting I didn't know it all and I didn't – *or would ever* – have it all together.

The *Perfect Conditions* I used as roadblocks and interruptions only ended up detouring and delaying me, making the first steps infinitely harder and heavier for all the added weight I was now carrying, heavy with guilt and self-disgust.

I'd get caught in the loop of wanting to move forward, riding my automatic reactions of avoiding and delaying, beating myself up for not having quit yet, feeling even more feelings of guilt and remorse, then running to the nearest bottle as quickly as possible to make those uncomfortable feelings known as *reality* go away as fast as I could.

The *Perfect Conditions* I was using to avoid the work I needed to do were just chameleons, transforming to look like necessary and natural parts of the whole picture. The only conditions they were perfect for, however, were adding to my already heavy heart, adding one more reason to degrade myself for stalling.

For delaying.

For avoiding.

Like *always*.

That's what the egoic voice inside all of us does.

It ridicules. It keeps us down and tethered to false truths about who we are (or who 'it' wants us to be - you know the 'it' - that hurt little kid inside, the abused spouse, the self-harmer, the anxious and insecure – we all have our *it*).

It sets us up to stay distracted in a desperate attempt to protect us from those feelings of discomfort and being out of our comfort zones, *because that's it's job.*

Its job is to ensure we stay out of danger.

Feelings of uncertainty, pain, discomfort, and disorientation *are* dangerous to our well-being, as far as the voice in our head is concerned.

So naturally, even *the idea* of getting rid of alcohol raised all the alarms inside me.

It sent all of its troops to the frontline to build walls and dig trenches, to do *anything and everything* they could to deter me from crossing over into uncharted, and scary, territory.

We are all much smarter than we care to admit.

We *know* when we're doing this.

We *know* when we're in avoidance mode, tossing jokes about procrastination around like it's a schoolyard game of dodgeball.

Except, eventually, the ball hits you smack in the face and *forces* you to pay attention.

It knocks you on your ass.

It knocked *me* on my ass.

It was almost as though my habit of aversion had a wicked sense of humour, and instead of delivering the elusive *Perfect Conditions* I was choosing to wait for, *It* brought to me the ultimate *Worst Conditions*, instead.

> "Midlife: When the universe grabs your shoulders and tells you
> 'I'm not f-ing around, use the gifts you were given."
> – *Brené Brown*

The Universe doesn't have all day to play your games.

It may entertain you for a while, and it may even play along. But eventually, a time comes along when the stakes are higher, and the game gets harder, and we aren't just playing anymore. What you're up against becomes *the real deal.*

It becomes a life-or-death situation, now swollen and bloated (and probably broke and surrounded by a lot of the really wrong people, since all the good ones left a long time ago) after all the time it's been sitting there festering, just *waiting for you to get started.*

So, what are you *actually* waiting for?

The First Few Days

Everything you need to accomplish your goals is in you already.

Whenever I am would begin a photoshoot with a new couple, I always started by asking them if they've ever done anything like it before. The answer was usually almost no, followed by me explaining to them that the first ten or fifteen minutes can feel really awkward, but then it becomes fun, and all they need to do is just relax into it and I'll guide them as we go.

I offer to you the exact same advice about getting sober.

After the first ten or fifteen minutes though, it becomes the first ten or fifteen *hours*.

Then days.

And weeks, and months.

Years.

The early days of getting sober can feel a lot like travelling back through time to middle school and suddenly becoming the most awkward, geekiest, nerdiest version of yourself complete with headgear, acne, and braces.

You know you're there to learn, but you can't focus because you're so fixated on your insecurities and differences, not to mention confined by strange and new restrictions, plus you feel as though *everyone is watching you,* and though you're in the company of so many other people, there's just something *different about you,* now.

Getting sober *will,* indeed, make you the odd man out for a while.

For some it will be more obvious if your circle of "friends" drink as much as you do, or if your taste for alcohol was born from a home life riddled with addiction, trauma, and neglect. For others, it may just be one more dirty little secret that you're adding to your pile behind closed doors, kept hidden with your collection of dust-ridden skeletons, covering it up like *it never happened,* no different than a cat crapping in a litterbox.

What we *do* share – and what *everyone* in recovery goes through – is feeling like the odd man out, displaced *in your own storyline.*

Suddenly, the script will have changed.

Suddenly, your character is getting completely rewritten.

Suddenly, the whole plot has twisted and you're no longer sure how the story will end.

Or if it ever will.

You step from one moment feeling as though you're standing on solid ground – despite it being shaky as hell – to the next, and then, into total and absolute *groundlessness.*

I'll tell you right now: *not drinking is the easy part.*

And I'll remind you again: *it isn't alcohol you need to recover from.*

It's from your *addiction to escaping reality.*

Keep both of those notes in your back pocket throughout your journey, and refer to them often, because I guarantee you'll forget them over and over and over again.

You're going to fixate on wanting a drink.

Needing a drink.

You do NOT need a drink.

You *need* to look at the *feelings* that you're trying to *drown with a drink.*

And for once in God-only-knows-how-long, you're going to be able to feel those feelings *without* the anesthetic of alcohol and hear what they're asking for *without* the sirens blaring in your head and your heart like they always do.

Now don't get me wrong – there *will* be sirens, and they'll start going off at the worst of times. They're going to blast out of nowhere and scare the hell out of you, and they're going to call to you with their sweet and irresistible song.

It is *not* your job to *ignore* them.

It is your job to learn how to hear them for what they really are.

The way that all this works is that you need to start recognizing that everything you *think* you know, everything you *believe* you see, and all that you *think* you understand – about alcohol, yourself, and the world – is for the most part *untrue*.

It's just our monkey mind painting pictures and creating illusions, so things fit neatly into our storyline, so our ego stays harbored, safe and protected.

Honestly – it's just doing its job.

This is where the hard part starts.

You can (and you will) *not* have a drink. You *won't* go to the liquor store, or the fridge, or wherever you hide your favourite poison. You *will* make it through the craving and the urge and be pretty darn smug with yourself.

Except that *the sirens will still be blaring*, and there will still be an overall, off-putting uneasiness that will still be writhing beneath your skin.

It will all still be there because *drinking is not the actual problem* you are here to fix.

You are here to practice how to stop yourself from falling down the same rabbit hole over and over, and you're here to learn how to stop running every time things get a little too close for comfort.

The smoke alarms will stop going off once you've found – and begin to put out – all the *real* fires that are creating the smoke.

This is the beginning of where you start to understand the polar difference between *not drinking* and not *wanting* to drink.

So, on one hand, you have your body demanding alcohol because it is chemically expecting it, and on the other hand, you have your soul demanding sobriety because it is *begging* for it. It's relatively easy to deal with physical cravings and pain. It's also relatively easy to sweat through the clammy withdrawal window of 3 or 4 days, even though while it's happening, *the rest of yourself* – notably your mind and your non-stop inner dialogue, and the *really real* you who hasn't found their voice yet – they're all going to be *inside*, coordinating a riot.

The physical discomforts will pass, so treat them the same as if you're holding your breath while you're at the doctor's office about to get a needle. (This analogy may be triggering and counterproductive for addicts who shoot up – in which case, I'd recommend you just skip to the next paragraph). A little prick, a little pressure, and sooner than you'd imagine – the worst part is over.

What's important is that you *allow yourself* to have a no-holds-barred pity party for yourself if you want to. And yes, that inner voice will pipe up and tell you to stop it.

Spoil yourself freaking *rotten*. And yes, that inner voice will start chirping and tell you that you don't deserve it. Nap. Despite that voice telling you there's so much stuff you *should* be doing, instead. Eat all the chocolate. Cry. Take a bath. Go to bed. Read, read, read, and then read some more – the world of sober literature (that's what you're reading right now, if you didn't know) is vast and growing, and full of magical little nooks and crannies jam-packed with goodies and treats you never imagined.

There is no level of self-care that you don't deserve during these first few days, or weeks, or months.

Or ever.

What is also crucial is that you stay firmly planted in your resolve to *never drink again,* and to treat your sobriety as though *it is your full-time job.*

You can't do this half-ass.

You can't do this by shuffling towards the end of the diving board without ever jumping in. Get wet. Drenched in it. Dripping for once in something other than alcohol or whatever your poison happens to be. *Because we all have our poisons.*

You have to take a leap of faith – in *yourself.*

So how you do you begin to stop – or prevent – the riots? Where do you look to start putting out the fires that keep sounding the alarms? How do you train yourself to shift your gaze, so you're no longer fixated on what feels like you're now going without?

You begin to look *beneath* everything.

You learn to start peeling back the layers of everything you *think* you know and everything you *think* you see, and hear, and read, and most importantly, *think and feel.*

You start to open tiny spaces between *what is actually happening* and *how you're reacting,* where you can pause and revisit what you *think* you're thinking.

You start asking yourself at every trigger, craving and curveball – *is what I'm thinking or telling myself true?* And if I believe it actually is, then asking next *how can I really know that it is, without a doubt, as true as I'm convincing myself it is?*

In a nutshell, stop trusting your thoughts and your feelings until you've seen their true colours.

They aren't serving you like you think they are.

Your mind is going to start racing with thoughts of having "given up" alcohol. You're going to start running through every possible, and now terrifying, scenario that you once used alcohol as a crutch to get through. That is, until *now*. You'll imagine all the challenges and tight situations you're going to find yourself in, and you're going to wonder what the hell you've gotten yourself into, and if you have the strength to stick with it after all. You're going to imagine the worst.

So, you need to plan for the worst and expect the best.

You're going to start feeling as though your best friend just died.

Well, here's another reminder, and toss this one in your back pocket, too, that best friend was nothing ever than a wolf in sheep's clothing, just waiting to huff, and puff, and blow your whole house down.

That best friend reliably stabbed you in the back every time you turned around.

That best friend did *nothing* other than pour fuel on your fires.

That best friend kept slipping lies into your liquor, and you drank it down, day after day after day.

You are not *giving up* alcohol. It is *not* a sacrifice.

You are getting rid of it.

You are *getting rid* of it, because that's what we do with garbage and things that no longer serve us: *we get rid of them.*

Without fail, the cravings will return. Sometimes they'll arrive like subtle waves lapping at your feet, and sometimes they'll rush ashore like a violent and greedy tsunami that wants nothing more than to pull you back out to sea.

You need to be prepared – *always* – for both.

Walk *through* it.

Step by step.

Walk yourself through the inevitable chain of events that is going to happen if you *do* decide to have a drink – because let's face it, you've proven *almost every time you drink* that it *never* ends at *just one* drink. Or weekend. Or month. Or year.

Generally, it never ends well at all.

You need to catch yourself in the craving, when you find your mind wandering to the liquor store or playing a slideshow of the rare, *rosy* memories of drinking and ask yourself, "And *then* what happens?"

And then what happens.

Exactly.

What happens is what *always* happens.

What happens are all the things that drove you to read this book. To not want to get out of bed. To want to cancel plans and stop wanting to make plans at all. To feel like a bag of absolute shit every day. What happens is the ground beneath you gets slippery and you slide, like you always have, back down into the rabbit hole, to some newer rock bottom and shallower lower low, and the sad black hole inside you grows somehow even bigger.

That is what happens.

So go ahead and have a drink if you want one, after proving to yourself you can predict the future – because now you know *exactly* what is going to happen once you take that first insidious sip.

Always. Walk. Yourself. Through. It.

When the cravings hit and the spoiled brat inside you is throwing the tantrum of all tantrums, take yourself by the hand, take a deep breath, and walk the predictable path of where this is headed if you don't start pumping the brakes.

What is also happening while you're rationalizing your way out of a craving, is you're allowing room for *The Pause.*

That magical split second made up of sliding doors and alternate outcomes. It's the ultimate crossroads, where quite literally *anything is possible.*

Even healing.

Melting

There's a story of two men who went hiking up a mountain.

Each with a bottle of water, but one man froze his before their hike. After climbing for hours in the sweltering heat, the two men break for a rest. The man who had frozen his water bottle takes a final swig and is left with nothing but a chunk of ice, rattling around against plastic.

The other man, who didn't freeze his bottle, found his water too hot to drink.

Since one had ice, they tried and tried to chip away at the ice, so they could slowly pass slivers to the other bottle in order to help cool it down and make it drinkable. In a moment of clarity and pause, one man suggests to the other that rather than chiseling away at the hard ice and trying to *get it out*, they could just *pour the warm water in* to the bottle with the ice instead, and they could then both drink cool water from the same bottle.

The lesson here is that instead of chipping away at the cold, hard stuff, sometimes it makes more sense to let new, warm things in.

To allow the warmth of things *outside yourself* to melt your frozen parts.

We do a very good job of isolating ourselves while in the throes of deep, active addiction, building walls that would give Trump a hard-on. Walls always serve two purposes: they prevent things from *getting in,* but also they slow down the chance of our feral parts *getting out.*

The wild parts.

The parts we don't ever want anyone to see.

The parts of ourselves we shamefully keep hidden behind tall walls and closed doors.

And the walls grow taller the longer we stay behind them. Or maybe, it's that we just grow smaller.

Alcohol worked like a liquid microscope for me, amplifying all my troubles, fixating on the small and insignificant things until they appear to be of mountainous proportions.

It kept me in a loop of looking too closely at all the wrong things, from the wrong angle, with a growing disability to look away.

We fixate. We dwell. We drink to the point of our words and emotions spinning off in a repetitive loop that create cyclones of tunnel vision. We go dangerously deep into dark rabbit holes that stop us from seeing that there are *always* alternatives.

That we have options.

That sometimes even just a little to the left, there has always been a different path we could follow. *A better, easier path.*

But we travel the same beaten paths, over and over and over, on thoughtless autopilot because it's the fastest route to a predictable destination. Our brains will always defer to what it already knows to keep traffic flowing, regardless of how the outcome is sorely disappointing every time.

It will always choose what is easiest, not necessarily what's best.

This is where learning to pause changes everything.

This is where you give yourself the time and space you need to detour your tired and self-deprecating repetitive patterns.

This is where you finally discover a way to walk *around* the rabbit hole, instead of falling into it, again and again.

This is where you begin to learn to question quite literally every thought, every word, every action, and every emotion that passes through you.

This is where you begin letting things in so you can more easily tame your feral secrets and more easily let things out.

Beautiful Failure

In hindsight, I can now say that my epic relapse after rehab was one of the most integral and important steps to getting myself to this point of sobriety.

Failure can become the exact steppingstone you didn't know you needed.

It not only drove the final nails in the coffin of my delusion that I could moderate, but it taught me that failure can also be poetically beautiful,

It taught me to remember to *pause*, so I could at long last learn how to interrupt my reckless autopilot.

It reminded me that we are never in control, like we struggle to believe we are.

It gave me a battery of evidence to dispel any myths I was still trying to convince myself of around my addiction, my alcoholism, and *my own role* in the destruction of anything meaningful in my life.

Having *"failed"* after rehab (and countless attempts before that) was ultimately the kick in the crotch I needed to once and for all *sincerely* knock me to knees. It buckled me into pieces, in total surrender and absolute humility. I wanted *the embarrassment and shame* of having given in and *failed* to be lifted from me, as though I'd been tarred and feathered by own actions.

And, in a way, I was.

Failing is fine, so long as you can figure out how to *fail forward* – which is how I learned that there's actually two kinds of failure.

First, there's the kind of failure that weighs you down, and then there's the *beautiful* kind of failure, that has the potential to lift you up. The type of failure you experience, however, is entirely dependent on the angle at which you *choose* to look at how and why you've fallen.

Without having taken my first ill-fated sip of wine 3 short months after entering rehab, I would still be white knuckling my way through sobriety, coasting on the fumes of my willpower. I'm fairly certain I wouldn't even have maintained my sobriety much longer anyhow because I was on a crash course toward failure from the moment I stepped foot off the plane.

Without having failed in my first, sincerely earnest attempt at getting rid of alcohol, I would still be holding space for all the *what-ifs and maybe's* that are so easy to pad and soften even the sharpest of good intentions.

I'd still be standing with one eye on the emergency exit door.

I'd still be juggling the possibility that maybe I *could* actually moderate my drinking. Maybe I did have it in me to *just have one* (despite having failed miserably in every prior attempt, ever). I'd always be wondering if maybe the danger and disease had left me once and for all, and it was finally safe to go back in the water.

But, since my arrogance got the best of me and the undertow claimed me once again,

I was given a priceless gift disguised as a failure, and that is the irrevocable and unquestionable knowledge that *those waters will never be safe.*

This is a good thing.

This is *certainty*, and what an addict needs most of all is some sort of decisiveness and surety and fewer massive, gaping question marks.

My "failure" and remarkable face plant after rehab which landed me smack at the bottom of the bottle again gave me a platform to raise myself up on, to make my next attempt wiser and no longer weighed down by what-ifs.

Looking back, it's easy for me to make out how my entire path has been paved by my failures, creating a new space for me to be both grateful for them and my own, at times faltering, resilience. Each flimsy house of cards I've tried to build that always collapsed in on itself has just been a trial run for the real deal. They've each given me new approaches to balance things better, to plan for the inevitable bumps that will, inevitably, send it toppling, not to mention a great deal of very much-needed practice in being *patient*.

It was, after all, my collection of failures I was looking at from the wrong angle that perpetuated my drinking and my addiction.

And, looking at failure from the wrong angle can not only be hard on the eyes but heavy on the heart.

So much of recovery involves turning things inside out and upside down.

It's no different when it comes to roadblocks or falling flat on your face in a skin-tearing skid that never looks or feels good in the end. The key is to quiet your mental reflex that points fingers and calls you names, *to pause,* breathe, step back and take a slow walk around what happened. And *how.*

You can allow it to be woven into your tired storyline, and wallow in the mud you've found yourself in. You can let it keep you there until you're heavy and caked and all dried up. Or you can remind yourself that failure – along with quite literally everything – is *no big deal.*

Failure is a gift if you allow yourself to see it as one.

What *is* a big deal though is not trying again. Giving up.

That's the only *real* kind of failure.

Forfeit out of fear.

So maybe you drank after two days sober, or twenty weeks, or thirty years. Maybe you told yourself you wouldn't drink on weekdays anymore, yet here you are half in the bag at 3 pm.

The key here is that these are not failures.

You have the power to turn them into *beautiful* failures.

They're beautiful because they are lessons and answers dressed up as disappointment. They have much to teach you if you're able to step back and finally see them for what they are. And more importantly, *why and how they happened.*

It would have been easy for me to wallow in my faltering after rehab – and, indeed, I did for a solid 8 months, or roughly 960 more bottles of wine. I could have stayed there, pickling myself for eternity in a jar I put myself in because I was too afraid to accept the truth that I don't – and will never – have it all figured out.

The truth is that I tested the waters, and found that for me, they would always be filled with sharks.

And that's okay. That is not failure.

That is transforming an err in judgement and the consequences of my wild curiosity into wisdom.

Strange New Places

**To get myself to sit down and finally write this damn book
I had to pick myself up and put myself into a strange new place.**

I found myself a quiet cottage in the woods on Airbnb where I could hide away for a week, *alone*, without distraction, and put on my literary blinders and focus on writing.

I had to do the same thing – *uproot myself* – to ultimately get rid of alcohol, to find my husband, to change careers, and to slowly learn how to leave things behind.

You see, life only moves forward through strange new places.

The uncomfortable, unknown, anxious tightness of having no reference point.

Of having no ground under your feet.

Of feeling the strangeness of never having been somewhere before.

Surroundings.

Relationships.

Sobriety.

It's in that *moving through to what's new* that our eyes begin to open.

It's ridiculous what I packed to come here – so many things, when all I ever needed was a pen and paper.

And that's what we do - *we carry things around.*

We carry things to work, to the park, from the car to your kitchen, from your trepidatious youth to wherever you find yourself today. We've stashed so much away inside ourselves that we've forgotten what's even at the back of the closet anymore, and that spills into our real world where we just drag shit we don't need *but helps us feel secure* with us everywhere we go.

We carry so much that we feel the need to numb our sore muscles and soul.

Then, all it does is water-log our already too heavy hearts, saturating what is already sometimes too much on its own, and it weigh us down.

It wears us down.

It addicts us to itself in a twisted and dark, codependent ballet.

This whole "I'm going to write a book" thing (which I've procrastinated on for more years than I care to count) is one of these strange new places. Uncharted and uncertain, and absolutely fucking terrifying.

But only when I think about it because *thinking* doesn't usually end very well.

Everything we carry with us – the boxes and bags of stuff I needed to bring to this cottage so I could "be somewhere new" (without it feeling like somewhere new), for example.

Anything to make it familiar.

To make it more *comfortable.*

To give me *things* to tend to and *stuff* to worry about on my outside so my attention doesn't get an opportunity to rest for too long and tend to the dark ballet being performed with gusto on the *inside.*

So many things, just to avoid feeling out of my element in a strange new place, to help it feel, somehow, maybe a little less strange.

Getting sober is the strangest of all the strange new places, because it's full to the brim and overflowing with all the old things we've been carrying around.

It's the most overcrowded, dusty, and creepy antique shop full of your most treasured fears, and biggest, brassiest regrets. It's busting at the seams with all the things you've tried to hide away, which have only left your heart aching, over and over *and over* again.

What's new though, is how everything begins *to look* once you're sober, and the world is no longer viewed through merlot-coloured glasses. The strangeness of new places becomes a little less scary, and a lot more exciting. The idea of *going without* disappears, and you start to view your sobriety as *having got rid of,* instead. Sobriety turns your mind into a sort of acrobat, with a newfound ability to contort your thoughts so you can wrap them around what used to be so slippery and finally hold on for a change.

The best *strange new places* are never places you can actually *go.*

They're mindsets.

Ideas.

Points of view.

Steps taken just beyond the edges of your comfort zone.

It's when we stay saddled between what we know, what is predictable, and what is safe (as far as we're concerned) that stagnation and sadness can find us.

Life moves forward through strange places.

The first few days of *existing* without alcohol were not only strange, but they were disorienting. My up was down, my left was right, and I felt totally outside of my skin.

That's how I knew it was exactly what I was supposed to be doing.

When you find yourself out of sorts and surrounded by conditions that make you uncomfortable – know that you are on the right path. It's the mindless, commonplace, everyday things we do that perpetuate our patterns, but it's in the things we haven't tried before, the tastes we haven't explored, and the paths we've never taken that lead us to places we never could have aimed for.

Places where we belong.

The key is to be aware enough, instead of afraid enough.

Our habits and monkey mind push us to run when there's danger – and as far as our instincts are concerned, the unknown is always to be considered dangerous. But our instincts are using an operating system that was designed millennia ago, when we needed to know our routes and hiding places, where there was life-threatening danger around every corner.

You know. Like, dinosaurs and shit.

But it's 2019 (at the time of writing this. Please disregard that it's now 2023 when I'm publishing this book. *Finally.*)

Other than getting hit by a distracted driver while crossing the street, our day-to-day dangers, for lucky ones, like myself, are limited.

We're allowed to relax into the unknown, it's just that our instincts haven't caught up with us yet, and they still need to update their operating system.

Our innate fear of strange new places needs to be transformed into excitement. Adventure. Possibility. Opportunity.

And that's what my journey through recovery has been like, so far. It hasn't been the dreadful nightmare my ego prepared me for and tried so hard to make me avoid. The strange newness of sobriety has been a welcome rebirth in what was an otherwise monotonous loop.

It's No Big Deal

My addiction turned me into a loudspeaker, with the annoying ability to amplify the smallest things into epic and overwhelming proportions.

It wasn't always out loud – most of the screaming happened in my head – but I'd pull whoever I could into the cyclone of my criticism.

You know the kind.

The nattering.

The incessant, negative inner – and sometimes outer – chatter.

The overwhelming pull to be drawn into dramas of my own creation.

And, I'd get stuck hook, line and sinker in yet another blown out-of-proportion storyline that whipped around me like an evil spell, mesmerized by all then *"and thens"* and *"how could theys"* and *"as ifs."*

Deservedly or not (it was almost always not) – everything was a *Very Big Deal.*

I don't believe this is unique to addicts.

I feel it's more of a tendency of our human nature, and it's one of our biggest assignments. Learning to catch ourselves as we get hooked by our habit of inflating importance can be one of the most beneficial tools not only while getting sober, but also for anyone who thinks life can be a whole lot easier.

Alcohol just poured more fuel on my already chronic dissatisfaction.

It enabled what should have only been a simple spark and engulfed it. It turned flames into infernos, and my built-in *Addicts Defense System* would kick into high gear, and I'd raise war flags and charge headlong into whatever conflict I as of yet had no idea I was creating.

It just sort of happened.

All the time.

This is what happens when you don't *pause*.

You miss out on the first, and easiest, opportunity to stop and revisit what you believe you're looking at and ask yourself if what you're *thinking* actually reflects what is really, actually, *happening* – *and* then check yourself to see if how you're *reacting* is appropriate for how you are actually, truly *feeling*.

I'm going to tell you now, that once you drill down through the surface of whatever ignited your inferno, you'll see that in reality, it's not even *close* to what you thought, imagined, or created in your mind that it was.

And it will almost always fall into the category of *No Big Deal*.

I began paying attention, for likely the first time in my life, to how I was physically feeling when I got myself *all worked up* – so I could begin to recognize when it was happening, like seeing storm clouds on the horizon so I can prepare for the imminent rain.

The rising shoulders, the tense jaw, a smoldering heat rising up through my neck to flush my cheeks, the instant distraction from whatever I was doing, the pounding heartbeat, and *always* the desire to *tell someone*.

Or *everyone*.

To broadcast my disapproval of whatever the hell was happening, so I could find someone who agreed with me to satisfy my ego's need for approval.

We all do it.

"OMG I told Tina, and she totally agreed."

We use the agreement and approval of others to legitimize our claim and build our case on why we are *so hard done by*.

For alcoholics, this is our playground.

Except it's a playground littered with used syringes and broken glass.

There is no better (and obnoxious) storyteller than a drunk.

We get hooked into this loop by the smallest of things, from everyday traffic to simple interruptions to Whole Foods being sold out of the damn TTLA sandwich. The voice in our head starts to rant and rave and off we go to the races. This is why the internet and social media is full of rant and rave pages; for people to vent behind anonymous screens, puffed up with their indignation over what is always *never a Very Big Deal*, usually at the expense of innocent small business owners or someone who cut them off at an intersection, just like they themselves did to someone else just hours before.

All of it is just one more way our ego tries to convince us that we're separate, we're alone, we're one against millions, and that it's our *duty* to defend ourselves when things aren't *exactly how we like them.* It's just one more way we suffer when faced with the unwavering truth that nothing can be controlled, nothing can remain the same, and nothing will ever be the same as it was, as it is, or as it ever will be again.

And that sort of groundlessness can be terrifying.

What we're trying to do when we turn something into a *Very Big Deal* is pin it down in time and freeze our *current* drama so we can just keep staring at it and discussing how wrong it is. We want to use it as a stage to parade all our pent-up resentments and disapprovals.

It's also a vain attempt to simply hold onto something that lights us up, that gets our dopamine kicking and adrenaline rushing.

To hold onto *anything* because we can't come to terms that *there is nothing we can hold on to.*

The moment you notice yourself escalating, the very second you feel the hook pulling you away, you need to remind yourself that whatever is happening, whatever criticisms are bubbling up inside you, it is *No Big Deal.*

Remind yourself of this immediately and *first,* to at least put a lid on the boiling pot of your blistering emotions, then walk through and explain to yourself *afterwards* why it is in fact, *Not a Big Deal* after all.

Sometimes, you may not catch yourself until you're so twisted up you're mostly made up of knots. And that's okay, too. What's important is that you *notice eventually.*

In the big scheme of things – there are very few things that are indeed *Very Big Deals.*

The *problem* is not the problem.

The problem is what we do *next.*

We spin-off.

We catastrophize.

We get swept away and we get caught up in the storyline and chatter of our internal conversation, full of judgements, embellishments, and labels about what's happening.

It's rare that any of it is true.

When you're able to catch yourself, when you're able to feel the hook in your cheek pulling you down the dark and uncertain hole of *what could happen next* – it's *then* that you need to pause, breathe, and start asking yourself some very basic questions.

This is critical.

If you don't, it's no different from turning your back to a fire and pretending it's been put out. You need to lean into the hot parts of your frustration and figure out what started the blaze.

First – put it into perspective. Is what's happening *as* much of a *Very Big Deal* as you're making it out to be? In the land of *actual Very Big Deals*, how does this (likely paling in comparison) measure up? Don't be surprised when it's difficult to see, because whatever you're freaking out about likely falls into the shadow of things that are *Truly Big Deals* to your soul.

Next – reel it in and come back. Our emotions drag us around like kites in a hurricane, tossed this way and that, and anywhere but *right here and right now*. There's a simple formula to decipher where in time you've been lost: if you're anxious, get out of the *future*, and if you're sad, get out of the *past*. It's impossible to be present – for ourselves, for our loved ones, for our screaming emotions that just want to be soothed – when we're constantly being dragged away. If you are able to recognize that your inner dialogue is entirely made up of *make-believe endings and resurrected hurts,* that what's happening right now is *far* from a *Very Big Deal* and see that at this moment everything is honestly okay and you have everything you need, you'll have taken a huge step in pulling your kite out of the hurricane.

Then – walk through it. Dissect it. Turn over all the tiny pieces of your spontaneous drama in your hands and see how small and harmless they really are. Ask yourself "Okay, what just happened?" and maybe your answer will be "I fell." And then you ask, "And then what happened?" And maybe your answer will be "I scraped my knee – but it wouldn't have happened if Tina hadn't left her bag where I've told her before to stop leaving it!" And then you notice again that your kite has taken off and you're being pulled back into the hurricane. So, you ask yourself once more "Tell me again, what happened?" And you answer, "I fell." And you ask yourself again and again and again "And then what happened?" You keep repeating this question-and-answer session with yourself until your focus dials back and you stop magnifying your sensitive, stored-up hurts and resentments, slapping them onto whatever sent your kite flying and you started treating it like a *Very Big Deal*.

Keep asking yourself what happened until you can recount what is happening *without the storyline*.

Keep asking yourself to explain, step by step, what happened and what's happening, until you can talk yourself down from the ledges of the past and the future, and bring yourself to how *actually okay* you are *right now*.

Keep asking yourself as many times as you need to until the actual events at hand shrink back to their normal size, until your kite comes back to earth, and you can see clearly that it's *No Big Deal* after all.

What happens next, happens naturally.

You move on.

You move through the fresh and new open space that is made available when you lose the storyline and see clearly that the only *Very Big Deal* was the one you were *creating*.

You move through without the self-absorption. Without highlighting how whatever just happened poked you in all your sore spots.

You move on better prepared to recognize sooner when the hook has landed in your cheek, and when your kite is getting whisked away by the pull of another windstorm brewing inside you.

You move on understanding that there is only one true *Very Big Deal*.

And that's how when you find yourself accepting the present moment and all its conditions *as is, without wishing they were different,* you'll see that you have everything you need.

That everything is *more okay* than your storyline would like to lead you to believe.

And *that* is a Very Big Deal.

Twenty-Six Letters

It's a bit of a mind–fuck to think that all books (in the English language)
and all the moving prose that stir your dusty soul, all the soaring
lyrics to songs that resonate deep into the core of your being – are
just 26 letters, juggled, rearranged, and in turn, redefined.

Twenty-six letters that when properly arranged hold the power to change lives or destroy them, to build up or tear down, to enlighten or delude and confuse.

Often, the small, everyday things we take for granted and overlook harbor the most power if we can learn how to use them skillfully.

The longer I'm sober, the more I'm realizing that I *always had* the tools at my disposal to plan and orchestrate my escape from addiction.

I always had the same twenty-six letters that I have now.

It's just that I was arranging them in all the wrong ways.

My p's & q's were confused, and all my t's were dotted, and my i's were crossed. Like most things end up in the chaotic underworld of addiction, everything was turned up upside down and inside out.

It was as though I was trapped in a never-ending game of Scrabble, and my tiles never seemed to spell *anything*. And, like most alcoholics, I was certain it was because the game was rigged, and all my opponents were against me (this of course is when I could actually *focus* on the letters in front me).

It never dawned on me then that these were the tiles I had drawn *for myself*, and even if they had been given to me or doled out like a hand of cards – it was *my* responsibility to rearrange them and play them as best as I can.

To make sense of them and give *meaning* to what was in front of me.

To look deeper, and to find a solution to the jumble of characters I had to work with.

In this big game of life, we are all given the same 26 letters to work with. We all draw from the same bag, and we all have the same board to play on. Granted, some tiles are harder to play than others, some of us are playing on boards that are battered and bruised with dog-eared corners and hand-me-down parts, and none of us have instructions on how to play the game.

Which is the essence of the game right there.

We make it work.

We play the letters we can when we can.

We learn that sometimes if we can hold out and hold on, the right letters land in our lap.

And we learn to be patient, not only with ourselves but with everyone else playing the game.

The thing with addiction is that it stops you from seeing what is in front of you, only showing the negative and reverse of everything: what is black appears white, and what is white turns to black. You stop seeing the letters you have to play with and only see the letters you wish you had.

Or worse, the letters you once had but don't have anymore.

It is up to you – and it is *always* up to you – as to how you choose to rearrange the letters you have to work with. It is up to you whether you choose to strengthen your patience, wait it out and pass, or trade in what is no longer working for you for the uncertainty, but the possibility, of better letters instead.

And it's up to you to learn how to see what you have to work with, instead of what you're working without.

Connection

Hubs has recently got into background acting for movies and tv shows.
You know, the people quite literally in the background of various scenes.
I've never in 18 years seen him as in his element or happier.

As photographers by trade, I know firsthand the exhaustion that comes from shooting all day (not to mention the decade I did it hungover as hell). It's not only physically, but mentally and oftentimes emotionally, draining. And then, once the day is over, come the hours and weeks and days of editing in front of a computer.

It's a rollercoaster of energy levels and emotions, and it's a creative's personal nightmare.

Since Hubs started acting, I've witnessed him drive 3 hours to film on 4 hours of sleep and be on set for 17 hours, only to drive home another 3 hours and do it all again the next day, somewhere else.

And his energy is through the roof.

I've also witnessed him leave for an engagement shoot 15 minutes away, shoot for 1.5 hours, and return drained, depleted, and exhausted.

His energy is through the roof these days because he's connected with his passion.

The things that swell our soul never drain us.

They *give* to us.

They *enable* us.

They *nourish* us.

When you connect with something that aligns with your spirit, it's like you've plugged yourself into the *Universal Battery Pack*.

You're constantly being recharged.

I cannot stress enough the absolute, life or death importance of connection in recovery and how it directly relates to addiction.

As addicts – and honestly, simply as humans – we treat it as though it's our full-time job to *disconnect.*

To separate.

To isolate and push away.

It's what we do, and we do it remarkably well.

It doesn't matter whether you're a super social drunk who is out at the clubs 7 days a week, or a closet alcoholic who hides their vodka in the toilet tank. Regardless of how we portray ourselves on the outside, our *hearts* remain disconnected, detached, and constantly longing for something we can't quite put our finger on.

And that thing, my friends, is *connection.*

As humans, we are innately ingrained with a need to bond. With our mother, our siblings, friends, flesh and blood real-life humans, animals, places, experiences, and sometimes, the right *things.*

When we have difficulty bonding, because of trauma, disability, isolation, or circumstance - the need doesn't go away. And so, we turn to whatever we can to create a pseudo-connection.

Sex, drugs, shopping, adrenaline – anything that makes us feel as though we are plugged in to *something.*

The problem is when our surrogate bonds begin to replace our real, authentic, face-to-face, and heart-to-heart connections we *need* to thrive.

It's exactly what happened to me, and how I catapulted from casual drinking to 4 liters of wine a day. These surrogate bonds are just *easier* in the interim. They're quick and they cut to the chase. They satisfy our inner cravings that growl louder and louder until we can't hear what they're hungry for anymore.

As I moved through my 20's and 30's, the complexities of life increased in proportion to my level of drinking.

It's possible the complexities of my life were being exacerbated by my drinking, but it's also possible that my drinking accelerated my mounting dilemmas. It's not only possible, but also highly likely.

What happened next is that I began pushing people away.

I began sabotaging opportunities.

I started burning bridges like I was a prodigal pyromaniac, the golden child of glorious infernos left behind me to mark where I've been.

It was almost as if the surrogate connection I had made with wine was jealous of any meaningful relationship outside of our codependent love affair. With each loss of a *real* connection, I'd find myself bonding faster and harder with one more bottle of wine, one more shot in my glass, one more puff of a joint.

The further I pushed myself from authentic and meaningful relationships, the deeper I dove into whatever numbing comfort I could find.

The kind that had no expectations of me.

These surrogate bonds we create are only meant to foster us, not adopt us. And in my case, and the case of so many addicts and alcoholics, we end up not only adopted, but *abducted*.

I'm not just making this stuff up over here.

There's a fascinating study that was done by Canadian psychotherapist Dr. Bruce Alexander in the late 1970's where the effects of opioid use by rats was compared between rats in isolation, and rats in what was dubbed "Rat Park" – essentially a rat's playground, where they were free to be social, have sex, and do whatever rats like to do.

The rats in both cages were given two water bottles – one with plain drinking water, and another with drinking water spiked with morphine. (Full disclaimer: I am vehemently against animal testing of any kind.)

The caged rats in isolation took to the morphine instantly, drinking 19 times more morphine than the rats in Rat Park, overdosing often. The rats in Rat Park – in the company of their friends and partners with objects to interact with and other rats to hump – resisted the morphine water, trying it occasionally, but always showing a preference for the plain water.

So, what does it mean?

In a nutshell, when given the choice, those in isolation almost always choose the poison.

Those in healthy environments and circumstances – and notably, in the company of others – would rarely, if ever, willingly choose the poison. Even rats that were given nothing *but* the morphine water for 57 days in isolation to force addiction, who were then moved to Rat Park, ended up reverting to the plain drinking water once they found themselves in situations that nurtured and provided healthy connections.

It comes down to understanding that the cure for addiction is not sobriety, but connection.

It supports my certainty that we are not addicted to alcohol, or drugs, or gambling, or sex.

We are addicted to escaping reality.

We are addicted to grasping at whatever connections and bonds we can, regardless of what's available to us, and regardless of how damaging our ultimate choice of bond becomes.

As I moved from active day drinking into recovery, some of the first truly memorable and therapeutic things I did for myself was to resurrect whatever old friendships I could.

I started gathering the charred timber from all my burnt bridges and mustered the humility to do my best to rebuild. I reached out, I offered apologies (the real kind, that don't have a "but" tethered to them) and I made efforts and promises – and I kept them.

I did everything in my power to fire up as many dried-up old connections as I could, and it recharged me. This was a welcome change from how I'd been plugged into a bottle for two decades, as all it ever did was drain me.

There Is Nothing Wrong with You

There's a tonne of research to back up the theory that addiction is not a substance use disorder – but a *social* one.

This ties into the definition of addiction itself, and what the opposite of addiction truly is. The opposite of addiction is not sobriety. The opposite of addiction is *connection*.

Having real, one-on-one, flesh and blood connections with other human beings, in meaningful and honest ways is the *actual* cure for addiction. Developing reasons to get out of bed in the morning that connect you with purpose and pride, whether it's a job you love or a person you can't live without – that's the soul-fulfilling connection a lot of addicts *need* in order to leave substance abuse behind.

And it's hard.

It's hard because we live in a society that is *saturated with ideals of perfection*.

From Instafamous strangers to Facebook/*friendquaintances* (I just made that word up, and I like it) every waking moment of our lives, our senses are overwhelmed by images and stories of *everyone else's* successes, perfectly curated so only the pretty parts show.

And here *we* are, broke-down and falling apart with so much *"wrong with us"* that we want to make right, wondering what the hell our problem is and wondering why we can't get out shit together like everyone else.

It feels like you arrived at the party underdressed and uninvited.

Well, here's a newsflash: *There is nothing wrong with you.*

Let me repeat.

There is Nothing. Wrong. With. You.

Read that again, and again, and again until it sinks in.

We've come to a point where *"things sucking"* no longer has anything to do with circumstance, but instead we believe it has *everything to do with us.*

If things suck, it has to be because *we* suck.

We believe that things in our life suck because we aren't *good enough.*

We haven't *tried* hard enough.

We don't *want it* enough.

We aren't *worthy* enough, *skinny* enough, *smart* enough or *pretty* enough.

The word *"enough"* used to mean sufficient, adequate, ample, and plentiful.

We're now in a world where *enough is no longer ever enough.*

We measure our worth in comparison to the curated perfection of complete strangers and wonder why we end up feeling inadequate.

And it's these feelings of inadequacy that stall our relationships. They make us underperform at work, in our marriages, our friendships, and in *actively participating in our very own lives.*

When our lives don't look just like the *unsucky lives* of everyone we see on social media (and tv, movies, magazines, billboards...) it's easy to feel disconnected, and most definitely *not good enough.* We isolate and withdraw, turning to self-sabotage and *connecting* with what we know best – drinking or whatever poison feeds our addiction. We turn to whatever feeds our primal need to feel connected and whatever makes our feelings of inadequacy fall to the wayside, at least for a little while.

Life sucks, and then it gets better, and then it sucks again.

If the opposite of addiction is in fact *connection*, then that would make addiction itself the same as *disconnection.* We disconnect from people and situations, we disconnect from our true selves, and we disconnect from accepting the reality that sometimes yes, *life sucks,* and there isn't anything we can do about it.

We don't do it consciously, but we also don't absorb the destructive ideas that we're not good enough consciously, either. It all happens without us noticing until things to start sucking even more, and the cycle repeats. We repel the idea that it's okay for things to suck sometimes, that it's okay to be struggling or stumbling because we're told we aren't good enough if our lives aren't tied up nicely into a perfect bow.

When our lives don't match the glossy ones we are being force-fed non-stop every day it's easy to ask yourself: *what is wrong with me?* And, when you start having thoughts like that, it's just easier to drink and make those uncomfortable feelings you don't have answers to go away. It's easier to get drunk than to accept the possibility that maybe, just maybe, there's *actually nothing wrong with you.*

Maybe there's something wrong with the image we've been sold of *what our lives should look like:* shiny, flawless, and definitely without any sucky parts.

Being famous on Instagram is like being rich in Monopoly.

It was my habit of refusing to accept the sucky parts of my life that drove me to drink in excess. The more I refused to accept that sometimes *things just suck,* the suckier things became. I made a career out of trying to drown out the shitty parts with bottles of wine instead of embracing them as part of the unpredictable, wonderful experience of being alive. Since my life seemed to be as far as humanly possible from the scale of success I adopted *was brainwashed into believing,* I defaulted to assuming I was forever flawed, and that was that.

I forfeited so many years of my life to drinking, because I felt I didn't know how to "do life" quite right, in comparison to everyone else, regardless of how hard I tried.

What we forget to remember, and what we are rarely told, is that sometimes life just sucks, *and that's okay.* What is *not* okay is believing that because some *things* may suck, that means *we suck,* too.

Sometimes the hands we're dealt are actually pretty shitty. Sometimes we make bad choices that in turn can make our lives suck even more for a little while. It's the inevitability of being alive: *things will suck. Things will never be perfect.*

Our job is to make it work anyways.

It's not only our job – it is our life's work. It's in the lining up of all those days of *"making it work anyways"* that add up to a life well lived, instead of a life well avoided.

Clinging to the social media induced ideal that we aren't allowed to be *beautifully imperfect* is the cornerstone of 21st century addiction. *Suffering* is a human condition – unchangeable and inevitable, and even the Instafamous and curated Facebook *friendquaintances* experience suffering in their lives, every single day.

Here's the truth.

Sometimes life does suck. Sometimes other people will do *really sucky things* that will make your life suck in return. Sometimes we're *actually the person* doing the thing that sucks, and we make *other people's* lives suck as a result.

And what sucks most, is owning the shame that comes with believing that because things in life sometime suck, we do, too.

Trying to *remove the suck* from your life (or drowning it in booze, or wherever you find your escape) will forever and always only cause more feelings that everything sucks.

Putting your life on hold until things stop sucking is the same as saying you're never going to do it. Embrace the suck, because it's as much a part of being human as the air we breathe.

You can take all of this as the most depressing thing you've ever read, or you can take it as an inspiring and freeing way of looking at everything – *starting with everyone and everything you see on social media.*

You can allow yourself to embrace the sucky parts of life instead of hiding from them. You can admit to yourself that there is *nothing wrong with you.* What *is wrong* is our inability to allow the sucky parts of our life to shine, because I believe that's where we'll find the honest and true connections we're seeking, in others.

"Human connections are deeply nurtured in the field of a shared story."
– *Jean Houston*

Let go of comparing your life (however unconsciously) to the lives of strangers and *friendquaintances.* Stop clinging to ideals that in no way serve you. And most of all, find peace and balance with the sucky parts of your life. Don't immerse yourself in them, but also stop pretending they don't exist.

Accept the sucky parts, stop trying to control them, and stop defining yourself by them.

Suck happens.

If we all wore our *challenges* on our sleeves – instead of our accomplishments – what a beautifully supportive and humble world we'd live in.

Find your tribe.

Surround yourself with people who see that *stumbling and trying* is more beautiful and inspiring than perfection ever could be. That's the only place - *in the company of our tribe* - that we can find the true and real connections we are all looking for, and all that we all need.

That's where the real cure is.

Epilogue

This isn't the end, though.
Well, of this book it is.
But my story, and yours, doesn't end here.

Epilogue

FEBRUARY 16, 2023

If you look at the cover of this book, I didn't lie to you – there is no lack of messiness – but, *beautiful messiness* – in telling a story like this.

It's not a clean dotted line, with a clearly laid out plot, predictable characters, and a premeditated resolution to help you tie a neat little bow on it and close by return. No lock to fasten to close the diary of my dirty little secrets, or box to tuck it away in, forgotten.

Real life doesn't work like that.

No, *real life* – and I mean *really real* real life – is full of unpredictable surprises, and the beauty is hidden inside them if you learn how to pause and see below the surface of what has sprung up in front of you.

That's the beauty in the mess.

No, things *did not* go to plan, to say the least.

But could I have written a better ending, for myself, or this book? Absolutely not.

It's impossible, because this isn't the end. Like every other bookend, like every other *last page*, there is always another book, another story to tell, another adventure that will no doubt be just as messy and unpredictable and *beautiful* as I see every one that is tucked between these covers. Each one, to me, is like a person in a photograph, not stuck there but *remembered* there, and that is the beauty of photography and storytelling – both of which are intricately connected. To revisit all these characters again and see how much we've both grown since I visited them last is refreshing because I'm able to *see how far we've both come.*

Yes, the guy in those stories is indeed me, but then again – it isn't.

Not anymore.

And there in itself lies the beauty of recovery.

You find it in the transformation.

You find it in the washing off all the messiness, and watching it drain away – relieved that you're clean, but never regretting lessons you learned that led you here today, to the clearing on the other side of the Dark Forest.

xo

Shawn

About the Author

I'm not going to pretend I have some fabulous, fancy agent or rep who wrote this part.

This is me. This is Shawn aka SJ and these are also my words, like every other one tucked between the covers of this book. You'd think after writing nearly 500 pages about myself and my adventures that crafting this About the Author page would be easy. But, if it weren't necessary to include, I'd probably omit it entirely because if you don't know me yet after reading everything that came before this, nothing I write here can help you learn who I am or where I came from.

Once upon a time, someone reminded me that the question *"Who are you?"* is harder to define than it sounds. And the more I thought about it, the more complex and challenging it became.

Well, I'm a writer, photographer, Creative Director, and artist.

Nope. That's what I do.

Okay then, I'm married to a fabulous guy, I have three crazy dogs, and we live in a beautiful heritage home in St. Thomas, Ontario, Canada.

Nope. That's where I live, and who I live with.

Fine. I'm a deep thinker, who overthinks pretty much everything, uses creativity of all kinds to channel those thoughts, and transform them into palpable forms that are easier for me to process and share, whether it's by writing, or baking sourdough bread.

Still nope. That's who I think I am and what I enjoy doing.

This is annoying. Okay, I was with my ex-husband for 18 years, we had a wildly successful photography empire, I did this thing called The Drawing Hope Project which catapulted me to global fame and then it all fell apart because of my struggle with addiction, grief from too many losses, and really – just trying to survive.

Nope. Sorry. That's what you've done, and what you've been through.

So, you get it. This page is challenging. I can't write it because I still don't know the answer. So, just read every page before this one. It'll tell you more about the author than this page ever can.

xo Shawn

Printed in Great Britain
by Amazon

18810060R00312